S0-CCC-387

RINGOLD
3416 Tulane Drive
Apartment Number 31
Hyattsville, Maryland 20783

CAUSAL MODELS IN MARKETING

THEORIES IN MARKETING SERIES
GERALD ZALTMAN, EDITOR

CAUSAL MODELS IN MARKETING

Richard P. Bagozzi
MASSACHUSETTS INSTITUTE OF TECHNOLOGY

John Wiley & Sons
NEW YORK · CHICHESTER · BRISBANE · TORONTO

Copyright ©1980, by John Wiley & Sons, Inc.

All rights reserved. Published simultaneously in Canada.

Reproduction or translation of any part of
this work beyond that permitted by Sections
107 and 108 of the 1976 United States Copyright
Act without the permission of the copyright
owner is unlawful. Requests for permission
or further information should be addressed to
the Permissions Department, John Wiley & Sons, Inc.

Library of Congress Cataloging in Publication Data:

Bagozzi, Richard P
Causal models in marketing.
(Theories in marketing series)
Includes index.
1. Marketing research.   2. Marketing-
Mathematical models.   I. Title.   II. Series.
HF5415.2.B25   658.8'35   79-11622
ISBN 0-471-01516-4

Printed in the United States of America

10 9 8 7 6 5 4 3 2 1

. . . science is not common sense, and its most basic theoretical ideas and frames of reference require development through complex intellectual processes which involve not only interpretations of observation but also theoretical and partly philosophical conceptualization.

Talcott Parsons

to my mother and father

ABOUT THE AUTHOR

Richard P. Bagozzi is Associate Professor of Management Science at the Alfred P. Sloan School of Management, Massachusetts Institute of Technology. Previous to this he taught at the University of California, Berkeley.

Dr. Bagozzi received his Ph.D. in Marketing from Northwestern University in 1976, an M.B.A. in General Business from Wayne State University in 1972, an M.S. in Electrical Engineering and Mathematics from the University of Colorado in 1969, and a B.S.E.E. from General Motors Institute in 1970.

Dr. Bagozzi has authored or co-authored more than thirty articles in scholarly journals in the areas of social psychology, multivariate statistics, research methodology, and marketing theory. He is on the editorial boards of the *Journal of Marketing Research* and the *Journal of Consumer Research* and is a member of the American Psychological Association, the American Sociological Association, the Association for Consumer Research, and the American Marketing Association.

Among other honors, his dissertation was given a first place award in the national American Marketing Association competition, and in 1978 he was presented with the campus-wide Distinguished Teaching Award by the University of California, Berkeley.

PREFACE

My aim in this book is to provide a systematic, rigorous treatment of the theory construction and empirical inquiry phases of marketing research. To do this, I have taken a perspective that combines principles from the philosophy of science with methodological developments in econometrics, psychometrics, and sociology. The approach is a holistic one in that it integrates the theory construction process with the design, conduct, and analysis of research; the integrating theme throughout is the notion of cause and effect.

Previous works in marketing have tended to separate theory from both methodology and analysis, creating a lacuna in the literature that has hampered both the teaching and practice of marketing research. Although excellent books can be found dealing with theory, on the one hand (e.g., Zaltman et al., 1973; Hunt; 1976), or methodology and data analysis on the other (e.g., Green and Tull, 1975; Zaltman and Burger, 1975), the discipline lacks a treatment integrating metatheoretical criteria with methodological considerations. Marketers need a unified, yet scientifically precise, model for developing and testing theory.

The model developed in this book begins with one of the most dominant analytic concerns in the history of science: the problem of causation. Two fundamental schools of thought—the positivist and realist—are outlined in order to define causality and the related problems of explanation and confirmation. After these foundations are laid in the first chapter, succeeding chapters present the component parts of causal modeling. Among other topics, the discussion deals with the general linear model, construct validity, experimental and survey research, panel analysis, longitudinal studies, and marketing models. An attempt is made to help the reader think in a systematic way about the underlying cause-and-effect processes governing the behavior of marketing phenomena. Extensive examples are woven into the development of principles throughout the book. Moreover, much of the treatment presents original research in a number of substantive areas of marketing.

The general procedures outlined in this book owe their origin to quite recent developments in the behavioral sciences. In sociology, the approach is known as path analysis, and for elementary treatments the reader is referred to Duncan (1975) and Heise (1975). Somewhat more advanced sociological discussions may be found in Burt (1973), Blalock (1971, 1974), and Blalock et al. (1975). In economics, the orientation has been referred to as simultaneous equation systems or structural equation models. Detailed discussions may be found in Thiel (1971), Goldberger (1973, 1974), or Rothenberg (1973). Finally, perhaps the most developed treatments can be found in the psychometric literature usually under the rubrics of confirmatory factor analysis (e.g., Jöreskog, 1969; Lawley and Maxwell, 1971) or analysis of covariance structures (Jöreskog, 1970, 1973, 1974). Because Jöreskog's methods represent a major breakthrough for obtaining numerical solutions in maximum likelihood procedures and because sociological and econometric models can be shown to be special cases of Jöreskog's general model, I have chosen to follow the development due to Jöreskog wherever possible. Moreover, virtually all the numerical analyses performed in this book were done using the computer program LISREL, from Jöreskog and van Thillo (1972). This program and others are available from International Educational Services, P.O. Box A 3650, Chicago, Illinois, 60690.

A number of audiences should find the book helpful in their work. The principle audiences are marketing research, marketing models, or marketing theory students at the masters or doctoral level. Advanced undergraduates should be able to follow the development also, provided they are motivated enough. An introductory statistics course and an intuitive understanding of multiple regression are all that are assumed as background. The beginning reader unfamiliar with these topics might review an introductory textbook such as Kmenta's (1971), which provides an excellent summary of basic statistical and econometric theory. Students in economics, management science, and related fields will find *Causal Models in Marketing* general enough to aid them in approaching their problems. Finally, marketing researchers should find the book useful in the construction and analysis of research in the field. The procedures allow the researcher to model cause and effect, measurement error, and construct validity in the context of cross-sectional or longitudinal designs.

I owe an enormous debt to my teachers and colleagues. Professors Richard M. Clewett, Philip Kotler, and Sidney J. Levy of Northwestern University provided me with the initial stimulation and guidance to investigate the theoretical side of marketing. Professors Donald T. Campbell and Robert F. Boruch, also of Northwestern University, were very instrumental in helping me gain a better understanding of research methodology and model building. Discussions with Professors Leo A. Goodman (University of Chicago), Richard Westin (University of Toronto), and Dr. Jay Magidson (ABT Research) proved invaluable while I was learning the more quantitative side of causal modeling. My interest in the philosophy of science aspects of marketing thought result largely from the influence of Professors Gerald Zaltman (University of Pittsburgh), Reinhard Angelmar (INSEAD), and Christian Pinson (INSEAD). I have benefited greatly from my associations with Professors David Aaker, Ronald Burt, Francesco Nicosia, and Frances Van Loo at the University of California, Berkeley. Finally, I am indebted to Professors Lynn Phillips (Stanford University) and John Farley (Columbia) for detailed comments made on earlier drafts. To each of these friends I am most grateful.

RICHARD P. BAGOZZI

EDITOR'S PREFACE

Historically, marketing's intellectual concerns have focused predominantly on applied issues. Rather recently in the development of marketing, there has been greater understanding that applied or practice related issues are intertwined with theory: as one improves so does the other. Still, the amount of attention given to theory in marketing is relatively small, especially when compared to other disciplines. In fact, a common practice in marketing is to use theories developed in other disciplines. This practice has benefited marketing practitioners considerably and has advanced the discipline intellectually more quickly than the alternative route of independently discovering the presence of these theories in marketing phenomena. However, there are clear costs to heavy reliance on this approach. For example, insights unique to knowledgeable marketers may fail to be developed into theories. Additionally, phenomena unique to marketing may fail to be developed into theories.

One way of avoiding these costs is to be more venturesome with regard to theory building. This, in turn, requires certain tools in developing and refining theory. Richard P. Bagozzi, in an extraordinary and landmark effort, provides in this volume a general model for the construction and testing of theory. He uses the concept of causality as the core theme of his book. In the process of providing understanding of this concept he provides the reader with skills for articulating his or her own insights about marketing phenomena. Thus Professor Bagozzi not only makes his own contribution to theory in marketing but, more importantly perhaps, may stimulate and enable others to do so as well. It is appropriate that *Causal Models in Marketing* be the first volume in this special series of books intended to help foster the development of theory in marketing. Other volumes will explore other issues and present other perspectives relating to thinking and action in marketing. It is hoped that collectively the different volumes will stimulate more creative and exciting thinking and practice in marketing which, after all, is what good theory is about.

Gerald Zaltman
Pittsburgh, PA

CONTENTS

ONE
CAUSATION AND CAUSAL THEORIES   1

TWO
BASIC CONCEPTS IN CAUSAL MODELING   33

THREE
CONSTRUCTING CAUSAL MODELS   62

FOUR
STRUCTURAL EQUATIONS AND THE GENERAL LINEAR MODEL   83

FIVE
CONSTRUCT VALIDITY   113

SIX
ESTIMATING AND TESTING SIMPLE CAUSAL MODELS   165

SEVEN
STRUCTURAL EQUATION MODELS IN EXPERIMENTAL RESEARCH   189

EIGHT
LONGITUDINAL AND PANEL ANALYSIS   221

NINE
BUYER BEHAVIOR   240

TEN
CAUSAL MODELS IN SURVEY RESEARCH: THE CASE OF AN
INDUSTRIAL SALESFORCE   251

AUTHOR INDEX   293

SUBJECT INDEX   297

ONE

CAUSATION AND
CAUSAL THEORIES

if there be any relation among objects which it imports us to know perfectly, it is that of cause and effect. On this are founded all our reasoning concerning matter of fact or existence. By means of it alone we attain any assurance concerning objects which are removed from the present testimony of our memory and senses. The only immediate utility of all sciences, is to teach us, how to control and regulate future events by their causes. Our thoughts and enquiries are, therefore, every moment, employed about this relation [David Hume, 1777].

Perhaps no single concept is more pervasive and important in marketing than the notion of cause and effect. Marketing practitioners depend on it in their planning and implementation of programs designed to obtain responses from consumers. Ideas of advertising affecting sales, opinion leaders influencing the adoption of new products, or promotion activities producing interest and preferences for one's wares all rely implicitly on mechanisms of cause and effect. Marketing scholars and researchers find causality at the heart of phenomena they attempt to understand and explain. Our propositions, theories, and methodologies are all fundamentally based on the concept of causality. Even consumers find cause and effect essential in their dealings with marketers. Through bargaining, letters of complaint, protest, boycotts, picketing, and other activities, people strive to influence marketers and obtain desired responses. Whether one wishes to understand the world or to change it, causality will invariably play a central role.

This monograph attempts to develop a general model for the construction and testing of theory. To do this, the concept of causality is used as a basic unit of analysis for achieving explanation and meaning of behavior in the market-place. Concept formation, hypothesis generation, theory building, and empirical confirmation (or falsification) are all shown to build upon the notion of causation. This introductory chapter lays the conceptual foundation for the design and testing of theory to be developed throughout the text. Its purpose is to analyze the concept of causality in greater depth and place it in a proper perspective. Although the nature of causality has perplexed philosophers and scientists since at least the time of the ancient Greeks, it is essential that marketers grasp the meaning of cause and effect, its underlying structure, and its implications for research, theory, and practice.

History and Importance of the Concept

The idea of causality is, at first glance, simple enough. To say that x causes y is to say that x and y are related, and the relation involves some notion of mechanism, force, production, or the like between x as cause and y as effect. Thus, marketers often have images of cause and effect in mind when they search for the determinants of sales, the factors producing satisfaction/dissatisfaction with a product or service, the conditions facilitating positive attitudes toward or preferences for a particular brand, or the variables under-lying conflict in the channel of distribution.

Commonsense notions such as these, however, provide little insight into the fundamental nature of causality. To say that "x causes y" means "x produces y," "x determines y," and so on begs the question as to the meaning of the causal relation itself, since such verbs of activity as produce, determine, force, and so forth merely substitute one synonym of causality for another. To discover the meaning and role of causality in scientific investigation, it will be necessary to examine the elements and structure of the causal relation in great detail. Before this analysis can be performed, however, it will prove useful to trace briefly the evolution of the concept itself.

Early Developments

Aristotle (1930) provides perhaps the first detailed analysis of a cause, dividing it into four types[1]: (1) the definable form, (2) an antecedent which *necessitates* a consequent, (3) the efficient cause which started the process, and (4) the final cause. By definable form, Aristotle meant, roughly, the shape, pattern, nature, or structure of a thing functioning as a cause. For example, Ivancevich and Donnelly (1975) discovered that salespeople in flat (versus salespeople in medium or tall) organizations perceive more satisfaction with respect to self-actualization and autonomy, perceive lower amounts of anxiety stress, and perform more efficiently. This finding suggests that organizational structure in the form of the number of levels of supervision acts as a determinant of behavior and feelings in salespeople.

Aristotle's second causal type refers to "that out of which (*ex hou*), as a constituent, something is generated" (Wallace, 1972, p. 14). When the marketer notes that awareness is a necessary condition for internalizing an advertisement and developing positive attitudes toward a product, he or she is referring to a necessary antecedent cause in Aristotle's second sense.

The efficient cause is perhaps the most intuitive. The third type refers to the source of change or its cessation as exemplified in the actions of a social actor or an external physical force. The influence of a salesperson or the impact of shortages on price are two examples.

Finally, by final cause, Aristotle meant the purpose or end for which a thing is done. When marketers study decision making as a purposeful, goal-directed activity, they are examining the process in Aristotle's sense of final cause.

Aristotle also wrestled with the concept of explanation. For him, to explain the occurrence, nature, or implications of any phenomenon is to answer the question: "Why?"—Why did this event occur? Why is this thing structured as it is? Why does this variable have this consequence? And so forth. Significantly, Aristotle claimed that the most comprehensive answers to "why" questions—the fullest explanations—are those achieved in terms of the identification of the four types of cause. Aristotle felt that knowledge is the goal of scientific explanation and this, in turn, depends fundamentally on the nature of causality.

Probably the next most important development in the concept of causality occurred during the Middle Ages as an outgrowth of medieval science. Three centers of learning in Europe proved to be instrumental in determining early facets of the concept: Oxford University, the University of Paris, and the University of Padua. Scholars in these institutions pioneered the notions of scientific explanation and experimentation in which the causal relation was central.

Going back to the medieval precursors of modern science, one finds that they consistently associated the Latin term *scientia* with causal knowledge. *Scientia est cognito per causas*. It was precisely on this basis that they differentiated *scientia* from other forms of knowledge: science was concerned with causes, whereas other types of knowing were not. To have scientific knowledge was to know perfectly, *scire simpliciter*, to know that something is so because it could not be otherwise and this, in turn, because of the causes that make it be as it is. Thus, the early understanding of science—from which the modern notion grew—was that it must be concerned with a search for causes. And the explanations for which science was ultimately searching ... were causal explanations [Wallace, 1972, vol. I, p. 6].

Galileo (e.g., 1974) was a leading proponent of causality as the foundation of science in the postmedieval period. He attempted to find the true causes, *verae causae*, of phenomena and concluded that these consist of the necessary and sufficient conditions for the occurrence or appearance of an object or event. Galileo emphasized the role of mathematics as a model of science and as an instrument for discovering the true causes of natural phenomena. Unlike Aristotle, who seemed to emphasize the nature of a cause as crucial for understanding its power in producing an effect, Galileo presented an early analysis of the logic and empirical requirements connecting cause to effect. In advocating a procedure akin to the modern experimental method, Galileo noted that a cause is always followed by an effect and that removal of the cause will make it such that the effect will disappear. Such reasoning can be seen to underly later empiricist and positivist conceptions of causality as involving only relations among observable phenomena. Galileo appears to be one of the first to have suggested that the causal relation entails contiguity and constant conjunction between cause and effect.

Contributions in the Classical Period

The concept of causality underwent its most thorough development in the classical period which spanned the beginning of the 18th century until the end of the 19th. The contributions of David Hume, Immanuel Kant, and John Stuart Mill are particularly noteworthy.

David Hume. The modern notion of causation is perhaps indebted most to the work of Hume.[2] Drawing on the analogy of the interaction of billiard balls, Hume succinctly identified three elements of any causal relation—namely, contiguity in time and place, temporal priority of cause and effect, and constant conjunction:

Here is a billiard-ball lying on the table, and another ball moving towards it with rapidity. They strike; and the ball, which was formerly at rest, now acquires a motion.... There was no interval betwixt the shock and the motion. *Contiguity* in time and place is therefore a requisite circumstance to the operation of all causes. 'Tis evident likewise, that the motion which was the cause, is prior to the motion, which was the effect. *Priority* in time, is therefore another requisite circumstance in every cause. But this is not all. Let us try any other balls of the same kind in a like situation, and we shall always find, that the impulse of the one produces motion in the other. Here, therefore is a *third* circumstance, viz., that of a constant conjunction betwixt the cause and effect. Every object like the cause, produces always some object like the effect. Beyond these three circumstances of contiguity, priority, and constant conjunction, I can discover nothing in this cause ... [Hume, 1739, from the abstract].

Hume's insights are deceptively simple and deserve further comment. The author intended causality to apply between events; event x produces a change in event y. Unlike Aristotle and certain modern theorists (described below), Hume denied that things can be causes (for example, through their natures, characteristics, powers, etc.). Rather, it is changes in events, or processes, that are causes. The only empirical content in the statement of a causal relation, in the Humean view, is the fact of the occurrence and regularity of events. All we know or can know in the world is that event y followed, and has always followed, event x in the appropriate circumstances. The idea of a cause producing an effect is held to be an illusion, a psychological phenomenon, a subjective feeling in the mind of the observer. The notion of a necessary connection between cause and effect is taken to be not one of natural necessity but rather one of conceptual necessity. Continuing Hume's billiard-ball analogy:

In the considering of motion communicated from one ball to another, we could find nothing but contiguity, priority in the course, and constant conjunction. But, besides these circumstances, 'tis commonly suppos'd, that there is a necessary connexion betwixt the cause and effect, and that the cause possesses something, which we call a *power*, or *force*, or *energy*. The question is, what idea is annex'd to these terms? If all our ideas or thoughts be derived from our impressions, their power must either discover itself to our senses, or to our internal feeling. But so little does any power discover itself to the senses in the operations of matter . . . [further] our own minds afford us no more notion of energy than matter does . . . . Upon the whole, then, either we have no idea at all of force and energy, and these words are altogether insignificant, or they can mean nothing but that determination of the thought, acquired by habit, to pass from the cause to its usual effect [Hume, 1739, from the abstract].

Hume did not stop at specifying the elements of the causal relation but proposed procedures or "rules by which to judge causes and effects." He thus anticipated later developments by John Stuart Mill and others in regard to the experimental method. Three of his rules deserve mention[3]:

Rule 4. The same cause always produces the same effect, and the same effect never arises but from the same cause. This principle we derive from experience, and is the source of most of our philosophical reasonings. For when by any clear experiment we have discovered the causes or effects of any phenomenon, we immediately extend our observation to every phenomenon of the same kind, without waiting for that constant repitition, from which the first idea of this relation is derived [Hume, 1739].

In this rule, Hume makes a couple of important points about causality and how one may determine its occurrence. The notion of same cause/same effect seems to imply that the regularity between cause and effect is lawlike. That is, Hume suggests that the causal relation is accompanied by universal laws relating generic events: if an event of type x occurs, an event of type y will follow. Further, these implied laws are taken to hold true for all times and places. On the other hand, Hume claims elsewhere that it may be possible to detect causality with a single experiment: "we may attain the knowledge of a particular cause merely by one experiment, provided it be made with judgment, and after a careful removal of all foreign and superfluous circumstances" (Hume, 1739). As Ducasse (1966) notes, however, this creates an ambiguity in Hume's account, since "it is paradoxical to suppose that a *single* experiment—unless it reveals a genuine *connection* between events of the kinds that figure in it—can inform us that in all past and future cases of an event similar to the first, an event similar to the second *did,* or *will* follow" (p. 144). The problem with Hume's claim is that it provides no explanation for an observed regular sequence, making it difficult to distinguish between accidental and causal sequences. As noted below, Mill and modern methodologists have improved upon Hume's arguments somewhat.

Consider, next, Hume's fifth and sixth rules:

Rule 5 [the principle of Agreement].   There is another principle, which hangs upon this, viz., that where several different objects produce the same effect, it must be by means of some quality, which we discover to be common amongst them. For as like effects imply like causes, we must always ascribe the causation to the circumstances, wherein we discover the resemblance.

Rule 6 [the principle of Difference].   The following principle is founded on the same reason. The difference in the effects of two resembling objects must proceed from that particular in which they differ. For as like causes always produce like effects, when in any instance we find our expectation to be disappointed, we must conclude that this irregularity proceeds from some difference in the causes [Hume, 1739].

These rules suggest other qualities of the causal relation that will be shown later to be central to modern views of causation. First, note that, in Rule 5, Hume makes reference to the fact that the circumstances surrounding cause and effect are essential to its meaning. He is explicit in separating cause, effect, and circumstances. Next, note that Hume *seems* to refer to properties or characteristics of a cause and an effect as being somehow instrumental in the emergence and production of the relation itself. References to "by means of some quality" (Rule 5) and "objects must proceed from that particular in which they differ" (Rule 6) connote the presence of notions of "power" in the cause and/or "liability" in the effect, respectively. Yet, it should be stressed that Hume is quite clear in virtually all of his writings that such ideas have no foundation in nature, but reside in the cognitions of the observer. Nevertheless, other theories of causality rest fundamentally on explicating the character of the natural necessity connecting cause to effect (c.f., discussion below and Harré and Madden, 1975).

Immanuel Kant. Although it has not always been possible to understand exactly what Kant meant in his writings or whether he was disagreeing with or supporting Hume's views on causation, he did raise a number of very important issues that underlie contemporary controversy into the nature of causation.[4]

Before his position may be presented, however, it will be necessary to introduce the reader to four concepts in philosophy—namely, the notions of analytic, synthetic, a priori, and a posteriori statements.

The difference between analytic and synthetic statements is, according to one view, based upon logical criteria (e.g., Carnap, 1966; Kahane, 1973). An analytic statement is one in which its predicate is "contained in" or is "part of" the concept of its subject. For example, the statement, "all drop-shippers are limited-function wholesalers" is analytic, since the meaning of the predicate "limited-function wholesalers" is part of the meaning of the subject term "drop-shippers." Analyticity depends only on the meaning relations of the concepts in the sentence. An analytic sentence or proposition can only be logically true or false, not factually so. A synthetic statement, in contrast, is one in which the meaning of the predicate is not contained in the concept of the subject. Rather, a synthetic statement has factual content, that is, it refers to a particular event or state of affairs in the world of experience. Thus, the statement "all drop-shippers are motivated by expected profits" is synthetic, since the meaning of "motivated by expected profits" is not contained in the meaning of the subject term, "drop-shippers." Rather, it is possible to subject the statement to empirical validation. As Carnap (1966, p. 178) notes in regard to synthetic statements, their meaning "goes beyond the assigned meanings of the terms. It tells something about the nature of the world." Analytic and synthetic statements both address the question of *what kinds* of sentences or propositions one can know.

A priori and a posteriori statements, on the other hand, ask *how* things are or can be known. Distinctions between these terms are epistemological differences between two types of knowledge. An a priori statement is "one whose truth value can be known before, or without the need of, any experience of the things which the sentence discusses" (Kahane, 1973). Its truth or falsehood is established on strictly logical or semantic grounds. For instance, to use a famous example, many philosophers claim that the statement "$7 + 5 = 12$" is an a priori one. This is so since, given conventions of numbers and elementary arithmetic and algebra, it is possible to know its truth or falsity independent of experience. An a posteriori statement, in contrast, is "one whose truth value cannot be known before experience of things of the kind which the sentence or proposition is about" (Kahane, 1973). Take the sentence, "At least 50 percent of the manufacturers of breakfast cereals in the United States practice the marketing concept." Assuming it is possible to operationalize the "practice" of a principle such as the marketing concept, the truth or falsity of this statement can only be known by examining the behavior of the manufacturers. This proposition is said to be knowable only a posteriori.

Given the distinctions between analytic and synthetic and between a priori and a posteriori, it is possible to categorize all knowledge into the types shown in Figure 1.1. Notice that all a posteriori statements are synthetic, and all

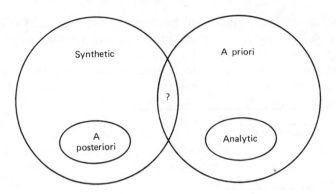

Figure 1.1 Four key concepts in the nature of human knowledge.

analytic statements are a priori. These points are generally conceded by most contemporary philosophers. Of considerable controversy even among philosophers of today, however, is the claim that some knowledge can be both synthetic and a priori. In Kant's view certain classes of knowledge about facts in the world can be known with certainty without relying on our experiences. These aspects of knowledge have been termed Kant's synthetic a priori in the literature. For example, Kant claims that the statement "7 + 5 = 12," which most would agree is a priori, is also synthetic since the concept of "12" is not part of the concept of "7 + 5." Ayer (1973, p. 199) disagrees, however, claiming that "the equation follows from suitable definition of the numbers and of the signs of addition and equality; and ... this is sufficient to make it analytic." This controversy will be shown later in the chapter to have significance for many deterministic marketing models involving definitions, axioms, and optimization procedures such as found in economic theory. For the present, the reader should merely note the distinctions in knowledge illustrated by Figure 1.1.

We are now in a position to present Kant's ideas about causation. Kant attempted to show that the principle of causality is a synthetic, necessary statement (Suchting, 1967). It is synthetic because the concept of a cause is logically independent of the concept of an event. This is so because any particular cause and effect contain distinct factual information. Of more interest is Kant's claim that there is a necessity between cause and effect. Unlike Hume, who posited that the necessity is a psychological one, Kant seemed to say that the connection between cause and effect involves "a form of nonlogical, nonempirical necessity and that this necessity is a prerational pattern imposed by the mind" (Beauchamp, 1974). In the author's words, the schema of cause is "the real upon which, whenever posited, something else always follows. It consists therefore in the succession of the manifold in so far as that succession is subject to a rule" (Kant, 1961).

To better understand Kant's perspective, it will prove useful to contrast Hume and Kant as to their conceptions of apprehension. Hume had a predominantly mechanistic view of man and how one experiences the world. For Hume, the fundamental unit of human experience is the impression. Whether the impression arises from external stimuli or not, it induces ideas in the individual, and the relationships between ideas (contiguity, constant conjunction, priority) constitute all that there is to causality. Although the connection or relationship of cause to effect is denied to have ontological status by Hume (i.e., the relation itself has no empirical content), the impressions of antecedent and consequent events experienced as stimuli do contain empirical content. For Kant, in contrast, the fundamental units of human experience are not impressions stimulating ideas but rather the active process of the individual synthesizing and constructing his or her interpretation of the world.

For Kant, perception and thought are to be construed as activities we perform, rather than responses produced in us. To describe experience as the passive reception of sensory inputs is, on the Kantian view, to misdescribe it, because seeing something is constructing a spatio-temporal object from the inputs on the basis of rules. Neither experience nor thought can be understood as things that happen to us, but only as things we do, because they are synthetic activities that involve construction according to a rule [Harré and Secord, 1972, p. 37].

Kant believed that the mind imposes rules or laws upon the interpretation of the occurrence of so-called objective events and phenomena, and that through this process, the individual actively participates in the interpretation of the meaning of cause and effect as distinct from noncausal happenings.

Two examples from Kant illustrate how these principles can be used to detect a causal from a noncausal relationship. Consider first the act of an individual apprehending a house. One may begin by observing different parts of the house in some sequence. Thus, one might begin at the basement and eventually end by observing the roof. Alternatively, the sequence may be reversed or conducted in some other order. Whatever sequence is used, it would not be correct to say that the individual moments of apprehension represent any relationship of necessity between the sequence of perceptions. There is only one objective event perceived in any sequence of apprehensions of the house, and this is the event of the perceived presence of the house. The order of apprehensions is irrelevant. On the other hand, consider the example of an individual apprehending the passage of a boat going downstream. Here the sequence of perceptions is important for understanding the phenomenon. One first observes the boat upstream and later sees it at a point farther downstream. One cannot apprehend the boat first downstream and then upstream and claim that this represents the same event (as was possible with the house). The order of successive perceptions for the understanding of the passage of the boat downstream is a necessary one according to Kant. Furthermore, the author claims that the necessity proceeds from a rule imposed by the individual perceiver, and the notion of causality is presupposed in the judgments of the perceiver.[5] The distinction between objective and accidental and/or subjective successions of events is taken to lie in the necessity connecting cause to effect. Although Kant failed to fully explain this necessity, as noted below, a number of modern theorists have attempted to discover the nature of necessity and the mechanisms underlying the causal relationship.

John Stuart Mill. The contributions of Mill (1959) are primarily methodological in character in that he attempted to derive procedures for both discovering and demonstrating causal relationships.[6] For the most part, standards of modern experimental research derive directly from those proposed by Mill (compare Mill, 1959, Book III, chs. 8–10, originally published in 1872, to Campbell and Stanley, 1963).

Mill suggested five methods of experimental inquiry: the method of agreement, the method of difference, the method of concomitant variation, the joint method of agreement and difference, and the method of residues. Since the latter two methods are somewhat redundant, only the first three will be outlined here. Each of Mill's canons strives to establish causation by eliminating rival hypotheses in one way or another.

The *method of agreement* can be briefly stated as follows: "If two or more instances of the phenomenon under investigation have only one circumstance in common, the circumstance in which alone all the instances agree is the cause (or effect) of the given phenomenon" (Mill, 1959). For example, if two consumers expressing a desire for a new product were both previously exposed to a persuasive advertisement, but had in other ways different tastes, backgrounds, and so on, such that the exposure to the ad was the only factor common to both, then one may conclude that the ad was a cause of the expressed desire. The problem with the method of agreement is that, when applied as the only means of causal inference, the method can rarely guarantee that the instances of a phenomenon have only one variable in common. The method of agreement depends on the possibility of choosing as cause that common element in a set of otherwise different attributes of two or more things (objects, actors, etc.). Yet, when dealing with people, institutions, products, and so forth, as marketers do, the researcher will often find more than one single element common to instances of these phenomena and may even discover some elements common to some groups and others common to yet other groups. For this reason, the following method is often employed to augment the method of agreement.

Mill's *method of difference* can be described as follows: "If an instance in which the phenomenon under investigation occurs, and an instance in which it does not occur, have every circumstance in common save one, that one occurring in the former; the circumstance in which alone the two instances differ, is the effect, or the cause, or an indispensable part of the cause, of the phenomenon" (Mill, 1959). Thus, for example, if two groups are randomly formed, one a treatment and the other a control group, and a persuasive message is given to the former but not the latter, then one may conclude that a difference in attitudes or preferences toward a product would be due to the message as cause. The method of difference identifies as the cause that phenomenon which is present in instances where the effect occurs but which is missing in instances where the effect fails to occur. The method of difference finds considerable application in present-day research in marketing and the behavioral sciences, particularly in the experimental method. One of the major problems with the approach in the behavioral sciences is that it is often difficult to separate the effect of a planned stimulus from unintended influences such as evaluation apprehension, demand characteristics, and other artifacts (cf., Rosenthal and Rosnow, 1969).

Finally, the *method of concomitant variation* states: "Whatever phenomenon varies in any manner whenever another phenomenon varies in some particular manner, is either a cause or an effect of that phenomenon, or is connected with it through some fact of causation" (Mill, 1959). The canon says that if two variables are correlated, they will be causally connected. This method of Mill has perhaps received the most criticism in that "correlation does not necessarily imply causation." The reason two variables may be correlated could, for example, be due to a third factor causing parallel variation in the other two. Yet, since causation implies correlation, by definition, this third method of Mill is often used with other criteria (e.g., temporal priority, logical considerations) to establish the presence of a causal relation.

Mill's methods have done much to provide the researcher with procedures for inferring causality. Refinements in the procedures over the years have contributed to greater rigor in sociology (e.g., Smelser, 1976), psychology (e.g., Campbell and Stanley, 1963), and marketing (e.g., Green and Tull, 1975; Zaltman and Burger, 1975). Yet, for all their elegance, the methods of Mill have done little to unveil the fundamental nature of the causal relation itself. At best, they operationalize the model of Hume (i.e., temporal priority, constant conjunction, contiguity in space and time) without addressing the question as to the nature of the necessity or mechanisms connecting cause to effect. Modern causal theorists have addressed these problems, however, and it is to their contributions that we now turn.

Modern Theories of Causation and their Role in Scientific Inquiry

In some ways, inquiry into causation nearly came to a halt in the twentieth century.[7] Philosophers such as Bertrand Russell relegated the concept to the domain of myth, not worthy of serious investigation:

All philosophers, of every school, imagine that causation is one of the fundamental axioms or postulates of science, yet, oddly enough, in advanced sciences . . . the word "cause" never occurs . . . . The law of causality, I believe, like much that passes muster among philosophers, is a relic of a bygone age, surviving, like the monarchy, only because it is erroneously supposed to do no harm . . . [Russell, 1912–1913, p. 180].

Before examining Russell's arguments, one might well ask if his claim is true that "in the advanced sciences . . . the word 'cause' never occurs." A colloquium of philosophers of science recently met to discuss this issue and concluded, among other things, that although the *term* cause is often absent in contemporary research papers in the natural sciences, "the *idea* for which it stands continues to have wide currency" (Lerner, 1965). More compelling evidence is provided by Suppes (1970) in his review of the literature:

Contrary to the days when Russell wrote [his] essay, the words "causality" and "cause" are commonly and widely used by physicists in their most advanced work. There is scarcely an issue of *The Physical Review* that does not contain at least one article using either "cause" or "causality" in its title . . . discussions of causality are now very much a part of contemporary physics [pp. 5–6].

Similarly, causality is now at the center of inquiry in sociology, psychology, economics, marketing, and other areas of the behavioral sciences (e.g., Blalock, 1971; 1974; Goldberger and Duncan, 1973; McClelland, 1975).

Of particular interest with regard to the utility of the concept of causality is Russell's claim that science is not fundamentally concerned with the nature of regularities in events or even with the mechanisms producing such regularities (if such mechanisms exist). In the author's words such concerns belong to the "infancy of science" in that "every advance in a science takes us away from the crude uniformities which are first observed into greater differentiation of antecedent and consequent, and into a continually wider circle of antecedents recognised as relevant" (Russell, 1912–1913, p. 188). Rather than searching for causal relations in the classical sense, Russell proposed that scientists look for functional relationships between variables and represent the relationships of interest through differential equations. Russell believed that the functional relationship represented a different and more advanced form than the causal relationship. Today, contemporary philosophers of science largely reject Russell's arguments. Although beyond the scope of this monograph, it should be stressed that it is possible to show that causation in the sense advocated by Russell is a limiting case of the causal sequence as interpreted, for example, by modern theorists such as Ducasse (1968, 1969); and, at best, the functional conception of causality can be interpreted as a refinement and extension of the classical concept, not a difference in kind (e.g., Mackie, 1974, chs. 6 and 7). Von Wright (1974) makes somewhat similar arguments in his analysis.

Modern notions of causation may be conveniently analyzed as presented in two dominant schools of thought: the regularity theory and modern necessity approaches.[8] Following discussion of these perspectives, the related topics of explanation and confirmation are briefly presented.

The Regularity Theory

Over the years, theorists have worked to improve Hume's pioneering analysis of causation. Probably the most important advances have been made first in regard to the nature of the lawfulness observed in regular sequences of antecedent and consequent events and second with respect to specifying the necessary and sufficient conditions accompanying cause and effect. These developments may be loosely grouped under the rubric, "the regularity theory."

Laws of Nature. Consider first the use of laws by the regularity theorist. Following Hume, the regularity theorist asserts that the causal relation consists of a cause and an effect and the fact that the sequence exhibits an observed regularity (i.e., law) in nature. In general, the regularity theorist usually claims that a law of nature must satisfy four conditions (Molnar, 1969):

D_1: p is a statement of a law of nature if and only if:

 (i) p is universally quantified; and

 (ii) p is omnitemporally and omnispatially true; and

 (iii) p is contingent; and

 (iv) p contains only nonlocal empirical predicates, apart from logical connectives and quantifiers.

In symbolic form, a law may be written as

$$(x)(Px \to Qx)$$

which, in words, reads "for all x, if x has property P, then it has property Q." The universal quantifier asserts that all entities of a particular category have some property or properties. A law, in the regularity theory view, is intended to apply for all times and places. It is contingent in that the truth or falsity of the law depends on empirical test rather than logic. Finally, the terms or variables in a law refer to classes of observable phenomena (things, events) rather than particular or single instances. Laws are tentative assertions about regularities in the world.

Proponents of the regularity theory disagree on the issue of necessity in laws of nature. Some philosophers assert that the necessity is a logical one. Most reject this view, however, and in keeping with Hume, claim that any necessity is in the mind of the observer. A few philosophers, while accepting the general Humean and regularity theory view of causality, reject the claim that laws are merely statements of universal generalizations. Kneale (1950, 1961), for example, argues that laws involve a natural necessity in addition to the observed general regularities. Natural necessity for Kneale is regarded as a primitive statement, not further explicable. It is expressed in modal statements, and the laws so represented are termed nomological generalizations. Although Popper has not always been clear in his discussions of laws of nature, he also emphasizes laws in his interpretation of causality: "To give a *causal explanation* of an event means to deduce a statement which describes it, using as premises of the deduction one or more *universal laws*, together with certain singular statements, the *initial conditions*" (Popper, 1968, p. 59). In recent times, Popper has tended to shift from what can be largely termed a Humean view of necessity in laws to a position advocating a stronger, but logically modified, notion of natural necessity (cf., Beauchamp, 1974, part two). Unfortunately, Popper has not further examined the nature of this necessity.

Although the notion of lawlikeness is central to both the regularity theory and the related positivist model of explanation (presented below), it is not without faults.[9] When the idea of lawlikeness is restricted to the regularity observed in antecedent and consequent events, one is immediately confronted with the problem of characterizing and distinguishing a law of nature from an accidental generalization. Since both the law of nature and accidental generalization are characterized by the regular sequence of the Humean account, that criterion cannot serve to differentiate one from the other. Actually, there are two related problems with lawlikeness that complicate the distinction between a lawlike generalization and an accidental one. The first stems from the problem of induction which says that no amount of evidence can establish the truth of a law in the regularity sense since any future piece of information could disconfirm the law. More on this problem will be said in the next section. The second problem deals with the issue of contrary-to-fact conditionals. Briefly, a number of authors (e.g., Chisholm, 1955) contend that a lawlike generalization will support a contrary-to-fact conditional (also often referred to as a counterfactual inference or a counterfactual conditional), while an accidental generalization will not. To see this, consider the following two generalizations as examples of lawlike and nonlawlike (accidental) statements, respectively:

L1. Everyone who purchases a product and subsequently discovers it to be defective, poorly constructed, or unsafe is dissatisfied.

N1. For all people, if they are salespersons in Company A, they will be men.

Both express observed regularities—the first derived perhaps from survey responses, the second from, say, interviews. Next consider the following subjunctive statements derived from the above sentences and termed contrary-to-fact conditionals:

L1'. If x had purchased a product and found it defective, poorly constructed, or unsafe, then he or she would have been dissatisfied.

N1'. If x were a salesperson in Company A, then x would have been a man.

Notice that it is possible to argue that there are strong reasons to believe that the first contrary-to-fact conditional, L1', depicts a lawlike relation while the second does not. That is, based on psychological theories of cognitive dissonance, say, one might anticipate that, should another person purchase an unsatisfactory product, there are grounds to predict dissonance. No lawlike connection appears present in the second instance, however. The fact that all salespersons in Company A have been men is, given no further information, most likely accidental.

Kneale (1950, 1961), on the other hand, presents compelling logic showing that unrestricted universal statements [e.g., Humean laws of the form $(x)(Px \rightarrow Qx)$] do not sustain contrary-to-fact conditionals. Consider the above statement, L1, which may be written symbolically as

$$(x) \cdot (\text{purchase of defective product})(x) \rightarrow (\text{dissatisfaction})(x)$$

Kneale (1950) shows that statements in the above form may be translated to the following equivalent form:

$$\sim (\exists x) \cdot (\text{purchase of defective product})(x) \cdot \sim (\text{dissatisfaction})(x)$$

which may be read "there has never been a person purchasing a defective product and later finding it defective who has not experienced dissatisfaction, and there will never be." This statement, in turn, is analyzable as a conjunction of the following three temporally distinct statements:

1. All past purchases of defective products were followed by dissatisfaction.
2. All present purchases of defective products are followed by dissatisfaction.
3. All future purchases of defective products will be followed by dissatisfaction.

Since the conjunction of these statements will not, according to Kneale (1950; Beauchamp, 1974), support a contrary-to-fact conditional such as L1', it cannot be a law of nature. Because of this, Kneale (1961) proposes a natural necessity solution in order to distinguish lawlike from accidental generalizations. As noted above, however, the author takes such necessity as given and does not attempt to account for and analyze it further.

Finally, there are a number of other problems with lawlike statements in the regularity theory that deserve mention. In order to not limit laws to specific temporal and spatial regions, modern theorists in the regularity tradition stress that lawlike sentences must be unrestricted universals. Yet, regularities in the behavioral and management sciences have seldom been found applicable to all periods of time or all localities. To circumvent this fact, some theorists have suggested that there are behavioral "laws" that are "relatively" general in space and time. The difficulty with claims such as these, however, is that no criteria can be found demarcating a behavioral "law" from an accidental universal. It is difficult, ambiguous, and somewhat arbitrary to designate any law as "relatively" universal in time and space. A second problem with law-like statements arises when one attempts to explain why a lawlike generalization holds. Theorists in the regularity tradition typically assert that a law can be designated as such only if one can show that it is derivable from still other universal generalizations (e.g., Taylor, 1970, p. 18). This solution, of course, only has meaning if one already knows what constitutes a law in the first place. Moreover, in addition to begging the question, one is not provided with criteria for judging the most general universal generalizations but is, instead, asked to search for more and more general laws in an infinite regress. Harré and Madden (1975) term this second problem the "epistemic–deductive criterion" and argue that one has no reason to accept it, and further, from the natural necessity perspective, this criterion neglects certain semantical and explanatory dimensions. Recall in the above statement, L1, that the alleged law could be assumed to be entailed by an existing body of knowledge such as the psychological theory of cognitive dissonance. By doing so, however, one might counterargue that the lawlike status of the statement L1 then rests on the lawlikeness of cognitive dissonance that may or may not be a universal generalization and which in any event would be *assumed* by L1. Further, as natural necessity theorists and others might argue, the nature of the connection or mechanism between the occurrence of the experience of a defective product in L1 and the feelings of dissatisfaction has not been demonstrated in the regularity theory approach. One does not know why and how the regularity occurs.

It is important to place the above criticisms in the proper perspective. The regularity theory has received considerable analysis in recent years and thus much criticism. Despite this fact, it is probably the most widely accepted viewpoint in contemporary philosophy of science. It is certainly the most applied model in the behavioral sciences, though most researchers do not acknowledge the philosophical and conceptual roots of their approaches in their writings. An understanding of the alleged shortcomings of the approach can help marketers construct better theories, and it was in this spirit that the above discussion was presented.

Conditions and Causality. A causal relation seldom, if ever, occurs in isolation. As Bridgman (1927, p. 83) once noted, "We do not have a simple event A connected with a simple event B, but the whole background of the system in which the events occur is included in the concept, and is a vital part of it." There are a number of ways to represent the conditions or circumstances surrounding a causal relation. Here we will only note a few.[10]

Ducasse (1951) proposes that the causal relation be represented in a triadic model. That is, it consists of a cause, an effect, and the circumstances (i.e., conditions) present at the time of the relation. The author defines these components as follows:

> The *cause* of an event B was an event A which, in the then existing circumstances, was *sufficient to* the occurrence of B; and therefore, conversely.
> The *effect* of an event A was an event B which, in the then existing circumstances, was *necessitated by* the occurrence of A. Again:
> A *condition* of an event B was an event A which, in the then existing circumstances, was *necessary to* the occurrence of B; and therefore, conversely.

To take a simple example, consider the observed change in sales as a result of a sharp drop in prices. In this situation, the drop in prices could be considered a cause, the change in sales the effect, and the existence of disposable income, a product delivery system, and so on, the conditions. Typically, the cause and the effect will occur as changes in the situation, while the conditions will not. Unlike Hume, however, Ducasse claims that one need not have a constant conjunction to infer causality. Rather, one need only observe a change in a single event followed by a change in another.

Mackie (1974) has further clarified the meaning of conditions and causality. Using X and Y to represent types of events or situations, the following distinctions are made: "'X is a necessary condition for Y' [means] that whenever an event of type Y occurs, an event of type X also occurs, and 'X is a sufficient condition for Y' [means] that whenever an event of type X occurs, so does an event of type Y" (Mackie, 1974, p. 62). With these distinctions in mind, it is possible to present Mackie's (1965) notion of one important class of causal relations, the "INUS condition." The INUS condition reads: a cause may be regarded as an insufficient but necessary part of a condition that is itself unnecessary but sufficient for the result. Formally,

A is an INUS condition of a result P if and only if, for some X and for some Y, (AX or Y) is a necessary and sufficient condition of P, but A is not a sufficient condition of P and X is not a sufficient condition of P [Mackie, 1965].

In addition to that stated in the definition, it should be noted that AX by itself and Y by itself are sufficient but not necessary for P. As an example, let us examine the claim sometimes made by marketers that brand image (measured by the brand name) affects the perception of quality. When marketers make this claim they are not saying that the brand image is a necessary cause or condition for the attribution of quality. One may judge a product as high or low in quality without knowing the brand. Similarly, marketers are not claiming that the brand image is sufficient for the perception of quality since one must at least attend to, be aware of, and evaluate the brand name before such an attribution can be made. Rather, the brand image may be regarded as an INUS condition in that it is an insufficient but necessary part of a condition that is itself unnecessary but sufficient for the result. Many of the causal relations investigated by marketers are of this sort.

The final theory which in some ways deals with the conditions surrounding causation is the manipulability theory.[11] Consider von Wright's (1971, 1974) definition of causality: "p is a cause relative to q, and q an effect relative to p, if and only if by doing p we could bring about q or by suppressing p we could remove q or prevent it from happening." Notice that this definition relies on the idea of human action. A human agent must actually control things so as to bring about something, or at least an agent must be able to do so in principle. However, von Wright (1974) is clear in specifying that the relation between cause and effect is one between events and that this relation is extrinsic to cause and effect. One merely becomes aware of a causal relation through an actual or hypothetical interference by an agent. The relation between an action by an agent and the result is an intrinsic, logical one:

I am anxious to *separate* agency from causation. Causal relations exist between natural events. When by *doing p* we *bring about q*, it is the *happening* of p which *causes q* to come. And p has this effect quite independently of whether it happens as a result of action or not. The *causal* relation is between p and q. The relation between the agent and cause is different. The agent is not "cause of the cause," but the cause p is the *result* of the agent's action. The effect q is a *consequence* of the action .... The relation between the result and the action is intrinsic. The result must be there, if we are to say correctly that the action has been performed [von Wright, 1974, p. 49].

Although von Wright's thesis is not strictly in the regularity tradition, his emphasis on events, nomic necessity as intrinsic to the cause and effect relation, counterfactual conditionals, and the history of states of events shows him to overlap somewhat with modern versions of Humean causality. In addition, the author makes a contribution to the conditions surrounding exchange by defining the *frame* as the conjunction of features in the situation in which a causal law holds. The frame includes not only those things which remain constant on an occasion of cause and effect and which are necessary for the law to hold, but also *counteracting* causes which could prevent an effect from occurring.

In summary, the regularity theory may be cogently phrased as follows:

"x is the cause of y" means "there is a set of initial conditions x, a set of (temporally) subsequent states of affairs y, and there is a law or a set of laws L, and a set of meaning postulates, definitions, semantic rules etc. M, such that the conjunction of the statements of the laws, meaning postulates etc., with a description of the conditions entails a statement describing the states of affairs which are the effect, provided that no one of these items can be omitted from the premises of the entailment in whole or part" [Harré and Madden, 1975, p. 29].

Natural Necessity and Realist Approaches

A number of theorists reject the Humean view of causation and instead strive in some way to discover the nature of the connection(s) between cause and effect. The arguments are complex and only an outline will be presented here. For well-reasoned introductions to the natural necessity and related realist approaches, see Harré and Madden (1975), Keat and Urry (1975), Anscombe and Geach (1973), Wallace (1974), and Bhasker (1975).

Typically, the natural necessity theorist begins by defining a cause as a material particular that produces or generates something. The cause may be an event, a state of affairs, or a material substance (Harré and Madden, 1975). The cause is said to produce the effect on the basis of its powers, capacities, or liabilities, and these, in turn, are said to reside in the nature of the causal particular. The relation between the nature of the causal particular and its powers, capacities, and liabilities is a necessary, noncontingent one, however. The nature of things is discovered a posteriori, and unlike nominal essences that reveal the surface characteristics of things, a posteriori real essences rest on some model or analogue of the internal structure of the cause. As Harré and Madden (1975, pp. 86–87) note:

"X has the power to A" means "$X \genfrac{}{}{0pt}{}{\text{(will)}}{\text{(can)}}$ do A, in the appropriate conditions, *in virtue of its intrinsic nature.*" . . .

(1) To ascribe a power to a thing or material is to say something specific about what it *will* or *can do*, but it is not to assert any specific hypotheses about the nature of the thing. To ascribe a power to a thing asserts only that it can do what it does in virtue of its nature, whatever that is. It leaves open the question of the exact specification of the nature or constitution in virtue of which the thing, person, or material has the power. It leaves open to be discovered by later empirical investigation, should that prove to be possible.

(2) But to ascribe a power is to say that what the thing or material does or can do is to be understood as brought about not just by the stimuli to which it may be subject or the conditions which it finds itself in, i.e., by extrinsic conditions, but in some measure by the nature or constitution of that thing or material, i.e., by intrinsic conditions.

To account for the nature of causes and the corresponding powers, capacities, and liabilities, the natural necessity theorist represents these properties through the structure (and characteristics of the constituent parts of the structure) of the material particular functioning as a cause. The causal relation, then, consists of a cause, its nature (e.g., powers), an effect, its liabilities, and the surrounding conditions. The concept of the field of potential, which is adopted from physics, is sometimes used to model the nature and powers of a cause.

As a simple example of the natural necessity model of causality, consider the customer–salesperson encounter. Looking at a particular relationship at one point in time, one might notice such things as (1) the presentation of the offer by the salesperson, the responses and questions by the potential customer, and other communication and interpersonal dynamics occurring during the encounter; (2) the impact of norms such as formal rules and procedures each actor must take into account in their role enactments and informal understandings that evolve during the exchange (e.g., the norm of reciprocity, deference and demeanor, etc.); (3) the facilitating and constraining aspects of the situation such as time pressures, physical surroundings, the presence of significant others, the importance and complexity of the objects for exchange, and so forth; and (4) other aspects of the transaction. To explain the outcome of the encounter, the natural necessity theorist claims that it is not sufficient to note antecedent and consequent events, stimuli and responses, or even the alleged lawlike behavior connecting these sequences. Rather, it is also required that the nature of the actors and relationship be specified so that the underlying mechanisms of the encounter can be analyzed. This might entail modeling the cognitive, motivational, or personality structures of the actors and the interface of these structures. It might also consist of modeling the theoretical structure and processes in the encounter using, for example, the social influence model of Tedeschi et al. (1973). In any case, according to the natural necessity theorist, it is necessary to go beyond the notion of regularities in sequences of events and discover the power, capacities, and liabilities producing or generating the flow of actions in the exchange relationship and its outcome.

Explanation and Confirmation in Scientific Inquiry

Perhaps the widest usage of the term explanation lies in its meaning as an answer to the why question.[12] Scientists disagree, however, on the appropriate form and content for scientific explanation. In the following paragraphs, a number of the more important models of scientific explanation are scrutinized, and the related topic of confirmation is discussed. Although causality can be seen to be an important part of each model, disagreement exists among scholars as to its primary role. Some see causality as a special case of the deductive–nomological model; some view it in a probabilistic sense; a few claim that to explain is to identify the causes of phenomena; and still others see causality as the primary concept and explanation as a derivative. Whatever one's preferences as to school of thought, it should be recognised that causality and explanation will be closely connected in any theory construction and research endeavor.

The Positivist Model of Explanation. One of the most elegant and important approaches in scientific explanation is the deductive–nomological (D–N) model due to Hempel (1965).[13] Hempel's model may be conveniently summarized in the following schematic:

$$\text{Explanans} \begin{cases} C_1, C_2, \ldots, C_k & \text{Antecedent conditions} \\ L_1, L_2, \ldots, L_r & \text{Laws} \end{cases}$$
$$\text{Explanandum} \quad E$$

In this schema, explanation is conceived as a deductive argument. The conclusion or phenomenon to be explained is known as the explanandum statement, E. The explanandum is explained through two premises, termed, explanans, which consist of certain explanatory factors. The antecedent conditions, $C_1, C_2, \ldots, C_k$, entail statements as to particular facts (usually the occurrence of events, changes of state, etc.), while $L_1, L_2, \ldots, L_r$ are uniformities or regularities in phenomena that are expressed as general laws. As Hempel (1965, p. 337) notes, the model

answers the question "*Why* did the explanandum-phenomenon occur?" by showing that the phenomenon resulted from certain particular circumstances, specified in $C_1, C_2, \ldots, C_k$, in accordance with the laws $L_1, L_2, \ldots, L_r$. By pointing this out, the argument shows that, given the particular circumstances and the laws in question, the occurrence of the phenomenon *was to be expected*; and it is in this sense that the explanation enables us to *understand why* the phenomenon occurred.

To take a simple example, consider the explanandum statement "The man purchased a glass of lemonade from a salesperson for $0.25." In order to explain this particular exchange using the D–N model, one might first note the following antecedent conditions:

1. The man was very thirsty (C_1).
2. He heard the salesperson's offer, that is, sales pitch (C_2), and saw it as an attractive solution to his need for liquid (C_3).
3. He recognized that he had the means to purchase the drink, that is, $0.25 ($C_4$).
4. The salesperson observed the man as a potential customer and made an offer (C_5).
5. The offer was such, in the eyes of the salesperson, that it covered costs, provided an adequate contribution to expected return on investment (C_6), and so on.

The laws in this example might be of a social, psychological, or economic nature, perhaps expressing regularities of the following types:

1. The greater the deprivation from liquid and other bodily necessities, the greater the drive to satisfy that need (L_1).
2. The greater the physical and social attraction of the salesperson, his or her location and facilities, communication media (e.g., advertisements), and so forth, the more one is motivated to approach that person (L_2).

3. Social behavior is, say from the perspective of the purposive behavior model of Tolman or Lewin, a goal-directed activity where means–ends relationships and evaluation of objects govern actions (L_3), and so on.

Thus, the procedure in using the D–N model is to identify the phenomenon to be explained, the occurrence of antecedent conditions and circumstances, and the laws from which the observed regularities are assumed to be derived. The explanandum statement, "the man purchased a glass of lemonade ...," is explained by deducing its occurrence from the premises. That is, the circumstances and laws are such that the explanandum follows as a valid conclusion. It should be stressed that the above example is, of course, highly abbreviated, and a full explanation would require detailed analysis of the circumstances, phenomenon to be explained, and laws connecting these events. The reader is reminded also of the shortcomings noted earlier with respect to the use of laws of nature and lawlike behavior in marketing and the social sciences.

Hempel (1965) and other theorists in the positivist tradition have further refined explanation into causal explanation and statistical explanation. Since these represent important, frequently used approaches in marketing and elsewhere, they will be briefly reviewed here.

For Hempel, causal explanation is considered to be a special case of the D–N model. A "cause" is claimed to consist of the circumstances or events implied in $C_1, C_2, \ldots, C_k$, while laws are asserted to subsume the regular occurrence of antecedent and consequent events such that the antecedent events provide the sufficient conditions for the occurrence of the explanandum:

Let me restate the point in more general terms. When an individual event b is said to have been caused by another individual event a, then surely the claim is implied that whenever "the same cause" is realized, "the same effect" will occur. But this claim cannot be taken to mean that whenever a recurs then so does b; for a and b are individual events at particular spatiotemporal locations and thus occur only once. Rather, a and b must be viewed as particular events of certain *kinds* ... of which there may be further instances. And the law tacitly implied by the assertion that b, as an event of kind B, was caused by a as an event of kind A is a general statement of causal connection to the effect that, under suitable circumstances, an instance of A is invariably accompanied by an instance of B. In most causal explanations the requisite circumstances are not fully stated; the import of the claim that b was caused by a may then be suggested by the following approximate formulation: Event b was in fact preceded by event a in circumstances which, though not fully specified, were of such a kind that an occurrence of an event of kind A under such circumstances is universally followed by an event of kind B [Hempel, 1965, p. 349].

Hempel feels it important to distinguish causal explanation from other modes of explanation in the D–N model since, according to the author, the former involves *laws of succession* while the latter entails *laws of coexistence*. An example of a law of succession can be found in the statement "the greater the repetition of a message in an advertisement, the greater will be the awareness of the product in the ad for members in the audience." The law implied here is one of psychological learning, and the reference to antecedent events (repetition and exposure to ad) and consequent events (percent of audience aware) presupposes this law of succession. An example of a law of coexistence can be found in the equation relating quantity demanded of a product Q to some marketing decision variable X such as price:

$$Q = aX^b$$

where a and b are constants governing the shape of the response. Assuming this equation underlies the observed regularity found for occurrences of Q and X, the law of coexistence expresses a mathematical relationship between quantity demanded and price. Hempel also separates causal explanation from "explanation of a general law by deductive subsumption under theoretical principles." For example, if the marketer were to explain the law relating quantity demanded to price (such as represented by the above power function) by subsuming it under still more general laws or principles (e.g., the "law" of supply and demand), then he or she would be using a D–N model of explanation but not a causal one.

Statistical explanation is the second broad class of explanatory models offered by Hempel (1965) and others (cf., Salmon et al., 1971) as fundamental to scientific inquiry. By statistical explanation, Hempel means "any explanation that makes use of at least one law or theoretical principle of statistical form." Laws or theoretical principles of statistical form "are statements to the effect that the statistical probability for an event of kind F to be also of kind G is r." As an example, the following statement represents a law of basic statistical form: "the probability that a consumer selected at random from group k (event F) will purchase brand X (event G) is 0.12 (probability r)."

The statistical explanation of greatest interest in marketing and the behavioral sciences is known as inductive statistical (IS) explanation and may be written diagramatically as follows (cf., Kahane, 1973):

1. The probability of G, given F, equals r
2. The probability of G, given not F, equals s (where r is "significantly" greater than s)
3. f is an instance of F
∴ 4. Probably, f is a case of G

In the IS explanation, statements 1 to 3 constitute the explanans, while statement 4 is the explanandum statement deduced from the explanans. Notice that statistical inference in this model, while in the form of a deductive argument, does not fit the structure of the D–N model in every detail. Rather than implying the conclusion with certainty, the explanans in the IS model imply the explanandum with "high probability." Or, as Hempel (1965) puts it, "the argument may be said to show that on the information provided by the explanans, the explanandum event was to be expected with 'practical' certainty, or with very high likelihood" (p. 389). To take a simple example, if the probability of purchase of brand X in period y (event G) is 0.90, given that one has purchased X in the past and expresses positive attitudes and preference for the brand (event F), and if the probability of purchase of X in period y, given that one has not purchased X in the past and does not express positive attitudes and preferences, is 0.08 (event not F), and if person A purchased X in the past and expresses positive attitudes and preferences for X, then the probability that A will purchase X in period y is 0.90. Under these circumstances, and under the IS model, one concludes that the purchase of X by A is explained.

An important question to answer is whether the IS model actually accomplishes the task of explanation. Hempel claims that an event, the explanandum, is explained by the IS model by demonstrating that it is supported with a high degree of probability by the explanans. However, it may be argued that the IS model is limited to *predictions* inferred from the frequency of events of a particular kind. Returning to the above example, suppose that one observes person A purchasing X, and the facts are as stated in the previous paragraph. Can one "explain" the particular purchase by A (or any other individual) with the IS model? Donagan (1966, p. 133) argues persuasively that one cannot:

In cases of this sort the obvious thing to say is that there is *no* explanation of any individual outcome. You will be deceived into imagining that there is only if you confound what it was reasonable to expect with what has been explained. Reasonable expectations and explanations differ fundamentally. It is more reasonable to expect at the first attempt to toss heads with a coin than to win roulette on a given number; but the grounds why it is more reasonable do not *explain* why you succeeded in tossing heads and failed to win at roulette. After all, you might have won at roulette and tossed tails. *With respect to explanation*, chance situations where the odds are equal do not differ from those where the odds are fifty to one or a thousand to one.

Donagan maintains that one should not base explanation on the arbitrary standard of differing degrees of probability wherein premises that make a conclusion "highly" probable are considered adequate whereas those that fail to do so are not. Although the degree of inductive probability in the IS model provides the researcher with a rationale for *predicting* the occurrence of *a* phenomenon, it does not supply one with the *grounds* or conditions for *explaining* why the phenomenon did or did not occur. To explain an event requires that one relate *other* phenomena or events to the one in question along with the laws and/or mechanisms underlying the change in state of the event to be explained. Another problem with the IS model is that it does not easily handle phenomena or events which, by their nature, have low probabilities. Events that are intrinsically improbable deserve explanation, yet the IS model is limited, by definition, to accounting for phenomena that can be represented as occurring "with very high likelihood." The IS model, for instance, cannot easily explain such marketing phenomena as the emergence of consumer movements, consumption of fads and fashions, impulse buying, consumer fetishes, and other unusual or infrequent behaviors in the marketplace. Finally, although beyond the scope of this monograph, there is reason to question the very possibility of inductive inferences of the type found in the IS model (e.g., Carnap, 1950; Salmon, 1971).

A number of authors defend the use of statistical or probabilistic models in scientific inquiry. Salmon et al. (1971) suggest the statistical relevance (SR) model: "an explanation is an *assembly of facts statistically relevant* to the explanandum, *regardless of the degree of probability* that results." As the authors stress, "To say that a certain factor is *statistically relevant* to the occurrence of an event means, roughly, that *it makes a difference to the probability of occurrence*—that is, the probability of the event is different in the presence of the factor than in its absence." The criteria for assessing the explanatory value of a theory relies on concepts from information theory and involves quantification of the reduction in uncertainty achieved, the increase in information attained, and the degree of prediction provided by a theory. Rather than evaluating the adequacy of a specific explanation of a particular event, however, the SR model has the more limited aim of explaining types of events such as the percentage of people purchasing a particular brand or the aggregate amount of switching among brands. Bass' (1974) stochastic preference and brand switching model is one marketing example that roughly fits the SR model.

Finally, it should be noted that there may not be a dichotomy between deductive and/or causal explanation on the one hand and statistical explanation on the other. Suppes (1970), for example, presents a rigorous derivation of causality based on probability theory. The author builds upon Hume's analysis, abandoning, however, reliance on constant conjunction: "Roughly speaking, the modification of Hume's analysis I propose is to say that one event is the cause of another if the appearance of the first event is followed with a higher probability by the appearance of the second, and there is no third event that we can use to factor out the probability relationship between the first and second events" (Suppes, 1970, p. 10). As the reader will see in later chapters, the above distinctions among explanatory frameworks will prove useful in understanding and using causal models in marketing research.

The Realist Model of Explanation. To a certain extent, the evolution in models of explanation parallels that occurring in paradigms of causality. The positivist model of the explanation owes its impetus to the work of David Hume and John Stuart Mill. It relies fundamentally on the identification of the event to be explained, appropriate antecedent events and conditions, and relevant laws (whether these be deterministic or probabilistic). A parallel school of thought has arisen in recent years to challenge the positivist conception. This framework, termed here the realist model, differs in a number of ways from the positivist account.[14] Although arriving on the scene somewhat later than the positivist view, the realist model owes its origins to the work of Aristotle, Locke, and Kant. Discussion will be limited here to a brief summary of the general orientation as found in contemporary writings.

The realist model of explanation accepts some of the features of the positivist approach in that it views its task as accounting for phenomena in nature (thus emphasizing the role of empirical observations). Like the positivist approach, the realist model assumes that scientific inquiry is an objective, rational process subject to certain rules and norms from the philosophy of science. Further, both approaches stress the role of answering "why" questions as the defining characteristic of explanation.

Differences between the positivist and realist models may also be identified. These center around the idea of laws of nature, the nature of necessity in the explanatory structure, and the meaning of theoretical terms. Since the latter issue is discussed in depth in the chapter on construct validity, only the first two points will be touched upon here. In addition, it should be stressed that although some authors in the positivist tradition separate causal from other forms of explanation, the realist orientation views explanation in much the same way as modern necessity theorists conceive of causation (see earlier discussion on natural necessity and realist approaches to causality).

The realist begins by rejecting the very foundation of the positivist model. First, the notion of Humean causality is rejected as being inadequate. For reasons similar to those discussed earlier, reliance on laws of nature is disputed as being a useful way to represent the link between antecedents or conditions on the one hand and the phenomenon to be explained on the other. Second, the realist often chides the positivist for providing *some* grounds for expecting why or when a phenomenon has or will occur (i.e., fulfilling some grounds for prediction) without necessarily specifying the mechanism or process of how it did or will in fact occur. Explanation in the positivist model does not truly answer why a phenomenon occurred, according to the realist, but is merely concerned with predictable regularities between antecedent and consequent events.

Given these objections, the realist then proposes that the key to explanation lies within the causal processes generating the phenomenon to be explained. To explain the occurrence of a phenomenon, the realist strives to delineate the characteristics of the connection between the causes of a phenomenon and its change in state. Typically, this will involve a modeling of natural necessity, the structure of the relationships between cause and effect, or some other aspect of the mechanism producing a change in a phenomenon. The natural necessity model of Harré and Madden (1975) mentioned earlier would be one example of explanation in this sense. As these authors note, "To ascribe a power to a particular which is seen to be causally productive of some effect is to offer a schematic explanation of that effect, and in the growth of knowledge of the natures and constitution of things the explanation schema is filled out" (Harré and Madden, 1975, p. 91).

In general, the realist claims that to fully answer why questions one must identify *how* a cause and set of circumstances bring about a change in the phenomenon of interest. This, in turn, will be a function of the nature or characteristics of the cause and its relationship to the phenomenon to be explained. A number of approaches in the behavioral sciences in recent years have assumed the realist posture. These include, among others, efforts at modeling information processing of people, structural theories of behavior, models of social action, and some theories viewing social behavior as an exchange, symbolic interaction, dramaturgical encounter, or rule-following activities. Marketers are only now beginning to use some of these approaches in their work. The shift from the positivist to the realist orientation in marketing and the social sciences has involved a move from basically stimulus–response theories to S–O–R models and more interactive, social paradigms.

Confirmation and Testability. Scientists generally acknowledge explanation as the primary objective of scientific inquiry in general and theory construction in particular. An important question to address, then, is how may one evaluate the adequacy of one's explanations? This problem, in turn, is embedded in the general question of how one comes to experience, know, and understand the meaning of phenomena in the world. It is in this regard that considerable controversy exists. Some theorists, termed conventionalists, see reality as determined largely by the construction of the individual and groups of individuals with vested interests. Competition and power among scientists, the transmitters and users of knowledge, and others is felt to shape the content of what is known and accepted as truth. Conventionalists have opened an important line of inquiry in scientific thought by viewing science as a social system. As the viewpoint crystallizes, it should contribute much to our understanding of the dynamics involved in the evaluation of scientific explanations. Discussion here, however, will be limited to the more traditional views of the positivist and realist approaches.[15]

Positivists and realists both believe that reality exists independently of the attempts to explain that reality. Since explanations strive to tell us something about the structure of the world as it is, one must rely on observation and empirical evidence as the means for judging how good one's explanations are. Two schools of thought dominate contemporary standards for evaluating explanations. The confirmationist school reasons that empirical evidence provides indirect and varying degrees of support for the truth of one's explanations. The support is indirect in that it is impossible to verify the truth of the theory on which an explanation rests solely on the evidence of past and present observations. Any future piece of evidence could conceivably disprove a theory or explanation. Again, this has come to be known as the problem of induction. Further, evidence consistent with an explanation is regarded as providing partial, temporary support by the confirmationist. Part of the logic behind the doctrine of replicating research findings in the natural and behavioral sciences is that greater confirmation of theories is provided the more the number of supporting instances. Confirmationists typically attempt to obtain confirming evidence for a hypothesis in controlled conditions and then later broaden the generality of the hypothesis by varying the setting, time, and sample of people involved. This is especially the modus operandi for positivists, since their explanations rest fundamentally on universal generalizations (i.e., laws).

A slightly different point of view is provided by the falsificationist school. This school argues that the truth of a theory or explanation can only be falsified by the evidence at hand. Popper (1968) nicely points out the features of this point of view:

We may if we like distinguish four different lines along which the testing of a theory could be carried out. First there is the logical comparison of the conclusions among themselves, by which the internal consistency of the system is tested. Secondly, there is the investigation of the logical form of the theory, with the object of determining whether it has the character of an empirical or scientific theory, or whether it is, for example, tautological. Thirdly, there is the comparison with other theories, chiefly with the aim of determining whether the theory would constitute a scientific advance should it survive our various tests. And finally, there is the testing of the theory by way of empirical applications of the conclusions which can be derived from it.

The purpose of this last kind of test is to find out how far the new consequences of the theory ... stand up to the demands of practice .... With the help of other statements, previously accepted, certain singular statements—which we may call "predictions"—are deduced from the theory .... From among these statements, those are selected which are not derivable from the current theory .... Next we seek a decision as regards these (and other) derived statements by comparing them with the results of practical applications and experiments. If this decision is positive, that is, if the singular conclusions turn out to be acceptable, or *verified*, then the theory has, for a time being, passed its test .... But if the decision is negative, or in other words, if the conclusions have been *falsified*, then their falsification also falsifies the theory ....

It should be noticed that a positive decision can only temporarily support the theory, for subsequent negative decisions may always overthrow it. So long as a theory withstands detailed and severe tests ... we may say it has "proved its mettle" or that it is "*corroborated*" by past experience [pp. 32–33].

Popper and other falsificationists couch their view of confirmation in the form of a deductive argument. Empirical evidence never proves a theory but can only disprove it. Like many confirmationists, however, falsifications usually rely on universal statements of regularities in nature as the basis for their explanations. It is these regularities that are thought to be falsifiable. Confirmation and testability are generally considered essential characteristics of any theory (e.g., Zaltman et al., 1973).

Summary

The notion of causality is at the heart of human understanding. We cannot hope to interpret and explain behavior without confronting the very essence and meaning of causality itself. Yet the concept defies simple representation, and it has provoked considerable controversy as to its nature and role in scientific inquiry.

This chapter has explored classic and modern conceptualizations of causation. It began by tracing the development of the concept from the seminal works of Aristotle through important contributions by Galileo and classical thinkers such as Hume, Kant, and Mill. Considerable time was spent on recent refinements culminating in two competing schools of thought: the regularity theory and modern necessity theories. The former builds directly upon the framework of Hume in that it makes contiguity in time and place, temporal priority, constant conjunction, and the idea of a cognitive or psychological necessity between cause and effect the defining structure of causality. The regularity theory also places primary emphasis on scientific laws, or universal generalizations, which state that whenever an event of type x occurs (the cause), an event of type y happens also (the effect). The characteristics of laws as links between cause and effect were investigated, and a number of shortcomings were pointed out. The treatment of modern necessity theories focused on the mechanisms or processes connecting cause to effect. Rather than assuming these to be general laws that are, in turn, subsumed under still more general laws, modern necessity theorists typically strive to represent the powers, capacities, and liabilities of causal agents and phenomena involved in the causal relationship. The relationship itself is viewed as a necessary, noncontingent one. The nature of the causal agent is given primary attention, and its ability to produce the effect is modeled through its internal structure and the characteristics of the constituent parts of that structure. The analogue of the physicists' concept of the field of potential is often used in this approach. The chapter closed with a discussion of the concepts of explanation and confirmation and their intimate relation to the notion of causality.

An understanding of causality and its role in the theory construction and research phases of scientific inquiry is essential if one is to avoid two of the most common faults in contemporary marketing research: blind empiricism and sterile tautologies. The researcher commits the first error when he or she fails to test an underlying theory in his or her research. Instead of investigating theoretical cause-and-effect processes in an explanatory context, the practitioner of blind empiricism limits inquiry to relationships among observable variables. The converse of this practice is expressed in the construction of sterile tautologies. Unlike blind empiricism which focuses entirely on empirical phenomena, the practitioner of sterile tautologies deals entirely with mathematical or logical relationships. In contrast, scientific explanation demands that the researcher model cause and effect and the laws and/or mechanisms producing the phenomenon to be explained. This, in turn, requires theoretical statements and testing of behavior in the world of experience. Discussion in succeeding chapters elaborates on the causal modeling process, presenting numerous illustrations of its use.

Notes

[1] For a historical treatment of causality including the contributions due to Aristotle, see the two excellent volumes by Wallace (1972, 1974). The labels for Aristotle's types of causes were first proposed by medieval philosophers.

[2] The quality and importance of Hume's writings on causality cannot be overestimated. The student of causality will find Hume's treatments in his *Treatise of Human Nature* and *An Enquiry Concerning Human Understanding* quite rigorous and timely. For modern treatments of causality, including new thoughts on Hume's contributions, the reader is referred to Mackie (1974), Beauchamp (1974), Sosa (1975), and Harré and Madden (1975).

[3] These rules are taken from the quotes appearing in Ducasse (1966). Ducasse presents additional comments and criticisms of Hume's ideas.

[4] Most of Kant's (1961) thoughts on causality may be found in his *Critique of Pure Reason*, particularly the second and third analogies. For analyses of his arguments, see Suchting (1967), Beck (1967, 1969), and Murphy (1969). For discussions of *a priori, a posteriori, synthetic, analytic,* and *necessity,* on which portions of the following discussion are based, see Carnap (1966, pp. 177–183), Kahane (1973, pp. 316–324), Kneale (1961), Molnar (1969), Beauchamp (1974), and Harré and Madden (1975, pp. 19–21, 70–81).

[5] In the words of Kant, a sequence of perceptions consisting only of the perceptions of two events, A and B, may be interpreted as follows:

In an appearance which contains a happening . . . B can be apprehended only as following upon A . . . . The order in which the perceptions succeeded one another in apprehension is . . . determined (bestimmt) . . . . In the series of . . . perceptions [of, for example, a house, there is] no determinate (bestimmte) order specifying at what point I must begin in order to connect the manifold empirically. But in the perceptions of an event there is always a rule that makes the order in which the perceptions (in the apprehension of this appearance) follow upon one another a *necessary* order . . . . The objective succession will therefore consist in that order of the manifold of appearance according to which *in conformity with a rule,* the apprehension of that which happens follows upon the apprehension of that which preceeds . . . . In conformity with such a rule there must lie in that which precedes an event the condition of a rule according to which this event invariably and necessarily follows. I cannot reverse this order, proceeding back from the event to determine (bestimmen) through apprehension that which precedes. For appearance never goes back from the succeeding to the preceding point of time. The advance, on the other hand, from a given time to the determinate (bestimmte) time that follows is a necessary advance. Therefore, since there certainly is something that follows, I must refer it necessarily to something else which precedes it and upon which it follows in conformity with a rule, that is, of necessity. The event, as the conditioned, thus affords reliable evidence of some condition, and this condition is what determines (bestimmt) the event . . . . In order that . . . the *objective relation* of appearances that follow upon one another . . . be known as determined (bestimmt) the relation between the two states must be so thought that it is thereby determined (bestimmt) as necessary which of them must be placed before, and which of them after, and that they cannot be placed in the reverse relation. But the concept which carries with it a necessity of synthetic unity can only be a pure concept that lies in the understanding, not in perception; and in this case it is the concept of the *relation of cause and effect*, the former of which determines (bestimmt) the latter in time, as its consequence . . . [Kant, 1961, quoted in Suchting, 1967].

[6] For excellent summaries and analyses of these procedures, see Mackie (1974, appendix) and Kahane (1973, pp. 261–264).

[7] For a discussion of some of the arguments against the inclusion of the concept of causality in scientific inquiry, see Bunge (1959, pp. 91–98) and Wallace (1972, vol. 2, part 2).

[8] Discussions of modern Humean, Kantian, manipulability, singularist, and necessity orientations can be found in Beauchamp (1974). Perhaps the best presentations of the regularity and natural necessity approaches may be found in Mackie (1974) and Harré and Madden (1975), respectively.

[9] For counterexamples damaging to the regularity theory conception of laws, see Harré and Madden (1975, ch. 2).

[10] In addition to those presented below, the reader might find Davidson's (1967) treatment of causality informative. Among other things, Davidson analyzes Mill's and Ducasse's notions of the conditions surrounding causal relations and concludes it is important to distinguish between causes and the *features* of causal instances logically independent of cause and effect.

[11] For a review and original papers dealing with the manipulability theory, see Beauchamp (1974, part 4).

[12] The everyday use of "explanation" typically takes the form of a what explanation or a reason-giving explanation (c.f., Taylor, 1970). The what explanation specifies the occurrence of a phenomenon or a sequence of events. It describes what happened, not necessarily why. The reason-giving explanation is limited to an individual's beliefs and feelings as to his or her own behavior or characteristics. Rather than providing the causes of one's behavior, feelings, or beliefs, per se, a person will most often supply a reason-giving explanation in order to influence the judgments or evaluations that others form. Both what explanations and reason-giving explanations may be converted to or become part of scientific explanations. The discussion below is limited to an analysis of the nature, forms, and implications of scientific explanation, that is, those striving to answer why questions.

[13] Hempel's model and a number of offshoots are also referred to as the covering law model in the literature. Although not nearly as narrow and rigid as the philosophical school of logical positivism from which it is descended, the deductive–nomological model is still considered the archtype of modern positivist approaches in the philosophy of science (cf., Keat and Urry, 1975, ch. 1).

[14] For a review of the realist model contrasting it with other approaches, see Keat and Urry (1975). Although still largely identified with the positivist tradition, Hempel (1973) and Popper (1972) have broadened their outlooks in recent years, occasionally embracing what is largely a realist orientation. Except for fundamental differences in regard to the role of laws of nature, natural necessity, and the meaning of theoretical terms, there has been a noticeable trend toward convergence and synthesis among various positivist and realist writings in the past few years.

[15] The conventionalist philosophy may be found in Kuhn (1970), Merton (1973), and Keat and Urry (1975, ch. 3). Feyerabend (1970) presents an anarchist view of science, while Berger and Luckmann (1966) outline the social processes involved in the construction of reality. For an approach integrating realist and conventionalist orientations in a marketing context, see Bagozzi (1976a).

TWO

BASIC CONCEPTS IN CAUSAL MODELING

Causal modeling provides the researcher with a systematic methodology for developing and testing theories in marketing. Before we can present the details of the approach, however, it will prove useful to outline a number of basic assumptions and conventions. The discussion begins with two fundamental areas in marketing where causal modeling is applicable; namely, the study of *human behavior* and the study of *social action*. After analyzing the distinction between behavior and action, the role of causality in both areas is explored in greater depth focusing on the structure of the causal relationship. Finally, the chapter closes with an introduction to various areas where causal modeling is appropriate. These include paradigms ranging from cause-and-effect at the level of the psychology of the individual to complex processes of interaction at the social level.

The researcher uses causal models to understand and explain phenomena in the marketplace. The particular structure of the causal model used in this sense will depend, in general, on three factors. First and foremost, the causal model will be a function of the phenomena to be explained, the scientific problems of interest. As developed below, the subject matter one studies constrains the type of causal model appropriate for achieving explanation and other scientific goals. Second, the specific antecedent conditions, laws, and/or mechanisms shaping the subject matter also influence the appropriate causal model. Third, the school of thought one assumes as a framework for study will contribute to the choice of causal model. Typically, the regularity theory, natural necessity approaches, or realist orientations will comprise the set of schools of thought for representing causation.

Human Behavior and Social Action

Scientific explanation in marketing addresses two generic phenomena[1]: behavior and action. Not only does the distinction underlie events and experiences as they occur in the marketplace, but it has been credited by philosophers of science as the quality separating the natural from the behavioral sciences. We explore this distinction in greater detail below.

Behavior refers to (1) the things people and organizations actually do and (2) the changes in material and nonmaterial entities people and organizations directly or indirectly bring about. The phenomena that constitute behavior can be either directly observed or inferred. In either case, it is the investigator or researcher who does the observation or inference.

Consider first the things people and organizations do. Probably the simplest things people and organizations do are to perform individual *acts*. Acts are physical movements or other events performed in a relatively short period of time. People search and shop for goods, make purchases, complain about advertisements, clip and save coupons, return products to retailers, discuss aspects of new products, and many other acts too numerous to mention. Organizations make sales, grant credit, place ads, incur expenses, deliver goods, offer promotions, change prices, and so on. When individuals acts are repeated, occur over relatively long periods of time, or are part of sequences of different acts, they are often termed *activities*. Common examples are brand loyalty, decision making, consumption and use of products, planning, implementing, and controlling a marketing effort, marketing research, transporting and storing goods, and so on. Finally, a third class of things people and organizations do is to participate in *relationships*. For example, giving and getting in exchange relationships entail observable things people do for or to others. Similarly, threats and promises in power or conflict relationships between members of the channel of distribution are instances of things done by organizations. It should be stressed that "relationships" as a category of *behavior* refers solely to the acts conducted reciprocally by the parties in an interaction. As will be shown below, relationships have a broader meaning when referring to *social action*.

Consider next changes in material and nonmaterial entities brought about by people or organizations. Typically, these include objects produced by people, the patterns or structure of behavior exhibited by people or organizations, or other aspects of social and collective behavior modeled by the investigator. In sociology and other behavioral sciences, these things are often referred to as social facts (cf., Ritzer, 1975). Examples of changes in material entities brought about by people in the marketing context include the diffusion of innovations, trends in sales response, marketing productivity, and market share differentials. Examples of changes in nonmaterial entities include life-style patterns, consumer movements, differentiation and integration of marketing functions, and the interaction between the environment on the one hand and the internal structure of marketing organizations on the other. These latter phenomena are listed under nonmaterial entities because they involve systems of abstract concepts. Although inferred from observable phenomena, they entail unobservable things such as structures, patterns, and functions.

Human behavior in the senses noted above comprises a large part of the subject matter of marketing. Marketers seek to explain changes in this subject matter in a variety of ways. Sometimes the marketing researcher will control or manipulate one kind of behavior (e.g., a change in price, advertising appeal, product offering) in order to see the effect on another kind of behavior (e.g., acts of inquiry, purchase, or brand switching by consumers). At other times, the researcher may merely search for patterns and changes in behavioral variables over time or in a cross-section study using correlational techniques. Occasionally, the marketer relies on simulations, judgments, or logical analyses to achieve an understanding of behavior in the marketplace. In all of these cases, however, explanation occurs through the modeling or representation of relationships among observable or inferred (by the researcher) variables. The subjective thoughts, feelings, experiences, and so forth, of the people comprising the subject matter of human behavior are not modeled in this approach. Rather, inquiry is concentrated on revealed preferences, actual purchases, and other things observed by the researcher.

In contrast to human behavior, *social action* refers to both what people are seen to do (or not do) and the meanings, reasons, and other subjective experiences they have for doing (or not doing) these things. Max Weber (1964) was one of the first to consider social action:

In "action" is included all human behavior when and in so far as *the acting individual* attaches a subjective meaning to it. Action in this sense may be either overt or purely inward or subjective; it may consist of positive intervention in a situation, or of deliberately refraining from such intervention or passively acquiescing in the situation. Action is social in so far as, by virtue of the subjective meaning attached to it *by the acting individual* (or individuals), it takes account of the behavior of others and is thereby oriented in its course [p. 88, emphasis added].

A number of points in Weber's account deserve mention. First, by including what people do, social action builds upon human behavior. Indeed, it often seeks to account for human behavior, to explain its occurrence. One could argue from the perspective of the philosophy of science, for example, that many attempts at explanation—using only variables from the human behavior category—do not adequately explain why a phenomenon occurs. As an illustration, take the case of an advertising response model relating a change in sales to a change in advertising effort. This model claims that one can, in principle, explain a change in sales as a function of advertising (and perhaps other behavioral variables). The assertion is often made that the better the fit or predictive ability of the model, the greater the degree of explanation. And from the viewpoint of the regularity theory of causality (see discussion in the first chapter), such a claim appears valid. However, from the perspective of natural necessity or realist approaches, scientific explanation may not be achieved in the sales response model because the mechanism or connection explaining why a change in advertising should lead to a change in sales has not been modeled *and* demonstrated. The fact that observations of changes in advertising and changes in sales confirm one's predictions (and perhaps have done so with a regularity approaching an empirical "law") does not provide information as to the processes (e.g., psychological, social, economic) linking these changes. Social action comprises one broad class of phenomena that can be used to model links between empirical associations of behavioral events.

A second point to notice in social action is the primary emphasis placed upon subjective experiences. These have to do with the reasons people give for doing what they do, the meanings they attach to their actions and that of others, the self-monitored following of rules that they may use (e.g., Harré and Secord, 1973), and the beliefs and affect that they experience. Yet, from a scientific viewpoint, one might well question the very existence of subjective experiences as well as their utility. These topics will be the subject for the next section and are postponed until then.

Finally, scientific explanation in the context of social action differs from that typically pursued with respect to human behavior. Sometimes the subjective experiences of people are the objects of inquiry, the dependent variables. For example, marketers often study personality structure, attitude change, attribution processes, and information processing phenomena as they relate to the consumption of products and services. The researcher might study these subjective experiences in their own right or in conjunction with such determinants as physical stimuli (e.g., product attributes) or social influence (e.g., persuasion). In other instances, marketers study the consequences or implications of subjective phenomena. For example, advertisers often investigate the effects of cognitive experiences (as a function of message or cummunicator characteristics) on subsequent purchase behaviors. In still other cases, marketers model structures or processes among subjective experiences. The relationship between cognitions and affect in the Fishbein attitude model or the interactions among perception, comprehension, memory, evaluations, and intentions in information processing models are two examples. Finally, subjective experiences in the form of shared meanings, social influence, and social interaction in general form yet another class of phenomena not directly accounted for in human behavior studies. In addition to the observable actions of the parties in a relationship, social interactions contain and are shaped by the individual and joint subjective experiences of the actors. This and related topics are discussed in the following section of the chapter.

Before investigating the issues involved in human behavior and social action in greater depth, it will prove useful to briefly discuss the distinction between the natural and behavioral sciences. The natural and behavioral sciences have much in common. Both aim to achieve explanation and understanding. Both utilize the scientific method and adhere to general philosophy of science standards. Moreover, both often employ similar methodologies and data analytic procedures (Bunge, 1973). The natural and behavioral sciences differ primarily in the subject matter they address. The former addresses movements, biophysical operations, and events. It generally includes the disciplines of physics, chemistry, biology, and their hybrids. The latter, in contrast, deals with the interactions of subjective experiences and their relation to physical movements and events. The disciplines in the behavioral sciences include sociology, economics, biology, political science, psychology, anthropology, and related fields such as organization behavior, marketing, and, on occasion, history. Kaplan (1964, pp. 32–33) states the distinction nicely:

Behavioral science deals with those processes in which symbols, or at any rate meanings, play an essential part . . . .

What is significant here is that the data for behavioral science are not sheer movements but actions—that is, acts performed in a perspective which gives them meaning or purpose. Plainly, it is of crucial importance that we distinguish between the meaning of the act to the actor (or to other people, including ourselves, reacting with him) and its meaning to us as scientists, taking the action as subject-matter. I call these, respectively, *act meaning* and *action meaning* . . . we may note that behavioral science is involved in a double process of interpretation, and it is this which is responsible for such of its techniques as are distinctive. The behavioral scientist must first arrive at an act meaning, that is, construe what conduct a particular piece of behavior represents; and then he must search for the meaning of the interpreted action, its interconnections with other actions or circumstances . . . . The difference [between the natural and behavioral sciences] is not that there are two kinds of understanding, but that the behavioral scientist has two different things to understand . . . .

Understanding of *social action* in marketing requires "a double process of interpretation" in that the marketing researcher must first discover the reasons why people do what they do, the meaning(s) of one's acts and those of others *for the people under study*, and so on, and second, relate these act meanings in an explanatory structure including the constraining and facilitating role of the situation and other conditions. The explanation of *human behavior* in marketing, in contrast, requires a similar process except that the act meanings of those under study are not modeled. Significantly, as shown below, causal modeling can be a means for achieving explanation in either domain when properly applied.

The Mind–Body Problem and Related Issues

All theories of human behavior and social action proceed from a foundation of assumptions as to the nature of the human body and human mind and the character of the relations between them. The issue is important because not only do the assumptions determine what kind of variables are allowable in one's models, they indirectly influence the form and content of the theories one uses to model interactions among people and between people and their environments. These constraints, in turn, affect one's choice of causal model.

The Mind–Body Problem in Perspective

Before addressing the question of whether mental events exist and are useful, it will prove helpful to examine the nature of the interaction between mental events and human behavior as posed by philosophers. The classical position by Descartes (1931-1934; 1966) provides a good starting point.[2] Descartes asserted that man consists of two essentially distinct substances, body and soul. This has come to be known as Cartesian dualism in the literature. For Descartes, the body is material in that it has properties of mass, position, volume, velocity, and so forth. The mind does not possess these attributes but rather is capable of three cognitive faculties: pure intellect, sense, and imagination. Over the years since Descartes first developed his ideas, philosophers have tended to polarize into schools of thought either accepting or rejecting a strict dichotomy between mind and body. Spicker (1970) points out that what has developed since Descartes as Cartesian dualism is, in fact, perhaps more extreme than Descartes intended. This can be seen in Descartes' claim that while pure intellect can be conceived apart from sense and imagination (i.e., pure intellect is the activity of the mind contemplating itself), the latter concepts can only arise in a mind through their union with a body. Thus, a modern reader of Descartes might interpret the mind in a somewhat organic and physiological sense, providing a bridge from body to soul.

The modern notion of the mind–body problem may be conveniently represented through a set of four incompatible propositions known as the "inconsistent tetrad" (Campbell, 1970):

1. The human body is a material thing.
2. The human mind is a spiritual thing.
3. Mind and body interact.
4. Spirit and matter do not interact.

Any three of the propositions "are mutually consistent and can all be true. But any three together entail that the fourth is false. It takes at least three of them to disprove the fourth, but any three are enough to dispose of the remaining one" (Campbell, 1970, p. 15). Since there are convincing arguments for thinking that each of the four propositions is individually true, the mind–body problem consists in determining which one is, in fact, false.

Many positions and arguments can be made in regard to the mind–body problem. Here we consider only two of the more persuasive. The first "solution" to the mind–body problem is that of the behaviorists. Behaviorists deny that the mind is a thing at all. Rather, it is claimed that all that may ever be known are overt actions and behaviors. Behaviors and events cause and are caused solely by other behaviors or events. For the behaviorist, it is meaningless to say that mental states cause other mental states or that mental events cause or are caused by physical events. Theory, in general, and causality, in particular, for the behaviorist rests fundamentally on the identification of stimuli and responses and the behavioral "laws" expressing the regularity between these two observable things.

A second school of thought diametrically opposed to the behaviorists is that of the causal theory of the mind. Campbell (1970, pp. 80–81) summarizes the features of this position as follows:

The Causal Theory of mind has two strands: that the various mental events and processes are postulated causes of segments of behavior belonging to various recognizable patterns, and that the mental causes are given their names in virtue of their postulated connection with those behavior patterns. The first strand admits the view that the mind is something inner, separate, and standing behind behavior. It thus allows for the existence of definite, nonbehavioral, nondispositional mental episodes and states, and so avoids one chief problem of Behaviorism. It also allows (indeed insists) that mental states are causally efficacious in behavior and so avoids the other chief problem [i.e., treating mental events only as effects of whatever causes human behavior and failing to account for certain logical and empirical grounds for believing mental events affect behavior]. The second strand, that mental terms get their meaning by reference to the behavioral effects of the mental states they denote, preserves the truth of Behaviorism that there is a conceptual connection of mind with behavior. But the connection between them is not that of referring to just the same facts.

The Causal Theory of mind views mental concepts as theoretical. The picture it paints is this: Men, confronted with the surprises of human (and animal) behavior in comparison with the activities of water, earth, and trees, have surmised that something inside them is causing their distinctive conduct. This something, of which little is known but its causal powers, is called a mind. And the mind is credited with as much complexity as there is complexity and differences in the characteristically human behavior of men. Talk about mental characteristics is talk of a theory (the theory of minds) about what makes men tick.

As noted below, there is an impressive body of research demonstrating the role of the mind in human behavior and social action.

One final caveat is in order. Following the argument of central-state materialism (cf., Campbell, 1970, ch. 5), one may reject psychophysical dualism as an ontological theory. In particular, the notion of the mind as a spiritual thing is rejected in favor of its conceptualization as a nonmaterial entity to be inferred from behavior and social action. Further, the connection of mind to body is regarded as one of neurophysiological mechanisms. However, as

Harré and Secord (1975, p. 302) stress (see also, Harré, 1972, ch. 8; Ayers, 1968, ch. 6):

> ... the direction of scientific development *must* always be toward the development of further knowledge of physiological mechanisms, the mechanisms by which we perform our various tasks. *But one must so construct one's conceptual system that this important truth does not encourage one in the fallacy of trying to reduce the tasks to physiology.* They remain social, cognitive, intellectual or motor tasks. Thus for us the social *performance* of human beings is to be described in a system of concepts that are not reducible to nonsocial concepts, either behavioral or, still further, physiological. But in order to ground our capacities or powers in these ways in physiological mechanisms we need the intermediate concept of a *grounded disposition* to behave in those ways, and the grounded dispositions of agents are their powers. [Emphasis added.]

The point the authors make is that the causal theory of the mind and social action have meaning in their own right and are frequently useful in the interpretation and explanation of phenomena such as that found in the marketplace.

Thus it appears that we are confronted with a choice between two views for interpreting the relation between mind and body: behaviorism and the causal theory of the mind. How is one to choose between them? Or must one choose at all? Before these questions may be answered, more basic questions must be addressed regarding the very existence of mental concepts and their utility for explaining behavior.

Mental Concepts and Marketing Research

In everyday speech and common sense reasoning, people make reference to mental events continuously. They use terms such as needs, wants, desires, tastes, goals, beliefs, preferences, and so on to explain or justify their actions in ordinary life situations. The same or similar terms are used to interpret the actions of others or events and happenings in the world. Our conversations are peppered with references to mental events, and, indeed, we take them for granted and assume them to be legitimate.

At a logical or conceptual level, mental events seem to cluster primarily into three categories. One category deals largely with the affective side of human nature, particularly as manifest in one's felt or experienced *relation* to things or others. For lack of a better term, philosophers typically indicate this category of mental events by the term "want." From a broad interpretation of the term and despite various nuances, "want" shares a common meaning with each of the following terms (among others): need, desire, taste, utility, motive, goal, preference, and like.[3] When consumers say they "need to buy a detergent," "desire to see a movie," or "prefer brand x," their statements reflect three things. First, the use of a want-term signifies some degree of affect that may vary considerably depending on context and user. Some want-terms may express relatively strong emotions such as reflected in a new salesperson's "need to make a sale." Other want-terms might contain only minimal amounts of affect such as seen in one's "preference for one brand of salt over another." Further, affect may be either positive or negative as well as varying in magnitude. One may like brand x, dislike brand y, or have no preference for a particular product or service. Second, a want-term expresses a relation between a person on the one hand and an object, event, or another individual on the other. It expresses how one feels about something or someone else. Finally, wants are usually action oriented, implying a motive of one sort or another. Thus, "to want to make a purchase" or "to place a high utility on a particular product" is to imply one will be motivated, in the proper circumstances, to perform an action of some kind in order to achieve positive affect (or avoid displeasure). The action might be a trial purchase, an increase in a standing order, or a switch in shopping behavior, to give specific examples.

   A second category of mental events deals with the thinking side of human nature and is labeled here cognitions. Cognitions are factual statements as to the existence or description of a thing or event. They frequently convey information of the form "x leads to y," but unlike wants, they are action neutral in the sense that they are not charged with the attractive or repulsive characteristics of affect. Further, they imply no compulsion to act as is the case for evaluative terms (discussed below). Common examples of cognitive terms include beliefs, expectancies, and subjective probabilities. Thus, when a person says "I believe breakfast cereal brand x has more nutritional content than brand y" or "using fertilizer z will accelerate the growth of one's lawn," he or she is expressing a cognition. Notice that cognitions express a statement of fact about some other person, object, practice, or thing. They may be proven true or false in an objective sense. Wants are not factual in this sense. Wants are relatively more person centered in that they convey information as to the subjective affect experienced by the communicator. Cognitions are relatively more object centered in that they express thoughts as to some factual content of an external thing or relationship between things. Although one may be mistaken in his or her beliefs, he or she can, in principle, come to discover the factual error in reasoning. Wants do not exhibit this quality.

   Finally, the third basic mental event is the moral belief or evaluation. Moral beliefs have two forms: (1) x ought (ought not) to be done and (2) x is good (bad). By definition, moral beliefs are action oriented; they advocate a policy. In addition, moral beliefs convey one's evaluation of another person, object, act, or thing in that they express degrees of favorableness or unfavorableness. Unlike wants or cognitions, moral beliefs always imply some third party, whether this be an internalized, powerful, or respected other, a body of law or rules, or "society" in general. As such, moral beliefs form an important part of persuasion, manipulation, and social control. Thus, when a person says "you ought to dine at Carlo's" or "to do business with firm x is bad because they discriminate against minorities," he or she is expressing a moral belief and indirectly or directly advocating some action.

In addition to common sense and logical reasons for accepting mental events, a number of empirical criteria may be cited. These criteria derive from psychological research and demonstrate that it is meaningful to speak of physical things affecting mental events and mental events affecting physical things. Consider first the impact of physical things upon mental events. Research in physiology indicates that the desire for food and sex is influenced, in part, by the actions of glands such as the hypothalamus. Psychological research clearly shows that physical stimuli affect such mental processes as comprehension, memory, learning, and information integration. Moreover, considerable evidence exists documenting the effect of stimuli upon emotional states ranging from fear, anxiety, and terror on the one hand to attraction, pleasure, and joy on the other. Finally, personality processes can be seen to depend, in part, upon social learning experiences (e.g., Mischel, 1973).

Research also clearly shows that mental events affect physical events, at least those connected to social action. In the area of perception, for example, people vary in attentiveness and selectively perceive and structure their environment. Mental experiences motivate individuals to behave in certain ways in that people consciously self-monitor their behaviors, adjust their activities to achieve goals according to rules, norms, and expectations, and in general function as agents initiating behavior as well as responding to stimuli and the desires of others. Behavioral scientists in recent years have developed many models of mental processes and their impact on behavior. A recent marketing example may be found in Bagozzi (1976b) where the personality structure of salespeople is shown to interact with situational factors and interpersonal variables to affect performance and satisfaction.

The three categories of mental events—wants, cognitions, and moral beliefs—can be seen to comprise the basic concepts upon which many psychological, social psychological, and other behavioral science theories are built. For example, modern theorists describe the concept of motivation as consisting of subjective affect and cognitive processes (e.g., Weiner, 1974). Some theorists also include physiological processes and social or cultural experiences as part of motivation. Similarly, contemporary conceptualizations of emotional behavior combine cognitive, affective, physiological, and normative processes. Even purposeful behavior is now believed to consist of both cognitive and affective components in that one must be aware of a particular goal and have a desire to approach or avoid that goal for a purpose to be inferred (Locke, 1969).[4] Economic theory, too, is concerned with mental events at least to the extent of decision making activities and the consequences of tastes, desires, and preferences.

Perhaps the most researched paradigm in marketing combining mental concepts is that of attitude theory.[5] Consider the following model representing an individual's attitude toward a particular act such as the purchase of a product (cf., Fishbein, 1967a; Lutz, 1975):

$$\text{A-act} = \sum_{i=1}^{n} B_i a_i$$

where A-act is one's attitude toward an act, B_i is one's belief that the act will have some consequence i, and a_i is one's evaluation of consequence i as good or bad. This formulation explicitly defines an attitude as the product of two mental events; namely, a cognition and moral belief.[6] The construct validity of this and other models of attitude will be examined further in Chapter 5. Other examples of models combining mental events in the marketing literature include recent attempts to represent causal processes among cognitive and affective components of attitudes (Lutz, 1976), information processing models (McGuire, 1976), and family decision making studies (Davis, 1976).

Causal Models of Human Behavior and Social Action

The goal in causal modeling is to achieve scientific explanation, and this may be accomplished whether one addresses human behavior or social action and whether one assumes a behaviorist or causal theory of the mind stance. However, the particular choice of scientific problems to be explained and the approach used to achieve explanation will vary depending on the circumstances. In the following paragraphs, four generic paradigms are presented for representing human behavior and social action.

The Stimulus–Response Model

Perhaps the most used and intuitive paradigm for explaining human behavior is the stimulus–response (S–R) model. The behavior of man in the S–R model is represented as a function of three classes of observable concepts: stimuli, responses, and reinforcements. By observing an individual's history of behavior in relation to the stimuli and reinforcements in one's environment, it is thought that behavior can be completely "explained."

The central concept in the S–R model is reinforcement. An addition to the environment that increases the probability of a particular behavior occurring in the future is termed a *positive reinforcer*, while an addition that decreases the frequency of a future response is labeled a *punisher*. Similarly, the removal of a stimulus that increases the likelihood of a specific behavior occurring in the future is called a *negative reinforcer*, while the subtraction of a stimulus that decreases the frequency of a future response is termed a *response cost*. Reinforcements are not defined a priori but achieve their identity by the consequences they produce. As Locke notes (1972, p. 176):

> A reinforcement is defined ... as any event which follows a response which makes a subsequent response more or less probable. Reinforcement is thus defined solely in terms of the events which follow it and has no essential or specific property of its own (e.g., such as being related to the organism's need satisfaction or being desired by the organism, etc.).

When a particular kind of behavior is regularly followed by reinforcing events, the phenomenon is known as operant conditioning.

Explanation in terms of the S–R model consists only in identifying spatial and temporal relations among stimuli, responses, and reinforcements. Typically, the relations are assumed causal in the Humean sense noted in Chapter 1 except for one slight modification: "The old 'cause-and-effect necessary connection' becomes a "functional relation.' The new terms do not suggest *how* a cause causes its effect; they merely assert that different events tend to occur together in a certain order" (Skinner, 1953, p. 4). Strict S–R theorists usually *assume* that there are S–R connections within the brain derived either genetically or through learning. So-called internal events such as emotions are taken to equal internal stimuli that are not directly modeled. In any case, the connections within the brain are termed S–R units:

> In a particular situation, there will be a physical event, usually the sensory reception of stimuli, which stimulates a matrix of S–R units, i.e., the S–R structure. Then this structure, all by itself, generates the response. The psychologists who advocated this simple scheme were also inclined to identify the theoretical S–R connection, the syntatical unit, with the empirical correlation that they found when they observed a response occurring in the experimental situation. That is, the S–R correlation became equated with a hypothetical neural S–R counterpart [Bolles, 1974, p. 5].

On balance, the S–R model is more concerned with the prediction of human behavior than its explanation. This is so because the identification of stimuli, responses, and reinforcements in any particular setting merely leads to the cataloging of antecedent and consequent events. It does not account for the connecting processes, structure, or reasons why a stimulus leads to a specific response. When lawlike statements are added to this description (e.g., learning processes), the model approaches the framework set forth in the regularity theory of causality discussed in Chapter 1, however.

The S–R model owes its origin and early development to the work of Watson (1930) and Skinner (1953). In recent years, it has broadened to account for more complex human responses while still retaining its central assumptions. For example, the model now accounts for the process whereby neutral stimuli become "secondary" reinforcers, functioning to increase or inhibit certain behaviors. Similarly, contemporary S–R models allow for the occurrence of broad classes of reinforcers such as money, status, and power that can become the means of acquiring other desirable things. As Bushell and Burgess (1969, p.38) note, these "generalized reinforcers"

... have great power and importance in social analysis because they retain their effectiveness in the absence of any specific deprivation. The term "generalized" refers to the fact that these stimuli stand for, represent, or provide access to, a wide range of other reinforcers, both unconditioned and conditioned, which may differ from time to time and from person to person.

Further, new generation S–R models illustrate that learning may occur vicariously through the observation of the behavior of others (e.g., Bandura, 1971). Finally, the S–R model is particularly suited as a means for shaping, modifying, or in some other way controlling behavior. Such processes are readily visible even in the more subtle processes of consumer socialization (Ward, 1974).

The modeling of cause-and-effect in S–R models is, in principle, quite simple. In the typical investigation, different people are exposed to different stimuli (or varying degrees of the same stimulus), and the responses of the people are recorded. If a change in the stimulus level is associated with a change in the response, a functional relation is said to exist. Assuming a proper experimental design or appropriate controls, the relation is interpreted as a causal one; that is, the stimulus is claimed a cause of the response. The regularity theory of causality is usually taken to be the one best model representative of the S–R relationship. Temporal priority, constant conjunction, and contiguity in space and time are the important elements for inferring causality in S–R relationships. In addition, the notion of a lawlike connection between stimulus and response is either assumed or demonstrated empirically.

A number of shortcomings of the S–R model may be identified.[8] First, the validity of the model appears to be tied to the truth of the Humean or regularity theory of causality. Thus, the criticisms discussed in Chapter 1 must also be addressed here. The most crucial issues are those dealing with the nature of the law-like behavior binding stimulus to response and the nature and quality of explanation achieved in the S–R model. The model seems to adequately account for the regular occurrence of antecedent and consequent events and thus describes what happens in the world. It seems adequate to the task of prediction. However, it does not fully address the why and how of human behavior, thus falling short of explanation. A second problem with the S–R model lies in the subject matter for which it does account. On the one hand, the model appears to capture learning of the simple trial and error or passive association types. These individual behaviors are indicative of classical conditioning findings, and the domain of their application is confined primarily to perceptual and elementary memory utilization situations. On the other hand, the S–R model fails to explain the more complex aspects of human action such as found in purposeful behavior, information seeking, cognitive processes, social relationships, and, in general, the dynamic, creative side of human behavior. Finally, the internal and external validity of the model has been challenged as a result of certain anomalies. As one psychologist notes commenting on the application of the model in behavior research:

> It was observed that the same stimulus and reinforcement preceded different responses in different persons and in the same person at different times, and that the same response could be preceded by different stimuli and reinforcements. Furthermore, some observed actions were not regularly associated with any observable stimuli or reinforcements [Locke, 1972, p. 181].

These inconsistencies have led theorists to modify the S–R model to encompass mental events; and, indeed, some have suggested other models. It is to these that we now turn.

Despite the problems associated with the S–R model, marketers have used it extensively.[7] In consumer research, for example, Jacoby, et al. (1974) investigated the effect of information load on various behaviors associated with brand choice. In particular, two stimuli (independent variables) were manipulated: package information load (number of brands and bits of information) and information mode (organized vs. disorganized; same vs. different). The three observed dependent variables (responses) included: performance accuracy ("the ability of the consumer to choose the 'best' brand"), performance speed, and certain subjective states (e.g., feelings of satisfaction, perceived risk, etc.). The hypothesis—which was largely confirmed—was that a finite limit exists as to the amount of information consumers can effectively use. As the total amount of information increased, a point was reached where accuracy decreased. The S–R model has been at the center of research into the effects of advertising and promotion on consumer behavior, communication models, attitude change approaches, and various models concerned with learned behavior. Moreover, the S–R model forms an integral part of most grand theories of consumer behavior (e.g., Nicosia, 1966; Howard and Sheth, 1969; Engel, Kollat, and Blackwell, 1973).

The Stimulus–Organism–Response and Response–Response Models

Skinner, Watson, Thorndike, and other behaviorists desired to represent human behavior through models as precise as those found in the natural sciences. They believed that mental events were "fictional," untestable, and in any case unnecessary for explaining human behavior. Their causal models were limited to the empirical representation of antecedent and consequent events, though they sometimes explicitly stated assumptions of lawlike relationships. In the years since the behaviorist model was first rigorously developed in the early decades of this century, behavioral scientists have found human behavior to be more complicated than that represented in S-R approaches. To better capture the forces underlying human behavior, some researchers proposed intervening processes or structures between observable stimuli and the responses of individuals. In general, these models have evolved in two directions. One theoretical tradition posits intervening variables that are *defined* in terms of overt behaviors of individuals, while a second hypothesizes intervening variables that are *inferred* from the behavior of individuals. Both traditions are often referred to as stimulus–organism–response (S–O–R) models. This section of the chapter will also address the off-shoot of the S–O–R model known as the response–response (R–R) model.

Consider first S–O–R models that define intervening variables in terms of overt behaviors. Two of the more well-known and influential models are those of Tolman and Hull.[9] Tolman (1932) proposed a purposive behavior model of man wherein the intervening variables between stimulus and response were thought to be of a cognitive and motivational nature. Specifically, Tolman suggested that one's behavior was a function of expectancy times value:

$$S \longrightarrow [\text{expectancy} \times \text{value}] \longrightarrow R$$

By expectancy, Tolman meant the beliefs one has that a particular course of action or an event will have some specific consequence. This is clearly a cognitive variable. By value, "demand," Tolman meant the belief-value matrix an individual has as part of his or her learned cognitive structure. Given an aroused need, certain objects produce cognitive and affective evaluations in the person with regard to different degrees of satisfaction or dissatisfaction. The model says that people judge the degree to which an action will lead to some outcome and also the affective significance of that outcome before making a particular response. Although the wording of Tolman's model would appear to rely on the mental concepts of want and cognition noted earlier, the author, in reality, preferred to define these constructs in terms of actual behaviors of the individual.[10] This procedure eliminates the semantic problem as to the connection between construct and operation since the operation becomes the construct. Further, Tolman proposed an explicit syntatical structure relating his theoretical constructs. The model is not an intervening variable one in the sense of both mental events and relationships among mental events acting between stimulus and response, but rather it is a hypothesis as to the structure of behavioral events between stimulus and response.

Hull (1943) proposed a S–O–R model that, while similar in general principle to Tolman's, differs in detail. In particular, the model claims that certain S–R constructs and motivation (drive) intervene between stimulus and response (e.g., Bolles, 1974):

$$S \longrightarrow \begin{bmatrix} S^H R \\ S^I R \\ \text{etc.} \end{bmatrix} [\text{Drive}] \longrightarrow R$$

The S–R constructs, $S^H R$ and $S^I R$, indicate habit and inhibitory conditioning, respectively. They are constructs defined in terms of the observed relationships between schedules of reinforcements and response behaviors and are independent of motivational (e.g., deprivation) conditions. The drive construct is a motivational or want concept reflecting an individual's needs. Hull (1943) attempted to model the process intervening between stimulus and response by postulating particular syntatical relationships between S–R constructs and drive (e.g., $S^H R$ and D_1 combine multiplicatively). However, his operationalizations of constructs were accomplished by defining them in terms of behaviors and reinforcements and thus avoided explicit reference to mental events. Neo-Hullians have improved upon the syntatical structure of the S–O–R model by refining the concept of drive into incentive motivation (e.g., anticipatory goal reaction), frustration, and fear motivation, among other developments (cf., Bolles, 1975).

The R–R model largely evolved from the S–O–R model. In the version descended from the more behaviorist approaches, the R–R model attempts to explain the responses of individuals based on the association or pattern that these responses have with other responses. For example, a marketer might observe the life styles of a set of consumers such as reflected in their choice of neighborhood, friends, or entertainment activities and then see if these correlate with purchases.

A number of S–O–R models infer, rather than define, the presence of intervening variables between stimulus and response. These models explicitly hypothesize that mental events, processes, structures, and so forth act upon incoming stimuli before the individual produces a particular response. The inference process imposes semantic problems for the researcher, however, and these topics will be discussed later along with syntatic issues in construct validity in Chapter 5. For now, it should be stressed that, in addition to syntatic relations among one's constructs (such as found in an axiomatic structure of hypotheses), one's theories should explicitly model the relations between constructs and observations (such as found in correspondence rules).

One of the earliest S–O–R type models to rely on the causal role of mental events is that of Lewin (1936, 1938). Lewin believed that behavior is determined by (1) the particular means–end relationships perceived by the person in a specific situation or life space and (2) a matrix of forces or tensions which compel one to seek particular goals. Although somewhat similar in structure to the model of Tolman, Lewin's approach differs fundamentally in that the constructs are mental events to be inferred from behavior.[11] Other early frameworks sharing the general orientation of representing mental events, processes, and so forth as intervening between stimulus and response include the work of Freud, Murray (1938), Kelly (1955), and Rotter (1954). Recent advances in motivation (e.g., Weiner, 1974), personality theory (e.g., Mischel, 1973), and cognitive views of emotions (Lazarus, 1974) are largely in this S–O–R tradition. In addition, some have suggested that explanation can be achieved by relating mental events in the R–R structure (e.g., Dulany, 1968).

Marketers have employed the S–O–R and R–R models at an increasing rate in recent years. This can be seen in attempts to model the role of the situation in consumer behavior (Belk, 1975), information processing behaviors (Bettman, (1975), personality variables and processes (McGuire, 1976), and the dynamics of attitude formation (Lutz, 1976).

The modeling of cause-and-effect in S–O–R or R–R models may take a number of forms. The former typically involves the representation of a structure of variables or a sequence of variables (e.g., process) between stimuli and responses. If relationships among variables are modeled in the regularity sense of causality, then lawlike statements as to physiological processes, genetic assumptions, learned behaviors, and so on will be included as a part of the associations of antecedent and consequent events. If, on the other hand, natural necessity or realist models of causality are employed, the nature of stimuli in conjunction with the characteristics of the person and situation will be modeled as they articulate in some structure of relationships. For instance, in Mischel's (1973) "cognitive social learning" theory of personality, the author proposes six generic processes governing behavior: cognitive and behavioral construction competencies, encoding strategies and personal constructs, behavior-outcome and stimulus-outcome expectancies, subjective stimulus values, and self-regulatory systems and plans. Finally, S–O–R causal models differ with respect to the representation of inferred, unobservable constructs. Some causal models limit inquiry strictly to observable behaviors and events, while others include the process of abstraction directly in their frameworks by modeling constructs, their operationalizations, and the semantic and syntatic rules connecting these variables. Causal models of R–R theories parallel the above distinctions except that stimuli are usually not represented. The responses may, however, be overt or covert.

The Organism–Response Model

Both the S–R and S–O–R models feature the role of stimuli in their frameworks. This has led some authors to critize both models as viewing man too much in a passive sense. Although the S–O–R model has broadened to capture the fact that man processes information from his environment, it still can be faulted for overemphasizing the reactions taken to stimuli at the expense of initiating, creative behaviors. Two similar models designed to express this active side of man are known as the organism–response (O–R) model and the S---O–R model. Bolles (1974, pp. 18–19) describes the former as follows:

There is a trend away from passivity; the subject does not just process information about the outcomes of his behaviors, he makes something of this information. He pigeon-holes and characterizes it, and makes what is, for him, cognitive sense of it. At the same time he characterizes and makes sense out of himself and the world around him. We can see that while the substance of these motivational propositions are cognitive, the effects of a particular kind of attribution can, in turn, affect the individual's motivation . . . we see quite clearly an interaction between the motivational determinants and the cognitive processes that have traditionally been viewed as structural determinants of the individual's behavior.

Similarly, Locke (1972, p. 195) views the S---O–R model in the following sense:

This writer believes that the most appropriate model for the study of man is . . . S---O–R with emphasis on the O–R. Men do exist in a physical and social environment, thus the environment is not irrelevant to a full understanding of their actions; but the dotted line between S and O emphasizes that there is no fixed inevitable relation between the environment and the individual's actions. The O–R aspect of the model stresses the fact that such actions will depend upon how the individual processes, interprets and evaluates environmental facts as well as conclusions he reaches on his own. Such conclusions will depend upon such factors as his knowledge and beliefs, his values, his subconscious premises and his methods of thinking.

Bowers (1973) presents still a third version of the O–R model emphasizing that behavior and reinforcement conditions are subject to the selection and guidance of biocognitive structures. Unlike the passive processing of information that occurs in the cognitive social learning views of personality, Bowers' theory stresses the active, dynamic side of behavior in a manner reminiscent of Kant's conception of causality (see discussion in Chapter 1). Lazarus (1974, pp. 24–25) states the position nicely in his description of cognition and emotion in theories of motivation: "People select the environments to which they must respond; they shape their commerce with it, plan, choose, avoid, tolerate, postpone, escape, demolish, manipulate their attention, and also deceive themselves about what is happening, as much as possible casting the relation- ship in ways that fit their needs and premises about themselves in the world."

Marketers have only recently begun to model behavior and action in this dynamic sense. For example, McGuire (1976) reviews new developments "on the internal characteristics of the person that affect exposure to and influence by these outside factors [i.e., product relevant communication through face-to-face contacts, past experiences with a product, and point-of-purchase

experience] when he or she is making purchase and consumption decisions."
The author addresses two broad classes of variables:

1. The structural characteristics of one's personality that channel the information
   processing of one's own experiences and of communications from other people
   through successive steps of exposure, perception, comprehension, agreement
   [retention, search and retrieval, decision making], to the ultimate purchasing act and
   consumption behavior.
2. The dynamic aspects of personality, that is, the energizing components of human
   personality—the motivational forces that activate and sustain this information
   processing and account for its termination [McGuire, 1976, p. 302].

In a parallel fashion, Chestnut and Jacoby (1977) outline a number of the
dimensions or "sectors" of the consumer information processing system
where, among other points, a distinction is made between "spectator" and
"participant" modes of problem solving. The former refers to the passive reception of encoded information while the latter stresses the active "decomposing,
manipulating, and testing" of information. (See also Posner, 1973.)

The modeling of cause-and-effect with the O–R model follows procedures
similar to that outlined above with the S–O–R models except for the addition
of structures and processes designed to capture the more active side of man's
behavior. Typically, this will include the representation of motivation, cognitive
processes, personality, and so on as the person both actively constructs his
or her reality and is buffeted by stimuli from his or her environment. The idea
is to view man as he or she interacts with the world.

The Social Models

For the most part, the S–R, S–O–R, R–R, and O–R models are limited to the
behavior or actions of individuals. The subject matter focuses on the person
as the unit of analysis. Marketers are also interested in explaining behavior
and relationships among individuals and institutions, however, and causal
models are appropriate here, too. For purposes of discussion, this level of
analysis is categorized as social interaction, small group, and macrosocial
phenomena. Each is briefly described below as it relates to causal modeling.

Social Interaction Models

The subject matter for social interaction models is typically the relationship(s)
between the actors in a dyad. The dyad may consist of two people, two groups,
two organizations, a person and an organization, and so on. The relationship
may be one of power, conflict, exchange, cooperation, conformity, bargaining,

interpersonal attraction, or some other social connection. In general, relationships are characterized by common experiences, shared meanings, interdependencies, alliances, and the like. Relationships are inferred from the behavior or actions transpiring between two parties, the pattern of events surrounding these behaviors and actions, and/or the stated experiences of the parties vis-à-vis each other.

Many social interaction models have been proposed over the years in the behavioral sciences. In sociology, for example, symbolic interactionism and related approaches have attempted to capture the dynamics underlying the relationships between people (e.g., Mead, 1934; Blumer, 1969; Meltzer et al. 1975; Goffman, 1959, 1974). Social psychologists have contributed perhaps the most numerous and rigorous models. The social influence model of Tedeschi et al. (1973), the social action model of Harré and Secord (1973), and models of bargaining and negotiation (e.g., Rubin and Brown, 1975) represent but a few of the more successful. Marketers, too, have employed social interaction orientations in their research. Evans (1963) was one of the first to view the sales situation as a dyadic interaction process. Similarly, Willett and Pennington (1966) used Bales (1970) interaction process analysis scheme to study the customer-salesperson dyad. Davis and Rigaux (1974) have viewed the husband-wife interaction from a social interaction perspective also.

Perhaps one of the most researched paradigms in the behavioral sciences for investigating social interaction is that of social exchange theory. Social exchange theory has developed somewhat independently in sociology, anthropology, psychology, organization behavior, and marketing.[12] Out of these traditions, one may identify fundamental characteristics of the exchange relationship that can aid in explaining social interaction (Bagozzi, 1978b). First, the parties in an exchange usually *share some values* or have *mutual interests*. They may want something the other has or in some other way be dependent on the other. Sometimes the mutuality in interests will take the form of cooperation, alliances, coalitions, or other relations. Often the interaction will involve a conflict of interest or disagreement over certain issues. These instances may involve relations of give and take, dominance or submission, or other social processes. Second, the dyad will invariably contain instances of *social influence* by one or both parties. This may entail the communication of promises or threats, warnings or mendations, or the attempt to control information or other cues (e.g., Tedeschi, Schlenker, and Bonoma, 1973). It may also consist of deception, flattery, ingratiation, or similar strategies and ploys. The parties to an exchange have a number of options available for influencing the outcome of the transaction. Third, forces in the *situation* may constrain or shape the nature of the relationship and its outcome. Among other factors, these might consist of sources of satisfaction outside the relation, the influence of a powerful third party, or socio-economic restrictions in the immediate environment. Fourth, the *characteristics of the actors* may affect the course of an exchange or certain aspects of the relationship. For instance, the history of reward mediation, personality characteristics, individual or organizational needs, internal structures or processes of an actor (such as cognitive conflict), or resources of an actor may all affect a relationship. Fifth, *normative variables* may play a decisive role in dyadic relations. Norms are shared conceptions of how one ought to behave, and they can invoke compelling behavioral expectations and demands upon parties in a dyad. Among the members of a buying center, for example, certain rules, procedures, policies, and standards of conduct often evolve as pragmatic, efficient means for social control. Similarly, in most sales-person-purchasing agent exchanges, norms of etiquette, reciprocity, deference, demeanor, and the like, can be identified. These often assume a ritual-like character (such as the courtesy call the industrial salesperson makes on his or her small buyers or those he or she "knows" will not buy at this time), but they fulfill expectations and serve other functions. Sixth, dyadic relations ebb and flow with the actions and *purposive behavior* of the parties. The actors in a social relationship have plans, goals, behavioral orientations, and intentions they hope to satisfy. Sometimes these are the object of negotiation. Invariably, they set restrictions on what is acceptable or not in an exchange and serve as a starting point of the course of give and take in the interaction. Finally, a common element in most dyads is the *uncertainty* in the relation. Not only is the final outcome problematic, but the on-going activities within the relation have a dynamic, ambivalent quality. The course of the relation—whether one of cooperation, conflict, escalation, de-escalation, and so forth—depends on the offers, counter offers, and mutual adjustments made by the parties in an on-going process of interpretation, evaluation, decision making, and exchange.

Causality in social interaction models may be represented in a variety of ways. Tedeschi et al. (1973), for example, rely on two broad representations of social influence. First, the behavioral and cognitive responses of the target of influence are modeled as a function of a sequence of variables in a "subjective expected utility theory of social influence." The hypothesized causal flow can be represented as: independent variables → target cognitions → subjective expected utility (believability of influence source and message) → subjective expected utility for decision alternatives → overt and covert responses. Independent variables include degree of attitudinal similarity, one's history of reward mediation, source expertise and legitimate authority, message credibility, and so on. Target cognitions encompass the attractiveness, perceived prestige, esteem, and status of the source, and expected utility of the message. Overt and covert responses entail compliance, conformity, attitude change, response frequency, imitation, and the like. This part of the influence model represents a formal elaboration of S–O–R relationships.

The second part of the Tedeschi et al. (1973) approach is more social in character. Here the actual pattern of communication and relationships between the actors in an interaction is modeled. The authors propose that social influence can be represented through the process and structure of influence modes transpiring between people. Four influence modes are suggested. One consists of influence attempts where the source does not strive to disguise his or her influence intentions (open influence) while at the same time mediating rewarding and/or punishing stimuli. These actions are termed threats and promises. A second mode that is also open but that does not entail the source directly mediating reinforcements involves acts of warning or the making of mendations. Persuasion is one important example of this mode of influence. The third mode is labeled reinforcement control, and here the communicator covertly and directly manipulates rewards and punishments. Finally, the fourth mode of influence, while covert, does not involve a direct mediation of rewards or punishments. The acts in this influence mode include cue control, the filtering of information, and, on occasion, warnings and mendations. By modeling the pattern of communication and responses between people using the above distinctions, it has been possible to explain the outcomes and course of interaction between people and groups (e.g., Bonoma, 1975; Angelmar, 1976). Cause-and-effect can be represented through longitudinal sequences of relationships or through simplex or circumplex models, among other approaches (e.g., Jöreskog, 1974).

Small Group Behavior

Moving to a more macro level of analysis beyond that of the dyad, one can identify relationships among limited numbers of actors as a second class of social phenomena where causal modeling is appropriate.[13] Although marketers have generally neglected this side of social behavior, small group phenomena comprise an important subject matter for study in such areas as family decision making, behavior in the buying center, the structure and processes among limited numbers of marketing organizations, and interactions among marketing managers and others in the firm. Discussion here will be limited to how causal modeling may be useful as a research method in these areas.

In general, small group behavior may be modeled in one of two broad ways. One method begins by discovering the subjective experiences for a set of individuals. These experiences might include evaluations of shared goals, expressions of affect or affinity for others, perceptions of role relations, and so on. Next, based on the responses made by individuals, relationships are inferred. Typically, this will involve the modeling of a pattern, structure, or process of associations among individuals. For example, using graph theory or similar methodologies (cf., Harary, 1969), behavioral scientists have represented the interconnections among people in social networks (Barnes, 1972; Whitten and Wolfe, 1973; Mitchell, 1974; Leinhardt, 1977). In another approach, Coleman (1973) has developed a mathematical framework for predicting the outcomes and degree of control social actors have for a set of collective actions in an exchange system. Building on economic theory, the model assumes rational actions in the sense that people are believed to maximize their utilities for certain goals by exchanging control they have over events of interest to others. The inputs to Coleman's model consists of (1) a matrix of control that each actor has for each event in a system of collective decisions and (2) a matrix of interests (importances) each actor has in each event (which are based on a function of utility differences). Given these quantities, Coleman derives the value of each event, the power of each actor, the final control that each actor has over each event, and the outcome of each event. Other frameworks in the above tradition include work in coalition formation (Caplow, 1968) and sociometric investigations.

The second broad tradition in small group research looks at group processes and structure and how these things affect individual behavior, collective or aggregate behaviors, or other aspects of group structure and social behavior. Many research streams may be identified. One body of work focuses on the effects of social influence on the conformity of group members; a second investigates the effects of group interaction on risk taking and other decision making behavior; a third explores communication patterns in small groups including their impact on task performance and problem solving; still another set of studies looks at the role of leadership in group decision making (e.g., Hare, 1976). Moreover, a considerable amount of research can be found investigating power, conflict, and other processes in groups as well as the influence environmental factors, social structure, technology, and task structure have upon human performance (e.g., Davis et al., 1976).

One of the newest approaches in small group research to emerge in recent years is social judgment theory (SJT). Social judgment theory is concerned with human judgment processes in situations involving two or more persons. Typically, the paradigm is employed in settings where cognitive conflict exists; that is, where there is "disagreement among persons trying to reach consensus in the face of uncertainty" (Rappaport and Summers, 1973). In the usual SJT study, two or more people interact so as to arrive at a joint judgment decision on some policy task. Conflict is created by either choosing and pairing subjects who differ in some way in the cognitive model they employ to reach decisions or else the subjects are trained prior to the encounter to use a particular model that differs from the person's model(s) for whom they will meet. The models used by subjects are called policies, and they may differ with respect to (1) the forms of functions relating stimulus cues to judgments, (2) the particular weighting of cues used by subjects, (3) certain organizing principles by which information is integrated, and (4) consistency. In the conflict encounter stage of SJT, the tasks for subjects are to study stimulus cues, make an individual judgment, communicate to the other, and decide on a joint decision. After this stage, the subjects are usually informed of the "correct" decision, and in some studies they are also asked to make a final individual judgment. The dependent variables in SJT are the individual judgments of the subjects in the group, their joint decision outcome, and the final (termed covert) judgment of each individual. The policy models are often represented through variants of the Brunswik lens model (e.g., Rapport and Summers, 1973). Many factors in group behavior have been studied using the SJT approach including the structure of the policy task, communication issues, group size, interpersonal influence, and others (Kaplan and Schwartz, 1975).

Causality in small group research can be represented in a variety of ways. For instance, the effects of environmental or structural variables on individual or group behavior can be modeled as independent variables. Conflict, power, and other interactions among group members can be depicted as many inter-related occurrences of influence attempts and responses (using techniques such as mentioned above with respect to the social interaction model). Often the causal processes are not modeled, per se, but rather antecedent and consequent events are observed, and causality is inferred using experimental design or other methodological criteria. Finally, causality may be inferred from the choices people make, the feelings they express relative to others, and so on when these behaviors are part of a mathematical or deductive theory (e.g., network theory approaches, Coleman's model).

Macrosocial Phenomena

Causal modeling can also be useful for explaining behavior and action at the more macro levels of social life. Taking human behavior as the subject matter, it is possible to identify at least three general areas for study: (1) the behavior of aggregates, (2) emergent phenomena, and (3) structures, processes, and patterns of behavior among groups, organizations, institutions, or collectivities. To date, marketers have not systematically investigated these phenomena, and they represent new frontiers for exploration (Bagozzi, 1976c).

Causal modeling may be used to explain the behavior of certain aggregates by relating these and other aggregates in antecedent/consequent relationships and identifying the reasons why one might expect such relationships (e.g., through lawlike generalizations). For example, suppose one desires to explain the variation in sales for automobiles across a sample of 60 cities of approximately the same population. In order to account for changes in this aggregative variable, one might use industry advertising, household income, the unemployment rate, and other measures as predictors. Economists, demographers, and marketers frequently use aggregative variables to explain other aggregative variables in their work. An obvious shortcoming in such research is that the processes linking independent to dependent variables are often vague, ambiguous, remote, and errorful. Nevertheless, in principle, causal modeling is sometimes appropriate.

Emergent phenomena are another class of dependent variables suitable for causal modeling. They are defined loosely as patterns of social relationships having properties and consequences different from the behaviors and actions of the individuals comprising those relationships. The properties in question refer to abstractions and constructs inferred from actions and the setting that may be useful in understanding social behavior. Blau's (1974) notions of status inequality, structural consolidation, and multiform heterogeneity are examples of properties of social relationships. Common instances of emergent phenomena include consumer movements, hording, fads, fashion, and other forms of collective behavior. Causality can be represented through the relations among variables comprising the structures of processes explaining emergent phenomena (e.g., Keat and Urry, 1975, pp. 96–97, 117, 126). For example, Smelser (1963) suggests a value-added model of collective behavior that specifies varying levels of necessary social conditions (determinants) for the occurrence of that behavior.

The final category of macrosocial phenomena consists of structures, processes, and patterns of behavior among groups, organizations, institutions, or collectivities. This is by far the largest class of social phenomena in terms of the number of studies in the behavioral sciences. In marketing, some research has been conducted at this macro level including that dealing with market structure, competition and conflict, relationships among firms, the interaction of firms with their environments, the determinants and implications of the internal structure of marketing organizations, the impact of technology on the organization, and marketing productivity studies. Causality has been modeled in these studies through regression models, structural equations, and the comparative method, among other approaches. In general, however, marketers have only recently begun to systematically investigate the macro side of marketing.

Conceptual Problems in Causal Modeling

We close this chapter with a discussion of three conceptual problems in scientific explanation that are not yet fully resolved and that pose problems for causal modeling. These problems are reductionism, reification, and explanation across levels of analysis.

Reductionism. Reductionism refers to the "idea that the principles explaining one range of phenomena are adequate for explaining a totally different range of phenomena—for example, the idea that human social behavior is ultimately psychological, or that human psychological behavior is ultimately biological" (Hoult, 1972, p. 267). Applied to marketing, one may identify at least two types of reductionism. One type suggests that all marketing phenomena at the social level can be reduced to dyadic exchanges. Bagozzi et al. (1977) take this position when they define and develop the dyad as the fundamental building block for marketing relationships. This position maintains that more complex patterns, structures, and processes of social behavior may be accounted for by the simplest, irreducible concept of social behavior, the dyad. The second type of reductionism goes even farther in that all marketing behavior is presumed reducible to the actions or characteristics of individuals, particularly as represented in psychological phenomena and laws.[14] Notice that such a claim involves a transition from one class of phenomena to another. That is, it explains essentially *social* phenomena involving two or more people, groups, or organizations by *psychological* phenomena restricted, by definition, to the thoughts, feelings, behaviors, and so forth of single individuals. The transition is one in kind, not degree. Theory building with dyadic exchange concepts, in contrast, is a matter of degree, not a difference in kind. Complex *social* behavior is explained with simpler *social* concepts. As a result, one has reason to question the second form of reductionism on a priori grounds since the validity of explaining social phenomena with psychological concepts and the transference or translation of social laws to psychological laws has not been demonstrated in theory or practice. From a conceptual standpoint, the first form of reductionism violates no problems in logic, and it has the virtue of receiving empirical support from various areas of the behavioral sciences (e.g., Bonoma et al., 1978).

Nevertheless, the issue of reductionism is one that remains yet to be fully resolved in the behavioral sciences. Well reasoned arguments have been marshalled in its favor (e.g., Addis, 1975; Homans, 1964) as well as in opposition (e.g., Webster, 1973; Koestler and Symthies, 1969; White, 1949, pp. 22, 29, 34–35).

For the researcher considering causal modeling, the issue of reductionism is important for a number of reasons. First, resolution will dictate which classes of concepts (psychological, sociological, etc.) are admissible in theories in both a logical and empirical sense. For the researcher following the second form of reductionism noted above, for example, it is unnecessary, and indeed even unscientific and misleading, to explicitly model shared or collective behavior, symbolic behavior, cause-and-effect among "social facts" such as structural variables, emergent phenomena, and cultural behavior. For those advocating the first form of reductionism and for those denying that reductionism is valid, however, the above phenomena legitimately comprise subject matters for study.

A second reason for addressing reductionism has to do with the issue of the proper structure for one's theories, particularly with regard to the relationship(s) between theoretical constructs and empirical observations. Two conflicting schools of thought may be identified. Methodological individualism is the doctrine that attempts to explain social behavior using theories wherein all social concepts are defined or derived from the behavior of individuals: "For a methodological individualist, the phenomena of interest are explained by propositions predicated on individuals and their behavior, and the concepts of the theory are concepts which inhere in individuals, not irreducibly in groups" (Webster, 1973, p. 260). Methodological holism, in contrast, is the doctrine that there are characteristics of groups and other social collections that are not definable in terms of the individuals comprising those groups. Although aspects of these doctrines will be discussed further in the following chapters, for now it is sufficient to note that causal modeling will differ depending on one's choice of method. For those following a strict methodological individualism, all social concepts will be explicitly tied to empirical observations of individual behavior or actions through correspondence rules. For those practicing methodological holism, some social concepts will be independent of the people contained within them in the sense of exhibiting properties not reducible to or of a different kind than those exhibited by people as individuals or aggregates. Some theoretical constructs in this approach, then, may be only indirectly tied to empirical concepts through other theoretical constructs.

Reification. Reification denotes "the ideological distortion by which social phenomena are seen not as constructions of human activity, but as material things having natural rather than social properties" (Keat and Urry, 1975, p. 138; Berger and Luckmann, 1966, p. 89). The problem of reification would appear to confront those attempting to model social behavior by omitting the act-meanings of those under study. Under these conditions, because of the paucity of research establishing lawlike generalizations, the representation of cause-and-effect is often tenuous. Moreover, the conceptual foundation of marketing itself has been criticized for exhibiting reification (Angelmar and Pinson, 1974). Thus, the marketing researcher should be cautious in inferring causality between aggregate or social constructs when these variables and the relationships between them are entirely abstractions in the mind of the observer and are lacking in lawlike or natural necessity content.

Explanation Across Levels of Analysis. The final unresolved problem, explanation across levels of analysis, arises when the researcher includes both social and psychological variables in his or her theories, attempting to explain one with the other. Cause-and-effect is presumed to occur between social and psychological variables when using this approach.

The issue of explanation across levels of analysis poses a dilemma to marketing scholars. On the one hand, the incorporation of explanatory concepts from other levels of analysis offers the promise of enriching theories, enhancing prediction, and aiding the decision maker or social planner who would strive to alter the performance of a marketing system. Organization behavior researchers have been perhaps the most active in such analyses, particularly in their study of joint programs among organizations. Hirsch (1975) briefly reviews some research in this area which deals with the "functions performed by coalitions [i.e., social cooperation] of . . . management organizations in negotiating at the institutional level on behalf of their respective members for societal resources and legitimacy" (see also, Zald, 1970; Parsons, 1960). A second line of inquiry in organization research that illustrates the analysis of behavior across levels of analysis is the new generation of organization-environment models. Three developments seem most promising for marketers. First, researchers have refined their definitions of the environmental phenomena that impinge on an organization and have empirically verified their effects. For example, environmental complexity, variability, and illiberality have been identified as important phenomena (e.g., Child, 1972; Duncan, 1972, Hirsch, 1975). Second, research has been conducted relating aspects of the environment to specific structures, processes, and practices within the organization. For instance, the environment has been found to affect the adaptability, decentralization, innovativeness, internal complexity, differentiation, and communication patterns of organizations in predictable ways (e.g., Lawrence and Lorsch, 1969; Aiken and Hage, 1968; and Galbraith, 1973). Finally, researchers have demonstrated that the organization not only reacts to its environment but may choose or change that environmental to better meet its needs and goals (e.g., Thompson, 1967; Child, 1972, pp. 13–16). All of the above represent examples of research relating concepts across categories of phenomena. Marketers have only recently begun to consider these determinants of marketing behavior.

The danger or dilemma in employing concepts across levels of analysis lies in the possibility of spurious relationships and false inferences. The researcher must be careful to specify the linkage or mechanism behind empirical associations of concepts from different levels of marketing phenomena. The cause-and-effect processes must be demonstrated since the correlation of systematic or environmental variables with, say, organization structural variables may be due to exogenous variables or unknown processes involving the modeled phenomena. The problem of spurious relationships is especially acute for the macromarketer because it is usually impossible, impractical, or unethical to experimentally manipulate variables to ascertain causality. Thus, the role of logic and theory in macromarketing is paramount.[15]

Summary

This chapter investigated the domain of causal modeling. The discussion began with an analysis of the distinction between human behavior and social action. The former refers to (1) the things people and organizations actually do and (2) the changes in material and nonmaterial entities people and organizations directly or indirectly bring about. The latter, in contrast, refers to both what people are seen to do (or not do) *and* the meanings, reasons, and other subjective experiences they have for doing (or not doing) these things. Human behavior and social action comprise the primary subject matter for causal modeling in marketing.

Next, a number of fundamental concepts used to construct theories for explaining human behavior and social action were presented. This included an introduction to the mind–body problem and an analysis of the role of mental concepts in marketing theory. Among other issues, the use of affect, cognitions, and moral beliefs were discussed as they relate to theories in the behavioral sciences and marketing.

The presentation then turned to an elaboration of five generic models of human behavior and social action; namely, the S–R, S–O–R, R–R, O–R, and social models. The structure of each model was investigated, and each was scrutinized in regard to its efficacy in explanation. Emphasis was placed on delineating how causality is represented.

Finally, the chapter closed with a brief introduction to a number of unresolved problems in the philosophy of science. These problems were reductionism, reification, and explanation across levels of analysis. In succeeding chapters, the methodology of causal modeling is developed and illustrated in greater detail.

Notes

[1] For excellent philosophical discussions on behavior and action, see Goldman (1970), Danto (1973), and Brand and Walton (1976). Keat and Urry (1975, ch. 7) present a nice introduction to social action. Harré and Secord (1973) provide a particular social-psychological perspective.

[2] Portions of the following discussion are drawn from the readings in the historical treatment due to Spicker (1970) and the contemporary analysis of Campbell (1970).

[3] For an insightful discussion on four types of affect or wants, see Ryle (1949, ch. 4).

[4] The classic model of purposeful behavior is that due to Tolman (1932). However, although Tolman claimed that purposeful behavior is cognitive, he clearly assumed a behaviorist position, attempting to eliminate mental concepts. According to Tolman, mental processes "are to be identified and defined in terms of the behaviors to which they lead." Locke (1969) believes that Tolman's position is fallacious: "The inconsistency . . . is that, if purposes are *defined in terms of* behavior then they must *be* behavior and there is nothing to infer." Locke (1969) feels that purposeful behavior can only be adequately represented through mental events *inferred* by the observer. As Locke puts it, "if purposes are *inferred from* behavior they must be something *different* from behavior and hence cannot be *defined in terms of* behavior." For a recent treatment of purposeful behavior in marketing, see Burnkrant's (1976) motivational model of information processing.

[5] For a review of attitude models in marketing, see Wilkie and Pessemier (1973).

[6] Sometimes attitude is represented as the product of cognition (belief) and affect with respect to an act or attitude object. Marketers sometimes overlook the distinction between

belief and moral belief using one to operationalize the other. For example, after giving a verbal definition of cognitions or beliefs, some have used good-bad scales to measure these.

[7] For an excellent introduction to the S–R model in marketing thought, see Nicosia (1966).

[8] Additional criticism may be found in Locke (1972) and Harré and Secord (1973).

[9] Analytical and historical discussions of S–O–R models due to Tolman, Hull, and others, may be found in Locke, (1969, 1972) and Bolles (1974, 1975).

[10] See Note 3. Also, it should be noted that Tolman sometimes confused goodness and badness (a moral belief) with differences in degrees of affect (a want). Although he referred to entries in one's value matrix in terms of goodness and badness (cf., Tolman, 1951, p. 293), he clearly had gratification or satisfaction in mind based upon his choice of examples: "given types of food are represented as having different degrees of positive values insofar as they are 'believed' to lead on successfully to hunger gratification and away from hunger deprivation" (Tolman, 1951, p. 293).

[11] For an analysis and critique of Lewin's model, see Bolles (1975, pp. 70–80).

[12] The literature on social exchange theory is enormous and growing day by day. Useful treatments may be found in Blau (1964), Homans (1974), Heath (1976), Emerson (1976), Sahlins (1965), Ekeh (1974), and Chadwick-Jones (1976). Recent discussions in marketing may be found in Cassady (1974) and Bagozzi (1974, 1975a, 1975b, 1976a, 1978b.)

[13] See Hare (1975) and David et al. (1976) for surveys of small group research. Bagozzi (1977a) presents additional theories related to small group processes in the marketing buying center.

[14] One could also posit that the psychological aspects of marketing can be reduced to physiology, then biology, then chemistry, and finally physics, but no one to the author's knowledge has suggested such positions.

[15] This is not meant to gloss over problems in methodology, however. Although beyond the scope of this monograph, many methodological issues deserve mention with respect to problems at the macro level and across levels of analysis (e.g., Smelser, 1976; Vallier, 1971).

THREE

CONSTRUCTING
CAUSAL MODELS

Before one can estimate parameters and test a theory, it is necessary to model the constructs, operationalizations, and propositions of the theory structure. This chapter investigates the form and logic behind such modeling. It begins with a discussion of the representation of causal theories including their structure, notational and diagramatical configurations, and other considerations. Next, an outline is presented of the theory construction, research, and testing phases of scientific inquiry from the perspective of causal modeling. These topics will also be scrutinized in greater detail in later chapters. The chapter then turns to a brief examination of the benefits of causal modeling. Finally, the discussion closes with an illustration of a theory that combines axiomatic and causal propositions in one overall systematization.

Representing Causality

In order to discover and test for the existence of a causal relationship, it is helpful to use the language of mathematics in conjunction with principles from the philosophy of science. Although the formal derivation of the procedures will be accomplished in the next chapter, discussion here will focus on the general conventions used to represent causal theories in the behavioral sciences.

The Structure of Theory

Any causal theory will consist of theoretical constructs (e.g., antecedent, intervening, or consequent variables), relationships of constructs to observations, and hypotheses or propositions connecting constructs. It will also usually contain assumptions as to lawlike generalizations among constructs or powers and liabilities of agents as manifest in the constructs. Philosophers of science have found it useful to represent the above elements in a conceptual network that makes explicit the hypotheses underlying one's theory. Consider the following account due to Hempel (1952) which has come in recent years to be known as "the standard construal:"

A scientific theory might . . . be likened to a complex spatial network: Its terms are represented by the knots, while the threads connecting the latter correspond, in part, to the definitions, and, in part, to the fundamental and derivative hypotheses included in the theory. The whole system floats, as it were, above the plane of observation and is anchored to it by rules of interpretation. These might be viewed as strings, which are not part of the network but link certain points of the latter with specific places in the plane of observation. By virtue of those interpretive connections, the network can function as a scientific theory: From certain observational data, we may ascend, via an interpretive string, to some point in the theoretical network, thence proceed, via definitions and hypotheses, to other points, from which another interpretive string permits a descent to the plane of observation (Hempel, 1952, p. 36).

Figure 3.1 illustrates one version of this conceptual network and is a modification of that due to Feigl (1970).[1] Theoretical constructs are related among themselves with hypotheses (i.e., nonobservational postulates or propositions). Theoretical constructs represent primitive concepts in the sense that they are not directly defined, nor do they contain observational terms. Rather, theoretical constructs are implicitly defined by their relationship with other theoretical constructs, defined (derived) concepts, and/or empirical concepts. Defined or derived concepts are those that obtain their meaning from empirical concepts; empirical concepts refer to objects, events, or things recognizable by one or more of the five senses. Empirical concepts are often termed observable, observational, or operational concepts. Definitions of constructs and concepts are typically extensional, intensional, or ostensive (e.g., Kahane, 1973).[2] The relationships connecting (1) theoretical constructs to either defined concepts or empirical concepts or (2) defined concepts to empirical concepts are called correspondence rules. Finally, empirical concepts achieve their meaning through operational definitions that specify procedures for measuring observations in the world of experience. The above concepts and principles will be discussed in greater depth in Chapter 5 where the standard construal will be slightly modified to better reflect recent developments in the philosophy of science.

In order to illustrate the standard construal, consider the example of the expectancy-value theory of behavior shown in Figure 3.2. Following the social learning model of expectancy-value theory (e.g., Rotter, 1954), one

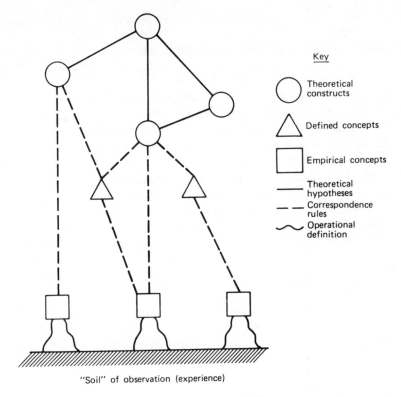

Key

Theoretical
constructs

Defined concepts

Empirical concepts

Theoretical
hypotheses
Correspondence
rules
Operational
definition

"Soil" of observation (experience)

Figure 3.1. The structure of theory.

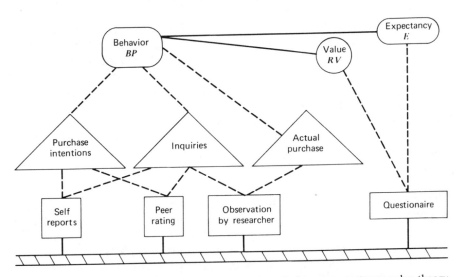

Figure 3.2. An example of the standard construal applied to an expectancy-value theory of consumer behavior.

theoretical hypothesis of interest might be the following:

$$BP_{x, S_1, R_a} = f(E_{x, R_a, S_1} \& RV_{a, S_1})$$

which in words reads, "the potential for behavior x to occur in situation 1, in relation to reinforcement a, is a function of the expectancy of the occurrence of reinforcement a following behavior x, in situation 1, and the value of reinforcement a in situation 1" (Lefcourt, 1976, p. 26). Suppose, for purposes of illustration, one desires to explain the purchase behavior of consumers using this theory. Three defined concepts of interest might include purchase intentions, inquiries with respect to the focal product's characteristics, and actual purchase actions (e.g., purchased or not, frequency of purchase over time, and so on). Note that the correspondence rules between the behavior construct and the defined concepts represent relationships between unobservable phenomena. The correspondence rules in this case might consist of logical relationships wherein the defined concepts are deduced from the behavior construct. For example, the following represents one possibility:

1. All mental events and actions having purchases as a referent are purchase behaviors (BP) in the sense noted above.
2. All purchase intentions are mental events. All product inquires and actual purchases are actions.

Therefore:

3. All purchase intentions, inquiries, and actual purchases are behaviors (BP) in the sense noted above.

Next, the defined concepts are related—again through correspondence rules—to empirical concepts. Three empirical concepts are suggested in the figure: self-reports, peer ratings, and direct observation by the researcher. Notice that correspondence rules here relate unobservable variables (the defined concepts) to observable ones (the empirical concepts). An example of a correspondence rule between inquiries and self-report is the following: "if x is an inquiry by person y, then when y is asked to record the number of occasions in the past week when he or she asked others about the price, quality, and so forth, of the focal product, he or she will respond with answer z." This and other forms of correspondence rules will be analyzed in greater depth in Chapter 5. An example of an operational definition for peer ratings of purchase intentions would be the following: "How often in the past eight hours have you heard co-worker x express his or her intention to purchase brand y: never _____, once or twice_____, three or more times_____?" Finally, expectancies and values are shown in Figure 3.2 to be related via correspondence rules to a questionnaire. With respect to expectancies, questions may be asked as to the subjective judgments of consumers that their actions (e.g., purchase) will lead to some reinforcement or need fulfillment. Similarly, the values placed on the act of purchase may be measured by the strength or importance of that reinforcement or need to the individual. Although not shown in Figure 3.2, a full specification of the expectancy-value theory also requires that one delineate the functional form relating behavior to expectancies and values.

Structural Equations and Causal Diagrams

After one has identified constructs, related these in hypotheses, and perhaps suggested correspondence rules, empirical concepts, and operationalizations, it is then possible to represent one's theory in a more precise fashion that lends itself to further refinement and test. In this section, the use of equations and diagrams are introduced as tools for model building in causal analysis.[3]

Consider the causal generalization "variable (y) is a function of variable (x)." One may rewrite this hypothesis in the following equation where, by convention, y is taken as the dependent variable (effect) and x is the independent variable (cause):

$$y = f(x) \tag{3.1}$$

In general, the variables x and y may be either or both stochastic or non-stochastic (i.e., deterministic), and the relation itself may be either stochastic or nonstochastic. A nonstochastic or deterministic relation between x and y occurs if for every value of x there is but one corresponding value of y. Similarly, a stochastic relation between x and y occurs if for each value of x there is a probability distribution of values for y. The deterministic function, $y = f(x)$, states that y is dependent on x in the sense that a change in x implies a change in y. The stochastic interpretation of $y = f(x)$ says that y is functionally dependent on x "if the probability distribution of y is not the same for all values of x" (Kmenta, 1971). Most of the models discussed in this monograph will deal exclusively with stochastic relationships.

By itself, Eq. (3.1) adds little to the verbal representation of the relationship between x and y. In order to give the relationship more precision, it is necessary to specify the mathematical form of the function. Typically, the functional form will consist of one of the following: the linear, log, power, modified exponential, Gompertz, or logistic function (e.g., Kotler, 1971, pp. 31–37). For example, the following equation establishes that y is a linear function of x:

$$y = \beta x \tag{3.2}$$

where β is a measure of the sensitivity of y to variation in x. This relation may be represented diagrammatically as follows:

$$x \xrightarrow{\beta} y$$

which may be read "a change in x causes a change in y." When representing the above linear relationship in Cartesian coordinates, it may be summarized through an intercept parameter α and the slope parameter β, which in equation form becomes

$$y = \alpha + \beta x \qquad (3.3)$$

Finally, reflecting the degree of uncertainty present in all domains of inquiry, the above model is often represented as the following linear hypothesis where the additional term u is added to reflect a disturbance:

$$y = \alpha + \beta x + u \qquad (3.4)$$

This equation, which is known as the linear regression model, may also be written using the following diagrammatical notation:

In general, the reasons for including the disturbance u in the linear model are threefold. First, u reflects the omission of other causes of y, perhaps left out of the original model because of an oversight or for practical considerations. Second, u represents a degree of randomness such as might be reflected in natural variability in the responses of individuals or in data collection and coding. Third, u contains errors in measurement as a result of the imperfect correspondence between construct and operationalizations. In contrast to the randomness of the second class of phenomena, measurement error is taken to be systematic.

Basic Assumptions of the Linear Regression Model.[4] Although Eq. (3.4) is used to represent cause and effect, strictly speaking this practice is somewhat misleading. From a technical point of view, Eq. (3.4) represents the conditional mean of **y** as a function of **x**. This fact, as will be shown below, is a consequence of certain assumptions, particularly that of a nonstochastic **x**. In much of explanatory research, however, one desires to go beyond measures of empirical association—beyond the mere variation in the mean value of **y** as **x** varies. Typically, this will involve assuming **x** to be a random variable, at least to the extent it serves alternatively as independent and dependent variables in a system of structural equations. As will be developed in the following chapter, one may represent causal relationships more accurately in structural equations. However, because the development there builds upon and parallels that in linear regression models, it will prove useful to discuss the assumptions of the linear regression model in greater depth.

The fundamental assumptions of the linear regression model in Eq. (3.4) are five in number (e.g., Thiel, 1971). First, the disturbance u is assumed normally distributed, and secondly it is assumed to have zero mean. Next, the assumption is made that every disturbance has the same variance which, nevertheless, is unknown. Disturbances of this kind are said to be homoskedastic. The fourth assumption is that the disturbances be nonautocorrelated, that is, that the $E(u_i u_j) = 0$ for $i \neq j$, where E stands for "expected value." Finally, it is assumed that the independent variable x is nonstochastic with values fixed in repeated samples; and for any sample size, n,

$$\frac{1}{n} \sum_{i=1}^{n} (x_i - \bar{x})^2$$

is a finite number different from zero (Kmenta, 1971). From these assumptions and Eq. (3.4), it follows that the mean and variance of the dependent variable y can be expressed as follows:

$$E(y) = \alpha + \beta x \tag{3.5}$$

$$\text{var}(y) = \text{var}(u) \tag{3.6}$$

When the regression model is extended to include more than one independent variable, it may be expressed as

$$y = \alpha + \beta_1 x_1 + \beta_2 x_2 + \cdots + \beta_k x_k + u \tag{3.7}$$

where k equals the number of independent variables. Or using the conventions of the causal diagram, Eq. (3.7) may be drawn as:

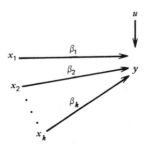

In addition to the assumptions noted above, the model of Eq. (3.7) also assumes that each independent variable is nonstochastic, that the number of observations is greater than the number of coefficients to be estimated, and that none of the independent variables is perfectly correlated with other independent variables or with any linear combination of other independent variables.

At this point, it is useful to consider the assumption of linearity made in the specification of the models; that is, the fact that the $E(y/x)$ is linear in x. First, from a pragmatic point of view, unless one has reasons to judge otherwise, the linear model represents a reasonable assumption. It is the simplest relationship between two variables, and if proven to accurately model the "true" relationship, it is the most parsimonious. When one does not know the functional form relating variables, the linear model is a useful first step in hypothesis testing and model building. A second reason for using the linear model is that many relationships in the world of experience are fundamentally governed by linear processes. There is considerable evidence in the behavioral sciences, for example, indicating that many basic psychological and social phenomena are linear or can be reasonably modeled as such (e.g., Dawes and Corrigan, 1974). Finally, since the linear regression model really only requires that there be linearity in the expected value of known *functions* of the explanatory variables, it is often possible to represent more complex processes using the linear model.[5] If one's model is nonlinear with respect to the variables in the model but linear with respect to the parameters to be estimated, it may be possible to transform the variables. For example, logarithmic or reciprocal transformations often allow one to use the linear regression model. If, on the other hand, one's model is nonlinear in both variables and parameters (and transformations are not possible), it may still be feasible to use maximum likelihood or other procedures under certain conditions.

Up to this point, the discussion has been primarily limited to issues of theory construction and model building. The issue of statistical inference has not been addressed. These issues are discussed as they relate to the general linear model in Chapter 4. Because the development of the general linear model assumes the reader is familiar with estimation procedures, the properties of estimators, and the problems involved in the violation of the basic assumptions in the linear model, it is suggested that the reader unfamiliar with these topics review a basic econometric text before proceeding (e.g., Kmenta, 1971; Thiel, 1971; Johnston, 1972).

Causal Diagrams. Over the years, researchers dealing with causal processes have developed conventions for representing their models. Figure 3.3 illustrates one of the more popular systems of notation used in the contemporary causal modeling literature (e.g., Jöreskog and Sörbom, 1976; Bagozzi, 1977a, 1977b). Assume, for purposes of discussion, that the model of Figure 3.3 is designed to represent the causes of variation in sales performance for salespeople in Company A.[6] Theoretical constructs are represented as circles in Figure 3.3, while squares indicate operationalizations. The model might hypothesize that sales performance (η_2) is directly caused by self-esteem (ζ) and motivation (η_1). These effects are represented by γ_4 and β, respectively. Similarly, self-esteem is shown to affect motivation directly through γ_3. Finally, motivation is shown also to be a function of two errorless exogenous variables, locus of control (x_1) and history of reward mediation (x_2). Following the conventions suggested by Jöreskog (e.g., Jöreskog and van Thillo, 1972), exogenous variables measured with error are shown as ξ, and endogenous variables

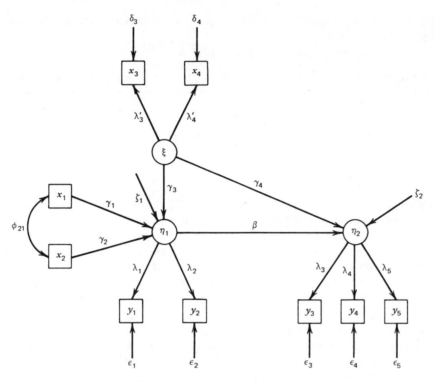

Figure 3.3. A simple causal model.

measured with error are modeled as η. Operationalizations of the former are drawn as x's, while those for the latter are represented as y's. Further, errors in variables for the x's are depicted as δ's while that for the y's are diagrammed as ε's. Errors in equations are shown as ζ's. Relationships between exogenous and endogenous variables are modelled as γ's, those between endogenous variables as β's, those between exogenous variables and their operationalizations as λ''s, and those between endogenous variables and their operationalizations as λ's. Finally, correlational relationships are drawn as curved line segments such as shown connecting x_1 and x_2. Such correlations are indicated by ϕ's.

The analysis in Chapter 4 will develop a procedure for building models such as shown in Figure 3.3 and for estimating parameters and testing hypotheses connected with these models. Each arrow bearing a parameter in Figure 3.3 represents one equation (i.e., causal relationship) in a system of simultaneous equations. For example, the direct causes of sales performance can be written algebraically as follows:

$$\eta_2 = \beta\eta_1 + \gamma_4\xi + \zeta_2$$

Likewise, the relationship between motivation and one of its operationalizations can be written as:

$$y_1 = \lambda_1 \eta_1 + \varepsilon_1$$

As will be developed in Chapter 4, the system of equations for models such as shown in Figure 3.3 can be expressed in the following general linear model:

$$\mathbf{B\eta} = \mathbf{\Gamma\xi} + \mathbf{\zeta}$$

where $\mathbf{B}$ and $\mathbf{\Gamma}$ are coefficient matrices, and $\mathbf{\eta}$, $\mathbf{\xi}$, and $\mathbf{\zeta}$ are as defined earlier.

Types of Causal Relationships

Certain classes of causal relationships occur with such regularity that it is useful to categorize them into types. A direct causal relationship exists between two variables if a change in one produces a change in the other and no third variable intervenes. An indirect causal relationship, in contrast, exists when one or more variables are intermediate between cause and effect. In Figure 3.3, the relationship between η_1 and η_2 is a direct one (represented as β), while that between x_1 and η_2 is indirect, being mediated by η_1. Another common distinction is that between recursive and nonrecursive systems of causal relationships: "A model is said to be recursive if all causal linkages run 'one way,' that is, if no two variables are reciprocally related in such a way that each affects and depends on the other, and no variable 'feeds back' upon itself through any indirect concatenation of causal linkages, however, circuitous" (Duncan, 1975, p. 25). A nonrecursive system of causal relationships contains at least one reciprocal causal path or an indirect feedback chain. Figure 3.3 represents a recursive system. However, if performance (η_2) were to also affect motivation (η_1), then the representation of this effect by an arrow from η_2 to η_1 would make the model a nonrecursive one. We will explore recursive and nonrecursive systems in greater depth in the following chapter.

Three final types of "causal" relationships of interest are those associated with spurious correlations, suppressor effects, or moderating variables. If an observed correlation between x and y were entirely due to the causal influence of a third variable z, then one would not want to infer causality between x and y but rather would term the association spurious. This can be diagrammed as follows:

If, on the other hand, one found that the absence of a zero-order correlation between x and y were a function of a third variable z, negatively related to one variable and positively related to the other, one might term the result a suppressor effect. Finally, if the relation between an independent variable x and dependent variable y were to depend on the level of a third variable z, then the latter would be termed a moderating variable. This is often referred to as an inter-action effect. Although subject to limitations, partial correlation analyses can aid in the detection of some spurious correlations and suppressor effects (e.g., Duncan, 1970). Similarly, moderating variables may be modeled using regression techniques to detect ordinal or disordinal interactions (cf., Kerlinger and Pedhazur, 1973, pp. 245–258).

Causality and the Process of Scientific Research

Scientific inquiry has many facets. One is the discovery and recording of facts. This is sometimes termed *descriptive science*. Another facet, somewhat more fundamental, is the construction and testing of hypotheses and theories. This aspect of inquiry is often labeled *theoretical science*. Although causal modeling is taken here to primarily encompass properties of theoretical science, it also involves a certain amount of description in that concepts are observed and modeled as they are manifested in the world of experience.

   A number of goals of theoretical science may be identified. The objective of *prediction* is to either deduce from known to unknown events in a conceptually static system or to make assertions about future outcomes "based on the observation of regularities among sequences of events of the past" (Zaltman et al., 1973). Perhaps the most fundamental goal of theoretical science is *explanation*. As discussed in Chapter 1, explanation strives to answer why some phenomenon (event, things, state of affairs) occurred. Typically, this is accomplished by representing cause-and-effect, antecedent-consequent events, lawlike generalizations, and so forth, in the deductive-nomological model, inductive-statistical model, realist model, or some other explanatory framework. The final objective of theoretical science is *control* of some phenomenon. Control means "the systematic manipulation of some element related to or contained within a system so as to effect a change in one or more elements in that system" (Zaltman et al., 1973, p. 174). The inclusion of control as an objective of theoretical science is a controversial topic. On the one hand are the views of many philosophers of science (both positivist and realist) who claim that reality exists independently of our beliefs and theories about that reality. While on the other hand are the views of conventionalists, scientific anarchists, and sociologists of knowledge who see our reality as something we socially construct and shape (e.g., Berger and Luckman, 1966; Keat and Urry, 1975; Bagozzi, 1976a). The issue of control is tied fundamentally to normative questions and questions of human values. Causal modeling represents a methodology for control as well as means for developing and testing theory.

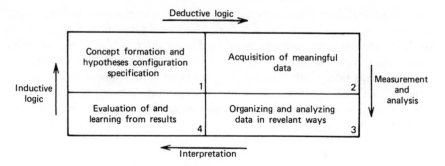

Figure 3.4. Basic processes in scientific research.

Source. Adapted from Zaltman et al., *Metatheory and Consumer Research,* New York: Holt, Rinehart & Winston, 1978, p. 18.

In achieving the above goals, scientific research can be seen to traverse at least eight basic processes or activities. The sequence usually begins with the development of concepts and the construction of hypotheses (see Figure 3.4). At this stage in the research process, one should be careful to specify the nature and rationale for the concepts in one's theory, the relationship(s) between concepts, the theoretical mechanisms behind hypotheses, and the conceptual and operational connections between concepts and observations. Typically, this involves the application of rules of logic and standards for determining the internal consistency of one's theoretical framework. It will also involve a determination of construct validity in conjunction with later stages in the research endeavor. Throughout the first stage and into the second, the process can be described as a deductive one. That is, the progression is one from general assertions to relatively particular or specific instances. The acquisition of meaningful data is accomplished after the initial activities of theory construction as shown in cell 2 in Figure 3.4. In general, the data should be internally consistent (e.g., have a high reliability) and be logically or causally tied to the concepts and constructs in one's theory. The third stage involves the organization and analysis of data in relation to the hypotheses stated in the beginning. This might entail the application of mathematical models or statistical procedures. The process of transition from the acquisition of data to its organization and analysis is labeled measurement and analysis in Figure 3.4. Next, through the process of interpretation, one evaluates the findings, learns from the results, and, in general, gains an understanding of the phenomenon to be explained. The scientific process achieves closure through the subprocess of induction wherein the learning attained through earlier stages is incorporated into one's theoretical framework. Induction involves the argument from particular instances to more general conclusions. Unlike the valid deductive argument that guarantees the truth of its conclusion given true premises, the valid inductive argument provides "good"—though not conclusive—grounds for accepting its conclusion. The scientific process outlined in Figure 3.4 is thus a continuous one, reflecting the tentativeness and uncertainty in our knowledge of the world.

Some Benefits of Causal Modeling

Causal modeling offers the theorist and researcher a number of benefits. First, the assumptions, variables, and hypothesized relationships in one's theory are made explicit. This is necessary if one is to avoid misunderstanding and ambiguities with respect to one's purposes and claims. Second, causal modeling adds a certain degree of precision to one's theory and research effort. The approach requires that the language for definitions of variables and operationalizations be specified clearly, and the functional relationships among variables be accurately represented. Should one's theory and hypotheses conflict with previous theory, past research, or empirical testing, one can then investigate whether the discrepancy lies in the precision of the proposed causal model. The precision of relationships, for example, can be seen to vary from relatively imprecise categorical statements such as "given x is either a or b and y is either c or d, if x is b, then y will be d," on the one hand, to more precise statements such as "a change in x of $t\%$ will produce a change in y of $r\%$ for $x_0 < x < x_1$ and $y_0 < y < y_1$," on the other hand. The more precise statement provides greater information and testability. Third, causal modeling allows the researcher to better represent complex social and psychological processes in the marketplace. Since these phenomena are often intricate, involving many sequences of interactions and feedback, causal modeling represents a useful method for capturing the system of true relationships. Finally, causal modeling is valuable because it formalizes many of the standards for inquiry specified in contemporary treatments of the philosophy of science. The causal model provides a framework for constructing and testing the internal consistency of one's theories and measurements as well as the degree of correspondence between theory and observation.

Representing Theories: An Illustration

Although there are a number of ways to systematically depict theories,[7] most formal theoretical structures utilize some combination of axioms and causal hypotheses. The overriding objective in theory construction is to represent one's assumptions, concepts, operationalizations, correspondence rules, and propositions in one meaningful system that is both internally consistent and testable.

As an illustration of one way to formally express a theory, consider the theory recently proposed by the author to explain the exchange relationships existing between a husband-and-wife dyad and the providers of goods and services (Bagozzi, 1978b). For purposes of analysis, the demand for goods or services by the dyad is divided into two sets of commodities: (1) focal goods or services (S_{SG}) and (2) a composite construct (S_{OG}) representing all other goods and services considered by the dyad. Given these assumptions, it is further presumed that the husband and wife attempt to maximize their joint satisfaction in their interactions with each other and with other social actors (including the providers of goods and services). That is, the husband and wife are assumed to maximize

$$U_d = U(S_{SG}, S_{OG}) \tag{3.8}$$

subject to

$$Y = I_{NL} + wL = p_1 x_{SG} + p_2 x_{OG} \tag{3.9}$$

$$T = t + L \tag{3.10}$$

and given the following production functions:

$$S_{SG} = f(t_{SG}, x_{SG}) \tag{3.11}$$

$$S_{OG} = f(t_{OG}, x_{OG}) \tag{3.12}$$

where U_d is the utility function of the husband-and-wife dyad, S_{SG} is the total satisfaction from focal goods, S_{OG} is the total satisfaction from other goods and services, Y is lifetime money income (i.e., permanent income), I_{nL} is the dyad's nonlabor wealth, w is the average hourly market wage received by the dyad, L is the number of hours the dyad works throughout marriage, x_{SG} is the total amount of tangible goods devoted to the production of satisfaction from subjective focal goods (i.e., S_{SG}), x_{OG} is the total amount of other goods devoted to the production of satisfaction from subjective other goods (i.e., S_{OG}), T is the dyad's life-span after marriage, t is the dyad's time available for home production (with t_{SG} the time input to S_{SG} and t_{OG} the time input S_{OG}), and p_1 and p_2 are the market prices of tangible focal and other goods, respectively. The subjective satisfaction from focal and other goods (i.e., S_{SG} and S_{OG}) is posited to consist of three classes of mental events: affect, cognitions, and conations.

Before presentation of the remainder of the theory, a few words of explanation are in order. Equation (3.8) expresses the idea that the subjective outcome of exchanges between the husband-and-wife dyad and other social actors will depend on the joint demand for certain abstract, yet subjectively experienced, human needs. Equations (3.9) and (3.10) represent the budget constraints that the dyad faces for money income and time, respectively. The former states that the amount of money spent on tangible goods used to produce S_{SG} plus the amount spent on tangible goods used to produce S_{OG} equals money income Y. The latter states that the total time T for the couple is divided between leisure t and labor, L. Equations (3.11) and (3.12) model the relationships between tangible goods and services on the one hand, and subjective commodities on

the other. The hypothesis is that the husband and wife combine tangible goods
and services with their time to "produce" the subjective "goods" S_{SG} and S_{OG}.

Taken together, Eqs. (3.8)–(3.12) specify the theoretical variables of interest
(where S_{SG} and S_{OG} are the two principal variables to be explained), the initial
assumptions in the theory, the decision rule used by the dyad in their exchanges,
the economic and time constraints faced by the dyad, and the means used by
the dyad to achieve satisfaction. With respect to the assumptions, it is assumed
that (a) $U(S_{SG}, S_{OG})$ is continuous and has continuous first and second partial
derivatives, (b) the indifference curves are strictly convex toward the origin and
do not intersect, (c) decision-making is for a specified period of time, and
(d) inputs to S_{OG} (i.e., t_{OG} and x_{OG}) do not jointly produce S_{SG}.[8] Further, the
husband-and-wife are assumed to use a utility maximization decision rule.
Next, unlike Becker (1965), Lancaster (1971), and others in the "new home
economics" tradition, subjective goods (S_{SG} and S_{OG}) are assumed to possess
"shadow" prices determined by the subjective costs of production experienced
by each individual dyad. Basically, shadow prices constitute perceived psychic
and social costs. With these assumptions and given that Y^* is the subjective,
anticipated permanent income (i.e., full wealth), the new budget constraint can
be written as

$$Y^* = \pi_1 S_{SG} + \pi_2 S_{OG} \qquad (3.13)$$

where π_1 is the shadow price of S_{SG} and π_2 is the shadow price of S_{OG}.

The interpretation of the theory up to this point is as follows. Theoretical
constructs include S_{SG}, S_{OG}, π_1, π_2, and Y^*; and the theoretical relationships
(i.e., nonobservational propositions) interconnecting these variables among
themselves are represented axiomatically through Eqs. (3.8)–(3.13). Notice
that this system of equations contains no operationalizations and correspondence rules for the theoretical variables, and therefore the theory is untestable as it stands. Nevertheless, the foundation is laid for the derivation of the
demand for S_{SG} and S_{OG}. The theory asserts that the demand for S_{SG} and S_{OG}
will be a function of the exchanges the dyad has and the unique combination
of time and tangible goods and services the dyad combines to produce their
utility. Consumption occurs subject to the psychic and social constraints on
the dyad's resources, given the desire of the husband and wife to produce a
combination of S_{SG} and S_{OG} placing them at the highest level of satisfaction.

The demand for S_{SG} and S_{OG} can be determined as follows. Forming the
Langrangian, taking partial derivatives, and setting these equal to zero yields
the following first-order conditions for a maximum:

$$V = U(S_{SG}, S_{OG}) + \lambda(\pi_1 S_{SG} + \pi_2 S_{OG} - Y^*) \qquad (3.14)$$

$$\frac{\partial V}{\partial S_{SG}} = U_{S_{SG}} + \lambda\pi_1 = 0 \qquad (3.15)$$

$$\frac{\partial V}{\partial S_{OG}} = U_{S_{OG}} + \lambda\pi_2 = 0 \qquad (3.16)$$

$$\frac{\partial V}{\partial \lambda} = \pi_1 S_{SG} + \pi_2 S_{OG} - Y^* = 0 \tag{3.17}$$

where $\lambda < 0$ is a Langrangian multiplier. To find the differentials for the demand for S_{SG} and S_{OG}, Eqs. (3.15)–(3.17) must be totally differentiated, and the resulting equations must be solved for the vector of differentials. Performing these operations and using Cramer's rule, it can be shown that the differentials are (with π_2 held constant)[9]

$$dS_{SG} = \frac{1}{\Delta}[(\lambda\Delta_{11}d\pi_1) - \Delta_{31}(dY^* - S_{SG}d\pi_1)] \tag{3.18}$$

$$dS_{OG} = \frac{1}{\Delta}[(-\lambda\Delta_{12}d\pi_1) + \Delta_{32}(dY^* - S_{SG}d\pi_1)] \tag{3.19}$$

where Δ is a particular determinant and Δ_{ij} are elements of a particular matrix both of which are not shown here for simplicity (see Bagozzi, 1978b, pp. 547–548). Equations (3.18) and (3.19) indicate that the demand for focal goods is a function of their shadow prices and the subjective anticipated permanent income. Finally, solution of the first-order conditions for λ, produces the following marginal utilities:

$$\frac{U_{S_{SG}}}{\pi_1} = \frac{U_{S_{OG}}}{\pi_2} \tag{3.20}$$

These results show that the husband and wife, as a producing and consuming unit, equate the ratios of the marginal utilities of S_{SG} and S_{OG} to their respective marginal costs. Hence, the husband and wife compare and weigh satisfaction from the number and quality of commodities produced from time and focal goods with that achieved from other sources of satisfaction. In this way, the mutual outcomes from the intra and extradyadic exchanges are maximized.

As a point of interpretation at this stage in the derivation, it should be noted that the theory does not explicitly model the social interaction processes within the dyad nor between the dyad and other social actors. Rather, it models the joint outcomes of these processes. The actual sources of interpersonal influence and external forces are not modeled directly. Thus, the theory omits important determinants of exchange and is limited in scope. Perhaps the most serious shortcoming is the fact that many of its assertions cannot be tested as the model stands. These deficiences must be corrected if one is to derive an explanatory theory of exchange.

To accomplish this goal, the theory needs to be refined in two directions. First, social psychological processes within the dyad and between the dyad and other social entities need to be introduced so as to model exchange as a function of the characteristics of the actors, social influence, and situational contingencies (Bagozzi, 1978b). This will be done by hypothesizing that four key theoretical constructs—S_{SG}, S_{OG}, π_1, and Y^*—will be functions of psychological and social variables. Second, operationalizations for variables need to be specified, and the entire network of measurement and causal relationships needs to be delineated.[10]

An outline of these refinements might consist of the following. Contemporary research in the behavioral sciences suggests that the four key subjective constructs in the theory can be related to antecedent social and psychological variables through[11]:

$$S_{SG} = f(\pi_1, y^*, \text{social influence, interpersonal attraction,} \tag{3.21}$$
source characteristics, power, and other relationships between husband and wife)

$$S_{OG} = f(\pi_1, Y^*, \text{social influence, interpersonal attraction,} \tag{3.22}$$
source characteristics, dependence, and other relations between the husband-and-wife dyad and the providers of goods and services)

$$\pi_1 = f(\text{norms, past experiences and satisfaction of husband} \tag{3.23}$$
and wife, social comparison processes)

$$Y^* = f(\text{norms, past experiences and satisfaction of husband} \tag{3.24}$$
and wife, social comparison processes)

Combined with the demand equation for S_{SG}, Eqs. (3.21)–(3.24) might translate into the following system of linear hypotheses:

$$\begin{bmatrix} 1 & 0 & -\beta_1 & -\beta_2 \\ 0 & 1 & -\beta_3 & -\beta_4 \\ 0 & 0 & 1 & 0 \\ 0 & 0 & 0 & 1 \end{bmatrix} \begin{bmatrix} S_{SG} \\ S_{OG} \\ \pi_1 \\ Y^* \end{bmatrix}$$

$$= \begin{bmatrix} \alpha_1 & \alpha_2 & \alpha_3 & \alpha_4 & 0 & 0 & 0 & 0 & 0 & 0 & 0 \\ 0 & 0 & 0 & 0 & \alpha_5 & \alpha_6 & \alpha_7 & \alpha_8 & 0 & 0 & 0 \\ 0 & 0 & 0 & 0 & 0 & 0 & 0 & 0 & \alpha_9 & \alpha_{10} & \alpha_{11} \\ 0 & 0 & 0 & 0 & 0 & 0 & 0 & 0 & \alpha_{12} & \alpha_{13} & \alpha_{14} \end{bmatrix} \begin{bmatrix} SI_w \\ A_w \\ SC_w \\ P_w \\ SI_b \\ A_b \\ SC_b \\ D_b \\ N \\ PB \\ SCP \end{bmatrix} + \begin{bmatrix} \zeta_1 \\ \zeta_2 \\ \zeta_3 \\ \zeta_4 \end{bmatrix}$$

$$\tag{3.25}$$

where SI is social influence, A is interpersonal attraction, SC is source character-istics, P is power, D is dependence, N is normative prescriptions, PB is past experience and satisfaction behaviors, SCP is social comparison processes, w indicates "within the husband-and-wife dyad," b signifies "between the husband-and-wife dyad and the providers of alternative sources of satisfaction," $\beta_1 - \beta_4$ are parameters expressing relations among endogenous variables, $\alpha_1 - \alpha_{14}$ are parameters relating endogenous to exogenous variables, and $\zeta_1 - \zeta_4$ are errors in equations.

Because the variables in Eq. (3.25) are theoretical constructs and the relation-ships implied by the equations are nonobservational propositions, it is necessary to tie at least a subset of the variables to measurements for the entire theory to be testable. Although the general form of the measurement equation is discussed in the following chapter, Eq. (3.26) represents an example for the endogenous variables:

$$
\begin{pmatrix} y_1 \\ y_2 \\ y_3 \\ y_4 \\ y_5 \\ y_6 \\ y_7 \\ y_8 \end{pmatrix} = \begin{pmatrix} \lambda_1 & 0 & 0 & 0 \\ \lambda_2 & 0 & 0 & 0 \\ 0 & \lambda_3 & 0 & 0 \\ 0 & \lambda_4 & 0 & 0 \\ 0 & 0 & \lambda_5 & 0 \\ 0 & 0 & \lambda_6 & 0 \\ 0 & 0 & 0 & \lambda_7 \\ 0 & 0 & 0 & \lambda_8 \end{pmatrix} \begin{pmatrix} S_{SG} \\ S_{OG} \\ \pi_1 \\ y^* \end{pmatrix} + \begin{pmatrix} \varepsilon_1 \\ \varepsilon_2 \\ \varepsilon_3 \\ \varepsilon_4 \\ \varepsilon_5 \\ \varepsilon_6 \\ \varepsilon_7 \\ \varepsilon_8 \end{pmatrix} \tag{3.26}
$$

where it is assumed for purposes of illustration that each endogenous variable $(S_{SG}, S_{OG}, \pi_1,$ and $Y^*)$ has two operationalizations. The equations in (3.26) relate eight empirical measures $\mathbf{y}$ to $S_{SG}, S_{OG}, \pi_1,$ and Y^* through the λ param-eters. The ε's represent random error in variables. Parallel equations would be required to operationalize the exogenous variables, $SI_w, A_w, \ldots, SCP.$ The general form for these latter measures is

$$
\mathbf{x} = \Lambda_x \boldsymbol{\xi} + \boldsymbol{\delta} \tag{3.27}
$$

where $\boldsymbol{\xi}$ is the vector of exogenous constructs. For a fuller description of the above theory, see Bagozzi (1978b).

Summary

Any causal theory may be represented as a formal network known as the standard construal. In this network, theoretical relationships are represented as nonobservational propositions between theoretical constructs. Theoretical constructs are related, in turn, to derived concepts or empirical concepts. These latter relationships are termed correspondence rules. Finally, empirical concepts are tied to observations through operational definitions. This model of causality was illustrated with an expectancy-value theory of consumer behavior.

In order to make the representation of causal theories more explicit, mathematical or statistical techniques were shown to be helpful. The example of the linear regression model was used to highlight the process of formalizing causal relationships, and the use of causal diagrams was illustrated. Brief mention was made of certain types of causal relationships including direct, indirect, recursive, nonrecursive, spurious, interactive, and suppressor cases. Finally, the chapter closed with an outline of the scientific process of research, the role and benefits of causal modeling, and an illustration of a theory combining axiomatic and causal hypotheses. We turn now to a derivation and discussion of the general linear model.

Notes

[1] For a slightly different perspective, see Zaltman et al. (1973, pp. 73–74).

[2] Following Kahane (1973, pp. 179–181), an extensional definition of a concept is a list of *all* things to which the concept applies. An intensional definition of a concept "lists a set of properties such that the term applies to all things having that set of properties, and to nothing else." An ostensive definition of a concept "is one which indicates the measuring of the term by providing a *sample* of the things denoted." Although controversial, criteria for "good" intensional definitions (the type most often used in scientific inquiry) include: a good definition must not be too wide or too narrow; it ought to avoid unnecessarily vague, ambiguous, obscure, or metaphorical language; it must not be circular; and it should state the essential properties of the things named by that term (Kahane, 1973, pp. 181–184). Finally, "good" definitions in formal systems should meet at least three criteria: (1) "a defined term must be eliminable from a system into which it is introduced. A term is said to be eliminable from a system if every sentence in the system in which it occurs can be replaced by an equivalent sentence in which that term does not occur," (2) "a good definition must not permit the proof of something which cannot be proved without it," and (3) "a good definition makes clear the form of the contexts in which the term is to be used" (Kahane, 1973, pp. 184–185, emphasis omitted).

[3] The classic treatment of causal diagrams and structural equation representation can be found in Simon (1957, ch. 1–3). Duncan (1975) and Heise (1975) present elementary treatments. A more rigorous approach will be sketched in Chapter 4.

[4] For an elementary treatment of the linear regression model, the reader is referred to Kmenta (1971). More advanced discussions may be found in Johnston (1972) and Thiel (1971).

[5] For discussions of ways to handle nonlinear models, see Kmenta (1971, pp. 451–472) and Johnston (1972, pp. 47–55).

[6] The figure is intended for illustration only and does not necessarily reflect cause-and-effect in the personal selling situation. For a test of some of the causal paths in the figure as well as other relationships, see Bagozzi (1976b).

[7] For a more detailed presentation of the example sketched in this section, see Bagozzi (1978b). For an analysis of different ways to express theories, see Zetterberg (1965), Reynolds (1971, ch. 5), and Nowak (1977, ch. 7).

[8] For a formal statement of assumptions as to transitivity, completeness, continuity, and strict convexity, see Lancaster (1971, pp. 20–21). Henderson and Quandt (1971) present the classic assumptions for the utility function and indifference curves.

[9] See Bagozzi (1978b, p. 547).

[10] Ultimately, one would like to incorporate the social psychological and other variables in the mathematical derivation developed in Eqs. (3.8)–(3.20). However, given the status of current theories in the behavioral sciences, the illustration here is presented in two stages. That is, the first stage builds on well-developed optimization procedures used in economics and the relatively sound new home economics model of decision-making. The variables derived in this stage become endogenous. The second stage introduces social psychological and other variables as exogenous factors. This is done because the theory relating these exogenous factors to the endogenous ones is not yet developed in sufficient detail to warrant inclusion in the axiomatic part of the overall theory represented in Eq. (3.8)–(3.20).

[11] For research supporting these and subsequent hypotheses, see McGuire (1969); Tedeschi, Schlenker, and Bonoma (1973); and Rubin and Brown (1975).

FOUR

STRUCTURAL EQUATIONS AND
THE GENERAL LINEAR MODEL

This chapter presents a general model for representing and testing causal theories. After presenting the overall philosophy and objectives of the approach, the discussion turns to the topics of specification, identification, estimation of parameters, and hypothesis testing. Next, a number of strengths and limitations of the general linear model are noted. Finally, the chapter closes with a simple illustration of the procedures. Throughout the discussion, an attempt is made to follow the notation and derivation due to Jöreskog (1969, 1970, 1971, 1973; Gruvaeus and Jöreskog, 1970; Jöreskog and van Thillo, 1972) wherever possible. Jöreskog's treatment represents perhaps the most general approach, and it has come to be widely used and discussed in the statistical, psychological, sociological, and, more recently, marketing literatures.

Philosophy and Objectives of the Approach

Causal Modeling is a broad general term for a diversity of scientific approaches dealing with the representation of cause and effect. As Goldberger (1973a, p. 1) recently noted:

In methodological terms, the models have been referred to as simultaneous equation systems, linear causal schemes, path analysis, structural equation models, dependence analysis, test score theory, multitrait-multimethod matrices, and the cross-lagged panel correlation technique.

Behind all this diversity of subject matter and terminology, several common features can be identified. One relates to the analysis of *nonexperimental data*; the absence of laboratory conditions demands that statistical procedures substitute for conventional experimental controls. A second one concerns *hypothetical constructs*; many of the models contain latent variables which, while not directly observed, have operational implications for relationships among observable variables. A third common element relates to *systems*: the models are typically built up of several or many equations which interact together.

These features call for statistical tools which are based upon, but which go well beyond, conventional regression and analysis of variance.

Actually, the procedures are even more general than Goldberger indicates. For example, causal modeling can be used in experimental research to better represent cause and effect, among other benefits (e.g., Bagozzi, 1977b). Before derivation of the general model, it will prove helpful to examine the role of the method in achieving explanation.

Explanation in Causal Modeling

In its broadest sense, the achievement of understanding in explanation can be seen to occur on various levels ranging from weak or descriptive explanation on the one hand to strong or "why" explanation on the other. As shown in Table 4.1, at least four levels of understanding in explanation may be identified

Table 4.1

Levels of Understanding in Explanation

Level of Understanding in Explanation	Explanation
One	Phenomenon z exists in state Q.
Two	The phenomenon is of the nature Q and is produced by factors $x_1, x_2, \ldots, x_n$.
Three	Factors $x_1, x_2, \ldots, x_n$ are interactive or have interacted in manner $y_1, y_2, \ldots, y_n$ to produce in some past or present time a phenomenon of the nature Q.
Four	Factors $x_1, x_2, \ldots, x_n$ interact in a manner $y_1, y_2, \ldots, y_n$ for reasons $w_1, w_2, \ldots, w_n$, thus producing a phenomenon of the nature Q.

Adapted with alterations from: G. Zaltman et al., *Metatheory and Consumer Research*, New York: Holt, Rinehart & Winston, 1973; p. 129.

(e.g., Doby, 1969; Zaltman et al., 1973). The first or most primitive level merely asserts that a certain phenomenon exists in a particular state. For example, the statement, "the level of sales in company A in year k for salespersons $p_1, p_2, \ldots, p_n$ is, respectively, $s_1, s_2, \ldots, s_n$," is an assertion as to the state of existence for sales achieved by a set of people. At this level of "explanation," one obtains a certain degree of descriptive understanding as to the nature of some phenomenon of interest. Although the first level is a necessary step in the theory construction process, it says nothing as to possible causes or consequences of variation in the phenomenon. The second level of understanding in explanation begins with the state or nature of some phenomenon of interest and then introduces antecedent variables that may serve as a basis for accounting for variation in the phenomenon. Thus, for example, one might identify the following as antecedents of the particular levels of sales performance (z) attained by each salesperson in company A: self-esteem (x_1), expectancies (x_2), motivation (x_3), role ambiguity (x_4), role conflict (x_5), and situational contingencies ($x_6, \ldots, x_m$). The first three variables represent vectors of characteristics of the salespeople; the next two attempts to capture certain interpersonal factors; and $x_6, \ldots, x_m$ depict situational influences on sales performance. Notice that this second level of understanding goes farther than the first in that variables are proposed that may serve as the foundation for theory construction. However, nothing is said as to the organization or ordering of relationships, nor is a rationale provided as to the mechanisms connecting the variables to sales performance.

The third level of understanding in explanation introduces, as a hypothesis, a particular structure of relationships among both the phenomenon to be explained and the set of explanatory variables. Typically, this will entail two dimensions. First, the articulation of all variables in some causal ordering will be made based upon theoretical considerations, past research, methodological factors, logical reasoning, or other information. Second, the functional form of each causal relationship must be specified. The model developed in this chapter is limited to linear relationships in the sense noted in the previous chapter.

The fourth and highest level of understanding in explanation occurs when one specifies the reasons why one expects a particular causal ordering and the hypothesized functional form(s) for relationships. As discussed in earlier chapters, the justification for the existence and form of relationships may be based on lawlike generalizations, natural necessity, or realist arguments. Invariably, the researcher will invoke theoretical reasoning as well as empirical support for his or her hypotheses. The fourth level of understanding in explanation attempts to specify how and why variables are related in the sense of elaborating on the mechanisms, laws, or structure of the connections binding causes to effects (see discussion in Chapter 1). A number of the chapters in the latter half of the monograph provide detailed illustrations of explanation at the third and fourth levels of understanding.

Unobserved Variables and Measurement Error

Although the standard regression model discussed in Chapter 3 assumes that variables are measured without error, this is often an unrealistic assumption. Rather, as a result of factors such as methods variance (cf., Campbell and Fiske, 1959), systematic influence in addition to the random disturbance will often be present in one's model. In general, the estimation of parameters in models where measurement error is present but not explicitly represented will not provide useful estimates. In order to see this, consider the models diagramed in Figure 4.1. Figure 4.1a presents the case where the independent variable x is assumed measured without error, while the true (i.e., unobservable) dependent variable η is assumed measured with error as y. The structural model for Figure 4.1a may be written as

$$\eta = \gamma x + \zeta \tag{4.1}$$

$$y = (1)\eta + \varepsilon \tag{4.2}$$

where η, ζ, and ε are assumed independently distributed with zero expectations. Multiplying the first equation by x and taking expectations yields the following:

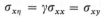

$$\sigma_{x\eta} = \gamma\sigma_{xx} = \sigma_{xy}$$

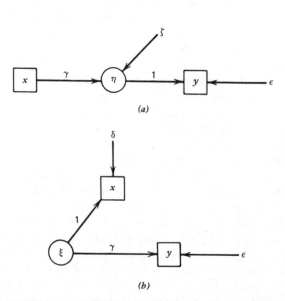

(a)

(b)

Figure 4.1. Two simple models with measurement error. (a) Errorless independent variable/error in the dependent variable. (b) Error in the independent variable/errorless dependent variable.

and

$$\gamma = \frac{\sigma_{x\eta}}{\sigma_{xx}} = \frac{\sigma_{xy}}{\sigma_{xx}}$$

since $E(\zeta x) = 0$. Hence, the parameter γ connecting the errorless independent variable x to the true dependent variable η is found to be the ordinary least-squares estimator and thus, even in finite samples, is unbiased and efficient. However, it should be noted that the standard error for γ will be a function of $\sigma_{\varepsilon\varepsilon}$, though this will pose no problems in large samples. In general, then, error in the dependent variables will not, by itself, adversely affect the estimation of the structural parameters of interest.

When there is error in the independent variable, on the other hand, the ordinary least-squares estimates will be both biased and inconsistent. To see this, consider the following structural equations for the model of Figure 4.1b:

$$x = (1)\xi + \delta \tag{4.3}$$

$$y = \gamma\xi + \varepsilon \tag{4.4}$$

where, as before, ξ, δ, and ε are assumed independently distributed with zero expectations. Solving for ξ in Eq. (4.3) and substituting the result in Eq. (4.4) yields

$$y = \gamma x - \gamma\delta + \varepsilon$$

or

$$y = \gamma x + u \tag{4.5}$$

where $u = \varepsilon - \gamma\delta$. Multiplying Eq. (4.5) by x and taking expectations produces the following:

$$\sigma_{xy} = \gamma\sigma_{xx} - \gamma\sigma_{\delta\delta} = \gamma(\sigma_{xx} - \sigma_{\delta\delta})$$

and

$$\gamma = \frac{\sigma_{xy}}{\sigma_{xx} - \sigma_{\delta\delta}}$$

If, instead of modeling the independent variable as a true unobservable plus error as shown in Figure 4.1b one merely regressed y on x directly, the estimated parameter would be the standard ordinary least-squares value:

$$\gamma' = \sigma_{xy}/\sigma_{xx}$$

Thus, given that the true model is that shown in Figure 4.1b and Eqs. (4.3) and (4.4), one would obtain a biased estimate for γ by failing to take into account measurement error in the independent variable. In particular, the parameter value given by ordinary least squares γ' will be an underestimate of the true value

γ. The instrumental variables approach or maximum likelihood procedures are usually used to estimate parameters when measurement error exists in the independent variable. The general model developed below is a maximum likelihood method and can be used to estimate parameters when measurement error is present in both independent and dependent variables simultaneously.

Although the representation of measurement error is one of the major benefits and motivations for using the structural equation approach, it places certain restrictions on what one may model. These restrictions stem from the necessity to be able to determine unique values for parameter estimates. The general issue is termed the identification problem in the literature. To illustrate the topic and prepare the reader for the derivation in the latter half of the chapter, it will prove helpful to consider the model consisting of a single unobservable variable η and its multiple operationalizations $y_1, y_2, \ldots, y_p$. This is represented in the causal diagram of Figure 4.2.

Consider first[1] the special case of the model of Figure 4.2 where $p = 2$ (i.e., there are two measurements for the unobservable). The structural equations for this model may be written as

$$y_1 = \lambda_1 \eta + \varepsilon_1$$
$$y_2 = \lambda_2 \eta + \varepsilon_2$$

where η, ε_1, and ε_2 are taken to be independently distributed with zero expectations. With the variance of η normalized at unity (i.e., $\sigma_{\eta\eta} = 1$), the observable moments may be related to the structural parameters through the following equations:

$$\sigma_{11} = \lambda_1^2 + \theta_{\varepsilon_1}^2, \qquad \sigma_{12} = \lambda_1 \lambda_2$$
$$\sigma_{22} = \lambda_2^2 + \theta_{\varepsilon_2}^2$$

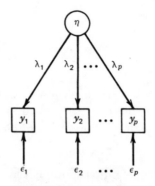

Figure 4.2. A causal model for one unobservable and p indicators.

where the σ_{ii}'s represent variances of the y_i's, the σ_{ij}'s stand for covariances for the y_i's and y_j's, and the θ_ε^2's are error variances for the y_i's. But notice that there are only three equations to determine four unknown parameters, that is, λ_1, λ_2, $\theta_{\varepsilon_1}^2$, and $\theta_{\varepsilon_2}^2$. Hence, the model is underidentified since it is impossible to determine unique estimates for the parameters.

Consider next the case with three indicators of η in Figure 4.2. The equations for this model may be written as

$$y_1 = \lambda_1 \eta + \varepsilon_1$$

$$y_2 = \lambda_2 \eta_2 + \varepsilon_2$$

$$y_3 = \lambda_3 \eta_3 + \varepsilon_3$$

with η and $\varepsilon_1 - \varepsilon_3$ taken to be independently distributed with zero expectations. Given the variance of η to be normalized as above, it follows that the observable moments may be related to the structural parameters through the following equations:

$$\sigma_{11} = \lambda_1^2 + \theta_{\varepsilon_1}^2, \qquad \sigma_{12} = \lambda_1 \lambda_2, \qquad \sigma_{13} = \lambda_1 \lambda_3$$

$$\sigma_{22} = \lambda_2^2 + \theta_{\varepsilon_2}^2, \qquad \sigma_{23} = \lambda_2 \lambda_3$$

$$\sigma_{33} = \lambda_3^2 + \theta_{\varepsilon_3}^2$$

Notice here, however, that there are six equations and six unknown parameters, that is, $\lambda_1, \lambda_2, \lambda_3, \theta_{\varepsilon_1}^2, \theta_{\varepsilon_2}^2$, and $\theta_{\varepsilon_3}^2$. Thus, solving for the parameters, one discovers that

$$\lambda_1 = \left(\frac{\sigma_{12}\sigma_{13}}{\sigma_{23}}\right)^{1/2}, \qquad \lambda_2 = \left(\frac{\sigma_{12}\sigma_{23}}{\sigma_{13}}\right)^{1/2}, \qquad \lambda_3 = \left(\frac{\sigma_{13}\sigma_{23}}{\sigma_{12}}\right)^{1/2}$$

$$\theta_{\varepsilon_1}^2 = \sigma_{11} - \lambda_1^2, \qquad \theta_{\varepsilon_2}^2 = \sigma_{22} - \lambda_2^2, \qquad \theta_{\varepsilon_3}^2 = \sigma_{33} - \lambda_3^2$$

Models such as this are termed just-identified.

Finally, consider the general case for the model in Figure 4.2 where there are p indicators of η. The structural equations for this model may be represented as:

$$\mathbf{y} = \lambda\eta + \varepsilon \tag{4.6}$$

where $\mathbf{y}$ is a $p \times 1$ vector of observable indicators, λ is a $p \times 1$ vector of parameters relating measurements to the true unobservable η, which is a scalar (with its variance assumed normalized at unity), $E(\eta\varepsilon) = 0$, and ε is a $p \times 1$ vector of disturbances with $E(\varepsilon\varepsilon') = \theta_\varepsilon^2$, a diagonal matrix of error variances. It then follows that the implied population covariance matrix of the observable indicators is

$$\mathbf{\Omega} = E(\mathbf{yy'}) = E[(\lambda\eta + \varepsilon)(\lambda\eta + \varepsilon)'] = \lambda\lambda' + \theta_\varepsilon^2 \tag{4.7}$$

Goldberger (1974) shows that since there are $l = p(p + 1)/2$ distinct elements in Ω and only $k = 2p$ nonzero elements in λ and θ_ε^2, there are $r = l - k = p(p - 3)/2$ restrictions on Ω. For $p > 3$, there are r overidentifying restrictions on Ω.

The model of Figure 4.2 is a special case of the factor analysis model with one common factor, p indicators, and p independent disturbances (specific factors). It may be extended to the general factor analysis model with k common factors (unobservables) as follows (cf., Goldberger, 1974; Lawley and Maxwell, 1971):

$$y = \Delta\eta + \varepsilon \tag{4.8}$$

where $E(\eta\varepsilon) = 0$, $E(\varepsilon\varepsilon') = \theta_\varepsilon^2$ is a diagonal matrix of error variances, y is a $p \times 1$ vector of indicators, Δ is a $p \times k$ matrix of factor loadings (structural coefficients), η is a $k \times 1$ vector of common factors, and ε is a $p \times 1$ vector of specific factors (disturbances). The implied population covariance matrix of the observable indicators may be written as

$$\Omega^* = E(yy') = \Delta\psi\Delta + \theta_\varepsilon^2 \tag{4.9}$$

where $\psi = E(\eta\eta)$. It can be shown that Eq. (4.9) represents f equations in q unknowns, where $f = p(p + 1)/2$, the number of distinct elements in Ω^*, and $g = p(k + 1) - k(k - 1)/2$, the number of free parameters (e.g., Goldberger, 1974, p. 198). For $r' = f - g$, the model will be identified if $r' \geq 0$; and if $r' > 0$, there will be r' overidentifying restrictions on Ω^*.

Simultaneity

When reciprocal causation or feedback exists in one's model, certain explanatory variables will be correlated with disturbances (assuming that the explanatory variables are stochastic). Under these conditions, estimation of parameters by ordinary least-squares procedures will produce biased and inconsistent estimates. To illustrate the problem further,[2] consider the following simultaneous equation system that is diagramed in Figure 4.3:

$$y = \gamma x + \varepsilon$$

$$x = \beta y + \delta$$

where ε and δ are assumed independent. Solving for y and x as a function only of ε, δ, and the parameters yields

$$y = \frac{\gamma\delta + \varepsilon}{1 - \gamma\beta}$$

$$x = \frac{\beta\varepsilon + \delta}{1 - \gamma\beta}$$

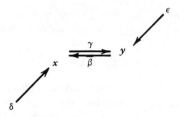

Figure 4.3. A simple simultaneous equation system.

From these, one may then obtain the following population moments:

$$\sigma_{xx} = \frac{\sigma_{\delta\delta} + \beta^2\sigma_{\varepsilon\varepsilon}}{(1 - \gamma\beta)^2}, \qquad \sigma_{xy} = \frac{\gamma\sigma_{\delta\delta} + \beta\sigma_{\varepsilon\varepsilon}}{(1 - \gamma\beta)^2}$$

$$\sigma_{yy} = \frac{\gamma^2\sigma_{\delta\delta} + \sigma_{\varepsilon\varepsilon}}{(1 - \gamma\beta)^2}$$

As a result of this analysis, the regression of y on x may be written as

$$E(y/x) = \left(\frac{\sigma_{xy}}{\sigma_{xx}}\right)x = \left(\frac{\gamma\sigma_{\delta\delta}}{\sigma_{\delta\delta} + \beta\sigma_{\varepsilon\varepsilon}} + \frac{1}{\beta\left(1 - \dfrac{\sigma_{\delta\delta}}{\sigma_{\delta\delta} + \beta\sigma_{\varepsilon\varepsilon}}\right)}\right)x = \Delta^*x$$

Now, since the ordinary least-squares regression of y on x will estimate Δ^*, one will not know the value of the true structural parameter of interest γ. Econometricians have developed two-stage least-squares and other procedures for arriving at the correct estimates, however (e.g., Thiel, 1971). For an introduction to two-stage least squares, the reader is referred to Duncan (1975) and James and Singh (1978). The procedures developed below present a maximum likelihood approach to the problem posed by simultaneity. The approach is general enough to handle both measurement error and simultaneity in one system of equations.

Specification of the Model

In this section of the chapter, a general linear model will be derived for representing causal relationships among variables. The model was first developed by Jöreskog (1966, 1967, 1969, 1970, 1971, 1973, 1974; Jöreskog and van Thillo, 1972) and has been referred to variously as analysis of covariance structures, confirmatory factor analysis, and the LISREL Model, among other terms. It is applicable to recursive and nonrecursive models.

The general model for representing a set of recursive or simultaneous linear structural relations may be written as follows (e.g., Jöreskog and van Thillo, 1972):

$$\mathbf{B}\boldsymbol{\eta} = \boldsymbol{\Gamma}\boldsymbol{\xi} + \boldsymbol{\zeta} \tag{4.10}$$

where $\boldsymbol{\eta}' = (\eta_1, \eta_2, \ldots, \eta_m)$ is a random vector of true unobservable dependent variables; $\boldsymbol{\xi} = (\xi_1, \xi_2, \ldots, \xi_n)$ is a random vector of true unobservable independent variables; $\mathbf{B}$ is an $m \times m$ matrix of parameters; $\boldsymbol{\Gamma}$ is an $m \times n$ matrix of parameters; and $\boldsymbol{\zeta}' = (\zeta_1, \zeta_2, \ldots, \zeta_m)$ is a vector of random residuals (also known as errors in equations). The specification of the model of Eq. (4.10) is complete with the following assumptions: $E(\boldsymbol{\eta}) = \mathbf{0}$, $E(\boldsymbol{\zeta}) = \mathbf{0}$, $E(\boldsymbol{\zeta}) = \mathbf{0}$, $\boldsymbol{\xi}$ and $\boldsymbol{\zeta}$ are uncorrelated, and $\mathbf{B}$ is nonsingular.[3]

The interpretation of the model of Eq. (4.10) may be stated as follows. The m true dependent variables $\boldsymbol{\eta}$ are related among themselves through the parameters in $\mathbf{B}$ and are related to the n true independent parameters $\boldsymbol{\xi}$ through the parameters in $\boldsymbol{\Gamma}$. This is consistent with the development in earlier chapters wherein causal relationships were modeled as connections between theoretical constructs. The parameters in $\mathbf{B}$ and $\boldsymbol{\Gamma}$ represent linear relationships to be estimated. Finally, the disturbance term $\boldsymbol{\zeta}$ captures the random error in the system of equations.

Since Eq. (4.10) is limited to theoretical variables and the relationships among them, it is necessary to consider the role of observations in the model. Recall from the discussion in Chapter 3 that theoretical variables are related directly or indirectly to observations through correspondence rules. Thus, the unobserved theoretical constructs $\boldsymbol{\eta}$ and $\boldsymbol{\xi}$ can be tied to observations as follows[4]:

$$\mathbf{y} = \boldsymbol{\mu}_y + \boldsymbol{\Lambda}_y\boldsymbol{\eta} + \boldsymbol{\varepsilon} \tag{4.11}$$

$$\mathbf{x} = \boldsymbol{\nu}_x + \boldsymbol{\Lambda}_x\boldsymbol{\xi} + \boldsymbol{\delta} \tag{4.12}$$

where $\mathbf{y}' = (y_1, y_2, \ldots, y_p)$ and $\mathbf{x}' = (x_1, x_2, \ldots, x_q)$ are, respectively, vectors of observed dependent and independent variables; $\boldsymbol{\mu}_y$ and $\boldsymbol{\nu}_x$ are the respective vectors of means for $\mathbf{y}$ and $\mathbf{x}$; $\boldsymbol{\Lambda}_y$ and $\boldsymbol{\Lambda}_x$ are regression (factor) matrices of order $p \times m$ and $q \times m$, respectively; and $\boldsymbol{\varepsilon}' = (\varepsilon_1, \varepsilon_2, \ldots, \varepsilon_p)$ and $\boldsymbol{\delta}' = (\delta_1, \delta_2, \ldots, \delta_q)$ are vectors of errors of measurement (also known as unique factors) in $\mathbf{y}$ and $\mathbf{x}$, respectively. Further, it is assumed that $E(\boldsymbol{\varepsilon})=\mathbf{0}$, $E(\boldsymbol{\delta})=\mathbf{0}$, $E(\boldsymbol{\eta}\boldsymbol{\varepsilon}')=\mathbf{0}$, $E(\boldsymbol{\xi}\boldsymbol{\delta}')=\mathbf{0}$, and $E(\boldsymbol{\varepsilon}\boldsymbol{\varepsilon}') = \boldsymbol{\theta}_\varepsilon^2$, and $E(\boldsymbol{\delta}\boldsymbol{\delta}') = \boldsymbol{\theta}_\delta^2$, where $\boldsymbol{\theta}_\varepsilon^2$ and $\boldsymbol{\theta}_\delta^2$ are diagonal matrices.

The true variables $\boldsymbol{\eta}$ and $\boldsymbol{\xi}$ may be regarded as common factors explaining variation in the observed variables $\mathbf{y}$ and $\mathbf{x}$. However, unlike what is known in the literature as exploratory factor analysis, some relationships between the common factors and their indicators may be specified a priori. Moreover, $\boldsymbol{\eta}$ and $\boldsymbol{\xi}$ may be correlated in the model. These restrictions may be treated as hypotheses to be confirmed or disconfirmed, and the rationale for their specification in the model depends on methodological, theoretical, logical, or empirical considerations.

As a simple example of the system of equations specified in (4.10), (4.11), and (4.12), consider the model of Figure 4.4. Following the conventions for writing equations noted in Chapter 3, it is possible to summarize the system of causal relationships and correspondence rules as shown below:

$$
\begin{pmatrix} 1 & -\beta_1 & 0 \\ -\beta_2 & 1 & 0 \\ 0 & -\beta_3 & 1 \end{pmatrix}
\begin{pmatrix} \eta_1 \\ \eta_2 \\ \eta_3 \end{pmatrix}
=
\begin{pmatrix} 0 & \gamma_1 & \gamma_2 & \gamma_3 \\ 0 & \gamma_4 & 0 & 0 \\ \gamma_5 & 0 & 0 & 0 \end{pmatrix}
\begin{pmatrix} \xi_1 \\ \xi_2 \\ \xi_3 \\ \xi_4 \end{pmatrix}
+
\begin{pmatrix} \zeta_1 \\ \zeta_2 \\ \zeta_3 \end{pmatrix}
\tag{4.10'}
$$

$$
\begin{pmatrix} y_1 \\ y_2 \\ y_3 \\ y_4 \\ y_5 \\ y_6 \\ y_7 \end{pmatrix}
=
\begin{pmatrix} \lambda_1 & 0 & 0 \\ \lambda_2 & 0 & 0 \\ 0 & \lambda_3 & 0 \\ 0 & \lambda_4 & 0 \\ 0 & \lambda_5 & 0 \\ 0 & 0 & \lambda_6 \\ 0 & 0 & \lambda_7 \end{pmatrix}
\begin{pmatrix} \eta_1 \\ \eta_2 \\ \eta_3 \end{pmatrix}
+
\begin{pmatrix} \varepsilon_1 \\ \varepsilon_2 \\ \varepsilon_3 \\ \varepsilon_4 \\ \varepsilon_5 \\ \varepsilon_6 \\ \varepsilon_7 \end{pmatrix}
\tag{4.11'}
$$

$$
\begin{pmatrix} x_1 \\ x_2 \\ x_3 \\ x_4 \\ x_5 \\ x_6 \end{pmatrix}
=
\begin{pmatrix} \lambda'_1 & 0 & 0 & 0 \\ \lambda'_2 & 0 & 0 & 0 \\ 0 & \lambda'_3 & 0 & 0 \\ 0 & \lambda'_4 & 0 & 0 \\ 0 & 0 & 1 & 0 \\ 0 & 0 & 0 & 1 \end{pmatrix}
\begin{pmatrix} \xi_1 \\ \xi_2 \\ \xi_3 \\ \xi_4 \end{pmatrix}
+
\begin{pmatrix} \delta_1 \\ \delta_2 \\ \delta_3 \\ \delta_4 \\ 0 \\ 0 \end{pmatrix}
\tag{4.12'}
$$

Note that variables x_5 and x_6 are represented as having no error; hence, the identities in (4.12'). This is done to stress the fact that it is permissible to have some variables in one's models operationalized by only single indicators. The derivation of (4.10'), (4.11'), and (4.12') from Figure 4.4 is left as an exercise for the reader.

Continuing the development of the general model, one may partition the variance-covariance matrix of the unobservable variables $(\boldsymbol{\eta}', \boldsymbol{\xi}')'$ as (cf., Jöreskog and Sörbom, 1977)

$$
\boldsymbol{\Omega} = \begin{pmatrix} \boldsymbol{\Omega}_{\eta\eta} & \boldsymbol{\Omega}_{\eta\xi} \\ \boldsymbol{\Omega}_{\xi\eta} & \boldsymbol{\Omega}_{\xi\xi} \end{pmatrix}
\tag{4.13}
$$

With $\boldsymbol{\Phi}(n \times n)$ and $\boldsymbol{\psi}(m \times m)$ specified to be the variance-covariance matrices of $\boldsymbol{\xi}$ and $\boldsymbol{\zeta}$, respectively, it is possible to express $\boldsymbol{\Omega}$ as a function of the parameters in $\mathbf{B}, \boldsymbol{\Gamma}, \boldsymbol{\Phi}$, and $\boldsymbol{\psi}$ as follows:

$$
\boldsymbol{\Omega}_{\eta\eta} = \mathbf{B}^{-1}\boldsymbol{\Gamma}\boldsymbol{\Phi}\boldsymbol{\Gamma}'\mathbf{B}'^{-1} + \mathbf{B}^{-1}\boldsymbol{\psi}\mathbf{B}'^{-1}
$$

$$
\boldsymbol{\Omega}_{\eta\xi} = \boldsymbol{\Omega}_{\xi\eta} = \mathbf{B}^{-1}\boldsymbol{\Gamma}\boldsymbol{\Phi}
$$

$$
\boldsymbol{\Omega}_{\xi\xi} = \boldsymbol{\Phi}
$$

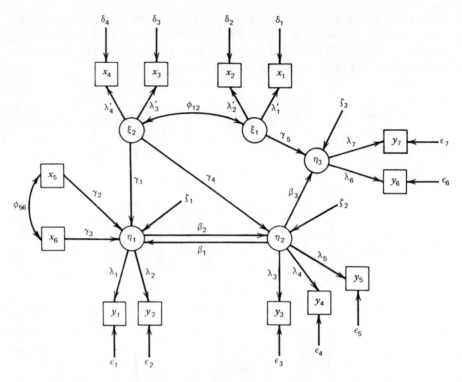

Figure 4.4. A causal model illustrating a structural equation system. Covariances among x_5 and x_6 and ξ_1 and ξ_2 are omitted to keep the diagram simple.

Note that in Eq. (4.13) only $\boldsymbol{\Omega}_{\xi\xi}$ is treated as a parameter by itself, and $\boldsymbol{\Omega}_{\eta\eta}$ and $\boldsymbol{\Omega}_{\eta\xi}$ are functions of the other parameters in Eq. (4.10).

The variance-covariance matrix of the observed variables $\mathbf{z} = (\mathbf{y}', \mathbf{x}')'$ may be partitioned as follows:

$$\boldsymbol{\Sigma} = \begin{pmatrix} \boldsymbol{\Sigma}_{yy} & \boldsymbol{\Sigma}_{yx} \\ \boldsymbol{\Sigma}_{xy} & \boldsymbol{\Sigma}_{xx} \end{pmatrix} \tag{4.14}$$

where

$$\boldsymbol{\Sigma}_{yy} = \boldsymbol{\Lambda}_y \boldsymbol{\Omega}_{\eta\eta} \boldsymbol{\Lambda}_y' + \boldsymbol{\theta}_\varepsilon^2$$

$$\boldsymbol{\Sigma}_{yx} = \boldsymbol{\Sigma}_{xy}' = \boldsymbol{\Lambda}_y \boldsymbol{\Omega}_{\eta\xi} \boldsymbol{\Lambda}_x'$$

$$\boldsymbol{\Sigma}_{xx} = \boldsymbol{\Lambda}_x \boldsymbol{\Omega}_{\xi\xi} \boldsymbol{\Lambda}_x' + \boldsymbol{\theta}_\delta^2$$

Performing the appropriate substitutions, one may write Eq. (4.14) as a function only of the parameters in the model; that is, a function of the elements in $\boldsymbol{\Lambda}_y$,

Λ_x, $\mathbf{B}$, Γ, Φ, ψ, θ_ε^2, and θ_δ^2:

$$\Sigma = \begin{pmatrix} \Lambda_y(\mathbf{B}^{-1}\Gamma\Phi\Gamma'\mathbf{B}'^{-1} + \mathbf{B}^{-1}\psi\mathbf{B}'^{-1})\Lambda_y' + \theta_\varepsilon^2 & \Lambda_y\mathbf{B}^{-1}\Gamma\Phi\Lambda_x' \\ \Lambda_x\Phi\Gamma'\mathbf{B}'^{-1}\Lambda_y' & \Lambda_x\Phi\Lambda_x' + \theta_\delta^2 \end{pmatrix} \quad (4.14')$$

where Σ is of order $(p + q) \times (p + q)$. Returning to the model of Figure 4.4 as an example, one may write the parameter matrices for Φ, Ψ, θ_ε^2, and θ_δ^2 as follows [the parameter matrices for Λ_y, Λ_x, $\mathbf{B}$, and Γ, are, of course, included in Eqs. (4.10'), (4.11'), and (4.12')]:

$$\Phi = \begin{pmatrix} \phi_{11} & & & \\ \phi_{21} & \phi_{22} & & \\ \phi_{31} & \phi_{32} & \phi_{33} & \\ \phi_{41} & \phi_{42} & \phi_{43} & \phi_{44} \end{pmatrix}$$

$$\psi = \begin{pmatrix} \psi_{11} & & \\ 0 & \psi_{22} & \\ 0 & 0 & \psi_{33} \end{pmatrix}$$

$$\theta_\varepsilon^2 = \begin{pmatrix} \theta_{\varepsilon_1}^2 & & & & & & \\ 0 & \theta_{\varepsilon_2}^2 & & & & & \\ 0 & 0 & \theta_{\varepsilon_3}^2 & & & & \\ 0 & 0 & 0 & \theta_{\varepsilon_4}^2 & & & \\ 0 & 0 & 0 & 0 & \theta_{\varepsilon_5}^2 & & \\ 0 & 0 & 0 & 0 & 0 & \theta_{\varepsilon_6}^2 & \\ 0 & 0 & 0 & 0 & 0 & 0 & \theta_{\varepsilon_7}^2 \end{pmatrix}$$

$$\theta_\delta^2 = \begin{pmatrix} \theta_{\delta_1}^2 & & & & & \\ 0 & \theta_{\delta_2}^2 & & & & \\ 0 & 0 & \theta_{\delta_3}^2 & & & \\ 0 & 0 & 0 & \theta_{\delta_4}^2 & & \\ 0 & 0 & 0 & 0 & 0 & \\ 0 & 0 & 0 & 0 & 0 & 0 \end{pmatrix}$$

where only the lower half of symmetric matrices are presented.

The specification of any structural equation model, then, is accomplished by constructing the variance-covariance matrix of Eq. (4.14') to represent one's theoretical causal relationships. This will involve the modeling of some parameters to be estimated and tested and others to be restricted, a priori, to known values. In general, the parameters in Eq. (4.14') are of three kinds (Jöreskog and van Thillo, 1972, p. 3): "(i) *fixed parameters* that have been assigned given values, (ii) *constrained parameters* that are unknown but equal to one or more other parameters, and (iii) *free parameters* that are unknown and not constrained to be equal to any other parameters." The basis for restricting parameters to be fixed or constrained or for allowing them to be free depends on prior theoretical knowledge, logical criteria, empirical evidence, or methodological or experimental design considerations. The distinction between kinds of parameters may be illustrated through the model of Figure 4.4. Looking at Eq. (4.10'), one may note that free parameters to be estimated include β_1, β_2, β_3, γ_1, γ_2, γ_3, γ_4, and γ_5. The zero entries in the **B** and Γ matrices represent fixed parameters. For example, the zero in the first row of **B** indicates that the causal path from η_3 to η_1 is hypothesized to be absent. Although not shown in Figure 4.4, it is possible to constrain parameters to equal certain other parameters. For example, if one had reason to believe that $\lambda_6 = \lambda_7$ in the model, then this information could be represented in Jöreskog's approach (e.g., Jöreskog and van Thillo, 1972). The role of prior knowledge can also be seen in experimental design considerations. Suppose that the researcher were able to manipulate an independent variable in the model (say x_5) and then observe a change in a dependent variable (say η_1). This fact allows the researcher to fix the parameter representing a causal relation from η_1 to x_5 equal to zero, since it is impossible for an effect to occur prior to its cause. Hence, only the path from x_5 to η_1 can logically occur. Finally, it should be noted that there is a fourth class of prior information consisting of empirical evidence from previous samples. Rothenberg (1973) shows that such prior information can be taken into account by finding the joint probability function of previous and current samples. Unlike the three cases noted above, this fourth class of information requires that changes be made in the likelihood function prior to estimation.

The foregoing illustrates the problem of model specification in causal analysis. In general, any causal model may be misspecified for one or more of the following reasons:

1. The mathematical form of the structural equations is incorrect.
2. Error terms are misrepresented or are not well behaved.
3. Important independent or dependent variables are omitted or extraneous ones are included.
4. Relevant causal paths are omitted or irrelevant ones are hypothesized.
5. Variables in the model are measured on nominal or ordinal levels rather than interval or ratio. Measurement error is not modeled.

The model of Eq. (4.10) assumes linear relationships among theoretical constructs. If the underlying structure of causal relationships that one desires to test is nonlinear and cannot be transformed to a linear function as discussed in the previous chapter, then one's estimates of structural parameters will, in general, be biased and inconsistent. Depending on the degree of nonlinearity, the magnitude of the bias may or may not be a problem.[5] Second, the specification of the general model in Eqs. (4.10)–(4.14') depends on the following assumptions as to error terms: ζ is a random vector of residuals uncorrelated with ξ, $E(\eta\varepsilon') = \mathbf{0}$, and

$E(\xi\delta') = 0$. Again, if these assumptions are violated, parameter estimates will be biased and inconsistent.

The third and fourth issues refer to problems in specifying cause and effect and what is to be included in one's model. Provided that the functional form and errors are specified correctly, one should be able to easily eliminate extraneous variables and irrelevant paths. The parameters representing an irrelevant path (whether from an extraneous or essential variable in one's model) can be tested for, in principle, using the procedures discussed later in this chapter and in subsequent chapters. Omitted variables and/or causal paths may pose problems, however. If an omitted independent variable is correlated with included independent variables, one's estimates of parameters will be biased and inconsistent.[6] If, on the other hand, the omitted independent variable is not correlated with included independent variables, the parameter estimates for causal paths, while unbiased, will have an upward bias on their variances. Although omitted paths in asymmetric causal models can often be tested for by using procedures to be developed later, the failure to model simultaneity when present will, as shown above, not produce estimates of the true parameters. In any case, one constraint on being able to test for these things is whether one's model is identified or not (see discussion below). Finally, one's model may be misspecified if it is assumed that variables in the model are interval or ratio scaled when, in fact, they are nominal or ordinal. Nominal independent variables pose no problems since they may be handled as dummy variables, but it may be incorrect to use the model of Eqs. (4.10)–(4.14') when the dependent variable is a dichotomy. This is so since the residual variances are heteroskedastic by definition, violating the assumptions of the general linear model. The occurrence of ordinal variables in one's model may also pose problems (e.g., Blalock, 1971; 1974). Causal modeling with nominal and ordinal variables will be discussed more fully in Chapter 9. It should be stressed that, due to the complexity and newness of structural equation models in the behavioral sciences, a number of qualifications and exceptions apply to the above comments on specification. For discussions of some of the relevant issues, the reader is referred elsewhere (e.g., Thiel, 1971). Also, though perhaps obvious to the reader, it should be emphasized that the specification of one's model depends fundamentally upon the theory one hopes to represent and test and upon previous research findings. Thus, the specification of any model is intimately connected to the theory construction stages outlined in the earlier chapters.

The Issue of Identification

Once the researcher has specified his or her model, another important problem to address is whether it is possible to obtain unique solutions for the parameters in Σ. We have already touched upon this problem in regard to the special case of the general linear model consisting of a single unobservable and its multiple operationalizations. Recall, as shown in the example of Figure 4.2, that there were just as many pieces of information to solve for the values of parameters as there were unknowns when $p = 3$, that is, when there were three indicators or observables for the single unobservable. Such a system is said to be just identified. For $p < 3$, the system is said to be underidentified (i.e., the number of structural parameters to be estimated exceeds the information provided); while for $p > 3$, the system is said to be overidentified (i.e., the information provided exceeds the number of parameters to be estimated).

Unlike the simple model of Figure 4.2, however, the solution of the identification problem for the general linear model is not so straightforward. Jöreskog and Sörbom (1977) introduce the general problem of identification for such models as follows:

We assume that the distribution of the observed variables is sufficiently well described by the moments of first and second order, so that information contained in moments of higher order may be ignored. In particular, this will hold if the distribution is multivariate normal. The distribution of $(y', x')'$ is therefore generated by the parameters in $\Lambda_y, \Lambda_x, \mathbf{B}, \mathbf{\Gamma}, \mathbf{\Phi}, \mathbf{\Psi}, \mathbf{\Theta}_\varepsilon, \mathbf{\Theta}_\delta$. Let $\mathbf{\Theta}$ be a vector of all the independent, free and constrained parameters (i.e., counting each distinct constrained parameter once only) and let s be the order of $\mathbf{\Theta}$. The identification problem is the problem of whether or not $\mathbf{\Theta}$ is uniquely determined by Σ. Every $\mathbf{\Theta}$ generates one and only one Σ but two or more $\mathbf{\Theta}$'s could possibly generate the same Σ. If within the model there is only one $\mathbf{\Theta}$ for every Σ, then $\mathbf{\Theta}$ is identified and we say that the whole model is identified. If, on the other hand, there are several $\mathbf{\Theta}$'s generating the same Σ, we say that all such $\mathbf{\Theta}$'s are equivalent. If a parameter in $\mathbf{\Theta}$ has the same value in all equivalent $\mathbf{\Theta}$'s, we say that this parameter is identified. If a parameter is not identified it will not be possible to find a consistent estimator of it.

As the authors note, since there are $(\frac{1}{2}) (p + q) (p + q + 1)$ equations and s unknowns in $\mathbf{\Theta}$, a necessary condition for identification of all parameters is

$$s \le (\tfrac{1}{2})(p + q)(p + q + 1)$$

The solution for sufficient conditions for identification of the general linear model has not been solved. A number of authors have examined the identification problem for special cases of the general linear model, however. Fisher (1966) provides the classic treatment for simultaneous equation systems but does not discuss the problem for models allowing for measurement error and multiple indicators of unobservables. Geraci (1974) analyzes a number of special cases of the general model including those allowing for measurement error. He does not, however, treat the cases of prior restrictions on the covariance matrix of ζ (i.e., $\mathbf{\Psi}$), the covariance matrix of unobserved exogenous variables (i.e., $\mathbf{\Phi}$), correlated measurement errors, or certain dynamic models. Hsiao (1975, 1976)

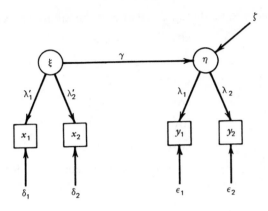

Figure 4.5. One theoretical variable causing a second—both operationalized by two indicators.

derives the identification criteria for a linear dynamic system with measurement error in both endogenous and exogenous variables and for a particular contemporaneous system. To date, no sufficient criteria exist for the most general model consisting of unobservable endogenous and exogenous variables with multiple operationalizations and allowing for correlated errors in equations and correlated errors in variables in longitudinal contexts.

As a result, until the most general criteria are derived, the researcher must demonstrate identification for each model tested on an individual basis. Two examples serve to illustrate the general principles involved.[7] Consider first the model of Figure 4.5 where one unobservable ξ is shown causing another unobservable η. Both theoretical variables are operationalized with two indicators. The structural equation for the system of Figure 4.5 can be written as

$$\eta = \gamma \xi + \zeta$$

and the equations relating observables to unobservables are

$$\begin{pmatrix} y_1 \\ y_2 \end{pmatrix} = \begin{pmatrix} \lambda_1 \\ \lambda_2 \end{pmatrix} \eta + \begin{pmatrix} \varepsilon_1 \\ \varepsilon_2 \end{pmatrix}$$

$$\begin{pmatrix} x_1 \\ x_2 \end{pmatrix} = \begin{pmatrix} \lambda'_1 \\ \lambda'_2 \end{pmatrix} \xi + \begin{pmatrix} \delta_1 \\ \delta_2 \end{pmatrix}$$

Information in this system of equations consists of the four variances and six covariances produced by the four observable variables, y_1, y_2, x_1, and x_2. This must be used to determine estimates for the following 11 parameters: λ'_1, λ'_2, $\Phi = \text{var}(\xi)$, $\theta^2_{\delta_1}$, $\theta^2_{\delta_2}$, γ, λ_1, λ_2, $\psi = \text{var}(\eta)$, $\theta^2_{\varepsilon_1}$, and $\theta^2_{\varepsilon_2}$. Assuming the variances of ξ and η to be standardized at one, the following six equations

$$\text{cov}(x_1, x_2) = \lambda_1' \lambda_2'$$
$$\text{cov}(y_1, y_2) = \lambda_1 \lambda_2$$
$$\text{cov}(x_1, y_1) = \lambda_1' \gamma \lambda_1$$
$$\text{cov}(x_1, y_2) = \lambda_1' \gamma \lambda_2$$
$$\text{cov}(x_2, y_1) = \lambda_2' \gamma \lambda_1$$
$$\text{cov}(x_2, y_2) = \lambda_2' \gamma \lambda_2$$

determine λ_1', λ_2', λ_1, λ_2, and γ with one overidentifying restriction. Finally, given the above, the error variances for the observables may be computed from

$$\text{var}(x_1) = \lambda_1'^2 + \theta_{\delta_1}^2$$
$$\text{var}(x_2) = \lambda_2'^2 + \theta_{\delta_2}^2$$
$$\text{var}(y_1) = \lambda_1^2 + \theta_{\varepsilon_1}^2$$
$$\text{var}(y_2) = \lambda_2^2 + \theta_{\varepsilon_2}^2$$

Thus, the model of Figure 4.5 is overidentified with one independent restriction on Σ. For the general model consisting of one unobservable affecting another where the first is indicated by q observables and the second by p observables, the degree of overidentification (or underidentification) is given by $t = (\frac{1}{2})(p + q)$ $(p + q + 1) - 1 - 2(p + q)$ (e.g., Hauser and Goldberger, 1971, p. 90).

As a second somewhat more complicated situation illustrating the determination of identification, consider the model of Figure 4.6. In this model, an observable x is shown affecting an unobservable η_1, which, in turn, has an impact

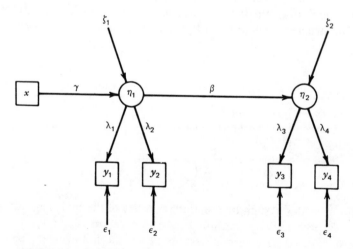

Figure 4.6. A causal model of an experimental design with two operationalizations of the dependent variable.

upon another unobservable η_2. The system of Figure 4.6 might represent an experimental situation where an independent variable x affects a dependent variable η_2 and the validity of the manipulation is represented through η_1, a manipulation check factor. The observables y_1 and y_2 might model manipulation checks, while y_3 and y_4 could be operationalizations of the dependent variable. The experimental interpretation of the model will be discussed further in Chapter 7.

The structural equations for the system of Figure 4.6 may be conveniently summarized as

$$\begin{pmatrix} 1 & 0 \\ -\beta & 1 \end{pmatrix} \begin{pmatrix} \eta_1 \\ \eta_2 \end{pmatrix} = \begin{pmatrix} \gamma \\ 0 \end{pmatrix} \xi + \begin{pmatrix} \zeta_1 \\ \zeta_2 \end{pmatrix}$$

and the equations relating observables to unobservables may be written as

$$\begin{pmatrix} y_1 \\ y_2 \\ y_3 \\ y_4 \end{pmatrix} = \begin{pmatrix} \lambda_1 & 0 \\ \lambda_2 & 0 \\ 0 & \lambda_3 \\ 0 & \lambda_4 \end{pmatrix} \begin{pmatrix} \eta_1 \\ \eta_2 \end{pmatrix} + \begin{pmatrix} \varepsilon_1 \\ \varepsilon_2 \\ \varepsilon_3 \\ \varepsilon_4 \end{pmatrix}$$

$$x = (1)\xi + 0$$

where the latter equation is presented to show that x is measured without error. In order to determine identifiability, it is convenient to begin with the following reduced form equations:

$$\eta_1 = \gamma x + \zeta_1$$

$$\eta_2 = \eta_1 \beta + \zeta_2$$

$$\eta_2 = \gamma \beta x + \beta \zeta_1 + \zeta_2$$

$$\eta_2 = \alpha x + u$$

where $\alpha = \gamma\beta$ and $u = \beta\zeta_1 + \zeta_2$. Assuming ζ_1 and ζ_2 are uncorrelated, the model contains 13 parameters to be estimated: $\lambda_1, \lambda_2, \lambda_3, \lambda_4, \gamma, \beta, \phi = \text{var}(x), \psi_{11} = \text{var}(\zeta_1), \psi_{22} = \text{var}(\zeta_2), \theta_{\varepsilon_1}^2, \theta_{\varepsilon_2}^2, \theta_{\varepsilon_3}^2,$ and $\theta_{\varepsilon_4}^2$. Information for the solution of these parameters is provided by the five variances and ten covariances among the observables y_1, y_2, y_3, y_4, and x.

Beginning with the covariance between x and the other observables, we find the following:

$$\text{cov}(x, y_1) = \lambda_1 \text{cov}(x, \eta_1) = \lambda_1 \gamma \phi$$

$$\text{cov}(x, y_2) = \lambda_2 \text{cov}(x, \eta_1) = \lambda_2 \gamma \phi$$

$$\text{cov}(x, y_3) = \lambda_3 \text{cov}(x, \eta_2) = \lambda_3 \gamma \beta \phi$$
$$= \lambda_3 \alpha \phi$$

$$\text{cov}(x, y_4) = \lambda_4 \text{cov}(x, \eta_2) = \lambda_4 \gamma \beta \phi$$
$$= \lambda_4 \alpha \phi$$

where $\phi = \text{var}(x)$ is determined from the data. Similarly,

$$\text{cov}(y_1, y_2) = \lambda_1 \lambda_2 \, \text{var}(\eta_1) = \lambda_1 \lambda_2 (\gamma^2 \phi + \psi_{11})$$
$$\text{cov}(y_3, y_4) = \lambda_3 \lambda_4 \, \text{var}(\eta_2) = \lambda_3 \lambda_4 (\alpha^2 \phi + \text{var}(u))$$

where $\text{var}(u) = \beta^2 \psi_{11} + \psi_{22}$. Finally,

$$\text{cov}(y_1, y_3) = \lambda_1 \beta \lambda_3$$
$$\text{cov}(y_1, y_4) = \lambda_1 \beta \lambda_4$$
$$\text{cov}(y_2, y_3) = \lambda_2 \beta \lambda_3$$
$$\text{cov}(y_2, y_4) = \lambda_2 \beta \lambda_4$$

The ten observed covariances determine λ_1, λ_2, λ_3, λ_4, γ, β, ψ_{11}, and ψ_{22} with two overidentifying restrictions (the solution for these parameters is left as an exercise for the reader). Finally, given the above parameter solutions, one may solve for the error variances $\theta_{\varepsilon_1}^2 - \theta_{\varepsilon_4}^2$ from the formulas for the variances of observables (i.e., $\text{var}(y_i) = \lambda_i^2 + \theta_{\varepsilon_i}^2$ for $i = 1, 2, 3, 4$). Thus, the model of Figure 4.6 is overidentified with two independent restrictions on Σ.

Given that one has specified his or her model correctly and determined if it is identified or not, the next stage in the analysis should be the estimation of relevant parameters. It is to this topic that we now turn.

Estimation of the General Model

In order to estimate the parameters in the general model, it is useful to employ the maximum likelihood technique.[8] The procedures outlined below were first developed by Jöreskog (cf., 1966, 1967, 1969, 1970, 1973; Jöreskog and van Thillo, 1972; and Gruveaus and Jöreskog, 1970). Except for a number of elaborations and expansions, the development follows Jöreskog's notation and treatment as closely as possible.

The vector of observations $\mathbf{z} = (\mathbf{x}', \mathbf{y}')$ is assumed to have a multivariate normal distribution with mean vector $(\mathbf{u}', \mathbf{v}')$ and variance-covariance matrix Σ. With M observations of $\mathbf{z}(\mathbf{z}_1, \mathbf{z}_2, \ldots, \mathbf{z}_M)$ and $\bar{\mathbf{z}} = (\bar{\mathbf{y}}', \bar{\mathbf{x}}')'$ representing the maximum likelihood estimates of the mean vector, the sample variance-covariance matrix may be written as follows:

$$\mathbf{S} = \frac{1}{N} \sum_{\alpha=1}^{N} (\mathbf{z}_\alpha - \bar{\mathbf{z}})(\mathbf{z}_\alpha - \bar{\mathbf{z}})'$$

where $N = M - 1$.

These definitions and those presented earlier allow one to write the logarithm of the likelihood function as follows (omitting a constant term):

$$\log L = -\tfrac{1}{2}N[\log|\mathbf{\Sigma}| + \text{tr}(\mathbf{S\Sigma}^{-1})]$$

where tr stands for the trace and log stands for the natural logarithm (cf., Anderson, 1958, p. 159; Lawley and Maxwell, 1971, p. 25). The likelihood is regarded as a function of $\mathbf{\Sigma}$; that is, $\mathbf{\Lambda}_y, \mathbf{\Lambda}_x, \mathbf{B}, \mathbf{\Gamma}, \mathbf{\phi}, \mathbf{\psi}, \mathbf{\theta}_\varepsilon^2$ and $\mathbf{\theta}_\delta^2$. The objective is to find values for the independent distinct parameters in $\mathbf{\Sigma}$ that maximize the value of log L. An equivalent but more convenient procedure is to minimize the following function F, which is $-2/N$ times the log L (plus the constant term):

$$F = \log|\mathbf{\Sigma}| + \text{tr}(\mathbf{S\Sigma}^{-1}) - \log|\mathbf{S}| - (p + q)$$

Since the values of the parameters in $\mathbf{\Sigma}$ that minimize F cannot be found analytically, an iterative procedure was developed by Jöreskog and his colleagues to numerically determine the maximum likelihood estimates (e.g., Jöreskog, 1973; Jöreskog and van Thillo, 1972; Gruveaus and Jöreskog, 1970). Briefly, the minimization method is based on an algorithm due to Fletcher and Powell (1963), which makes use of the first-order derivatives and large sample approximations to the elements of the matrix of second-order derivatives to achieve minimization. Lawley and Maxwell (1971, pp. 26–34 and Appendices I and II) present a derivation of a procedure that is essentially the same as that presented by Jöreskog, and the reader is referred there for additional details. The computer program LISREL developed by Jöreskog and his colleagues will calculate the maximum likelihood and standardized estimates of the parameters in $\mathbf{\Sigma}$ as well as their standard errors.

A number of advantages are provided through maximum likelihood estimators (e.g., Thiel, 1971, pp. 392–397). First, the estimators can be shown to be consistent and asymptotically normally distributed with a variance equal to the lower bound of the Cramér–Rao inequality (i.e., they are asymptotically efficient). Second, the maximum likelihood method is independent of the scales of measurement for the variables in one's model (e.g., Lawley and Maxwell, 1971, p. 33). Third, maximum likelihood estimates are robust over nonnormality (e.g., Howe, 1955, cited in Burt, 1973, p. 187). Finally, as developed below, a convenient statistic may be derived for testing one's model.

Hypothesis Testing

In order to derive a formal test for the adequacy of one's model, one may employ the likelihood ratio test criterion. Consider first the null hypothesis H_0, which states that one's specification for $\mathbf{\Sigma}$ with fixed, constrained, and free parameters is the true one. Letting L_{H_0} denote the maximum of L in Σ under H_0, we have

$$\log L_{H_0} = -\tfrac{1}{2}N[\log|\hat{\Sigma}| + \mathrm{tr}(S\hat{\Sigma}^{-1})]$$

where $\hat{\Sigma}$ stands for the value of parameters that maximize the value of L. Similarly, for the alternative hypothesis H_1 that Σ is any positive definite matrix, one may write:

$$\log L_{H_1} = -\tfrac{1}{2}N[\log|S| + p + q]$$

since $\log L$ achieves its maximum under H_1 when $\Sigma = S$. Forming the likelihood ratio $\lambda = L_{H_0}/L_{H_1}$, it can be shown (e.g., Thiel, 1971, pp. 396–397) that $-2 \log \lambda$ is distributed approximately χ^2 for large samples if H_0 is true. Further, performing the appropriate substitutions, it is easily shown that

$$-2 \log \lambda = NF_0$$

where F_0 is the minimum value of F as defined in the previous section. As Jöreskog notes (Jöreskog and van Thillo, 1972, p. 8), the χ^2 test is distributed with degrees of freedom equal to

$$\text{d.f.} = \tfrac{1}{2}(p + q)(p + q + 1) - t$$

where t is the total number of parameters to be estimated under H_0. The appropriate one-tailed test of significance is

$$\chi^2 \geq \chi^2_{\alpha;\,\text{d.f.}}$$

where large values of χ^2 lead to a rejection of H_0 at the α level, while small values lead to its acceptance.

Following Box (1949) and Bartlett (1951), the χ^2 approximation may be improved by using the correction factor $N - (2p + 2q + 5)|6$ with N and $(p + q)$ replaced by $N - (m + n)$ and $(p + q) - (m + n)$, respectively, to yield

$$\begin{aligned}\chi^2 &= [N - \tfrac{1}{6}(2p + 2q + 5) - \tfrac{2}{3}(m + n)]F_0 \\ &= N^*F_0\end{aligned}$$

where, as defined earlier, $N = M - 1$, $M =$ number of observations, $p =$ number of observable endogenous variables, $q =$ number of observable exogenous variables, $m =$ number of true endogenous variables, and $n =$ number of true exogeneous variables. As a rule of thumb, Lawley and Maxwell (1971) suggest that the χ^2 approximation "can probably be trusted" if $N - (p + q) \geq 50$.

The interpretation of the χ^2 goodness-of-fit statistic for the general linear model is as follows. Given that one's hypothesized structure Σ is true,

$$\chi^2 = N^*F_0$$

with d.f. $= \tfrac{1}{2}(p + q)(p + q + 1) - t$. A $\chi^2 \geq \chi^2_{\alpha;\,\text{d.f.}}$ causes one to reject the hypothesized structure, while $\chi^2 < \chi^2_{\alpha;\,d.f.}$ leads one to accept it. In testing H_0 against H_1, one may think of the test as measuring whether the residual correlations or residual variance-covariance values differ from zero. This information in conjunction with the standard errors of parameter estimates allows the researcher to determine how well a particular set of data fits one's model. In addition to calculating the maximum likelihood and standardized parameter estimates, standard errors of estimates, and χ^2 values, Jöreskog's program LISREL provides the probability p for the χ^2 test. This probability refers to the probability of obtaining an χ^2 value larger than that actually obtained, given that one's hypothesized model holds. Hence, the higher the value of p, the better the fit. In practice, adequate fits are usually obtained when the value of χ^2 is below the 10 percent significance level, that is, when $p > 0.10$ (e.g., Lawley and Maxwell, 1971, p. 42).

One of the major benefits of the above hypothesis testing procedure is that it may be used to ascertain the significance of the structure of parameters in Σ for one's overall model or for parts thereof. This aspect of the procedure has two consequences. First, one may test a specific hypothesis dealing with one's model as a whole or in part versus some more general alternative hypothesis.

Suppose H_0 represents one model under given specifications of fixed, free, and constrained parameters. To test the model H_0 against any more general model H_1, estimate each of them separately and compare their χ^2. The difference in χ^2 is asymptotically a χ^2 with degrees of freedom equal to the corresponding difference in degrees of freedom. In many situations it is possible to set up a sequence of hypotheses such that each one is a special case of the preceding and to test these hypotheses sequentially [Jöreskog and Sörbom, 1977].

Although such a procedure does not take into account the fact that each hypothesis in the sequence is dependent on the rejection of all predecessors, in practice this will not pose a problem in interpretation since the probability p will be close to the true value (e.g., Lawley and Maxwell, 1971, pp. 37–39). The general procedure will be illustrated in later chapters.

The second implication of the general test statistic is that it may be used in less structured research situations to discover and investigate potentially testable hypotheses. As Jöreskog and Sörbom (1977) described the method,

In a more exploratory situation the χ^2-goodness-of-fit-values can be used as follows. If a value of χ^2 is obtained, which is large compared to the number of degrees of freedom, the fit may be examined by an inspection of the residuals, that is, the discrepancies between observed and reproduced variances and covariances. The results of an analysis in conjunction with subject-matter considerations may suggest ways to relax the model somewhat by introducing more parameters. The new model yields a smaller χ^2. A large drop in χ^2, compared to the difference in degrees of freedom, supports the changes made. On the other hand, a drop in χ^2 which is close to the difference in number of degrees of freedom indicates that the improvement in fit is obtained by capitalizing on chance.

Costner and Schoenberg (1973), however, demonstrate that such a procedure can lead to misleading inferences when improperly applied. This method will also be illustrated further in later chapters.

There is a problem with the χ^2 test statistic that deserves mention. On the one hand, N must be sufficiently large [recall the rule of thumb, $N - (p + q) \geq 50$] for the test statistic to approximate the χ^2 distribution. While on the other hand as N increases, a point may be reached where one would be led to reject virtually any hypothesis. This will most likely pose no problems when looking at alternative hypotheses in the comparative sense noted above. Again, as Jöreskog (1974, p. 4) states:

... the statistical problem is not [in these situations] one of testing a given hypothesis (which a priori may be considered false), but rather one of fitting various models with different numbers of parameters and of deciding when to stop fitting. In other words, the problem is to extract as much information as possible out of a sample of given size without going so far that the result is affected to a large extent by "noise" .... In such a problem the differences between χ^2 values matter rather than the χ^2 values themselves.

Tucker and Lewis (1973) derive a reliability coefficient that is not as sensitive to sample size as the χ^2 test obtained from the likelihood ratio criterion. Following Burt (1973, pp. 148–149), the reliability coefficient may be conveniently written as

$$\rho_K = \frac{T_0 - T_K}{T_1 - E(T_K)} =$$

$$\frac{\text{the amount of covariation explained by a proposed structure}}{\text{the amount of covariation available to be explained by a proposed structure}}$$

where

$$T_0 = \frac{\sum_{i=1}^{(p+q)-1} \sum_{j=i+1}^{(p+q)} s_{ij}^2}{(p + q)(p + q + 1)/2}$$

s_{ij} = off-diagonal elements of the observed variance-covariance matrix, S

$$T_K = \frac{F_0}{\text{d.f.}}$$

$$E(T_K) = \frac{1}{N} = \frac{1}{M - 1}$$

As Burt (1973) notes, the sampling distribution of ρ_K is not known, and ρ_K is best thought of as a descriptive, rather than a test, statistic.

Some Strengths and Limitations of the General Linear Model

On the one hand, the general linear model offers many benefits. First, and foremost, it satisfies certain criteria for theory construction and testing as reflected in contemporary standards in the philosophy of science. The general linear model is a comprehensive scheme for representing all of the elements and relationships of a theory in a single structure. That is, it explicitly permits the modeling of theoretical, derived, and empirical concepts; nonobservational propositions (i.e., theoretical hypotheses); correspondence rules; and operational definitions. By formally representing the components of the theory construction process, the general linear model increases the likelihood that one's theory is accurate. Furthermore, the general linear model provides one with direct measures of the degree to which theoretical constructs are related, the extent of errors in equations and variables, and the relationships between constructs and operationalizations. To the author's knowledge, no other approach in the behavioral sciences yields as much information.

Other benefits may be noted. Since the approach is a maximum likelihood procedure, parameter estimates are independent of scales of measurement for the variables in the model. Moreover, Jöreskog's program, LISREL, provides a test statistic for one's entire model. As shown in later chapters, this fact allows the researcher to determine how good one's model is and to diagnose an incorrect specification of cause and effect. It also provides a useful way to build theory. Finally, as Burt (1973) indicates, maximum likelihood estimates from procedures such as LISREL are "optimally efficient ... over variable sample sizes" and are "robust over nonnormality."

Despite these advantages, however, a number of shortcomings deserve mention. The general linear model assumes interval scaled data, yet variables of interest are often only ordinal or nominal. Although LISREL can accommodate discrete or qualitative exogeneous variables, because of the violation of the assumption of homoskedasticity in error terms, there are problems of estimation and prediction when either an endogenous variable or operationalization is binary. In general, parameter estimates will not be efficient, predictions will be imprecise, tests of significance will not apply, and estimated standard errors will not be consistent.

When the researcher has a binary dependent variable in a single equation system, he or she may use the probit or logit model (cf., McFadden, 1974; Nerlove and Press, 1973). For example, given that consumers are to choose between two products x and y, the probability that person i chooses x will be a function, say, of person i's attitudes toward x, z_{ix}, and attitudes toward y, z_{iy}. This may be expressed as the following logit model:

$$P_{ix} = \frac{e^{\beta z_{ix}}}{e^{\beta z_{ix}} + e^{\beta z_{iy}}}$$

where β is a vector of weights relating attitudes to the dependent variable of product choice. A number of computer programs are available for obtaining maximum likelihood estimates of the β's as well as providing useful test statistics (e.g., Wills, 1974). The logit model has been extended in recent years to incorporate the polytomous dependent variable (i.e., one consisting of three or more categories) as well as the multivariate case of a number of polytomous dependent variables.

A second problem with the general linear model lies in the assumption of linear functional relationships among variables. Since some phenomena in marketing are most likely governed fundamentally by nonlinear processes, it may be inappropriate and misleading to use linear structural equations to represent them (see, however, the discussion in Chapter 3 for exceptions). The prediction-logic model (Hildebrand et al., 1976) and the multivariate analysis of qualitative data approach of Goodman (1970) do not assume linearity.

The general linear model contains a number of other shortcomings. It assumes that observations are obtained from a multivariate normal distribution. The estimates of parameters are efficient only for large samples. The χ^2 goodness-of-fit test, which is a large sample approximation, is directly sensitive to sample size. In addition, the program LISREL is limited to models containing 15 or less operationalizations of endogenous variables, and a maximum of 30 independent parameters (Jöreskog and van Thillo, 1972, p. 23).[9]

A final limitation with the general linear model lies in the requirement that one have a theory in mind to test or at least specific hypotheses. The approach is best suited for testing models that have been previously formulated. It also may be used, however, in a model building sense by testing sub-models following the hierarchical procedure noted earlier. Jöreskog and his colleagues have developed other programs more exploratory and inductive in orientation (e.g., EFAP and COFAMM).

Table 4.2
Product-Moment Correlations Among Variables for the Affect-Behavioral Intentions Model

Variables	y_1	y_2	x_1	x_2
y_1—Behavioral Intentions (likert)	1.000			
y_2—Behavioral Intentions (Thurstone)	0.792	1.000		
x_1—Affect (Guilford)	0.582	0.701	1.000	
x_2—Affect (Semantic Differential)	0.688	0.727	0.800	1.000

A Simple Example

In order to illustrate some of the principles discussed above, consider the model of Figure 4.5 where one theoretical variable causes another and both are operationalized by two indicators. Suppose, for purposes of discussion, one desires to test whether affect toward the church (ξ) affects behavioral intentions (η).[10] Affect can be operationalized by the self-reports of individuals on a Guilford (x_1) and a semantic differential (x_2) scales. Similarly, behavioral intentions can be measured with, say, Likert (y_1) and Thurstone (y_2) scales.

Table 4.2 presents intercorrelations among these observable variables for a sample of 62 respondents. The application of Jöreskog's methodology yields solutions to the following parameters in the general linear model:

$$\mathbf{\Lambda}_y = \begin{pmatrix} \lambda_1 \\ \lambda_2 \end{pmatrix}$$

$$\mathbf{\Lambda}_x = \begin{pmatrix} \lambda_1' \\ \lambda_2' \end{pmatrix}$$

$$\mathbf{B} = I = 1$$

$$\mathbf{\Gamma} = \gamma$$

$$\mathbf{\Phi} = \phi_{\xi\xi} = 1.0$$

$$\mathbf{\Psi} = \psi_{\eta\eta} = 1.0$$

$$\mathbf{\theta}_\varepsilon = \begin{pmatrix} \theta_{\varepsilon_1} \\ \theta_{\varepsilon_2} \end{pmatrix}$$

$$\mathbf{\theta}_\delta = \begin{pmatrix} \theta_{\delta_1} \\ \theta_{\delta_2} \end{pmatrix}$$

Figure 4.7 presents a summary of the maximum likelihood standardized parameter estimates using Jöreskog's program LISREL. The positive relation between affect and behavioral intentions (γ) can be seen to conform to that predicted by theory (cf., Bagozzi and Burnkrant, 1978).

The adequacy of the theoretical structure in Figure 4.7 for explaining the observed pattern of data may be determined as follows. First, note that the parameter estimates are each at least twice their standard errors. Second, the goodness-of-fit $\chi^2 = 2.77$ with 1 d.f. and $p = 0.10$. Third, as illustrated in Table 4.3, the estimated parameters faithfully reconstruct the variances and covariances of the observed variables within the context of the model. Finally, the reliability coefficient,[11] $\rho \simeq 0.991$, indicates an "adequate" fit. Overall, the model fits the data very well.[12]

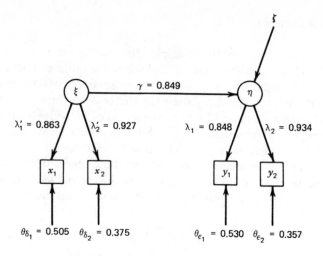

Figure 4.7. Maximum-likelihood standardized estimates for affect-behavioral intentions Model.

Table 4.3
Residuals, $S - \Sigma$, for the Model of Figures 4.4 and 4.7 and the Data of Table 4.2

Variables	y_1	y_2	x_1	x_2
y_1	0.000			
y_2	0.000	0.000		
x_1	0.040	−0.016	0.000	
x_2	−0.020	0.008	0.000	0.000

Summary

The focus of this chapter was on the general linear model. The discussion began with the overall philosophy and objectives for using the general linear model as a means for developing and testing theory in marketing. It was shown to represent one vehicle for achieving a high level of understanding in explanation. That is, it formally operationalizes the following structure concerned with why any phenomenon Q acts or behaves the way it does:

Factors $x_1, x_2, \ldots, x_n$ interact in a manner $y_1, y_2, \ldots, y_n$ for reasons $w_1, w_2, \ldots, w_n$, thus producing a phenomenon of the nature Q.

As an additional intuitive rationale behind the general linear model, the topics of unobserved variables, measurement error, and simultaneity were examined.

Next, following the development due to Jöreskog and his colleagues, the structure of the general linear model was presented. Special emphasis was given to the problem of specification, that is, the representation of one's variables and hypotheses in an overall theoretical structure. Given such a structure, the presentation then turned to the issue of how one might uniquely determine estimates of the structural parameters from the population moments of the observable variables. This is the problem of identification. Subsequently, a maximum likelihood method of parameter estimation was outlined, and the logic and form of hypothesis testing was investigated. The chapter closed with a simple example illustrating some of the principles developed throughout the treatment. Subsequent chapters extend the general linear model and illustrate its use in concept formation, hypothesis development, and theory testing contexts.

Notes

[1] Portions of the following discussion on measurement error and simultaneity were stimulated by work done by Goldberger (1973a, 1974).

[2] For a somewhat more extended example showing the upward bias in the estimation of the slope when using ordinary least-squares procedures, see Johnston (1972, pp. 341–344).

[3] For a general discussion as to the meaning and rationale of these assumptions in simultaneous equation models, see Thiel (1971).

[4] This system of correspondence rules represents perhaps the simplest structure. It should be regarded as a hypothesis to be tested, however, since other functional forms could conceivably relate the unobservables to observables. To the author's knowledge, however, this aspect of correspondence rules has not been dealt with in the literature.

[5] Thiel (1971, ch. 11) presents an interesting analysis of misspecification due to an incorrect mathematical form, as well as other problems.

[6] Goldberger (1974, p. 4) presents a simple example illustrating this point. See also Kmenta (1971, pp. 392–395).

[7] Jöreskog and Sörbom (1976) handle other models, and the reader is encouraged to read their article to gain a better perspective as to the identification problem.

[8] For a review of the general maximum likelihood principle, see Morrison (1976), Thiel (1971), or Lawley and Maxwell (1971).

[9] A larger version of LISREL is now available which effectively doubles the number of variables and parameters handled by the model. Descriptions and copies of Jöreskog's programs can be obtained from International Educational Services, P.O. Box 3650, Chicago, Illinois 60690.

[10] The theoretical rationale for this hypothesis and related others can be found in Bagozzi and Burnkrant (1978a).

[11] The reliability coefficient was calculated as follows:

$$\rho = \frac{T_0 - T_K}{T_0 - E(T_K)}$$

$$T_0 = \frac{(0.792)^2 + (0.582)^2 + (0.688)^2 + (0.701)^2 + (0.727)^2 + (0.800)^2}{10}$$

$$T_0 = 3.099$$

$$E(T_K) = \frac{1}{N} = \frac{1}{M-1} = \frac{3}{62} = 0.0161$$

$$T_K = \frac{F_0}{dF} = \frac{(2.77)}{(1)(62)} = 0.0447$$

$$\rho = \frac{3.099 - 0.0447}{3.099 - 0.0161} = \frac{3.0543}{3.0829} \simeq 0.991$$

As Burt (1973) notes, the reliability coefficient in restricted factor analytic models (such as Jöreskog's) can exceed positive one. However, "it should exceed positive one only when the fit of a model to a set of data is extremely good and will only exceed positive one by a small margin" (Burt, 1973, p. 188).

[12] It should be stressed that the analysis here is only a necessary one for determining the adequacy of one's theory. Ideally, the researcher would like to determine causality by manipulating independent variables and observing changes in dependent variables in a controlled setting. If, as in the case of many studies, it is impossible, impractical, or unethical to manipulate independent variables, then quasi-experimental techniques may be called for (e.g., Cook and Campbell, 1976). For the data analyzed in this simple example, one would have liked, at a minimum, to fit the model on a portion of the data and then test it on the withheld sample. Since the sample size of the illustration was only 62, however, this technique could not be employed here.

FIVE

CONSTRUCT VALIDITY

As discussed in Chapter 3, the scientific research process begins with the formation of the concepts comprising one's hypotheses and theory. This chapter examines a set of formal criteria—termed construct validity—that may be used to ascertain the adequacy of variables in one's theory. After discussing the dimentions of construct validity, the chapter explores two leading methodologies for determining construct validity: the multitrait-multimethod (MM) matrix and causal modeling approaches. The procedures are then illustrated with data from attitude studies performed by Ostrom (1969) and Kothandapani (1971). Finally, the chapter closes with some further issues related to construct validity, including the notion of interpretational confounding (e.g., Burt, 1976).

Construct Validity Defined

Construct validity has been defined variously as:

1. The extent to which an operationalization *measures* the concept that it purports to *measure* (Zaltman et al., 1973, p. 44).
2. Trait validity and nomological validity (Campbell, 1960).
3. Discriminant and convergent validity (Campbell and Fiske, 1959).
4. "Confounding"—the possibility that the operational definition of a cause or effect can be construed in terms of more than one construct (Cook and Campbell, 1976).

As will become clear below, however, each of these captures only a portion of construct validity. Further, the entire set neglects some important dimensions of the concept.

For purposes of analysis, construct validity is defined here as the degree to which a concept (term, variable, construct) achieves theoretical *and* empirical meaning within the overall structure of one's theory. Six components of construct validity are proposed:

1. Theoretical Meaningfulness of Concepts
2. Observational Meaningfulness of Concepts
3. Internal Consistency of Operationalizations
4. Convergent Validity
5. Discriminant Validity
6. Nomological Validity

The first two are semantic criteria and refer to the internal consistency of the language used to represent a concept and the conceptual relationship(s) between a theoretical variable and its operationalization(s), respectively. The third criterion is a strictly empirical one designed to determine the degree of internal consistency and single factoredness of one's operationalizations. Criteria 4 and 5 are the traditional objects of the MM matrix approach. By employing independent measurement procedures for concepts and examining the pattern of correlations among them, these criteria attempt to ascertain the extent of (1) agreement among different attempts to measure the same concept, and (2) divergence among different concepts measured with like procedures, respectively. Finally, nomological validity denotes the degree to which predictions are confirmed from a formal theoretical network containing the concept under scrutiny. Unlike the previous criteria, nomological validity entails syntatical considerations in one's theoretical structure, as well as certain empirical considerations. The achievement of construct validity, it is asserted, requires satisfaction of all six of the above criteria. Indeed, as will be demonstrated later in the chapter, misleading inferences can arise when one fails to consider the entire set. Construct validity is a necessary prerequisite for theory development and testing.

The Theoretical Meaningfulness of Concepts

A concept may be defined as the basic unit of thought (e.g., Zaltman et al., 1973; Hempel, 1952). It represents a mental construct or image of some object, thing, idea, or phenomenon. More formally, concepts achieve their meaning through their relationships with terms and objects (where objects are construed broadly

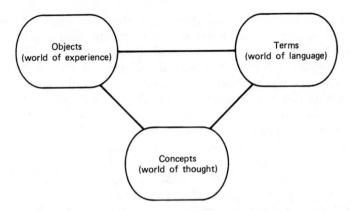

Figure 5.1. The relationships among concepts, terms, and objects.
Source: After Caws (1965).

to include physical things, events or happenings, etc.). As shown in Figure 5.1, it is possible to represent these relationships as connections among three systems or worlds of meaning. The relationship between a concept and term is one between the world of thought and the world of language. This connection is often labeled one of designation, that is, "a concept is designated by a word or group of words" (Zaltman et al., 1973). Further, there is not necessarily a one-to-one correspondence between concepts and terms. A concept may be designated by a number of terms (e.g., the concept, product, is often thought to consist of "physical objects," "ideas," "services," etc.); while a term may designate a number of concepts (e.g., the term "exchange" can mean a utilitarian or physical transfer of things, a symbolic relationship, or perhaps both, depending on the context).

The relationships between objects and terms and between objects and concepts entail the processes of abstraction and interpretation as shown in Figure 5.2 (e.g., Zaltman et al., 1973, pp. 27–32). That is, abstraction refers to the mental activity of deriving common theoretical content from a set of empirical objects. For example, the observed anger, statements of dissatisfaction, and expressed

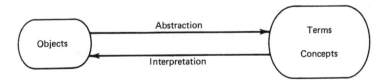

Figure 5.2. The processes of abstraction and interpretation.
Source: Zaltman et al. (1973, p. 28).

intentions to make a formal complaint by a consumer might each reflect a common element of cognitive dissonance stemming from a post-purchase discrepancy between expectations and actual product performance. The concept, cognitive dissonance, represents a mental construct intervening between experiences with the product and the observations of the three behaviors (i.e., anger, dissatisfaction, and complaint). Depending on one's school of thought in psychology, cognitive dissonance can be regarded here as either a concept common to all three behaviors, a concept indicated by all three behaviors, or a concept causing all three behaviors. Interpretation, on the other hand, is the process of deriving or defining the meaning of a term or concept (e.g., Kahane, 1973, ch. 10; and footnote 2, in ch. 3, of this monograph). Typically, interpretation will involve specification of the sense of a term or concept as well as its reference. More on these aspects of meaning will appear below under the discussion of observational meaningfulness.

It is useful to identify three main groups of concepts in science: classificatory, comparative, and quantitative (Carnap, 1966, ch. 5). A classificatory concept places objects or terms in a particular category or grouping. For example, marketers have classified products according to the way they are bought as follows: convenience goods (those purchased immediately, impulsively, or with a minimum of effort), shopping goods (those for which consumers compare alternatives for price, quality, etc.), specialty goods (those which consumers insist upon and seek-out), and unsought goods (those which the consumer is unaware of, avoids, and so on). The classificatory concept makes relatively weak statements about objects or terms, at least when compared to the other two types of concepts. As a result, it conveys less information, and it is not as useful for forming hypotheses and other relationships among concepts.

The comparative concept goes farther than the classificatory concept in that it allows for the specification of qualitative relations between concepts[1] (e.g., more than, less than, or equality). Comparative concepts are related through a logical structure of relations. For example, consider consumer satisfaction and the comparative concepts greater, less, and equal in satisfaction. With two or more products and a sample of consumers, one can apply the following rules to determine how products compare with respect to these three comparative concepts:

1. If the consumer rates his or her satisfaction with two products as indifferent, they are of equal satisfaction.
2. If the consumer rates his or her satisfaction with one product as higher (lower) than another, then that product is greater (less) than the other in satisfaction.

Hempel (1952; see also Carnap, 1966, p. 57) notes that there are four conditions that equality (E) and less than (L) (or its compliment, greater than, G) must satisfy to be termed comparative concepts:

1. E must be an equivalence relation (i.e., it must be symmetric, transitive, and reflexive).
2. E and L (or G) must exclude each other. No two products, for example, can be rated as equally satisfactory by a consumer while at the same time be related so that one is less satisfactory than another.
3. L (or G) must be transitive. If product x is rated less in satisfaction than product y, and product y is rated less than product z, then x must be rated less than z.
4. For any two objects, x and y, one of the following must hold:
   (a) E holds between the two objects.
   (b) L (or G) holds between x and y.
   (c) L (or G) holds between y and x.

Finally, quantitative concepts introduce functor symbols, that is, symbols for functions that have numerical values. The quantitative concept typically evolves, at least indirectly, out of the rules or procedures associated with measuring it. As discussed below under observational meaningfulness, however, a number of alternative rules and procedures have arisen in science for constructing quantitative concepts.

Before proceeding to an analysis of the theoretical meaningfulness of concepts, it will prove useful to introduce Carnap's (1966; 1956) conception of scientific language. Taking the position that there is a sharp distinction between analytic and synthetic statements, Carnap (1966) divides the terms of a scientific language into three main groups:

1. Logical terms, including all the terms of pure mathematics.
2. Observational terms, or O-terms.
3. Theoretical terms, or T-terms (sometimes called "constructs") (p. 258).

Logical terms are variables or symbols defined explicitly to be used in a system of logical or mathematical relations (e.g., "if", "and", "not", "equals", etc.). As such, they contain no empirical content. The observational terms, however, refer to things that may be directly observed. Typically, these include physical objects and things detectable with the five senses. Theoretical terms usually refer to things not directly observed such as mental events, dispositions, hypothetical constructs, ideal types, and so on. As will become apparent below, however, theoretical terms are connected to observational terms either (a) directly through correspondence rules, (b) indirectly through derived concepts and correspondence rules, or (c) indirectly through other theoretical terms which are eventually related to observational terms through correspondence rules.

We are now in a position to give a formal definition of the *theoretical meaningfulness* of a concept. The *theoretical meaningfulness* of a concept refers to the nature and internal consistency of the language used to represent the concept. It addresses the formal adequacy of the logical and theoretical terms comprising one's theory. In general, this semantic requirement of construct validity specifies particular properties of the object predicates[2] of a concept. Some of the more important properties include the sense, scope, range, or degree of specificity of a concept.

Perhaps the most developed set of standards for evaluating the theoretical meaningfulness of a concept has been developed by Lachenmeyer (1971). Lachenmeyer (1971) suggests four linguistic problems for any theoretical language. The first is vagueness.

A term is said to be *vague* when the range of object predicates forming a term's referential meaning has not been specified: the term's connotative meaning is greater than its denotative meaning.

As an example, consider the following sentence: "marketing is any activity which actualizes the potential market relationship among the users of economic goods and services" (McInnes, 1964, p. 57).[3] This definition can be criticized for being vague because the object predicates and referential meaning of "activity," "market relationship," and "economic goods and services" are not specified.

A second linguistic problem is ambiguity.

Any term is *ambiguous* when more than two but a finite number of object predicates have been specified as equiprobable members of the set comprising its referential meaning.

When looking at the discipline of marketing as a whole, one would have to conclude that the image of its subject matter is ambiguous, since, among other terms, the object predicates of marketing include "business activities," "study of transactions," "activities directed as facilitating and consummating exchanges," the "system which will direct an economy's flow of goods and services from producters to consumers," "a process of demand and supply adjustment," and "the creation of time, place, and possession utilities."

Opacity is a third problem with the theoretical meaningfulness of terms.

Opacity refers to the failure of a term's reference function because there is no referent object of the sort represented by the term's object predicate.

The use of opaque terms usually occurs in one of two ways. Perhaps the least common occurrence of opaque terms is to be found in the practice of reification (see discussion in Chapter 2). When the theorist models social or unobservable phenomena as material things having natural or observable properties, he or she is also introducing opacity into the theoretical language. The definition of marketing as a process whereby society adjusts its supply and demand to meet human needs is an example of the conduct of opacity in this sense. The second and more common use of opaque terms occurs through the omission or misuse of a term. This happens when a nonprimitive term is used without being defined.

The usage of the term, "marketing concept," is a common example in the literature of an opaque construct since it has rarely been explicitly defined.

A final problem threatening the theoretical meaningfulness of one's concepts
is contradiction.

Contradiction is a special case of ambiguity that occurs when a term has two different,
equiprobable object predicates specified as its referential meaning and these object
predicates are logically inconsistent. In this case, the predicates cannot both stand in
identity relation with the nominal, since they both cannot be equivalent to the nominal.
The most common form of contradiction is the assertion that a thing is both something
and not something, one being the converse of the other . . . .

As a somewhat more extended example of the notion of theoretical meaningfulness, consider the concept of attitudes. Attitudes have been defined as a
learned predisposition to respond to an object or class of objects in a preferential
or evaluative manner (cf., Allport, 1935; Rokeach, 1968). The object predicate
in this definition is a compound one, that is, "a learned predisposition to
respond . . . in a preferential or evaluative manner." It may be criticized for being
vague since the specific content and range of the object predicate is not identified.
To take a portion of the object predicate as an example, one may note that it is
possible to "respond evaluatively" in a variety of ways: through attributions of
good or bad, moral judgments, expressions of likes and dislikes, approach or
avoidance actions, and so on. Unless one adequately specifies the class of object
predicates for a concept, it must be regarded as an open set—implying every-
thing or anything—depending on the whim of the definer rather than upon the
scientific criteria of internal consistency and intersubjective confirmation
(Campbell, 1963).

Theoretical meaningfulness appears to be at the center of another controversy
concerning the attitude construct. Perhaps in order to overcome vagueness in
the definition of attitudes, authors have defined the concept variously as (1)
beliefs intended to have an action-oriented function (Rokeach, 1968), (2)
"implicit evaluative responses" (Fishbein, 1967a), and (3) "likes and dislikes"
(Bem, 1970). Notice that each of these definitions represents a distinct category
of psychological behavior (see discussion in Chapter 2 on Mental Concepts and
Marketing Research). The first represents a mental concept in that a belief is a
statement of fact held cognitively by an individual. Thus, a belief may be subject
to refutation and proved to be true or false in an objective sense. By definition, it
does not necessarily imply a "predisposition to action" as some claim (Rokeach,
1968), and it is often action neutral. The second conception of attitude (i.e.,
"implicit evaluative responses") has been conceived in at least two ways. Early
work by Fishbein (1967a) seemed to place the concept of attitude more in the
behavioristic category by emphasizing "implicit" responses rather than affect or
cognitions, per se. Attitudes are, in this view, to be ultimately inferred from
behavior (e.g., approach or avoidance tendencies) without recourse to mental

representations. Later work by the author, however, clearly shows that evaluations are taken as good or bad judgments of the consequences of performing
some behavior (e.g., Ajzen and Fishbein, 1973). The third definition of attitude
("likes and dislikes") represents still another aspect of human behavior, that is,
the mental concepts of affect or emotions. Unlike (a) beliefs that are relatively
object centered in that they express information about some fact external to the
person or (b) implicit responses that are, by definition, person centered, likes
and dislikes imply a relationship between a person on the one hand and an
object, action, or event on the other. Moreover, likes and dislikes cannot be
proven true or false even in principle as beliefs may be so proven. Nevertheless,
on balance each of the above definitions satisfies the semantic criterion of
theoretical meaningfulness in that is it not by itself vague, ambiguous, opaque,
or contradictory. The character of the attitude construct is not so clear, however,
when one considers recent formulations in marketing.

Consider the following attitude model due to Fishbein (1967b) which is used
extensively by consumer behavior researchers (cf., Lutz, 1975):

$$A\text{-act} = \sum_{i=1}^{n} B_i a_i$$

where A-act is an individual's attitude toward a particular act (e.g., purchase of a
product), B_i is one's belief that the act will have some consequence i, and a_i is
one's evaluation of consequence i as good or bad. This formulation explicitly
defines an attitude as the product of (1) cognition and (2) an evaluation which
may or may not be regarded as a pure cognition depending upon one's viewpoint. Recall from the discussion in Chapter 2 that there are conceptual grounds
for not defining evaluations of good or bad as cognitions expressing statements
as to matter of fact. Evaluations were shown, instead, to comprise an aspect of
moral beliefs in that they are action oriented, they indirectly or directly advocate
a policy, and they may imply a third party. However, Lutz (1975) treats evaluation as a cognition and calls the multiplicative summation ($\sum B_i a_i$) "an index
of the *cognitive structure* underlying A-act." Fishbein (1967a) has not been
consistent in his usage of evaluation, often connotatively implying either affect
or cognition. But how is one to regard evaluation—as a cognition, an emotion,
a moral belief, or combinations of these concepts? Rokeach (1968, pp. 121–122)
presents compelling reasons for distinguishing cognitive and affective dimensions of attitudes:

While everyone agrees that an attitude leads to a preferential (or discriminatory)
response, the basis for the preferential response is not clear. Is a positive or negative
preference due to the fact that the attitude object or situation is affectively liked or
disliked, or because it is cognitively evaluated as good or bad?

The conceptual difficulty arises from the fact that the two dimensions of *like-dislike*
and *goodness-badness* need not necessarily go together. In speaking of the "pro-con"
dimension, often said to be *the* defining characteristic of attitude, we do not know

whether the preferential response of approach or avoidance is due to the fact that it is liked or disliked or because it is seen to be good or bad. It is possible to like something bad, and to dislike something good . . . there is no necessary one-to-one relation between affect and evaluation. Whether the preferential response will be positive or negative will depend on the relative strength of one's evaluative beliefs and one's positive or negative feelings. A person will make a "pro" response to an object toward which he harbors negative feelings if he believes the object to be sufficiently good for him.

Until the distinctions among affect, cognitions, and evaluation are better defined, one must regard the A-act definition and other similar versions of attitude as vague and ambiguous. Recent work by Lazarus (1974) relating cognition to emotion and by others relating cognition to motivation (e.g., Weiner, 1974) may prove helpful in clarifying the meaning of these concepts (see also Bagozzi and Burnkrant, 1978).

Finally, the theoretical meaningfulness of the attitude construct may be questioned as perhaps superfluous. Doob (1947) and Campbell (1963), for example, suggest that the cognitive and action tendency aspects of attitudes have not been adequately distinguished from learning and motivation theories, respectively, and thus by implication have no unique content (at least none that cannot already be subsumed under existing concepts in psychology). For Doob (1947), an attitude is a type of conditioned response, while for Campbell (1963), it is one subset of all "acquired behavioral dispositions."

In summary, the theoretical meaningfulness of concepts attempts to capture the character and quality of the language used to represent the concepts. It is a measure of the internal consistency of the conceptual intention and significance of concepts. Further, because it is a necessary condition for the achievement of construct validity that one's concepts attain a high level of theoretical meaningfulness, it represents a basic component of theory design and research.

The Observational Meaningfulness of Concepts

The second dimension of construct validity is also a semantic criterion. Specifically, the *observational meaningfulness* of concepts refers to the relationship between theoretical variables (which are unobservable) and their operationalizations (which, of course, are observable). In the philosophy of science literature, the relationship is represented through correspondence rules.[4] Depending on one's school of thought, correspondence rules represent logical or conceptual relationships on the one hand, or causal relationships on the other. The former position is persuasively argued by the more positivistic scholars, while the latter is the orientation of contemporary realists.

The problem of observational meaningfulness arises because of the nature of theoretical concepts. Since theoretical concepts contain only logical terms and unobservable constructs, they must be tied, either directly or indirectly, to observable concepts if one hopes to develop theoretical laws and propositions with explanatory content. In general, there are three models that have been used in the scientific community to specify correspondence rules. One of the earliest approaches, termed the *operational definition model*, maintains that theoretical terms can be *defined* in terms of observational terms (e.g., Bridgman, 1927). The idea is that one can (must) always find—through test operations—a one-to-one correspondence between theoretical concept and observable concept. As Bridgman (1927) puts it, "[We] mean by any concept nothing more than a set of operations; *the concept is synonymous with the corresponding set of operations.*" Thus, the logical form of the operational definition model may be written symbollically as

$$Qx \equiv (C(x) \longrightarrow R(x))$$

which reads: "x has the theoretical property Q, by definition, if and only if our performing operation (i.e., test conditions) C implies result (response) R" (e.g., Petrie, 1971). The operational definition model states that a concept *is* its measure and nothing more. If, for example, one uses a Likert scale to indicate attitudes, the operational definition school of thought would equate the concept, attitude, with the scores obtained from the scale. In this sense, since the operation becomes the concept, the correspondence rule is collapsed, and the notions of theoretical and observational meaningfulness are subordinate to operational empirical criteria (discussed below). These aspects of the operational definition model deny that a theoretical concept can achieve meaning through its relation to other theoretical concepts in an overall theoretical structure. This implies that all theoretical terms must, from the point of view of this school of thought, be defined in terms of observables. Further, it is not clear whether it is meaningful to speak of a concept that is not operationalized or that appears as part of a counterfactual conditional, given this model (see discussion in Chapter I and Carnap, 1936, 1937, 1956). Marketers implicitly follow an operational definition model when they rely exclusively on observable variables in their theories, assume no error in measurements, or rely exclusively on empirical associations to model and test their theories.

Partly in answer to the shortcomings of the operational definition model, philosophers of science have proposed a second type of correspondence rule termed the *partial interpretation model*. Although the relationship between theoretical concept and observation is taken to be a logical one (as in the operational definition scheme), the connection is dependent on the context or manifestation of particular test conditions. In this sense, the empirical meaning of the concept is only partly specified. Thus, the logical form of the partial interpretation model may be written symbolically as

$$C(x) \longrightarrow (Qx \equiv R(x))$$

which reads "in performing operation (test condition) C, x will have the theoretical property Q if and only if it manifests result (response) R" (e.g., Petrie, 1971). As Keat and Urry (1975, p. 21) note:

... what we get here is a partial specification of the meaning of theoretical terms, that is, the meaning they have in certain test situations. Further specifications can then be given, by correspondence rules which give the meanings of the term in different situations.

In contrast to the operational definition school of thought which states that every theoretical term has one and only one operationalization associated with it, the partial interpretation framework advocates a doctrine of multiple operationalizations. Campbell (1969) suggests two arguments for such a policy: "one from theory, one from the authority of scientific practice."

First, the argument from theory: Measurements involve processes which must be specified in terms of many theoretical parameters. For any specific measurement process, we know on theoretical grounds that it is a joint function of many scientific laws. Thus, we know on scientific grounds that the measurements resulting cannot purely reflect a single parameter of our scientific theory [p. 14]. [Secondly] to move on to the argument from scientific experience: One of the greatest weaknesses in definitional operationism as a description of best scientific practice, was that it allowed no formal way of expressing the scientist's prepotent awareness of the imperfection of his measuring instruments and his prototypic activity of improving them . . . .

It is thus on the grounds of self-critical hard-headedness that we face up to our very unsatisfactory predicament: we have only other invalid measures against which to validate our tests; we have no "criterion" to check them against (Campbell and Fiske, 1959). A theory of the interaction of two theoretical parameters must be tested by imperfect exemplifications of each . . . great inferential strength is added when each theoretical parameter is exemplified in two or more ways, each mode being as independent as possible of the other . . . this general program can be designated multiple operationism [p. 15].

As a result, the partial interpretation model would, for example, allow attitudes to be operationalized variously, perhaps by semantic differential, Likert, Thurstone, peer ratings, or other methods. As will be shown below, this aspect of the model allows one to determine measurement error and methods variance for constructs.

Of particular significance is the fact that the partial interpretation model—unlike the operational definition scheme—does not ignore the distinction between a theoretical term and its operationalization(s); and it allows a theoretical construct to achieve its meaning first through its relation to both the language used to define the concept and other theoretical terms (e.g., Hempel, 1952; Feigl, 1970) and second, through the relation of the theoretical term to its operationalization(s) (in the conceptual sense noted above). The operational definition and partial interpretation models have been used most by the more positivistic philosophers of science and researchers. Although beyond the scope of this monograph, both approaches can be criticized for their overly restrictive reliance on a verificationist theory of meaning and an independent observation language, among other difficulties (Keat and Urry, 1975; Petrie, 1971; Hesse, 1970).

The correspondence rules in the operational definition and partial interpretation models are logical or conceptual in nature. For example, Zaltman et al. (1973, p. 59) show that the correspondence rule relating "attitude" to an attitude measurement instrument can be represented as follows:

Statement 1: The direction and strength of attitudes induces a systematic bias concerning beliefs about a social object.

Statement 2: The beliefs about social objects can be measured by an information test.

∴

Statement 3: The direction and strength of attitudes can be measured by the bias in an information test.

An alternative school of thought for representing correspondence rules has emerged in recent years. This approach, termed the *realist model*, avoids some of the pitfalls in the other orientations by rejecting the strict logical entailment implied in favor of a causal interpretation relating theoretical terms to observable phenomena. The realist model may be represented symbolically as follows:

$$Qx \longrightarrow (C(x) \longrightarrow R(x))$$

which reads "if x is Q, then performing operation (test condition) C will produce result (response) R." The rationale for the realist model is summarized nicely by Keat and Urry (1975, p. 38):

... positive results [for the realist model] provide only indirect, and logically non-conclusive, evidence for the truth of "x is Q." We postulate that x is Q, and argue that, if this is so, we should get R when we carry out C. If this is what happens, it gives us some reason to believe x is Q. But there are many reasons why R may happen, of which x's being Q is only one. Indeed, what is often involved in such cases is an argument from effects to causes (that is, from R as the effect of Q in C, to Q): but one can never be sure that there is only one possible cause for any given effect.
  Thus the realist regards "correspondence rules" ... as frequently expressing causal relations between theoretical entities and observable phenomena. It is because an entity of some kind exists, or has some property, that when the specified test conditions are carried out, the predicted results occur.

These characteristics of the realist model make the approach especially appealing from the standpoint of contemporary standards in the philosophy of science. First, the approach is consistent with the falsificationist school of thought which states that observations can only refute, and not confirm, one's theories (e.g., Popper, 1963). Second, the model allows for the fact that concepts may be multiply operationalized. This, in turn, facilitates the representation of measurement error and methods variance. Third, consistent with contemporary thinking on theoretical structures (e.g., Hempel, 1952; Carnap, 1966; Feigl, 1970), it is possible for theoretical concepts to achieve their meaning independently of direct test procedures (i.e., through their relationships with other theoretical terms and derived concepts). Finally, it should be noted that the distinction between the partial interpretation and realist models roughly parallels that between the alternative views on causality discussed in Chapter 1. That is, the partial interpretation approach is most often used in conjunction with theories containing Humean notions of causality, while the realist model is more compatible with modern natural necessity views on causality. Given the current state of thinking in the philosphy of science, the researcher can achieve observational meaningfulness of his or her concepts using either the partial interpretation or realist models of correspondence rules.

Internal Consistency of Operationalizations

The previous two criteria for construct validity are designed to ascertain the semantic quality of theoretical terms and the relationship between theoretical terms and observations, respectively. The *internal consistency of operationalizations* is a third criterion for construct validity and is concerned with the homogeneity or single factoredness of observations.

Since we will be dealing with quantitative observational concepts, it will prove useful to present a set of rules defining these concepts. Carnap (1966, ch. 6) suggests the following five rules for defining procedures of measurement[5] for these types of concepts:

Rule 1. This rule specifies an empirical relation E for magnitude M. "The rule states that, if the relation E_M holds between objects a and b, the two objects will have equal values of the magnitude M." In symbolic form:

$$\text{If } E_M(a, b), \quad \text{then } M(a) = M(b)$$

Rule 2. This rule specifies a second empirical relation L_M. "The rule says that, if the relation L_M holds between a and b, the value of the magnitude M will be smaller for a than b." In symbolic form:

$$\text{If } L_M(a, b), \quad \text{then } M(a) < M(b)$$

Rule 3. This rule "tells us when to assign a selected numerical value, usually zero, to the magnitude we are attempting to measure. It does this by specifying an easily recognizable, and sometimes easily reproducible, state and telling us to assign the selected numerical value to an object if it is in that state."

Rule 4. This rule "assigns a second selected value of the magnitude to an object by specifying another easily recognized, easily reproducible state of that object. This second value is usually 1, but it may be any number different from the number specified by Rule 3.

Rule 5. This rule specifies the precise form of a scale. "It specifies the empirical conditions ED_M, under which we shall say that two differences (D) in the values of the magnitude (M) are equal . . . . We want to specify empirical conditions under which we shall say that the difference between any two values of the magnitudes for *a* and for *b* is the same as the difference between two other values, say, for *c* and for *d*. This fifth rule has the following symbolic form:

$$\text{If } ED_M(a, b, c, d), \quad \text{then } M(a) - M(b) = M(c) - M(d)$$

The rule tells us that if certain empirical conditions, represented by "ED_M" in the symbolic formulation, obtain for four values of the magnitude, we can say that the difference between the first two values is the same as the difference between the other two values.

Given measurements on a quantitative concept such as sketched above, one would like to have some indication of the quality of those measurements. For example, if one used seven point scales ranging from extremely good to extremely bad to measure the evaluative aspect of A-act, it would be useful to determine the degree of unidimensionality of the multiple items for the evaluative aspect in order to gain one indication of the extent to which the operationalization achieved its intended representation. It is a matter of logical and empirical necessity that a variable be unidimensional and internally consistent. An operationalization that is internally inconsistent and/or multidimensional cannot, by definition, be considered a variable and hence must not be treated as such in one's theory or in MM matrix, experimental, or other procedures or analyses.

The determination of the internal consistency of operationalizations will depend on whether one has representational or index measurements. Briefly, a representational measurement is one that "involves the establishment of a two-way correspondence between: (1) some property of things being measured, and (2) some property of the measurement scale" (Dawes, 1972, p. 11). Examples of representational measurements in the behavioral sciences include magnitude techniques (e.g., Thurstone's method of comparative judgment), proximity techniques (e.g., Coombs' nonmetric proximity technique), interlocking techniques (e.g., Guttman scales), and unfolding techniques (e.g., unidimensional and multidimensional procedures). An index measurement, in contrast, establishes only a one-way correspondence between the property of the thing being measured and the measurement scale (Dawes, 1972). Semantic differential and Likert scales are two common examples.

The internal consistency of representational measurements are determined through the application of "consistency checks." In particular, it is possible to derive implications or predictions as to patterns of response from a scale under scrutiny and then compare the actual responses of people to that derived from logical considerations. The discrepancies or deviations from the logical predictions are then a measure of the internal consistency of the measurement. For various representational measurements, Dawes (1972) describes and illustrates consistency checks.

The internal consistency of operationalizations derived from index measurements can be examined in at least two ways. First, the unidimensionality of one's operationalizations may be determined with factor analysis or the general linear model derived in Chapter 4 (cf., Bagozzi, 1978c). These procedures will be touched upon near the end of the chapter (see also the discussion on measurement error in Chapter 4, and the discussion and illustration in Chapter 6). Second, one may gain an indication of internal consistency by examining the reliability of one's operationalizations. It is to this topic that we now turn.

In classical test score theory, the reliability of a scale or test is defined as the squared correlations (ρ^2) between observed score and true score (e.g., Lord and Novick, 1968, p. 61). This relation, which may vary in the interval from 0 to 1, can be expressed as the ratio of true-score variation to observed-score variation and also as the correlation between parallel measurements:

$$\rho_{xT}^2 = \frac{\sigma_T^2}{\sigma_x^2} = \rho_{xx'}$$

With σ_ε^2 used to represent measurement error, the reliability for any particular measurement can be expressed also as

$$\rho_{xT}^2 = \frac{\sigma_T^2}{\sigma_T^2 + \sigma_\varepsilon^2} = 1 - \frac{\sigma_\varepsilon^2}{\sigma_x^2}$$

In general, there are three types of procedures used for estimating reliability: the test-retest method, the split-half method, the internal consistency method (Lord and Novick, 1968, pp. 134–137). In the test-retest method, the same measure is given to respondents at two or more points in time. Reliability is then indicated by the correlation between the measurements. At least three problems may be identified with the test-retest method. First, because situational factors may systematically affect people, the correlation between measures may be a function of both the characteristics of people (for which the measurement is intended to capture) and the external influence. Yet, the usual test-retest procedure cannot separate these different factors. Second, because the psychological states of people change over time due to fatigue, maturation, learning, differences in motivation, and so on, the error in measurement from one time to another may also change systematically, producing biased results. Again, the test-retest correlation does not allow one to discriminate between such effects and the true relationship between concept and measurement. Third, demand characteristics, evaluation apprehension, and memory effects tend to be present at each measurement occasion, causing a correlation between errors in measurement and a corresponding bias in the observed correlation between measures. Lord and Novick (1968, pp. 134–135) present other problems with the test-retest method.

In the split-half method, the separate measurements of a variable are divided into equal parts (usually halves), and correlations between the parts are used to gain an indication of the reliability of the measures. The Spearman–Brown formula is most often used in this regard. Because the manner in which separate measurements of the same variable can be divided is largely arbitrary and because reliability can vary depending on this division, the procedure is no longer widely used. Also, the split-half method is subject to the first shortcoming noted above for the test-retest method.

The third method for assessing reliability—the internal consistency method—relies on an analysis of the variances and covariances of the component measurements of a variable. The Kuder–Richardson formulas for dichotomous items and the Cronbach α coefficients for interval data are two commonly used procedures. For example, with $x_1, x_2, \ldots, x_m$ measurements of a variable and $X = \sum x_i$. The Cronbach α coefficient may be expressed as

$$\alpha \equiv \frac{n}{n-1}\left[1 - \frac{\sum \sigma_{x_i}^2}{\sigma_X^2}\right]$$

where $\sigma_{x_i}^2$ is the variance of x_i and σ_X^2 is the variance of X. The Cronbach α coefficient ranges from 0 to 1 and has the desirable property of being a lower bound of the reliability for a variable (Lord and Novick, 1968, pp. 88–90). Further, the Spearman–Brown and Kuder–Richardson 21 formulas are special cases of α.

The major problems with α lie in its assumptions of equal units of measurement in each x_i and zero errors in measurement. The latter assumption, in particular, is quite restrictive since it prevents one from separating external influences from the effect of the underlying variable. Moreover, no explicit goodness-of-fit test exists for accepting or rejecting any particular application, nor can one ascertain the reasonableness of the equal units assumption. Chapter 6 presents a structural equation model that overcomes these deficits, however.

In sum, in order to determine the internal consistency of operationalizations—and thus establish one necessary condition for construct validity—one may use consistency checks for representational measurements and factor analysis and reliability indices for index measurements. Before discussing the fourth and fifth criteria for construct validity (i.e., convergent and discriminant validity), we turn now to the sixth criterion, nomological validity.

Nomological Validity

Nomological validity is the degree to which predictions from a formal theoretical network containing the concept under scrutiny are confirmed (Campbell, 1960). Recall from Chapter 3 that the structure of any theory may be represented through theoretical concepts, derived concepts, empirical concepts, nonobservational propositions, correspondence rules, and operational definitions. Within such a structure, any theoretical term will be related to other theoretical terms through nonobservational propositions. Nomological validity refers to the degree to which such nonobservational propositions are confirmed, given a set of observations and the processes of abstraction relating theoretical concepts to empirical concepts. This aspect of construct validity points out the essential incompleteness of the interpretation of theoretical terms. That is, it is not sufficient for determining construct validity to focus solely on semantic criteria of the language used to represent concepts and the relationship among concepts and operationalizations. Nor is it sufficient to examine only the empirical criteria of internal consistency of operationalizations or even convergent and discriminant validity. Rather, one must also consider the relationship of the concept under investigation to other concepts in an overall context of a theoretical structure. This will involve, as illustrated later in the chapter, the use of syntatic criteria in combination with the modeling of theoretical and empirical relationships.

The notion of nomological validity follows directly from contemporary representations of scientific theory (e.g., Hempel, 1952, 1965; Feigl, 1970; Carnap, 1966). Nomological validity can be interpreted as an extension of the earlier criteria for construct validity in that—given the satisfaction of theoretical and observational meaningfulness, the internal consistency of operationalizations, and convergent and discriminant validity—the meaning of a theoretical concept rests, in part, on its role in the sentences comprising the nonobservational propositions. Although Hempel (1970, 1973) recently argued that such sentences alone have no meaning, it is maintained here that theoretical hypotheses containing a concept under scrutiny can indeed be modeled using the general linear model. The procedures go beyond the representation of logical relationships by explicitly including the modeling of correspondence rules and observations in a complete structure of theory. This will be illustrated below.

Convergent and Discriminant Validity by the Multitrait-Multimethod Matrix Approach

Two final criteria for establishing construct validity may be identified. Convergent validity is the degree to which two or more attempts to measure the same concept through maximally different methods are in agreement; discriminant validity is the degree to which a concept differs from other concepts (Campbell and Fiske, 1959). The procedures for evaluating convergent and discriminant validity have evolved in two stages: The Campbell and Fiske Method and the Causal Modeling Method.

The Campbell and Fiske Method

As pioneered by Campbell and Fiske (1959), the MM matrix approach determines convergent and discriminant validity through an analysis of the pattern of correlations among two or more traits (i.e., variables, concepts, constructs) measured by two or more methods. For example, Table 5.1, which is adapted from Campbell and Fiske (1959, p. 82), presents a typical MM matrix where three traits (A, B, C) are each measured by three methods (1, 2, 3). Taking the concept, attitudes, as an illustration, traits A, B, and C might depict affective, behavioral, and cognitive components, respectively, while methods 1, 2, and 3 might represent Thurstone, Likert, and Guttman scales, respectively.[7] In Table 5.1, as

Table 5.1
A Multitrait-Multimethod Matrix for Three Traits and Three Methods

Traits		Method 1			Method 2			Method 3	
	A_1	B_1	C_1	A_2	B_2	C_2	A_3	B_3	C_3
Method 1									
A_1	$r_{A_1A_1}$								
B_1	$r_{B_1A_1}$	$r_{B_1B_1}$							
C_1	$r_{C_1A_1}$	$r_{C_1B_1}$	$r_{C_1C_1}$						
Method 2									
A_2	$r_{A_2A_1}$	$r_{A_2B_1}$	$r_{A_2C_1}$	$r_{A_2A_2}$					
B_2	$r_{B_2A_1}$	$r_{B_2B_1}$	$r_{B_2C_1}$	$r_{B_2A_2}$	$r_{B_2B_2}$				
C_2	$r_{C_2A_1}$	$r_{C_2B_1}$	$r_{C_2C_1}$	$r_{C_2A_2}$	$r_{C_2B_2}$	$r_{C_2C_2}$			
Method 3									
A_3	$r_{A_3A_1}$	$r_{A_3B_1}$	$r_{A_3C_1}$	$r_{A_3A_2}$	$r_{A_3B_2}$	$r_{A_3C_2}$	$r_{A_3A_3}$		
B_3	$r_{B_3A_1}$	$r_{B_3B_1}$	$r_{B_3C_1}$	$r_{B_3A_2}$	$r_{B_3B_2}$	$r_{B_3C_2}$	$r_{B_3A_3}$	$r_{B_3B_3}$	
C_3	$r_{C_3A_1}$	$r_{C_3B_1}$	$r_{C_3C_1}$	$r_{C_3A_2}$	$r_{C_3B_2}$	$r_{C_3C_2}$	$r_{C_3A_3}$	$r_{C_3B_3}$	$r_{C_3C_3}$

indicated in boldface type, correlations between the same traits across methods are known as validity diagonals. Similarly, heterotrait-monomethod triangles are shown as solid lines, while heterotrait-heteromethod triangles are drawn as broken lines.

Campbell and Fiske (1959, pp. 82–83) summarize convergent and discriminant validity in terms of the pattern of correlations as follows:

> Four aspects bear upon the question of validity. In the first place, the entries in the validity diagonal should be significantly different from zero and sufficiently large to encourage further examination of validity. This requirement is evidence of convergent validity. Second, a validity diagonal value should be higher than the values lying in its column and row in the heterotrait-heteromethod triangles. That is, a validity value for a variable should be higher than the correlations obtained between that variable and any other variable having neither trait nor method in common. This requirement may seem so minimal and so obvious as to not need stating, yet an inspection of the literature shows that it is frequently not met, and may not be met even when the validity coefficients are of substantial size . . . . A third commonsense desideratum is that a variable correlates higher with an independent effort to measure the same trait than with measures designed to get at different traits which happen to employ the same method. For a given variable, this involves comparing its values in the validity diagonals with its values in the heterotrait-monomethod triangles . . . . A fourth desideratum is that the same pattern of trait interrelationship be shown in all of the heterotrait triangles of both the monomethod and heteromethod blocks . . . . The last three criteria provide evidence for discriminant validity.

Table 5.2 presents a formal summary of the above criteria based upon the pattern of correlations shown in Table 5.1. Convergent validity is achieved when each of the nine correlations in the validity diagonals is statistically significant, greater than zero, and "sufficiently large." This is a necessary condition for convergent validity, but since significantly high correlations could be produced by methods variance, demand characteristics, or other extraneous factors, it is not a sufficient criterion. Thus, in addition to evidence for convergence, it is also necessary to examine discriminant validity. The first criterion for discriminant validity takes each validity diagonal correlation and compares its value to the adjacent row and column correlations in the corresponding heterotrait-heteromethod triangles. The idea here is that one expects two traits measured by two methods to be more highly correlated than each trait is with other traits measured by the same methods. The second criterion for discriminant validity takes each validity diagonal correlation and compares its value to the correlations obtained between each individual trait in the validity diagonal and the other traits when these are measured by the same method (i.e., in the adjacent heterotrait-monomethod triangles). Finally, the third criterion for discriminant validity claims that the pattern of correlations within all heterotrait triangles should be consistent. If, for example, the correlation between traits A and B as measured by method 1 is more highly correlated than that between traits B and

Table 5.2

Criteria for Convergent and Discriminant Validity in the Campbell and Fiske Multitrait Multimethod Matrix (three traits and three methods)

Convergent validity

Correlation Pattern	Criteria
(1) $r_{A_2A_1} > 0$ $r_{B_2B_1} > 0$ $r_{C_2C_1} > 0$ $r_{A_3A_2} > 0$ $r_{B_3B_2} > 0$ $r_{C_3C_2} > 0$ $r_{A_3A_1} > 0$ $r_{B_3B_1} > 0$ $r_{C_3C_1} > 0$	The correlations should be statistically significant, greater than zero, and "sufficiently large."

Discriminant validity

Correlation Pattern	Critera
(2) $r_{A_2A_1} > r_{A_2B_1}, r_{A_2C_1}, r_{B_2A_1}, r_{C_2A_1}$ $r_{B_2B_1} > r_{A_2B_1}, r_{C_2B_1}, r_{B_2A_1}, r_{B_2C_1}$ $r_{C_2C_1} > r_{A_2C_1}, r_{B_2C_1}, r_{C_2A_1}, r_{C_2B_1}$ $r_{A_2A_3} > r_{A_3B_2}, r_{A_3C_2}, r_{B_3A_2}, r_{C_3A_2}$ $r_{B_3B_2} > r_{A_3B_2}, r_{C_3B_2}, r_{B_3A_2}, r_{B_3C_2}$ $r_{C_3C_2} > r_{A_3C_2}, r_{B_3C_2}, r_{C_3A_2}, r_{C_3B_2}$ $r_{A_3A_1} > r_{A_3B_1}, r_{A_3C_1}, r_{B_3A_1}, r_{C_3A_1}$ $r_{B_3B_1} > r_{A_3B_1}, r_{C_3B_1}, r_{B_3A_1}, r_{B_3C_1}$ $r_{C_3C_1} > r_{A_3C1}, r_{B_3C_1}, r_{C_3A_1}, r_{C_3B_1}$	Differences in correlations should be in the proper direction and statistically significant.
(3) $r_{A_2A_1} > r_{B_1A_1}, r_{C_1A_1}, r_{B_2A_2}, r_{C_2A_2}$ $r_{B_2B_1} > r_{C_1B_1}, r_{B_1A_1}, r_{C_2B_2}, r_{B_2A_2}$ $r_{C_2C_1} > r_{C_1A_1}, r_{C_1B_1}, r_{C_2A_2}, r_{C_2B_2}$ $r_{A_3A_2} > r_{B_2A_2}, r_{C_2A_2}, r_{B_3A_3}, r_{C_3A_3}$ $r_{B_3B_2} > r_{C_2B_2}, r_{B_2A_2}, r_{B_3A_3}, r_{C_3B_3}$ $r_{C_3C_2} > r_{C_2B_2}, r_{C_2A_2}, r_{C_3A_3}, r_{C_3B_3}$ $r_{A_3A_1} > r_{B_1A_1}, r_{C_1A_1}, r_{B_3A_3}, r_{C_3A_3}$ $r_{B_3B_1} > r_{C_1B_1}, r_{B_1A_1}, r_{B_3A_3}, r_{C_3B_3}$ $r_{C_3C_1} > r_{C_1A_1}, r_{C_1B_1}, r_{C_3A_3}, r_{C_3B_3}$	Differences in correlations should be in the proper direction and statistically significant.
(4) Within all heterotrait triangles, the pattern of intertrait correlations should be repeated across triangles. For example, if $r_{B_1A_1} > r_{C_1A_1}$, then the following should also result: $r_{B_2A_1} > r_{C_2A_1}$, $r_{B_3A_1} > r_{C_3A_1}, r_{B_2A_2} > r_{C_2A_2}$, $r_{B_3A_2} > r_{C_3A_2}$, and $r_{B_3A_3} > r_{C_3A_3}$.	Differences in correlations should be in the proper direction and statistically significant

C and between A and C (also measured by method 1), similar patterns of ordinality should arise in the remaining eight correlational triangles.

It should be obvious that a considerable number of comparisons of correlations must be made in order to establish convergent and discriminant validity. If all of the criteria are satisfied in Table 5.2, then one may safely conclude that convergent and discriminant validity have been achieved. However, the procedure is not clear when, as often happens, some patterns of correlations do not satisfy the criteria while others do. In these instances, Campbell and Fiske (1959) suggest that a counting procedure be used where the number of exceptions to predicted patterns of correlations is determined and compared to that expected by chance. The authors state the procedure for the first criterion of discriminant validity as follows:

> If we take the validity value as fixed (ignoring its sampling fluctuations), then we can determine whether the number of values larger than it in its row and column is less than expected on the null hypothesis that half the values would be above it. This procedure requires the assumption that the position (above or below the validity value) of any of these comparison values is independent of the position of each of the others, a dubious assumption when common methods and trait variance are present [Campbell and Fiske, 1959, p. 98].

As will be demonstrated below through a re-analysis of data from two attitude studies (Ostrom, 1969; Kothandapani, 1971), the use of the above counting procedure is often arbitrary and can lead to erroneous conclusions. Further, the Campbell and Fiske (1959) procedures do not provide criteria for determining the degree to which operationalizations measure concepts, the amount of variance due to trait vs. method, or the adequacy of an entire MM matrix. The causal modeling and general linear model approaches described below can be used to achieve the above goals as well as the standard exploratory and confirmatory aspects of the MM matrix method.

The Causal Modeling Approach

Although the MM matrix model developed by Campbell and Fiske provides insights as to construct validity, a somewhat more intuitive and rigorous procedure has been suggested by Werts and Linn (1970), Althauser and Heberlein (1970), and Althauser et al. (1971). Building directly upon Campbell and Fiske (1959), these authors have attempted to pictorially represent construct validity as partitioned as trait, method, and error variance. Figure 5.3 illustrates a representative causal diagram for a system of three traits and three methods such as summarized in Table 5.1. In this diagram, the three traits are depicted as ξ_1, ξ_2, and ξ_3, while the three methods are shown as ξ_4, ξ_5, and ξ_6, respectively. Trait ξ_1 is shown operationalized by the three methods y_1, y_4, and x_1; and similar comments apply for traits ξ_2 and ξ_3. The relationships between

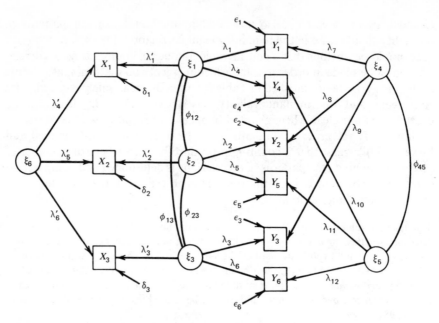

Figure 5.3. A causal diagram for a multitrait-multimethod matrix with three traits and three methods. *Note:* Curved line segments for the following covariances have been omitted from the diagram to simplify the presentation: ϕ_{14}, ϕ_{15}, ϕ_{16}, ϕ_{24}, ϕ_{25}, ϕ_{26}, ϕ_{34}, ϕ_{35}, ϕ_{36}, ϕ_{46}, ϕ_{56}.

traits and operationalizations are represented through the parameters λ_1–λ_6 and λ_1'–λ_3'. Similarly, the relative impact of each method on each operationalization is modeled through the respective parameters λ_7–λ_{12} and λ_4'–λ_6'. Error terms are shown as ε_1–ε_6 and δ_1–δ_3. These represent error in variables; that is, measurement error. The notation used in Figure 5.3 and the subsequent development is the same as introduced in Chapter 4. Although the notation for the general factor analysis approach is less confusing (cf., Bagozzi, 1978a), the present conventions are used in order to illustrate how the general linear model can be translated into a construct validity context.

As employed by Werts and Linn (1970) and Althauser and his colleagues (1970, 1971), the causal modeling approach for determining convergent and discriminant validity has been limited to the data analytic procedures associated with path analysis (e.g., Duncan, 1966). Briefly, path analysis uses multiple regression techniques to estimate parameters for each equation implied in Figure 5.3 (i.e., the parameters are λ_1–λ_{12}, λ_1'–λ_6', the nine variances for trait measures, and the variances and covariances among trait and method factors). Although useful information is provided by path analysis, it does not provide as much information nor lend itself to a full analysis of construct validity as the structural equation approach outlined in the previous chapter. Jöreskog's (e.g., 1971) procedures provide an efficient means for determining convergent and discriminant validity as illustrated below.

Using the conventions developed for structural equation models, the system of equations for Figure 5.3 may be written as follows (see Chapter 4):

$$\mathbf{B\eta} = \mathbf{\Gamma\xi} + \mathbf{\zeta} \tag{5.1}$$

with the parameter matrices defined to be

$$\mathbf{y} = \mathbf{\Lambda_y\eta} + \mathbf{\varepsilon} \tag{5.2}$$

$$
\begin{pmatrix} y_1 \\ y_2 \\ y_3 \\ y_4 \\ y_5 \\ y_6 \end{pmatrix} =
\begin{pmatrix}
\lambda_1 & 0 & 0 & \lambda_7 & 0 \\
0 & \lambda_2 & 0 & \lambda_8 & 0 \\
0 & 0 & \lambda_3 & \lambda_9 & 0 \\
\lambda_4 & 0 & 0 & 0 & \lambda_{10} \\
0 & \lambda_5 & 0 & 0 & \lambda_{11} \\
0 & 0 & \lambda_6 & 0 & \lambda_{12}
\end{pmatrix}
\begin{pmatrix} \eta_1 \\ \eta_2 \\ \eta_3 \\ \eta_4 \\ \eta_5 \end{pmatrix} +
\begin{pmatrix} \varepsilon_1 \\ \varepsilon_2 \\ \varepsilon_3 \\ \varepsilon_4 \\ \varepsilon_5 \\ \varepsilon_6 \end{pmatrix}
\tag{5.3}
$$

$$\mathbf{x} = \mathbf{\Lambda_x\xi} + \mathbf{\delta} \tag{5.4}$$

$$
\begin{pmatrix} x_1 \\ x_2 \\ x_3 \end{pmatrix} =
\begin{pmatrix}
\lambda'_1 & 0 & 0 & \lambda'_4 \\
0 & \lambda'_2 & 0 & \lambda'_5 \\
0 & 0 & \lambda'_3 & \lambda'_6
\end{pmatrix}
\begin{pmatrix} \xi_1 \\ \xi_2 \\ \xi_3 \\ \xi_6 \end{pmatrix} +
\begin{pmatrix} \delta_1 \\ \delta_2 \\ \delta_3 \end{pmatrix}
\tag{5.5}
$$

$$
\mathbf{\theta_\varepsilon^2} =
\begin{pmatrix}
\theta_{\varepsilon_1}^2 & & & & & \\
0 & \theta_{\varepsilon_2}^2 & & & & \\
0 & 0 & \theta_{\varepsilon_3}^2 & & & \\
0 & 0 & 0 & \theta_{\varepsilon_4}^2 & & \\
0 & 0 & 0 & 0 & \theta_{\varepsilon_5}^2 & \\
0 & 0 & 0 & 0 & 0 & \theta_{\varepsilon_6}^2
\end{pmatrix}
\tag{5.6}
$$

$$
\mathbf{\delta_\delta^2} =
\begin{pmatrix}
\theta_{\delta_1}^2 & & \\
0 & \theta_{\delta_2}^2 & \\
0 & 0 & \theta_{\delta_3}^2
\end{pmatrix}
\tag{5.7}
$$

$$
\mathbf{\Phi} =
\begin{pmatrix}
\phi_{11} & & & & & \\
\phi_{21} & \phi_{22} & & & & \\
\phi_{31} & \phi_{32} & \phi_{33} & & & \\
\phi_{41} & \phi_{42} & \phi_{43} & \phi_{44} & & \\
\phi_{51} & \phi_{52} & \phi_{53} & \phi_{54} & \phi_{55} & \\
\phi_{61} & \phi_{62} & \phi_{63} & \phi_{64} & \phi_{65} & \phi_{66}
\end{pmatrix}
\tag{5.8}
$$

$$\psi = 0 \tag{5.9}$$

$$B = I \tag{5.10}$$

$$\Gamma = I \tag{5.11}$$

$$\zeta = 0 \tag{5.12}$$

$$\eta \equiv \xi \tag{5.13}$$

Solution of the above equations using the procedures outlined in Chapter 4 allows the researcher to determine whether convergent and discriminant validity is achieved (using a maximum-likelihood ratio χ^2 test), the degree of measurement error, and the amount of trait and methods variance.

Some Illustrations Using the Attitude Construct as an Example

In order to illustrate the structural equation approach for determining convergent and discriminant validity, a series of reanalyses will be performed on the MM matrix data appearing in Ostrom (1969) and Kothandapani (1971). Each set of data nicely illustrates important facets of the procedures. For purposes of presentation, the methodology is divided into two phases: (1) analysis of congeneric and parallel forms and (2) analysis of discriminant validity and the partitioning of variance due to attitude components, measurement procedures, and error. For a somewhat different presentation and derivation of the general case where n traits are measured by m methods, see (Bagozzi 1978a).

Analysis of Congeneric and Parallel Forms

The first step for determining convergent and discriminant validity is to examine the model hypothesizing that traits are measured in a congeneric manner. To understand what is meant by congeneric measurements, consider the study conducted by Ostrom (1969). Ostrom measured the affective, behavioral, and cognitive components of people's attitudes toward the church using the methods of equal-appearing intervals (Thurstone), summated ratings (Likert), scalogram analysis (Guttman), and self-ratings (Guilford). The causal model for the three traits as measured by the four methods is shown in Figure 5.4 (omitting the methods factors). The structural equations for this system may be written as

$$B\eta = \Gamma\xi + \zeta \tag{5.14}$$

where

$$y = \Lambda_y\eta + \varepsilon \tag{5.15}$$

$$\begin{pmatrix} y_1 \\ y_2 \\ y_3 \\ y_4 \\ y_5 \\ y_6 \end{pmatrix} = \begin{pmatrix} \lambda_1 & 0 & 0 \\ 0 & \lambda_2 & 0 \\ 0 & 0 & \lambda_3 \\ \lambda_4 & 0 & 0 \\ 0 & \lambda_5 & 0 \\ 0 & 0 & \lambda_6 \end{pmatrix} \begin{pmatrix} \eta_1 \\ \eta_2 \\ \eta_3 \end{pmatrix} \begin{pmatrix} \varepsilon_1 \\ \varepsilon_2 \\ \varepsilon_3 \\ \varepsilon_4 \\ \varepsilon_5 \\ \varepsilon_6 \end{pmatrix} \tag{5.16}$$

$$\mathbf{x} = \mathbf{\Lambda}_x \mathbf{\xi} + \mathbf{\delta} \tag{5.17}$$

$$\begin{pmatrix} x_1 \\ x_2 \\ x_3 \\ x_4 \\ x_5 \\ x_6 \end{pmatrix} = \begin{pmatrix} \lambda_1' & 0 & 0 \\ 0 & \lambda_2' & 0 \\ 0 & 0 & \lambda_3' \\ \lambda_4' & 0 & 0 \\ 0 & \lambda_5' & 0 \\ 0 & 0 & \lambda_6' \end{pmatrix} \begin{pmatrix} \xi_1 \\ \xi_2 \\ \xi_3 \end{pmatrix} + \begin{pmatrix} \delta_1 \\ \delta_2 \\ \delta_3 \\ \delta_4 \\ \delta_5 \\ \delta_6 \end{pmatrix} \tag{5.18}$$

$$\mathbf{\theta}_\varepsilon^2 = \begin{pmatrix} \theta_{\varepsilon_1}^2 & & & & & \\ 0 & \theta_{\varepsilon_2}^2 & & & & \\ 0 & 0 & \theta_{\varepsilon_3}^2 & & & \\ 0 & 0 & 0 & \theta_{\varepsilon_4}^2 & & \\ 0 & 0 & 0 & 0 & \theta_{\varepsilon_5}^2 & \\ 0 & 0 & 0 & 0 & 0 & \theta_{\varepsilon_6}^2 \end{pmatrix} \tag{5.19}$$

$$\mathbf{\theta}_\delta^2 = \begin{pmatrix} \theta_{\delta_1}^2 & & & & & \\ 0 & \theta_{\delta_2}^2 & & & & \\ 0 & 0 & \theta_{\delta_3}^2 & & & \\ 0 & 0 & 0 & \theta_{\delta_4}^2 & & \\ 0 & 0 & 0 & 0 & \theta_{\delta_q}^2 & \\ 0 & 0 & 0 & 0 & 0 & \theta_{\delta_6}^2 \end{pmatrix} \tag{5.20}$$

$$\mathbf{\Phi} = \begin{pmatrix} \phi_{11} & & \\ \phi_{21} & \phi_{22} & \\ \phi_{31} & \phi_{32} & \phi_{33} \end{pmatrix} \tag{5.21}$$

$$\mathbf{\psi} = \mathbf{0} \tag{5.22}$$

$$\mathbf{B} = \mathbf{I} \tag{5.23}$$

$$\mathbf{\Gamma} = \mathbf{I} \tag{5.24}$$

$$\mathbf{\zeta} = \mathbf{0} \tag{5.25}$$

$$\mathbf{\eta} \equiv \mathbf{\xi} \tag{5.26}$$

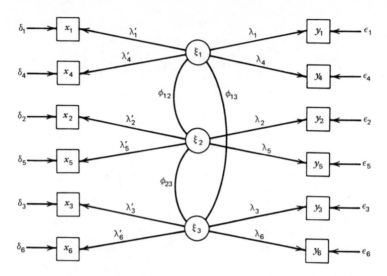

Figure 5.4. A causal model for three traits measured with four methods (methods factors omitted).

The above system of equations represents the variance due to the attitude components and measurement error alone. Before the concepts of congeneric measures can be defined and hypothesis tests derived, it is necessary first to consider the following four "working" hypotheses applied to Figure 5.4:

$$H_1: \quad = \lambda_1 = \lambda_4 = \lambda_1' = \lambda_4', \quad \lambda_2 = \lambda_5 = \lambda_2' = \lambda_5',$$

$$\lambda_3 = \lambda_6 = \lambda_3' = \lambda_6'$$

$$\theta_{\varepsilon_1}^2 = \theta_{\varepsilon_4}^2 = \theta_{\delta_1}^2 = \theta_{\delta_4}^2, \quad \theta_{\varepsilon_2}^2 = \theta_{\varepsilon_5}^2 = \theta_{\delta_2}^2 = \theta_{\delta_5}^2,$$

$$\theta_{\varepsilon_3}^2 = \theta_{\varepsilon_6}^2 = \theta_{\delta_3}^2 = \theta_{\delta_6}^2, \quad \phi_{12} = \phi_{23} = \phi_{13} = 1$$

$$H_2: \quad = \lambda_1 = \lambda_4 = \lambda_1' = \lambda_4', \quad \lambda_2 = \lambda_5 = \lambda_2' = \lambda_5',$$

$$\lambda_3 = \lambda_6 = \lambda_3' = \lambda_6'; \quad \theta_{\varepsilon_1}^2 = \theta_{\varepsilon_4}^2 = \theta_{\delta_1}^2 = \theta_{\delta_4}^2,$$

$$\theta_{\varepsilon_2}^2 = \theta_{\varepsilon_5}^2 = \theta_{\delta_2}^2 = \theta_{\delta_5}^2, \quad \theta_{\varepsilon_3}^2 = \theta_{\varepsilon_6}^2 = \theta_{\delta_3}^2 = \theta_{\delta_6}^2$$

$$H_3: \quad \phi_{12} = \phi_{23} = \phi_{13} = 1$$

$$H_4: \quad \Sigma \text{ is of the form of Eq. (4.14') with}$$

$$\lambda_1 - \lambda_6, \quad \lambda_1' - \lambda_6', \quad \theta_{\varepsilon_1}^2 - \theta_{\varepsilon_6}^2, \quad \theta_{\delta_1}^2 - \theta_{\delta_6}^2,$$

$$\phi_{12}, \quad \phi_{23}, \quad \text{and} \quad \phi_{13} \text{ unconstrained}$$

The fourth hypothesis, H_4, is the test of the model of Figure 5.4 versus the most general hypothesis that the variance-covariance matrix Σ is any positive-definite matrix. Hypotheses H_1, H_2, and H_3 are not of interest, per se, but rather are used along with H_4 to form the following two sets of hypotheses:

$$H_5:$$
$$H'_5 = H_1 - H_2$$
$$H''_5 = H_3 - H_4$$

$$H_6:$$
$$H'_6 = H_1 - H_3$$
$$H''_6 = H_2 - H_4$$

Hypothesis H_5 tests the hypotheses that $\phi_{12} = \phi_{23} = \phi_{13} = 1$; that is, that the traits are correlated unity. This is termed the test for congeneric measurements in the literature. It is a test of whether the four measurements of each of three components of attitude are measuring the same underlying construct, attitudes. Hypothesis H_6 (i.e., the test for parallel forms) examines the hypothesis that

$$\lambda_1 = \lambda_4 = \lambda'_1 = \lambda'_4, \quad \lambda_2 = \lambda_5 = \lambda'_2 = \lambda'_5, \quad \lambda_3 = \lambda_6 = \lambda'_3 = \lambda'_6$$

$$\theta^2_{\varepsilon_1} = \theta^2_{\varepsilon_4} = \theta^2_{\delta_1} = \theta^2_{\delta_4}, \quad \theta^2_{\varepsilon_2} = \theta^2_{\varepsilon_5} = \theta^2_{\delta_2} = \theta^2_{\delta_5},$$

and

$$\theta^2_{\varepsilon_3} = \theta^2_{\varepsilon_6} = \theta^2_{\delta_3} = \theta^2_{\delta_6}$$

that is, that the respective operationalizations are measured with equal reliability and have equal variances in the error term. As Jöreskog (1971, p. 113) notes,

Parallel tests have equal true score variances ... [and] can be used interchangeably. They have equal reliabilities and equal validities in predicting a given criterion and the most reliable composite is a simple sum.

The failure to reject H_5 suggests that the three components of attitude—ξ_1, ξ_2, and ξ_3—measured by the four methods, can be considered aspects of the same underlying concept, attitudes. The failure to reject H_6 suggests that the four measurements of the three components of attitude can be considered to be parallel measures as defined above. This outcome establishes that each component is unidimensional given the four measurements and considerations noted above. The degree to which the components covary can be determined from the Φ matrix. Should one reject either hypothesis H_5 or H_6, methods variance may be added to the model in order to see if this accounts for the poor fit (this step is discussed below). Because H_6 is not often a very realistic hypothesis, only the test for congeneric measurements will be examined in the illustration to follow.

The above analysis was performed on the data of Ostrom (1969). Table 5.3 presents the multitrait-multimethod matrix of correlations for Ostrom's data

Table 5.3
Multitrait-Multimethod Matrix of Correlations from Ostrom (1969)

		Thurstone			Likert			Guttman			Self-rating		
		A	B	C	A	B	C	A	B	C	A	B	C
T	A	—											
	B	57	—										
	C	63	62	—									
L	A	71	59	68	—								
	B	67	67	71	79	—							
	C	69	62	72	79	81	—						
G	A	54	39	49	58	51	56	—					
	B	59	61	58	60	69	60	43	—				
	C	63	50	63	69	67	71	49	56	—			
SR	A	65	63	69	72	73	72	54	66	65	—		
	B	61	51	56	62	68	64	53	52	56	76	—	
	C	56	48	60	63	66	66	46	48	62	77	68	—

The decimal point of each correlation has been omitted. N = 189, A = affective, B = behavioral, C = cognitive.

where it can be seen that—given the criteria set forth by Campbell and Fiske (1959)—convergent validity must be acknowledged. Convergent validity can be more rigorously ascertained using the structural equation methodology developed by Jöreskog, however. The results for $H_1 - H_5$ are shown in Table 5.4. First, note that none of the hypotheses in the left-hand portion of the table (H_1-H_4) individually indicates a satisfactory fit. This is indicated by the χ^2 tests and p values. Since each of these hypotheses is sensitive to sample size

Table 5.4
Congeneric Hypotheses for Ostrom's (1969) MM Matrix Data (four methods)

Hypothesis	No. of Parameters	χ^2	d.f.	p	Test of Hypotheses		
H_1	6	255.80	72	0.00	$\phi_{12} = \phi_{23} =$	$\chi^2_{72} = 255.80$	$\chi^2_{54} = 141.15$
H_2	9	250.12	69	0.00	$\phi_{13} = 1$		
H_3	24	141.15	54	0.00	$\phi_{12} \neq 1$		
H_4	27	135.48	51	0.00	$\phi_{23} \neq 1$	$\chi^2_{69} = 250.12$	$\chi^2_{51} = 135.48$
					$\phi_{13} \neq 1$		
					$H_5 \begin{cases} \chi^2_3 = 5.68 \\ p \cong 0.10 \end{cases}$	$\chi^2_3 = 5.67$	
						$p \cong 0.10$	

Table 5.5
Residual Matrix for Ostrom (1969)(four methods)

000											
−012	000										
−003	−057	000									
−029	028	014	000								
025	−012	−009	−021	000							
004	003	−007	−022	−034	000						
−048	056	011	−036	046	−006	000					
−020	−070	−005	031	−018	036	025	000				
−018	050	000	−012	015	−014	−001	001	000			
023	−019	−004	025	031	039	−002	−037	020	000		
−021	048	034	031	014	017	−060	049	020	−116	000	
040	059	017	034	011	022	020	070	−017	−113	−112	000

The decimal point in each residual has been omitted.

through the χ^2 test, however, it is more interesting to observe the difference in χ^2 tests afforded by H_5 (see discussion in Chapter 4 with respect to hypothesis testing). Looking at these hypotheses, we find that H'_5 yields a $\chi^2 = 5.68$ with 3 d.f. ($p \simeq 0.10$) and H''_5 produces a $\chi^2 = 5.67$ with 3 d.f. ($p \simeq 0.10$). In general, these are borderline fits, and judgment as to the achievement of construct validity or not must be temporarily withheld.

Given the above mixed results, the question then arises as to the reasons for the borderline fit.[8] An examination of the residuals $(S - \Sigma)$ for hypothesis H_4 may be enlightening in this context. Table 5.5 presents the residuals for H_4 where it should be noted that the discrepancies between actual and predicted variances and covariances are relatively low except for the measurements of the affective, behavioral, and cognitive components performed by the Guilford (self-rating) procedure (underlined in the table). This provides indirect evidence that the self-rating method perhaps contains an excessive amount of error and might be omitted from further analyses.[9]

Based on the above findings, the self-rating scale data were dropped, and a re-analysis was performed using only the Thurstone, Likert, and Guttman methods. Table 5.6 summarizes the congeneric and parallel forms tests for this reanalysis. An inspection of this hypothesis indicates that one must reject the tests for congeneric measurements. Specifically, for H_5, H'_5, and H''_5 yield, respectively, $\chi^2 = 16.37$ with 3 d.f. ($p \simeq 0.001$) and $\chi^2 = 16.37$ with 3 d.f. ($p \simeq 0.001$). Thus, rejection of H_5 indicates that some other nonrandom factors may be causing variation in the attitude responses. The next section develops the procedures for determining whether methods variance accounts for the lack of fit obtained for the congeneric and parallel forms tests. Finally, it should be noted that one cannot reject the model hypothesizing that the three

Table 5.6

Ostrom's (1969) MM Matrix Data Tested for Congeneric Hypotheses—Thurstone, Likert, and Guttman Methods Only

Hypothesis	No. of Parameters	χ^2	d.f.	p	Tests of Hypotheses		
H_1	6	142.56	39	0.00	$\phi_{12} = \phi_{23} =$	$\chi^2_{39} = 142.56$	$\chi^2_{27} = 43.45$
H_2	9	126.09	36	0.00	$\phi_{13} = 1$		
H_3	18	43.45	27	0.02	$\phi_{12} \neq 1$		
H_4	21	27.08	24	0.30	$\phi_{23} \neq 1$	$\chi^2_{36} = 126.09$	$\chi^2_{24} = 27.08$
					$\phi_{13} \neq 1$		
					$H_5 \begin{cases} \chi^2_3 = 16.47 \\ p \cong 0.001 \end{cases}$		$\begin{matrix} \chi^2_3 = 16.37 \\ p \cong 0.001 \end{matrix}$

components of attitude as measured by the Thurstone, Likert, and Guttman scales adequately represent the structure of attitudinal responses. This hypothesis is shown as H_4 in Table 5.6 (i.e., $\chi^2 = 27.08$ with 24 d.f. and $p \simeq 0.30$), and it is similar to the model of Figure 5.4 except that three operationalizations (say x_4, x_5, and x_6) should be omitted. The finding for H_4 provides evidence for convergent validity.

Analysis of Discriminant Validity and the Partitioning of Variance Due to Trait, Method, and Error

Given that one has rejected the hypotheses that the measurements of each trait (component) are congeneric, the next stage should introduce methods factors as shown in Figure 5.3.[10] The structural equations for this model are Eqs. (5.1)–(5.13). Solution of these equations using the methods of Chapter 4, yields a goodness-of-fit $\chi^2 = 5.03$ with 12 d.f. ($p = 0.96$), which represents a very good fit. However, an examination of the maximum likelihood estimates reveals that the methods factor due to the Guttman measure correlates nearly unity with the other measures. Since this indicates that the methods are collinear, only two methods factors were modeled. This produced a model with a goodness-of-fit $\chi^2 = 10.16$ with 14 d.f. ($p = 0.75$), which is also a good fit. Table 5.7 presents the residuals for this analysis providing further confirmation of the adequacy of the model. Thus, one may conclude that convergent and discriminant validity have been achieved for the data of Ostrom (1969) when the analysis is confined to the Thurstone, Likert, and Guttman methods for measuring the affective,

Table 5.7
Residuals for the Data of Ostrom (1969) with Three Methods and Two Methods Factors

000								
001	001							
016	−040	001						
006	−008	008	001					
000	005	−012	−003	001				
−002	−013	003	005	000	001			
−012	040	007	−011	029	−011	000		
−010	006	008	−007	−002	019	022	002	
−024	038	003	−013	019	−003	010	007	001

The decimal point in each residual has been omitted.

behavioral, and cognitive components of attitude. The principle advantage of using the structural equation approach versus the Campbell and Fiske (1959) procedures is that the former, unlike the latter, provides explicit, objective measures for accepting or rejecting convergent and discriminant validity.

Another advantage of the structural equation approach lies in its ability to determine the amount of variance due to trait, method, and error in any multi-trait-multimethod matrix. These variances may be determined as follows. Table 5.8 presents the maximum likelihood estimates of parameters for the model described above consisting of three attitude components (ξ_1, ξ_2, ξ_3) and two methods factors (ξ_4, ξ_5). The entries under the ξ columns express the estimates for the λ's and λ''s. The final column presents parameter estimates for the θ's and δ's, that is, the error in variables terms. Squaring the error terms yields the amount of error variance for each measurement of each attitude component. Similarly, the square of the appropriate λ's and λ''s produces the amount of variance due to each attitude component. Finally, the square of the appropriate λ's and λ''s for the methods factors yields the amount of variance due to each method.

Performing the above operations leads to the partitioning of the total variance due to trait, method, and error as shown in Table 5.9. A number of findings in this table deserve mention. First, note that affect is measured best by the Thurstone method and worst by the Guttman scale. A similar conclusion can be reached for the cognitive component but not to the same extent. The behavioral component is measured relatively uniformly by all three methods. Based on the amount of variance shown for each attitude component, however, one must conclude that all methods produce only moderately valid measurements. Second, note that the Likert scale contains a considerable amount of methods variance relative to the other procedures. Perhaps the Likert scale introduces response sets, demand characteristics, or other confounds into the measurement

Table 5.8
**Maximum Liklihood Estimates of Parameters for the Data of Ostrom (1969)
with Three Methods (Thurstone, Likert, and Guttman) and Two Methods
Factors**

	Trait Factors			Methods Factors		Error
	ξ_1	ξ_2	ξ_3	ξ_4	ξ_5	$\theta \& \delta$
Thurstone						
Affect A_1	0.76	0	0	0.35	0	0.55
Behavior B_1	0	0.73	0	0.28	0	0.63
Cognition C_1	0	0.71	0.71	0.40	0	0.58
Likert						
Affect A_2	0.66	0	0	0.62	0	0.43
Behavior B_2	0	0.68	0	0.65	0	0.34
Cognition C_2	0	0	0.66	0.62	0	0.42
Guttman						
Affect A_3	0.53	0	0	0	0.38	0.76
Behavior B_3	0	0.74	0	0	0.31	0.60
Cognition C_3	0	0	0.62	0	0.51	0.60

task. Finally, note that the Guttman scale and, to a somewhat lesser extent, the
Thurstone scale, show relatively high error components. The Likert method
exhibits relatively small error variance. In general, based on these findings, it
appears that the Thurstone procedure provides more valid measures.

Some Further Analyses

The analysis of the model in the previous section yielded two methods factors
that were highly correlated (i.e., $r = 0.94$). In order to test whether the two
methods factors are indeed different, one may use the hierarchical hypothesis
testing procedures outlined in Chapter 4. The appropriate test is whether
$\phi_{45} = 1$ or not. Performing this test produced the following χ^2 values for the
constrained and unconstrained models: $\chi^2 = 5.57$ with 9 d.f. and $\chi^2 = 2.75$
with 8 d.f. Since the difference between these values produces a $\chi^2 = 2.82$ with
1 d.f., which is significant beyond the 0.10 level, one may not reject the hypothesis
that the two methods factors are equivalent.

The entire set of procedures performed above for determining convergent and
discriminant validity of the data of Ostrom (1969) was repeated for the data of
Kothandapani (1971). The reanalysis of Kothandapani's data illustrates some

Table 5.9
Partitioning of Variance due to Attitude Component, Method, and Error for the Data of Ostrom (1969)—Three Methods and Two Methods Factors

	Variance Components		
	Attitude Component	Method	Error
Thurstone			
Affective	0.58	0.12	0.30
Behavioral	0.53	0.08	0.39
Cognitive	0.51	0.16	0.33
Likert			
Affective	0.43	0.39	0.18
Behavioral	0.47	0.42	0.12
Cognitive	0.44	0.39	0.17
Guttman			
Affective	0.28	0.14	0.57
Behavioral	0.54	0.09	0.37
Cognitive	0.38	0.26	0.36

features of the structural equation procedures not fully apparent in the earlier analysis. Kothandapani (1971) followed essentially the same procedures as Ostrom for ascertaining construct validity except that the attitude object was birth control. Table 5.10 presents the multitrait-multimethod data from Kothandapani (1971). Notice first that the validity diagonals show statistically significant values but that, in general, the correlations are considerably lower than that found by Ostrom. Perhaps more disconcerting, however, is the data relevant to discriminant validity. Taking the second criterion for discriminant validity as an example, one finds that at least 34 comparisons of values in the validity diagonal with the appropriate heterotrait-monomethod triangle values are in the improper direction.[11] Using the counting procedure discussed earlier, Kothandapani (1971, p. 329) concluded that the Thurstone and Guttman methods satisfied this criterion of discriminant validity, while the Likert and Guilford methods did not. The author also concluded, based in part on exploratory factor analyses, that the affective, behavioral, and cognitive components of attitude were distinct.

Using the more rigorous structural equation methodology leads one to question the conclusions made by the author, however. Table 5.11 presents the

Table 5.10

Multitrait-Multimethod Matrix of Correlations from Kothandapani (1971)

		Thurstone			Likert			Guttman			Guilford		
		A	C	B	A	C	B	A	C	B	A	C	B
T	A	—											
	C	26	—										
	B	19	43	—									
L	A	58	34	05	—								
	C	20	50	22	66								
	B	−03	08	49	31	65	—						
G	A	49	06	−06	60	20	04	—					
	C	20	28	09	41	44	24	48	—				
	B	18	−05	42	05	07	47	28	32	—			
SR	A	45	20	12	59	41	31	50	30	13	—		
	C	25	39	32	31	51	39	13	35	13	65	—	
	B	17	12	49	15	34	60	14	24	50	55	61	—

The decimal point of each correlation has been omitted. N = 100. A = affective, B = behavioral, C = cognitive.

Table 5.11

Congeneric Hypotheses for Kothandapani's (1971) Data(four methods)

Hypothesis	No. of Parameters	χ^2	d.f.	p		Tests of Hypotheses
H_1	6	992.71	72	0.00	$\phi_{12} = \phi_{23} =$	$\chi^2_{72} = 992.71 \quad \chi^2_{54} = 489.87$
H_2	9	775.54	69	0.00	$\phi_{13} = 1$	
H_3	24	489.87	54	0.00	$\phi_{12} \neq 1$ $\phi_{23} \neq 1$ $\phi_{13} \neq 1$	$\chi^2_{69} = 775.54 \quad \chi^2_{51} = 367.25$
H_4	27	367.25	51	0.00		
					H_5	$\chi^2_3 = 217.17 \quad \chi^2_3 = 122.62$ $p = 0.00 \qquad p = 0.00$

results of the congeneric hypotheses where it can be seen that both must be rejected based on the χ^2 values. Notice that the χ^2 values are much higher than those found for the data of Ostrom even though the sample size for the latter is greater (see Table 5.4). The poorer fit of the Kothandapani (1971) data is perhaps more evident when one compares the residuals (Table 5.12) with that obtained for the Ostrom (1969) data (Table 5.5). Notice that a considerable

Table 5.12
Residual Matrix for Kothandapani (1971)(four methods)

000											
−063	000										
−097	−260	000									
000	−001	110	000								
183	−008	115	001	000							
202	240	012	−013	−027	000						
−142	143	156	000	197	138	000					
−020	−050	067	−100	009	052	−294	000				
−093	212	−166	100	245	002	−190	−172	000			
−108	000	−026	000	−020	−135	−146	−117	−041	000		
−043	−124	−139	047	008	−053	084	−107	040	−439	000	
−057	090	−161	045	069	012	−023	−048	−191	−435	−389	000

The decimal in each residual has been omitted.

number of residuals in the former analysis are greater than 0.100 while only three residuals were large in the latter. The measurements of the affective, behavioral, and cognitive components by the Guilford method are especially errorful for the Kothandapani data (i.e., values −0.493, −0.435, and −0.389 in Table 5.12).

For purposes of comparison with the analysis performed on the data of Ostrom (1969), the self-rating method was omitted from Kothandapani's (1971) data, and the congeneric and parallel forms hypotheses were tested. These findings are shown in Table 5.13. Based on the χ^2 values in the table, one must

Table 5.13
Congeneric Hypotheses for Kothandapani's (1971) MM Data—Thurstone, Likert, and Guttman Methods Only

Hypothesis	No. of Parameters	χ^2	d.f.	p	Tests of Hypotheses
H_1	6	660.16	39	0.00	$\phi_{12} = \phi_{23} =$ $\quad \chi^2_{39} = 660.16 \quad \chi^2_{27} = 319.60$
H_2	9	524.05	36	0.00	$\phi_{13} = 1$
H_3	18	319.60	27	0.00	$\phi_{12} \neq 1$
H_4	21	202.97	24	0.00	$\left. \begin{array}{l} \phi_{23} \neq 1 \\ \phi_{13} \neq 1 \end{array} \right\} \quad \chi^2_{36} = 524.05 \quad \chi^2_{24} = 202.97$
					$H_5 \left\{ \begin{array}{ll} \chi^2_3 = 136.11 & \chi^2_3 = 116.63 \\ p = 0.00 & p = 0.00 \end{array} \right.$

Table 5.14
Residuals for Data of Kothandapani (1971) with Three Methods and Three Method Factors

005								
079	−047							
−051	012	058						
075	049	029	098					
106	−011	−025	083	027				
061	064	048	093	032	039			
−077	125	−015	026	126	042	−026		
−002	−002	−106	−068	−007	−099	021	052	
−189	099	012	−011	070	031	−072	−039	−041

The decimal point in each residual has been omitted.

reject the hypotheses that the measurements are congeneric. Notice that the χ^2 values in Table 5.13 are considerably greater than those found for Ostrom's data in Table 5.6. Next, three methods factors were introduced into the analysis of the data of Kothandapani in order to test the model of Figure 5.3. The results produce a goodness-of-fit $\chi^2 = 24.20$ with 12 d.f. ($p \simeq 0.02$). One must, therefore, reject the model. Table 5.14 presents the residuals for this model where it can be seen that five residuals exceed 0.100 (compare Table 5.14 to Table 5.7). In general, then, one must conclude that discriminant validity was not achieved for the data of Kothandapani (1971) and that the degree of convergent validity was weak.

Although the data of Kothandapani (1971) failed to confirm the validity of the attitude construct, it is interesting to observe the pattern of partioned variance due to attitude component, method, and error and compare the results to that found for the data of Ostrom (1969).[12] As shown in Table 5.15, the affective component is best measured by the Likert method and least effectively measured by the Guttman method. Again, the Likert method contains a considerable amount of methods variance, while the other procedures produce only somewhat less. On the other hand, the Likert scale shows very little error variance. The other procedures contain relatively high amounts of error.

Nomological Validity

As an example of nomological validity in the context of attitude theory, consider the recent study performed by Bagozzi and Burnkrant (1978). Using data from an investigation conducted by Fishbein and Ajzen (1974), Bagozzi and

Table 5.15

Partitioning of Variance due to Attitude Component, Method and Error for the Data of Kothandapani (1971)—Three Methods and Three Method Factors

	Variance Component[a]		
	Attitude Component	Method	Error
Thurstone			
Affective	0.48	0.03	0.50
Behavioral	0.45	0.60	0.00
Cognitive	0.39	0.22	0.35
Likert			
Affective	0.86	0.24	0.00
Behavioral	0.38	0.66	0.00
Cognitive	0.46	0.56	0.01
Guttman			
Affective	0.39	0.29	0.29
Behavioral	0.52	0.14	0.30
Cognitive	0.28	0.31	0.46

[a] The fractions do not total to 1.00 since the data failed to confirm the hypotheses of convergent and discriminant validity.

Burnkrant (1978) examined the ability of the affective and cognitive components of attitude for predicting behavioral intention and self-report behaviors. Two samples of respondents were obtained. In the first, 62 male and female undergraduates indicated which items from a set of 100 religious behaviors they had performed (the self-reported behaviors sample). The second sample was composed of 63 male and female undergraduates who indicated which items from a set of 100 religious behaviors they would perform (the behavioral intentions sample). In addition, all subjects completed five scales measuring attitudes toward religion: Guilford self-rating, semantic differential, and three religious scales. The first two scales measure the affective component, while the last three measure the cognitive component. Table 5.16 presents the product-moment correlations for both data sets.

Figure 5.5 presents the general model for testing nomological validity in the present context where A represents the attitude component (either affect or cognitions), and B stands for the scaled behavior criteria (either self-reported

Table 5.16

Product-Moment Correlations for Attitude Scales and Scaled Behavioral Criteria[a]

	1	2	3	4	5	6	7
Self-report (1)	1.000	0.800	0.519	0.652	0.584	0.451	0.582
Semantic Differential (2)	0.765	1.000	0.644	0.762	0.685	0.591	0.688
Religiosity #1 (3)	0.688	0.773	1.000	0.790	0.744	0.531	0.647
Religiosity #2 (4)	0.743	0.837	0.878	1.000	0.785	0.660	0.656
Religiosity #3 (5)	0.672	0.666	0.818	0.786	1.000	0.575	0.624
Scaled Behavior #1 (6)	0.444	0.517	0.501	0.563	0.483	1.000	0.776
Scaled Behavior #2 (7)	0.594	0.640	0.656	0.727	0.649	0.851	1.000

[a] Above diagonal for respondents indicating self-reported behaviors ($n = 62$); Below diagonal for respondents indicating behavior intentions ($n = 63$).

behaviors or behavioral intentions). The equations for this model can be written as

$$B = \gamma A + \zeta$$

$$\begin{pmatrix} y_1 \\ y_2 \\ y_3 \end{pmatrix} = \begin{pmatrix} \alpha_1 \\ \alpha_2 \\ \alpha_3 \end{pmatrix} A + \begin{pmatrix} \delta_1 \\ \delta_2 \\ \delta_3 \end{pmatrix}$$

$$\begin{pmatrix} y_4 \\ y_5 \end{pmatrix} = \begin{pmatrix} \lambda_1 \\ \lambda_2 \end{pmatrix} B + \begin{pmatrix} \varepsilon_1 \\ \varepsilon_2 \end{pmatrix}$$

where the dotted lines in the second equation are used to indicate that there are two measures for affect and three measures for cognitions.

The hypothesis implied by Figure 5.5 is that attitudes toward religion (as measured by the affective and cognitive scales) should predict self-reported religious behaviors and religious behavioral intentions. Acceptance of this hypothesis would provide evidence for nomological validity of the attitude constructs. However, based on past findings in marketing, one might question the predictive validity of the attitude-behavior relationship. Early research in consumer behavior typically employed a general attitude (e.g., attitude toward a product class) to predict the specific behavior of purchase or purchase predisposition (e.g., Hansen, 1969; Day, 1970; Hughes and Guerrero, 1971; Cohen and Ahtola, 1971). The weak relationships frequently obtained in this work might be attributable, in part, to a lack of correspondence between attitudinal predictors and behavioral criteria. Fishbein maintains (cf., Ajzen and Fishbein, 1977) that a strong relationship should be expected between attitude and behavior only when these two variables are measured at an equivalent level of specificity with respect to the action, target, context, and/or time at which the

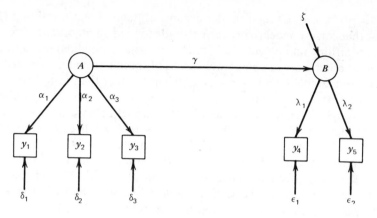

Figure 5.5. A causal diagram representing the relationship between attitudes and scaled measures of self-reported behaviors and behavioral intentions.

Table 5.17
Goodness-of-fit Tests and Parameter Estimates for Nomological Validity Models Relating Affect to Behavior

Parameter	Self-reported Behaviors G&L	Behavioral Intentions G&L
α_1	0.816	0.843
α_2	0.980	0.908
λ_1	0.813	0.851
λ_2	0.954	1.000
γ	0.737	0.705
θ_{δ_1}	0.578	0.539
θ_{δ_2}	0.197	0.419
θ_{ε_1}	0.582	0.525
θ_{ε_2}	0.300	0.000
ψ	0.458	0.503
Tests of Model	$\chi^2 = 1.01$ d.f. $= 1$ $p \doteq 0.32$	$\chi^2 = 1.38$ d.f. $= 1$ $p \simeq 0.24$

action is performed. Using a similar argument, Bagozzi and Burnkrant (1978) suggest that correspondence between attitude toward an object and behavioral criteria regarding that object will be high only when attitudinal predictors and behavioral criteria are at comparable levels of specificity and are derived from roughly comparable scaling procedures. Hence, rather than using attitudes to predict arbitrary single-act or multiple-act criterion behaviors, it is hypothesized that nomological validity will obtain best for scaled behavioral measures. The tests conducted below reflect this hypothesis (for a full description of the rationale and results, see Bagozzi and Burnkrant, 1978, 1979).

The model of Figure 5.5 was applied to the data of Table 5.16. Looking first at the relation between the affective component of attitude and the scaled behavior measures, it can be seen in Table 5.17 that nomological validity is established for both the self-reported behaviors ($\chi^2 = 1.01$, d.f. $= 1$, $p \simeq 0.32$) and behavioral intentions samples ($\chi^2 = 1.38$, d.f. $= 1$, $p \simeq 0.24$). Looking next at the relation between the cognitive component of attitude and the scaled behavior measures, it can be seen in Table 5.18 that nomological validity is again established for both the self-reported behaviors ($\chi^2 = 5.38$, d.f. $= 4$, $p \simeq 0.25$) and behavioral intentions samples ($\chi^2 = 6.35$, d.f. $= 4$, $p \simeq 0.17$). Notice further

Table 5.18
Goodness-of-fit Tests and Parameter Esti-
mates for Nomological Validity Models
Relating Cognitions to Behavior

Parameter	Self-reported Behaviors G&L	Behavioral Intentions G&L
α_1	0.861	0.935
α_2	0.918	0.938
α_3	0.857	0.857
λ_1	0.852	0.851
λ_2	0.911	1.000
γ	0.798	0.742
θ_{δ_1}	0.508	0.355
θ_{δ_2}	0.396	0.346
θ_{δ_3}	0.515	0.515
θ_{ε_1}	0.524	0.525
θ_{ε_2}	0.412	0.000
ψ	0.363	0.449
Tests of Model	$\chi^2 = 5.38$ d.f. $= 4$ $p \simeq 0.25$	$\chi^2 = 6.35$ d.f. $= 4$ $p \simeq 0.17$

that the value of the standardized parameter, γ, relating attitudes to behavior is large in each instance (γ ranges from 0.705 to 0.798).

In sum, evidence is provided for the nomological validity of the affective and cognitive components of attitude when relevant scaled behavior measures are used as criteria. For further analyses and issues related to the validity of the attitude construct, the reader is referred elsewhere (Bagozzi, 1978a; Bagozzi and Burnkrant, 1978, 1979; and Bagozzi, Tybout, Craig and Sternthal, 1979).

Interpretational Confounding

Theoretical concepts, as we have seen, achieve their meaning in a variety of ways. The internal consistency of the language used to represent a concept provides it with a portion of its meaning as does the relationship between the concept and its operationalization(s). Information about the internal consistency of operationalizations and the convergent and discriminant validity of measures also is helpful in determining the meaning of a concept. Finally, nomological validity broadens a concept's meaning to include its role in an overall theoretical structure. Burt (1973, 1976) has approached the problem of the meaning of unobservable variables by examining certain structural equation models. More specifically, he analyses theoretical terms through the mechanisms whereby meaning is assigned to them empirically. The author identifies the general problem of ascertaining the meaning of theoretical variables as "interpretational confounding." Interpretational confounding "occurs as the assignment of empirical meaning to an unobservable variable which is other than the meaning assigned to it by an individual a priori to estimating unknown parameters" (Burt, 1976, p. 4). The discussion below treats interpretational confounding and other issues as they relate to construct validity.

The Two-Concept Theoretical Structure

In order to provide a background for understanding interpretational confounding, consider the simple case consisting of one theoretical concept related causally to a second where both are operationalized with two measures (see Figure 5.6). If the diagram in Figure 5.6 represents one's true theoretical structure, then one would like the parameters reflecting the relationships between (1) the first theoretical variable ξ and its operationalizations x_1 and x_2 (represented as λ_1' and λ_2') and (2) the second theoretical variable η and its operationalizations y_1 and y_2 (represented as λ_1 and λ_2) to be entirely a function of the correspondence between the appropriate theoretical concept and its measures. Under certain circumstances, however, the estimation of λ_1' and λ_2' on the one hand, and λ_1 and λ_2 on the other, will not only be dependent on their respective

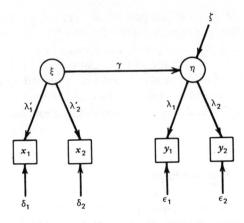

Figure 5.6. A two-concept theoretical structure—each concept operationalized with two
measures.

communalities (due to the theoretical concepts to which they relate) but these
parameter estimates may also be influenced by the pattern of covariation among
all observable variables in the model.

Figure 5.7, which is adapted from Burt (1973, p. 158), illustrates the problems
that may arise in the interpretation of theoretical variables. The four circles
represent the variances of x_1, x_2, y_1, and y_2, respectively, while the overlap of
each circle indicates covariance. The area marked with lines slanting downward
to the right shows the covariance of x_1 with x_2 that identifies the theoretical

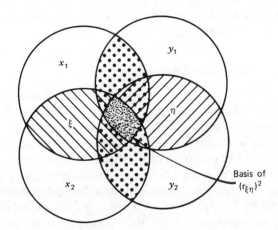

Figure 5.7. Sources of covariance empirically
describing the structure of Figure 5.6.

variable ξ. Similarly, the area marked with lines slanting downward to the left shows the covariance of y_1 with y_2 that identifies the theoretical variable η. The relationship between ξ and η (represented as γ in Figure 5.7) is based on the square root of the area common to the two theoretical variables (shown shaded in Figure 5.7). The problem in the interpretation of theoretical variables arises as a result of the covariance of operationalizations for one theoretical variable with that for another. This confounding covariance is drawn as the dotted area of Figure 5.7. As Burt (1973, p. 159) summarizes the problem,

Because the confirmatory factor-analytic model of estimation will consider all four observed variables simultaneously, it will take advantage of the covariance of the indicants of separate concepts to improve the fit of the model to the data set by allowing the covariance of the indicants of different concepts to influence the extraction of the unobserved variables. Thus, indicants of concept [ξ] which are strongly correlated with with the indicants of [η] will appear to be more significant in the conceptualization of concept [ξ]. What this means to the theorist is that the unobserved variables will not only be a function of the covariance of their constituent indicants, but will also be a function of the covariance of their constituent indicants with the indicators of other unobserved variables in a proposed structure. In this fashion, the confirmatory factor model can confound the interpretability of the unobserved variables it extracts.

Interpretational confounding will occur under one or both of the following conditions: "(1) The indicants of the unobserved variable have low covariances among themselves, and (2) the covariances of the indicants of the unobserved variable with the indicants of other unobserved variables in the model are widely different" (Burt, 1976, p. 10).

Interpretational confounding can be eliminated by first treating each theoretical concept and its operationalizations separately in a maximum-likelihood factor analysis and, second, solving the causal model containing the theoretical variables with relevant parameters in this model constrained to equal values obtained in the first step. For example, for the model of Figure 5.6, this would involve the following two steps. First, two separate maximum-likelihood factor analyses would be run for ξ and η, respectively. Second, the entire model of Figure 5.6 would be solved with λ_1', λ_2', δ_1, δ_2, λ_1, λ_2, ε_1, and ε_2 restricted to equal the values solved for in the first step.[13] This procedure keeps the interpretation of theoretical variables constant in the analysis and makes for a more accurate estimation of the relationship between the theoretical variables.

Interpretational Confounding In More Complicated Causal Models

In general, there are at least five sources of empirical meaning for the theoretical variables in one's model (Burt, 1976). Figure 5.8 graphically illustrates each of these sources of meaning for the particular model consisting of the inter-relationships among five theoretical variables (A, B, C, D, E) operationalized

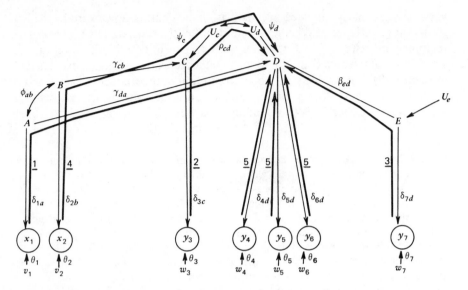

Figure 5.8. Sources of empirical meaning for unobserved variable D where dark paths indicate the compound paths through which each source can assign empirical meaning to D.

Source: Ronald S. Burt, "Interpretational Confounding of Unobserved Variables in Structural Equation Models," *Sociological Methods and Research*, Vol. 5 (August 1976, p. 5).

with seven indicators $(x_1, x_2, y_3, y_4, y_5, y_6, y_7)$. For purposes of discussion, it is assumed that the theoretical variable of interest is variable D. The five generic sources of empirical meaning for variable D are indicated by the dark paths in the figure and are marked with underscored numbers 1–5. These sources include:

1. The indicator variables of the concepts that cause variation in D (i.e., the indicator of variable A, x_1).
2. The indicator variables of the concepts that covary with D (i.e., the indicator of variable C, y_3).
3. The indicator variables of the concepts whose variation is caused by variation in D (i.e., the indicator of variable E, y_7).
4. The indicator variables of concepts that covary with those concepts whose variation causes, covaries with or is caused by variation in D (i.e., the indicator of variable B, x_2).
5. The indicator variables of the unobserved variables D itself (i.e., y_4, y_5, y_6) (Burt, 1976).

The final source is the one commonly discussed by researchers and theorists as defining the empirical meaning of a theoretical term. It represents essentially what was discussed earlier under observational meaningfulness and correspondence rules. The first and third sources correspond, in part, to the notion of nomological validity, which was also discussed earlier in the chapter. The second and fourth sources (and the first and third) follow directly from contemporary representations of the structure of theory (see Figure 3.1 and the discussion there and earlier in this chapter). That is, a theoretical variable also achieves its meaning through its relationships with other theoretical variables in a model and their relationships with observations. For the second and fourth sources, the theoretical variable D is tied indirectly to the observations of theoretical variables B and C through the covariance of U_c with U_d.

When a theoretical variable achieves its meaning primarily through its relationships to its operationalizations as described in the fifth source above, one may say that epistemic criteria determine the interpretation of the unobservable. Similarly, when a theoretical variable also achieves its meaning through its relationships with other theoretical variables and their operationalizations as in the first through fourth sources above, one may say that structural criteria play a role in the interpretation of the unobservable. Burt (1976) shows that, for a general structural equation system, the epistemic and structural criteria may be expressed algebraically as follows[14]:

$$\left.\begin{matrix} \text{epistemic} \\ \text{criteria} \end{matrix}\right\} \hat{s}_{ij} \cong \hat{\sigma}_{ij} = \sum_{p} \sum_{k} (\hat{\delta}_{ik} \hat{\phi}_{kp} \hat{\delta}_{jp})$$

for all $i, j \in Q$ and all $k, p \in R$, and

$$\left.\begin{matrix} \text{structural} \\ \text{criteria} \end{matrix}\right\} \frac{\hat{s}_{ik}}{\hat{\delta}_{iy*}} \cong \frac{\hat{s}_{jk}}{\hat{\delta}_{iy*}} \cong \frac{\hat{\sigma}_{ik}}{\hat{\delta}_{iy*}} = \frac{\hat{\sigma}_{jk}}{\hat{\delta}_{jy*}}$$

for all $i, j \in Q$ and all $k \in R$, where the $\hat{s}$'s and $\hat{\sigma}$'s are elements of S and Σ, respectively. The conditions expressed in the structural criteria say that the covariances among indicators of an unobservable $y*$ with indicators of other unobservables are proportional to the epistemic correlations (i.e., the $\hat{\delta}._{y*}$'s) of $y*$ with its indicators. As Burt (1976, p. 12) notes:

This proportionality is a general characteristic of observed variables combined according to structural criteria into linear composites which operate as "point variables." As discussed by Wright (1960, pp. 190–191 . . .), an unobserved variable fails to operate as a point variable within a structural equation model when the indicators of which it is a linear composite are of differential significance and/or sign in separate relations between the unobserved variable and other unobserved variables in the model.

Given that the empirical meaning of theoretical variables depends upon the relative emphasis of epistemic versus structural criteria in one's model and data and also upon the degree of covariance among indicators of the theoretical variable, Burt (1976) suggests that interpretational confounding occurs "when low communality in a set of indicators occurs simultaneously with low point variability in a linear composite constructed from the set of indicators." This is shown in Table 5.19. Thus, interpretational confounding will be a problem when the covariances among indicators of the theoretical variable of interest are low and the theoretical variable does not function as a point variable.

Interpretational confounding is relatively easy to discover. Using a two-stage procedure similar to that discussed above for the two-concept model, the researcher can first estimate the parameters for each unobservable and its indicators using a maximum-likelihood factor analysis and second, using these

Table 5.19

Relative Emphasis on Epistemic versus Structural Criteria in Constructing an Unobserved Variable Y^* from a Set of Indicators Y_i ($i \varepsilon Q$) under Four Conditions in a Structural Equation Model

Communality of Y_i $i \in Q$ as a Function of Covariance Among Indicators in the Set Q	Point Variability of Y^* when Epistemic Correlations are Solely a Function of Epistemic Criteria in Constructing Y^*	
	$\hat{s}_{ik}/\hat{\delta}_{iy^*}{}^\dagger = \hat{s}_{jk}/\hat{\delta}_{jy^*}{}^\dagger$ for all $i, j \in Q$ and all $k \in R$ High	$\hat{s}_{ik}/\hat{\delta}_{iy^*}{}^\dagger \neq \hat{s}_{jk}/\hat{\delta}_{jy^*}{}^\dagger$ for one or more $i, j \in Q$ and one or more $k \in R$ Low
High	*A* Epistemic criteria determine the interpretation of Y^*.	*C* Mixture of epistemic and structural criteria determine the interpretation of Y^* according to the extent to which communality is high while point variability is low.
Low	*B* Epistemic criteria determine the interpretation of Y^*.	*D* *Interpretational Confounding* Interpretation of Y^* in terms of covariances of indicators in set Q with indicators not in set Q. Structural criteria determine the interpretation of Y^* so that the usual interpretation of Y^* in terms of epistemic criteria is erroneous.

Source: Ronald S. Burt, "Interpretational Confounding of Unobserved Variables in Structural Equation Models," *Sociological Methods and Research*, Vol. 5 (August 1976,), p. 15.

estimates, solve the entire model containing all unobservables and indicators. If the parameter estimates from this procedure differ substantially from those found when the entire model is solved with no constraints made, then one may conclude that the empirical meaning of the unobservable(s) of interest in the latter analysis arises also from structural criteria rather than solely from epistemic criteria.

A final contribution made by Burt (1976) with respect to interpretational confounding occurs in regard to hypothesis testing procedures that may be used both to determine the degree of interpretational confounding and to remove it. The following is an outline of these procedures. For a fuller development and numerous illustrations and nuances associated with the approach, the reader is referred to Burt (1976). Consider first the general hypothesis H_0, which proposes that some model is the true population structure. Then, as developed in the previous chapter, the maximum-likelihood estimates of the unknown parameters will minimize

$$\chi_0^2 = N[\log|\Sigma| + \text{tr}(S\Sigma^{-1}) - \log|S| - (p + q)]$$ (5.27)

with the degrees of freedom given by

$$\text{d.f.}_0 = \frac{(p + q)(p + q + 1)}{2} - t_0$$ (5.28)

where t_0 is the number of independent unknown parameters to be estimated under H_0. To test whether the model specified under H_0 is a significant improvement over that specified under H_1 which has fewer restrictions, the following will be distributed χ^2:

$$\chi_{(0/1)}^2 = \chi_0^2 - \chi_1^2$$ (5.29)

where χ_1^2 is the value determined under H_1 and the number of degrees of freedom is given by

$$\text{d.f.}_{(0/1)} = \text{d.f.}_0 - \text{d.f.}_1 = t_1 - t_0$$ (5.30)

where t_1 is the number of independent unknown parameters to be estimated under H_1.

Next, the following is needed to develop the remaining hypotheses:

The set R of all unobserved variables in a model can be partitioned into P disjoint subsets or blocks: $R_1, R_2, \ldots R_P$, where each block contains one or more substantively similar unobserved variables. If parameters among unobserved variables within each block are estimated separately, then the estimation of parameters among unobserved variables in separate blocks is constrained via the equality of the ratios of predicted covariance over factor loadings in $\ldots$ [$\sigma_{ik}/\delta_{iy*} = \sigma_{jk}/\delta_{jy*}$ for all $i, j \in Q$ and all $k \in R$], i.e., via the criterion of point variability [Burt, 1976, p. 22].

Given the above, three types of hypotheses may be formulated. The first tests whether a specified structure of unobserved variables in block R_P is an adequate description of the indicators within block R_P. The appropriate χ^2 to be minimized is

$$\chi^2_{0(P)} = \text{Eq. (27) for the within block model } R_P \tag{5.31}$$

with degrees of freedom given by

$$\text{d.f.}_{0(P)} = \frac{(p + q)_P(p + q + 1)_P}{2} - t_{0(P)} \tag{5.32}$$

where $t_{0(P)}$ is the number of independent unknown parameters in R_P.

With the parameters determined as above, the next hypothesis to test is whether the entire structural equation model is the true population model when the above parameters are introduced as constraints. The χ^2 test to be minimized will then be

$$\chi^2_{0(P, P', PP')} = \begin{cases} \text{Eq. (27) for the model with within block parameters} \\ \text{fixed at their values estimated to yield the chi-square in Eq. (31)} \end{cases} \tag{5.33}$$

With the upper and lower limits for the degrees of freedom given by the following:

$$\text{d.f.}^{\text{lower}}_{0(p, p', pp')} \leq \text{d.f.}_{0(p, p', pp')} \leq \text{d.f.}^{\text{upper}}_{0(P, P', PP')} \tag{5.34}$$

where

$$\text{d.f.}^{\text{lower}}_{0(p, p', pp')} = \frac{(p + q)(p + q + 1)}{2} - t_0 + P$$

$$\text{d.f.}^{\text{upper}}_{0(P, P', PP')} = \text{d.f.}^{\text{lower}}_{0(p, p', pp')} + \sum_{P=1}^{P} [t_{0(P)} - 1]$$

Finally, in order to test whether the specified unobserved variables within each of the P blocks of unobserved variables operate as point variables relative to unobserved variables in separate blocks, the appropriate χ^2 approximation is

$$\chi^2_{0(PP')} = \chi^2_{0(P, P', PP')} - \sum_{P=1}^{P} [\chi^2_{0(P)}] \tag{5.35}$$

with the upper and lower limits for the degrees of freedom given by

$$\text{d.f.}^{\text{lower}}_{0(pp')} \leq \text{d.f.}_{0(pp')} \leq \text{d.f.}^{\text{upper}}_{0(PP')} \tag{5.36}$$

where

$$\text{d.f.}^{\text{lower}}_{0(pp')} = \text{d.f.}^{\text{lower}}_{0(p, p', pp')} - \sum_{P=1}^{P} [\text{d.f.}_{0(P)}]$$

$$\text{d.f.}^{\text{upper}}_{0(PP')} = \text{d.f.}^{\text{lower}}_{0(pp')} + \sum_{P=1}^{P} [t_{0(P)} - 1] = \text{d.f.}^{\text{upper}}_{0(P, P', PP')} - \sum_{P=1}^{P} [\text{d.f.}_{0(P)}]$$

Table 5.20 summarizes the eight possible types of hypotheses that may be made with respect to any structural model.

Table 5.20

Chi-square Tests for Eight Hypotheses Concerning the Adequacy of a Proposed Structural Equation Model as a Description of an Observed Variance–Covariance Matrix S

	Ignoring Interpretational Confounding	Removing Possible Interpretational Confounding		
	(Full information estimation of unknown parameters in overall model.)	(Limited information estimation of unknown parameters in model by: (1) estimating parameters within blocks of substantively similar unobserved variables with their indicators as distinct models, and then (2) estimating remaining unknown parameters in model while holding constant parameters estimated during step one.)		
	H_0: Specified model is an adequate description of S.	H_0: Specified model is an adequate description of S given the constraints on the sources of empirical meaning of unobserved variables.	H_0: Specified model is an adequate description of covariances among indicators of substantively similar unobserved variables in each of the P sets of substantively similar unobserved variables.	H_0: Specified unobserved variables operate as point variables in relation to substantively dissimilar unobserved variables in the model.
H_1: Specified model is less adequate than a just-identified model which perfectly describes S.	$\chi^2_0 = $ Eq. (27) d.f.$_0 = $ Eq. (28)	$\chi^2_{0(p,p',pp')} = $ Eq. (33) d.f.$_{0(p,p',pp')} = $ Eq. (34)	$\chi^2_{0(p)} = $ Eq. (31) d.f.$_{0(p)} = $ Eq. (32)	$\chi^2_{0(pp')} = $ Eq. (35) d.f.$_{0(pp')} = $ Eq. (36)
H_1: Specified model is less adequate than a known less restrictive model.	$\chi^2_{(0|1)} = $ Eq. (29) d.f.$_{(0|1)} = $ Eq. (30)	$\chi^2_{[0(p,p',pp')|1]} = $ Eq. (29) d.f.$_{[0(p,p',pp')|1]} = $ Eq. (30)	$\chi^2_{[0(p)|1]} = $ Eq. (29) d.f.$_{[0(p)|1]} = $ Eq. (30)	$\chi^2_{[0(pp')|1]} = $ Eq. (20) d.f.$_{[0(pp')|1]} = $ Eq. (30)

Source: Ronald S. Burt, "Interpretational Confounding of Unobserved Variables in Structural Equation Models," *Sociological Methods and Research,* Vol. 5 (August 1976), p. 26.

Summary

An integral part of the concept formation, theory construction, and testing phases of scientific research is the determination of construct validity. Construct validity may be defined as the degree to which a concept (term, variable, construct) achieves theoretical and empirical meaning within the overall structure of one's theory. In general, six components of construct validity may be identified: the theoretical meaningfulness of concepts, the observational meaningfulness of concepts, the internal consistency of operationalizations, convergent validity, discriminant validity, and nomological validity.

The theoretical meaningfulness of a concept refers to the nature and internal consistency of the language used to represent the concept. In addressing the formal adequacy of the logical and theoretical terms comprising one's theory, this semantic requirement specifies particular properties of object predicates such as the degree of vagueness, ambiguity, opacity, and contradictoriness. The observational meaningfulness of a concept, in contrast, refers to the relationship(s) between theoretical variables and their operationalizations. Three correspondence rules were discussed in this regard: the operational definition model, the partial interpretation model, and the realist model.

The internal consistency of operationalizations criterion attempts to ascertain the reliability and degree of unidimensionality of one's empirical measures. Consistency checks, test-retest reliability, internal analysis methods, and parallel forms tests are common procedures for determining this empirical standard. The following chapter illustrates a general structural equation approach for determining the internal consistency of operationalizations.

Convergent and discriminant validity are the commonly applied criteria for construct validity. The former is the degree to which two or more attempts to measure the same concept through maximally different methods are in agreement. The latter is the degree to which a concept differs from other concepts. Although the multitrait-multimethod matrix approach is the traditional method for ascertaining convergent and discriminant validity, structural equation procedures were shown to provide a more rigorous procedure. Finally, nomological validity denotes the degree to which predictions from a formal theoretical network containing the concept under scrutiny are confirmed.

After illustrating construct validity with the concept of attitudes, the notion of interpretational confounding was discussed. Interpretational confounding, following Burt (1976), "occurs when the sources of empirical meaning used to interpret an unobserved variable are different from those used to estimate parameters in terms of which the unobserved variable is interpreted."

Notes

[1] For a discussion using weights to illustrate comparative concepts, see Carnap (1966, pp. 53–58). Dawes (1972) presents a nice treatment in relation to scaling techniques.

[2] An object predicate is "any extralogical term in predicative position that refers directly to observable objects, properties, or relations" (Lachenmeyer, 1971, p. 11; see also, Hempel, 1952).

[3] Angelmar and Pinson (1974) provide a provocative analysis of some of the various definitions of marketing currently in vogue and problems associated with each.

[4] For enlightening treatments of correspondence rules, the reader is referred to Carnap (1936, 1937, 1956, 1966), Petrie (1971), and Keat and Urry (1975). For an alternative approach, however, see Smart (1968, ch. 5).

[5] Dawes (1972) presents an introductory treatment of attitude measurement. More advanced treatments of measurement may be found in Coombs (1964), Suppes and Zinnes (1963), and Coombs, Dawes, and Tversky (1970).

[6] Hempel (1970, 1973) terms such sentences "the postulates of the theoretical calculus, which are said to constitute 'implicit definitions' for its primitive terms."

[7] Campbell and Fiske (1959) propose two rules for selecting methods. First they suggest:

The several methods used to measure each trait should be appropriate to the trait as conceptualized. Although this view will reduce the range of suitable methods, it will rarely restrict the measurement to one operational procedure [p. 103].

Second, they caution:

Wherever possible, the several methods in one matrix should be completely independent of one another: there should be no prior reason for believing that they share method variance . . . . If the nature of the traits rules out such independence of methods, efforts should be made to obtain as much diversity as possible in terms of data-sources and classification processes. Thus, the classes of stimuli *or* background situations, the experimental contexts, should be different. Again, the person providing the observations should have different roles *or* the procedures for scoring should be varied [p. 103].

Given these rules of thumb, it might be better to use such methods as peer ratings, observation by the researcher, self-ratings, archival searches, physiological measurement, or various unobtrusive methods to measure attitudes rather than rely soley on Likert, Thurstone, or Guttman scales. This fact was pointed out to the author by Professor Michael Ray, Stanford University.

[8] Ordinarily, when a poor fit is obtained for the congeneric test, one should then add method factors (e.g., ξ_4, ξ_5, and ξ_6 in Figure 5.3). This was done for Ostrom's (1969) data, but since the addition produced a condition in the variance-covariance matrix where the iterations failed to converge in the program, the parameters could not be estimated. However, after the errorful self-rating measure was dropped (as discussed below), the full analysis was performed using the Thurstone, Likert, and Guttman measures. Similar conditions resulted for Kothandapani's (1971) data.

[9] The researcher should analyze residuals with care taking into account the pitfalls associated with such a procedure (e.g., Costner and Schoenberg, 1973).

[10] Following the convention adopted by Jöreskog (1971, 1974), covariances between traits and methods were constrained to equal zero in the analysis, that is, $\phi_{14} = \phi_{15} = \phi_{16} = \phi_{24} = \phi_{25} = \phi_{26} = \phi_{34} = \phi_{35} = \phi_{36} = 0$ (see Figure 5.3).

[11] In addition, the third criterion of discriminant validity is violated since a number of patterns within the heterotrait triangles are inconsistent.

[12] Since the data failed to confirm the model, however, the results should be taken in a rough, descriptive sense.

[13] For the two indicator factor analyses, the following equalities must be specified in order to make the system identified: $\lambda'_1 = \lambda'_2$, $\delta_1 = \delta_2$, $\lambda_1 = \lambda_2$, and $\varepsilon_1 = \varepsilon_2$. With three or more indicators for an unobservable in a two construct model, however, these restrictions are not required.

[14] When the y_i and y_j are indicators of the same theoretical concept y^*, the epistemic criteria become (Burt, 1976): $\hat{s}_{ij} \cong \hat{\sigma}_{ij} = \hat{\delta}_{iy^*} (1.0)\hat{\delta}_{jy^*}$.

SIX

ESTIMATING AND TESTING
SIMPLE CAUSAL MODELS

Causal modeling is applicable to a wide range of marketing phenomena. In this chapter, a number of fundamental models are developed and illustrated. The discussion begins with the case consisting of a single unobservable, theoretical variable influenced by multiple causes and measured by multiple indicators. This situation has come to be known as the multiple-indicator-multiple-cause (MIMIC) model in the literature (cf., Goldberger, 1974). The MIMIC model is then modified to include a second theoretical variable as a consequent to the first. Next, the causal modeling methodology is illustrated as a means for estimating and testing recursive models. Third, a general model for measuring reliability is derived. Finally, the chapter closes with a discussion of some issues and topics common to many investigations into cause-and-effect processes.

The Multiple-Indicator-Multiple-Cause Model

Consider the model of Figure 6.1 consisting of a single theoretical variable η influenced by q causes $\xi_1, \xi_2, \ldots, \xi_q$ and measured by p indicators $y_1, y_2, \ldots, y_p$. Using the principles developed in Chapter 4, one may write the structural equations for this model as follows:

$$\mathbf{B}\eta = \mathbf{\Gamma}\xi + \zeta \tag{6.1}$$

$$(1)\eta = (\gamma_1 \quad \gamma_2 \quad \cdots \quad \gamma_q)\begin{pmatrix} \xi_1 \\ \xi_2 \\ \vdots \\ \xi_q \end{pmatrix} + \zeta \tag{6.2}$$

$$\begin{pmatrix} y_1 \\ y_2 \\ \vdots \\ y_p \end{pmatrix} = \begin{pmatrix} \lambda_1 \\ \lambda_2 \\ \vdots \\ \lambda_p \end{pmatrix} \eta + \begin{pmatrix} \varepsilon_1 \\ \varepsilon_2 \\ \vdots \\ \varepsilon_p \end{pmatrix} \tag{6.3}$$

$$\boldsymbol{\theta}_\varepsilon^2 = \begin{pmatrix} \theta_{\varepsilon_1}^2 & & & & \\ 0 & \theta_{\varepsilon_2}^2 & & & \\ \vdots & 0 & & \ddots & \\ \vdots & \vdots & & & \\ 0 & 0 & \cdots & 0 & \theta_{\varepsilon_p}^2 \end{pmatrix} \tag{6.4}$$

$$\begin{pmatrix} x_1 \\ x_2 \\ \vdots \\ \vdots \\ x_q \end{pmatrix} = \begin{pmatrix} 1 & 0 & \cdots & & 0 \\ 0 & 1 & 0 & \cdots & 0 \\ 0 & 0 & & & \vdots \\ \vdots & \vdots & & \ddots & 0 \\ 0 & 0 & & \cdots & 0 & 1 \end{pmatrix} \begin{pmatrix} \xi_1 \\ \xi_2 \\ \vdots \\ \vdots \\ \xi_q \end{pmatrix} + \begin{pmatrix} 0 \\ 0 \\ \vdots \\ \vdots \\ 0 \end{pmatrix} \tag{6.5}$$

$$\boldsymbol{\theta}_\delta^2 = \mathbf{0} \tag{6.6}$$

$$\boldsymbol{\phi} = \begin{pmatrix} 1.0 & & & & \\ \phi_{21} & 1.0 & & & \\ \phi_{31} & \phi_{32} & & \ddots & \\ \vdots & \vdots & & & \\ \phi_{p1} & \phi_{p2} & \cdots & \phi_{p,p-1} & 1.0 \end{pmatrix} \tag{6.7}$$

$$\psi = 1.0 \tag{6.8}$$

The latter normalization $\psi = 1.0$ is needed to remove an indeterminancy in the system of equations (cf., Jöreskog and Goldberger, 1975). That this is the case can be shown as follows. From Eqs. (6.2), (6.3), and (6.5), one may

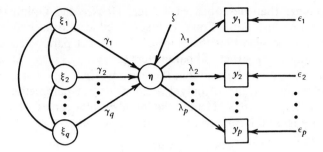

Figure 6.1. The multiple-indicator–Multiple-cause model.

solve for the reduced form equations relating observable variables such that

$$\mathbf{y} = \mathbf{\Lambda}_y(\mathbf{\Gamma\xi} + \mathbf{\zeta}) + \mathbf{\varepsilon}$$
$$= \mathbf{\Delta\xi} + \mathbf{u} \qquad (6.9)$$

where the reduced-form coefficient matrix is

$$\mathbf{\Delta} = \mathbf{\Gamma\Lambda}_y' = \begin{pmatrix} \gamma_1\lambda_1 & \gamma_1\lambda_2 & \cdots & \gamma_1\lambda_p \\ \gamma_2\lambda_1 & \gamma_2\lambda_2 & \cdots & \gamma_2\lambda_p \\ \vdots & \vdots & & \vdots \\ \gamma_q\lambda_1 & \gamma_q\lambda_2 & \cdots & \gamma_q\lambda_p \end{pmatrix} \qquad (6.10)$$

and the vector of disturbance is

$$\mathbf{u} = \mathbf{\Lambda}_y\mathbf{\zeta} + \mathbf{\varepsilon} \qquad (6.11)$$

The variance-covariance matrix of $\mathbf{u}$ may be written as

$$\mathbf{\Sigma}^* = E(\mathbf{uu'}) = E[(\mathbf{\Lambda}_y\mathbf{\zeta} + \mathbf{\varepsilon})(\mathbf{\Lambda}_y\mathbf{\zeta} + \mathbf{\varepsilon})'] = \psi\mathbf{\Lambda}_y\mathbf{\Lambda}_y' + \mathbf{\theta}_\varepsilon^2$$

$$\mathbf{\Sigma}^* = \begin{pmatrix} \lambda_1^2\psi + \theta_{\varepsilon_1}^2 & \lambda_1\lambda_2\psi & \cdots & \lambda_1\lambda_p\psi \\ \lambda_2\lambda_1\psi & \lambda_2^2\psi + \theta_{\varepsilon_2}^2 & \cdots & \lambda_2\lambda_p\psi \\ \vdots & \vdots & \ddots & \vdots \\ \lambda_p\lambda_1\psi & \lambda_p\lambda_2\psi & \cdots & \lambda_p^2\psi + \theta_{\varepsilon_p}^2 \end{pmatrix} \qquad (6.12)$$

Now, if $\mathbf{\Lambda}_y$ is multiplied by a scalar while $\mathbf{\Gamma}$ and ψ are divided by the same scalar, the parameters in $\mathbf{\Delta}$ will not be altered. By normalizing the variance of ψ at one, however, one may remove the indeterminancy in the structural parameters. Two alternative normalization strategies would be to fix the variance of η at one or to fix one λ at one in each column.

Although one may use the procedures developed in Chapter 4 to estimate the model of Figure 6.1, it is necessary to calculate the degrees of freedom in a different manner than described earlier (cf., Hauser and Goldberger, 1971). This may be done as follows. Consider first the reduced-form coefficient matrix Δ, where it can be seen that there are $q \times p$ distinct parameters expressible in terms of only $q + p$ structural parameters (i.e., $\gamma_1, \gamma_2, \ldots, \gamma_q, \lambda_1, \lambda_2, \ldots, \lambda_p$). Next, from (6.12), it can be seen that there are $\frac{1}{2}(p)(p + 1)$ distinct parameters in Σ^* expressible in terms of only $1 + 2p$ structural parameters (i.e., $\psi, \lambda_1, \lambda_2, \ldots, \lambda_p, \theta_{\varepsilon_1}^2, \theta_{\varepsilon_2}^2, \ldots, \theta_{\varepsilon_p}^2$). Hence, the number of degrees of freedom for the model of Figure 6.1 must be calculated as follows:

$$\text{d.f.} = [q \times p + \tfrac{1}{2}(p)(p + 1)] - (q + 2p)$$

$$= q(p - 1) + \frac{p(p - 3)}{2}$$

Jöreskog and Goldberger (1975) derive three useful quantities for the model of Figure 6.1. One quantity, Q_1, measures the proportion of variation in η which may be accounted for by the ξ's. This may be calculated as

$$Q_1 = \frac{\rho^2}{1 + \rho^2} = \frac{C - 1}{C}$$

where $\rho^2 = C - 1$ and $C = \hat{\Gamma}\hat{\phi}\hat{\Gamma}' + \psi$. A second quantity, Q_2, yields a scalar measure of the proportion of the variation in the y's accounted for by the ξ's. This may be represented as

$$Q_2 = 1 - \frac{|\Sigma^*|}{|\Sigma^* + \Gamma\phi\Gamma'\Lambda_y\Lambda_y'|}$$

Finally, the scalar measure of the proportion of the variation in the y's accounted for by η may be calculated as Q_3:

$$Q_3 = 1 - \frac{|\theta_\varepsilon^2|}{|\Sigma^* + \Gamma\phi\Gamma'\Lambda_y\Lambda_y'|}$$

When investigating a particular MIMIC model, it is often useful to examine the weaker, less restricted model consisting of the system of Figure 6.1 with the errors $\varepsilon_1, \varepsilon_2, \ldots, \varepsilon_p$ allowed correlated. The comparison in fit between the model of Figure 6.1 and the less restricted model allows one to test the restrictions made on Δ and Σ^* separately. The χ^2 test for the less restricted model can be used to test the restrictions on Δ. Given the restrictions on Δ, the restrictions on Σ^* may be tested by examining the difference in χ^2 values for the model of Figure 6.1 and for the less restricted model. The difference in χ^2 may be taken as distributed approximately χ^2 with degrees of freedom equal to the difference in the respective values for degrees of freedom. A large value for the difference in the χ^2 tests relative to the change in degrees of freedom leads one to reject the additional restrictions on Σ^*. Hauser and Goldberger (1971) present a derivation of the model of Figure 6.1 with $\varepsilon_1, \varepsilon_2, \ldots, \varepsilon_p$ allowed correlated. Jöreskog and Goldberger (1975) present an illustration of the test for restrictions on Δ and Σ^*.

Consider next the extension of the MIMIC model to include the presence of a second theoretical variable η_2 being caused by η_1. Figure 6.2 depicts this model where, for simplicity, there are three exogenous variables and three indicators for each unobservable.

The structural equations for this model may be written as

$$\begin{pmatrix} 1 & 0 \\ -\beta & 1 \end{pmatrix} \begin{pmatrix} \eta_1 \\ \eta_2 \end{pmatrix} = \begin{pmatrix} \gamma_1 & \gamma_2 & \gamma_3 \\ 0 & 0 & 0 \end{pmatrix} \begin{pmatrix} \xi_1 \\ \xi_2 \\ \xi_3 \end{pmatrix} + \begin{pmatrix} \zeta_1 \\ \zeta_2 \end{pmatrix}$$

$$\begin{pmatrix} y_1 \\ y_2 \\ y_3 \\ y_4 \\ y_5 \\ y_6 \end{pmatrix} = \begin{pmatrix} \lambda_1 & 0 \\ \lambda_2 & 0 \\ \lambda_3 & 0 \\ 0 & \lambda_4 \\ 0 & \lambda_5 \\ 0 & \lambda_6 \end{pmatrix} \begin{pmatrix} \eta_1 \\ \eta_2 \end{pmatrix} + \begin{pmatrix} \varepsilon_1 \\ \varepsilon_2 \\ \varepsilon_3 \\ \varepsilon_4 \\ \varepsilon_5 \\ \varepsilon_6 \end{pmatrix}$$

$$\theta_\varepsilon^2 = \begin{pmatrix} \theta_{\varepsilon_1}^2 & & & & & \\ 0 & \theta_{\varepsilon_2}^2 & & & & \\ 0 & 0 & \theta_{\varepsilon_3}^2 & & & \\ 0 & 0 & 0 & \theta_{\varepsilon_4}^2 & & \\ 0 & 0 & 0 & 0 & \theta_{\varepsilon_5}^2 & \\ 0 & 0 & 0 & 0 & 0 & \theta_{\varepsilon_6}^2 \end{pmatrix}$$

$$\begin{pmatrix} x_1 \\ x_2 \\ x_3 \end{pmatrix} = \begin{pmatrix} 1 & 0 & 0 \\ 0 & 1 & 0 \\ 0 & 0 & 1 \end{pmatrix} \begin{pmatrix} \xi_1 \\ \xi_2 \\ \xi_3 \end{pmatrix} + \begin{pmatrix} 0 \\ 0 \\ 0 \end{pmatrix}$$

$$\boldsymbol{\theta}_\delta^2 = \mathbf{0}$$

$$\boldsymbol{\phi} = \begin{pmatrix} 1.0 & & \\ \phi_{21} & 1.0 & \\ \phi_{31} & \phi_{32} & 1.0 \end{pmatrix}$$

$$\boldsymbol{\Psi} = \begin{pmatrix} \psi_{11} & \\ 0 & \psi_{22} \end{pmatrix}$$

In order to estimate the model of Figure 6.2, one must first solve the sub-model consisting of η_1 and its causes and indicators. Then, with the parameters of Figure 6.2 constrained to equal that found in this analysis, the parameters

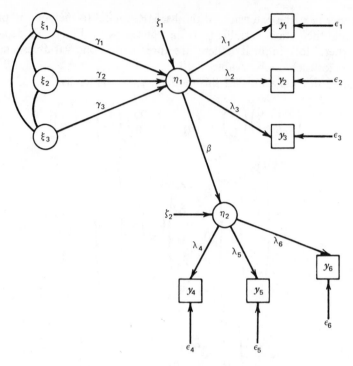

Figure 6.2. A causal model with three exogenous variables affecting one theoretical variable which in turn influences a second theoretical variable.

Table 6.1
**Product-Moment Correlations for Selected
Variables from Goldberg (1975)**

Variables	y_1	y_2	y_3	x_1	x_2
y_1	1.00				
y_2	0.62	1.00			
y_3	0.77	0.58	1.00		
x_1	0.54	0.42	0.59	1.00	
x_2	0.72	0.57	0.70	0.52	1.00

$M = 593.$

for the rest of the model may be solved. This procedure is needed because β would not be identified as the model stands.

In order to illustrate a MIMIC model, consider the model of Figure 6.3, which hypothesizes that the modernization orientation η of women in less developed countries will be a function of the women's place of birth ξ_1 (city or rural) and the women's education ξ_2.[1] The modernization orientation is measured by the truncated modernization index y_1, the modern objects scale y_2, and the media exposure index y_3. Drawing upon the raw data presented in Goldberg (1975), it is possible to test this hypothesis. Table 6.1 presents the product-moment correlations for the data. The structural equations can be expressed as

$$(1)\eta = (\gamma_1 \quad \gamma_2) \begin{pmatrix} \xi_1 \\ \xi_2 \end{pmatrix} + \zeta$$

$$\begin{pmatrix} y_1 \\ y_2 \\ y_3 \end{pmatrix} = \begin{pmatrix} \lambda_1 \\ \lambda_2 \\ \lambda_3 \end{pmatrix} \eta + \begin{pmatrix} \varepsilon_1 \\ \varepsilon_2 \\ \varepsilon_3 \end{pmatrix}$$

$$\boldsymbol{\theta}_\varepsilon^2 = \begin{pmatrix} \theta_{\varepsilon_1}^2 & & \\ 0 & \theta_{\varepsilon_2}^2 & \\ 0 & 0 & \theta_{\varepsilon_3}^2 \end{pmatrix}$$

$$\begin{pmatrix} x_1 \\ x_2 \end{pmatrix} = \begin{pmatrix} 1 & 0 \\ 0 & 1 \end{pmatrix} \begin{pmatrix} \xi_1 \\ \xi_2 \end{pmatrix} + \begin{pmatrix} 0 \\ 0 \end{pmatrix}$$

$$\boldsymbol{\theta}_\delta^2 = \mathbf{0}$$

$$\boldsymbol{\phi} = \begin{pmatrix} \phi_{11} & \\ \phi_{21} & \phi_{22} \end{pmatrix}$$

$$\boldsymbol{\psi} = 1.0$$

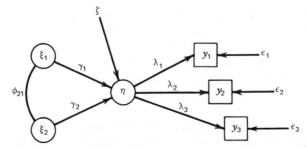

Figure 6.3. A mimic model with two causes and three indicators.

Table 6.2

Parameter Estimates and Standard Errors for the Model of Figure 6.3 and Data of Goldberg (1975)

Parameter	Maximum Likelihood Solution	Standard Errors
λ_1	0.46	0.02
λ_2	0.35	0.02
λ_3	0.46	0.02
γ_1	0.56	0.02
γ_2	1.25	0.08
θ_{ε_1}	0.47	0.02
θ_{ε_2}	0.73	0.02
θ_{ε_3}	0.49	0.02

$\chi^2 = 11.20$; d.f. $= 4$; $p = 0.03$.

Using the procedures developed in Chapter 4, LISREL yields the parameter estimates and standard errors shown in Table 6.2. Since $\chi^2 = 11.20$ with 4 d.f., one must reject the model of Figure 6.3. Notice, however, that all parameter estimates are twice their respective standard errors. The descriptive statistics were calculated from the results.

$Q_1 =$ Proportion of variation in η accounted for by ξ_1 and ξ_2 $= 0.72$

$Q_2 =$ Proportion of variation in y_1, y_2, and y_3 accounted for by ξ_1 and ξ_2 $= 0.64$

$Q_3 =$ Proportion of variation in y_1, y_2, and y_3 accounted for by η $= 0.88$

Thus, despite the significance of individual parameter estimates (see Table 6.2) and the relatively high proportion in variation explained by the descriptive statistics, one must still reject the entire model as representing the pattern of relationships among the variables, based on the overall χ^2 test.

In order to see why the model does not fit the data, one must examine the restrictions on Δ and Σ^* separately. This can be done by investigating the MIMIC model that allows the error terms of y_1, y_2, and y_3 to be correlated and then comparing this model to the MIMIC model of Figure 6.3. For the MIMIC model of Figure 6.3 allowing correlated errors in the indicators, the goodness-of-fit is $\chi^2 = 7.94$, 2 d.f., and $p \cong 0.00$. Thus, the restrictions on the reduced form path coefficients are not reasonable. However, looking at the difference in χ^2 values, we see that the restrictions on the error terms are justified since $\chi^2 = 3.26$, 2 d.f., and $p \cong 0.20$.

The MIMIC model discussed by Hauser and Goldberger (1971) and Jöreskog and Goldberger (1975) contains only a single latent variable. Stapleton (1977) recently treated the general MIMIC model with multiple latent variables. The system of relationships can be expressed as

$$\boldsymbol{\eta} = \boldsymbol{\Gamma}\boldsymbol{\xi} + \boldsymbol{\zeta}$$

$$\mathbf{y} = \boldsymbol{\Lambda}\boldsymbol{\eta} + \boldsymbol{\varepsilon}$$

where $\boldsymbol{\eta}$ is a vector of latent variables, $\boldsymbol{\xi}$ is a vector of causes, $\mathbf{y}$ is a vector of indicators, $\boldsymbol{\Gamma}$ and $\boldsymbol{\Lambda}$ are parameter matrices, and $\boldsymbol{\zeta}$ and $\boldsymbol{\varepsilon}$ are error matrices. Although LISREL can be used to estimate the parameters for this model, no general solution exists for the identification problem, and each particular solution must be solved on its own. Stapleton presents an illustration for three latent variables, 11 indicators, and 15 causes. There are 161 degrees of freedom in this model (Stapleton, 1977). For further illustrations of the MIMIC model in the advertising and consumer behavior context, see Aaker, Bagozzi, Carman, and McLaughlin (1980).

Recursive Models

The structural equation approach developed in Chapter 4 can also be used to estimate and test recursive models. In order to illustrate the procedures, consider the simple four-variable recursive model illustrated in Figure 6.4. This model examines the relationships among two behavioral outcomes experienced by outside salespeople—performance (η_1) and job satisfaction (η_2)—and two antecedents, specific self-esteem (ξ_1) and verbal intelligence (ξ_2). The hypotheses are:

1. The greater the specific self-esteem, the greater the performance and the higher the felt job satisfaction.
2. The greater the verbal intelligence, the lower the performance.
3. The greater the performance, the higher the felt job satisfaction.

These hypotheses are represented as γ_1, γ_2, γ_3, and β in Figure 6.4. Specific self-esteem is operationalized by a six-item scale measuring how individual salespeople rate themselves in relation to other salespeople in their company as to their sales performance, ability to reach quota, potential, quality of customer relations, management of time and expenses, and knowledge of own products, competitors' products, and customers' needs. The measures are shown as two sets of measures (i.e., x_1 and x_2) in Figure 6.4. Verbal intelligence

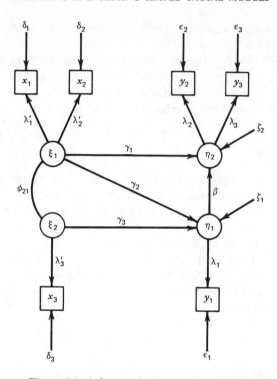

Figure 6.4. A four-variable recursive model.

is measured with a 30-item scale (x_3) developed by Borgatta. Performance is indicated by the dollar volume of sales that each person achieved (y_1). Finally, job satisfaction is measured by two sets of scales (y_2 and y_3) each comprised of four Likert items indicating each salesperson's respective feelings about promotion opportunities, job security, compensation, overall satisfaction, and related dimensions. The sample size is 122. For a discussion of the rationale

Table 6.3
Product-Moment Correlations for Recursive Model of Figure 6.4

	y_1	y_2	y_3	x_1	x_2	x_3
y_1	1.000					
y_2	0.418	1.000				
y_3	0.394	0.627	1.000			
x_1	0.544	0.281	0.324	1.000		
x_2	0.507	0.225	0.314	0.546	1.000	
x_3	−0.357	−0.156	−0.038	−0.294	−0.174	1.000

behind the hypotheses, supporting research, and the methodology and results for the entire study, the reader is referred to Bagozzi (1976b, 1979a, b). Table 6.3 presents the product-moment correlations for the variables.

The structural equations for the model of Figure 6.4 can be written as follows:

$$\begin{pmatrix} 1 & 0 \\ -\beta & 1 \end{pmatrix} \begin{pmatrix} \eta_1 \\ \eta_2 \end{pmatrix} = \begin{pmatrix} \gamma_2 & \gamma_3 \\ \gamma_1 & 0 \end{pmatrix} \begin{pmatrix} \xi_1 \\ \xi_2 \end{pmatrix} + \begin{pmatrix} \zeta_1 \\ \zeta_2 \end{pmatrix}$$

$$\begin{pmatrix} y_1 \\ y_2 \\ y_3 \end{pmatrix} = \begin{pmatrix} 1 & 0 \\ 0 & \lambda_2 \\ 0 & \lambda_3 \end{pmatrix} \begin{pmatrix} \eta_1 \\ \eta_2 \end{pmatrix} + \begin{pmatrix} 0 \\ \varepsilon_2 \\ \varepsilon_3 \end{pmatrix}$$

$$\theta_\varepsilon^2 = \begin{pmatrix} 0 & & \\ 0 & \theta_{\varepsilon_2}^2 & \\ 0 & 0 & \theta_{\varepsilon_3}^2 \end{pmatrix}$$

$$\begin{pmatrix} x_1 \\ x_2 \\ x_3 \end{pmatrix} = \begin{pmatrix} \lambda_1' & 0 \\ \lambda_2' & 0 \\ 0 & 1 \end{pmatrix} \begin{pmatrix} \xi_1 \\ \xi_2 \end{pmatrix} + \begin{pmatrix} \delta_1 \\ \delta_2 \\ 0 \end{pmatrix}$$

$$\theta_\delta^2 = \begin{pmatrix} \theta_{\delta_1}^2 & & \\ 0 & \theta_{\delta_2}^2 & \\ 0 & 0 & 0 \end{pmatrix}$$

$$\phi = \begin{pmatrix} 1.0 & \\ \phi_{21} & 1.0 \end{pmatrix}$$

$$\psi = \begin{pmatrix} \psi_{11} & \\ 0 & \psi_{22} \end{pmatrix}$$

There are $\frac{1}{2}(6)(7) - 15 = 6$ d.f. for this model.

Application of LISREL to the data yields the results shown in Table 6.4. Notice first that the overall model may be accepted based on the goodness-of-fit test: $\chi^2 = 7.44, 6$ d.f., $p \cong 0.28$. Next, as predicted, specific self-esteem is positively related to both performance ($\gamma_2 = 0.662$) and job satisfaction ($\gamma_1 = 0.242$); verbal intelligence is negatively related to performance, though relatively low in magnitude ($\gamma_3 = -0.146$); and performance is positively related to job satisfaction ($\beta = 0.341$). Notice further that the relative impact of specific self-esteem on performance is more than four times the impact of verbal intelligence on performance (0.662 vs. -0.146). Moreover, the effect of performance on job satisfaction is about 140 percent greater than that of specific self-esteem on job satisfaction.

Table 6.4
Parameter Estimates for the Re-
cursive Model of Figure 6.4

Parameter	Standardized Parameter Estimate
λ_1	1.000^a
λ_2	0.791
λ_3	0.792
λ'_1	0.776
λ'_2	0.705
λ'_3	1.000^a
γ_1	0.242
γ_2	0.662
γ_3	-0.146
β	0.341
θ_{ε_1}	0.000^a
θ_{ε_2}	0.611
θ_{ε_3}	0.610
θ_{δ_1}	0.631
θ_{δ_2}	0.709
θ_{δ_3}	0.000^a
ϕ_{21}	-0.319

$\chi^2 = 7.44$; 6 d.f.; p $\cong$ 0.28.
[a] Constrained parameter.

Causal Modeling and Reliability

Causal modeling can be used also to represent and test the reliability of measurements (cf., Bagozzi, 1978c). Before derivation of the general model, it is useful to briefly present the concept of a true score. In the classical test theory model (Lord and Novick, 1968), the observed, empirical measurement x_{ij} of person i on variable j is represented as a linear function of a true-score T_{ij} and an error-score random variable ε_{ij} as follows:

$$x_{ij} = T_{ij} + \varepsilon_{ij}$$

where it is assumed that all variables have zero expectations, the true-score is uncorrelated with the error variables, and the variance-covariance matrix of errors is diagonal. Given this model and the above assumptions, it follows that

$$E(x_{ij}) = E(T_{ij})$$

(that is, the mean of observations is an unbiased estimate of the mean of true-scores) and

$$\sigma^2_{x_{ij}} = \sigma^2_{T_{ij}} + \sigma^2_{\varepsilon_{ij}}$$

(i.e., the variance of observations is the sum of the variance of true-scores and the error). Given this specification, the reliability for any particular measurement x_{ij} at a given point in time can be defined as (Lord and Novick, 1968, p. 61):

$$\rho^2_{xT} = \frac{\sigma^2_T}{\sigma^2_x} = \frac{\sigma^2_T}{\sigma^2_T + \sigma^2_\varepsilon} = 1 - \frac{\sigma^2_\varepsilon}{\sigma^2_x}$$

where ρ^2_{xT} is the reliability coefficient, and the subscripts i, j have been dropped for convenience. The reliability coefficient is thus a measure of the degree of true-score variation relative to observed-score variation and will yield a number in the interval 0 to 1, depending on the values for the observed-score and error-score variances.

Consider the general case where $m \geq 2$ true-scores $T_1, T_2, \ldots, T_m$ are each measured respectively by $n_m \geq 2$ operationalizations $x_{11}, x_{12}, \ldots, x_{1n_1};$ $x_{21}, \ldots, x_{2n_2}; \ldots; x_{mn_1}, x_{mn_2}, \ldots, x_{mn_m}$. The basic model for the system of equations relating observed-scores to true-scores may be written as

$$\mathbf{x} = \mathbf{BT} + \mathbf{e} \tag{6.13}$$

where $\mathbf{x}$ is a vector of order $N = n_1 + n_2 + \cdots + n_m$ observed scores, $\mathbf{T}$ is a vector of order $m < N$ true-scores, $\mathbf{e}$ is a vector of N error terms, and $\mathbf{B}$ is a $N \times m$ matrix of parameters. Without loss of generality, it is assumed that $E(\mathbf{x}) = E(\mathbf{T}) = E(\mathbf{e}) = 0$, $E(\mathbf{Te}) = 0$, $E(\mathbf{TT'}) = \boldsymbol{\phi}$, and $E(\mathbf{ee'}) = \boldsymbol{\Psi}$, a diagonal matrix. As a result, the variance-covariance matrix of $\mathbf{x}$, $\boldsymbol{\Sigma} = E(\mathbf{xx'})$, can be expressed as

$$\boldsymbol{\Sigma} = \mathbf{B}\boldsymbol{\phi}\mathbf{B'} + \boldsymbol{\Psi} \tag{6.14}$$

The general model described by Eqs. (6.13) and (6.14) should be recognized as the basic factor analysis model (cf., Mulaik, 1972) applied to the particular measurement problem set out in this chapter. The elements of $\mathbf{B}$, $\boldsymbol{\phi}$, and $\boldsymbol{\psi}$ represent the parameters of the model to be estimated from the data. Figure 6.5 illustrates a causal diagram for the model of Eqs. (13) and (14).

In order for any particular structure of relationships represented by the model of Eqs. (13) and (14) to be identified, certain parameters in $\boldsymbol{\Sigma}$ must be fixed or constrained to equal other parameters. The choice of fixed or constrained parameters is made based on a priori information derived from logical considerations, past research, or methodological factors unique to the test situation at hand. For example, if two true-scores were each measured by two

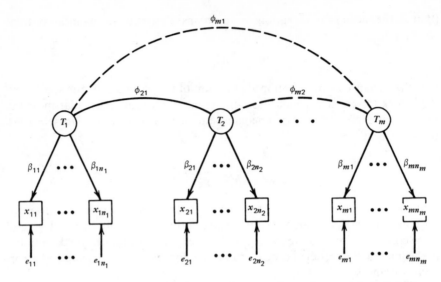

Figure 6.5. A causal diagram for the general structural equation model of reliability.

separate scales, the matrix of parameters **B** would appear as follows:

$$\mathbf{B} = \begin{pmatrix} \beta_{11} & 0^* \\ \beta_{12} & 0^* \\ 0^* & \beta_{21} \\ 0^* & \beta_{22} \end{pmatrix}$$

where the β's indicate free (unconstrained) parameters to be estimated, and the 0^*'s represent parameters fixed at zero as dictated by the specific measurement task at hand. In the general case, the degrees of freedom for any model may be computed from

$$\text{d.f.} = \tfrac{1}{2}(N)(N + 1) - (t_B + t_\phi + t_\psi) \tag{6.16}$$

where N is defined as above, and t_B, t_ϕ, and t_ψ indicate the number of parameters to be estimated in the respective **B**, $\boldsymbol{\phi}$, and $\boldsymbol{\Psi}$ matrices.

The parameters in the model of Eqs. (13) and (14) may be estimated as follows. Letting **S** represent the sample variance-covariance matrix for the **x**'s, the logarithm of the likelihood function may be written as (cf., Lawley and Maxwell, 1971; Mulaik, 1972, pp. 374–380):

$$\ln L = -\tfrac{1}{2}s^*[\ln|\Sigma| + \text{tr}(S\Sigma^{-1})] \tag{6.17}$$

where $s^* = s - 1$ and $s = $ sample size. Jöreskog (1967) shows that maximizing $\ln L$ is equivalent to minimizing

$$F = \tfrac{1}{2}[\ln|\Sigma| + \text{tr}(S\Sigma^{-1}) - \ln|S| - N] \tag{6.18}$$

Since the values for the parameters in Σ that minimize F cannot be found analytically, an iterative procedure based on the Fletcher–Powell (1963) algorithm may be used to find numerical solutions. LISREL may be used to estimate the parameters and test hypotheses.

To illustrate the model, the procedures will be applied to a set of measurements obtained on industrial salespeople. Three broad categories of job outcomes were measured. The first—termed task specific self-esteem—is a particular kind of personal construct that refers to the manner in which individuals attribute and infer dispositions in themselves (Kelly, 1963). These dispositions typically deal with attributions of personal competence and self-regard (Coopersmith, 1967; Wells and Marwell, 1976). They entail both cognitive and affective psychological processes in that the person must perform an act of conceptual self-identification and form an emotional evaluation thereof. The emotional content, which may be positive or negative, is directed toward specific experiences on the job and may vary in intensity, depending on the situation and the person's attributions in relation to it (Korman, 1970).

The second broad job outcome measured was job satisfaction that is defined herein as "the pleasurable emotional state resulting from the appraisal of one's job as achieving or facilitating the achievement of one's job-values" (Locke, 1969, p. 316). Typically, job satisfaction will be a function of the discrepancy between what one desires from one's job and what one perceives that the job offers. Job satisfaction differs from task specific self-esteem in the sense that the former denotes specific cognitive and affective reactions toward the job as an object of focus, while the latter refers to attributions toward the self as an object of scrutiny.

Performance refers to actual events resulting from a salesperson's efforts. Thus, they connote objective happenings under the influence of the salesperson. In this study, performance is operationalized through the actual sales generated and new business obtained.

Table 6.5
Observed Variance-Covariance Matrix Among the Variables

	x_1	x_2	x_3	x_4	x_5	x_6	x_7
x_1	4.6773						
x_2	2.4319	4.2481					
x_3	2.0846	1.5858	11.7388				
x_4	1.9697	1.8205	6.0344	7.9034			
x_5	4.1017	3.6426	4.9902	3.8575	12.1410		
x_6	2.2658	1.2519	0.6394	0.6197	2.8083	8.5023	
x_7	0.9161	0.3336	−1.0655	0.2694	−0.3900	4.1843	11.2304

$s = 122.$

Table 6.5 presents the variance-covariance matrix for observed variables: task specific self-esteem #1 (x_1), task specific self-esteem #2 (x_2), job satisfaction #1 (x_3), job satisfaction #2 (x_4), sales for the year (x_5), dollar value of new accounts (x_6), and number of new accounts (x_7). Four true-scores are hypothesized: $T_1 =$ task specific self-esteem, $T_2 =$ job satisfaction, $T_3 =$ sales, and $T_4 =$ new business. The latter two true-scores are included in the analysis primarily as control variables for T_1 and T_2.

Given the general model of Eqs. (6.1) and (6.2), the specific model for data treated in Table 6.5 can be expressed as follows:

$$
\begin{pmatrix} x_1 \\ x_2 \\ x_3 \\ x_4 \\ x_5 \\ x_6 \\ x_7 \end{pmatrix} = \begin{pmatrix} \beta_{11} & 0 & 0 & 0 \\ \beta_{12} & 0 & 0 & 0 \\ 0 & \beta_{21} & 0 & 0 \\ 0 & \beta_{22} & 0 & 0 \\ 0 & 0 & \beta_{31} & 0 \\ 0 & 0 & 0 & \beta_{41} \\ 0 & 0 & 0 & \beta_{42} \end{pmatrix} \begin{pmatrix} T_1 \\ T_2 \\ T_3 \\ T_4 \end{pmatrix} + \begin{pmatrix} e_{11} \\ e_{12} \\ e_{21} \\ e_{22} \\ e_{31} \\ e_{41} \\ e_{42} \end{pmatrix} \tag{6.19}
$$

$$\Sigma = \mathbf{B}\phi\mathbf{B} + \psi \tag{6.20}$$

$$
\phi = \begin{pmatrix} \phi_{T_1 T_1} & & & \\ \phi_{T_2 T_1} & \phi_{T_2 T_2} & & \\ \phi_{T_3 T_1} & \phi_{T_3 T_2} & \phi_{T_3 T_3} & \\ \phi_{T_4 T_1} & \phi_{T_4 T_2} & \phi_{T_4 T_3} & \phi_{T_4 T_4} \end{pmatrix} \tag{6.21}
$$

$$\psi = (\sigma_{e_{11}}, \sigma_{e_{12}}, \sigma_{e_{21}}, \sigma_{e_{22}}, \sigma_{e_{31}}, \sigma_{e_{41}}, \sigma_{e_{42}}) \tag{6.22}$$

These equations—given the appropriate specification of fixed, free, and constrained parameters—may be used to test at least three types of reliability: (1) the general model of reliability positing underlying true-scores, (2) the model hypothesizing equal units of measurements (which is equivalent to Cronbach α), and (3) the model proposing parallel forms.

The first model hypothesizes that the four true-scores explain the entire pattern of relationships among the seven observed measurements (except for random error). This is the model implied by Eqs. (6.19)–(6.22). In this model, it is convenient to restrict one parameter in each column of $\mathbf{B}$ at one (e.g., $\beta_{11} = \beta_{21} = \beta_{31} = \beta_{41} = 1$) so that the true-scores are scaled in the same units of measurement as their respective observed-scores. This specification does not affect the outcome of hypothesis testing but merely aids in the interpretation of results since it establishes the metric of true-scores. From Eq. (6.16) it can be seen that the model is overidentified with $\frac{1}{2}(7)(8) - (3 + 10 + 5) = 10$ degrees of freedom.

The second reliability model makes the stronger assumption that all observations have equal units of measurement. This is equivalent to assuming that the measures are "essentially tau equivalent" (Lord and Novick, 1968, p. 50). The hypothesis of equal units of measurement may be tested by restricting $\beta_{11} = \beta_{12} = \beta_{21} = \beta_{22} = \beta_{31} = \beta_{41} = \beta_{42} = 1$. This model is overidentified with 13 degrees of freedom. The difference in χ^2 values between the first two models of reliability is a test of the equal units of measurement hypothesis.

Finally, the third reliability model makes even stronger assumptions by both restricting the β's to equal 1 and constraining the error variances of indicators of common true-scores to be equal (i.e., $\sigma_{e_{11}} = \sigma_{e_{12}}$, $\sigma_{e_{21}} = \sigma_{e_{22}}$, $\sigma_{e_{41}} = \sigma_{e_{42}}$). This model is known as the parallel halves model in the literature and, for the particular example investigated, there are 16 degrees of freedom. The difference in χ^2 tests between the second and third models is a test of the equality of the reliabilities for the measurements of common true-scores.

To compute the individual reliabilities of each measurement as well as the composite, the following formulas may be used (cf., Werts et al., 1974b):

$$\hat{\rho}_{N*} = \frac{\beta_{N*}^2 \, \text{var}(T_m)}{\beta_{N*}^2 \, \text{var}(T_m) + \text{var}(\sigma_{e_{N*}}^2)} \tag{6.23}$$

$$\hat{\rho}_C = \frac{(\sum_{i=1}^{N*} \beta_i)^2 \, \text{var}(T_m)}{(\sum_{i=1}^{N*} \beta_i)^2 \, \text{var}(T_m) + \sum_{i=1}^{N*} \sigma_{e_i}^2} \tag{6.24}$$

where $\hat{\rho}_{N*}$ is the reliability of the corresponding measure, $\hat{\rho}_C$ is the reliability of the composite for a single T_m, each β_{N*} and $\sigma_{e_{N*}}^2$ is paired with its corresponding T_m only, and $N*$ is the number of corresponding measurements. The composite error variances may be computed from

$$\sigma_e^2 = \frac{(\sum_{i=1}^{N*} \sigma_{e_i}^2)}{(\sum_{i=1}^{N*} \beta_i)^2} \tag{6.25}$$

Results

The application of LISREL to the data and three reliability models yields the results summarized in Table 6.6. Notice first that the results for the general reliability model shown in the first column indicate that the model is consistent with the data since $\chi^2 = 11.50$ with 10 degrees of freedom and $p \cong 0.32$. Thus, the general reliability model positing that task specific self-esteem is measured adequately by x_1 and x_2, job satisfaction is measured adequately by x_3 and x_4, sales performance is measured adequately by x_5, and new business performance is measured adequately by x_6 and x_7 can be accepted. The presentation

Table 6.6
Parameter Estimates and Hypothesis Test for the Three Reliability Models

The General Model of Reliability Positing Underlying True-Scores

$$\beta = \begin{pmatrix} 1.000 & 0 & 0 & 0 \\ 0.821 & 0 & 0 & 0 \\ 0 & 1.000 & 0 & 0 \\ 0 & 0.827 & 0 & 0 \\ 0 & 0 & 1.000 & 0 \\ 0 & 0 & 1.000 & 0 \\ 0 & 0 & 0 & 1.000 \\ 0 & 0 & 0 & 0.492 \end{pmatrix}$$

$$\phi = \begin{pmatrix} 2.962 & & & \\ 2.263 & 7.299 & & \\ 4.215 & 4.825 & 12.141 & \\ 2.015 & 0.696 & 2.810 & 8.504 \end{pmatrix}$$

$$\psi = (1.309,\ 1.501,\ 2.107,\ 1.707,\ 0,\ 3.028,\ 0)$$

$$\chi^2 = 11.50$$
$$\text{d.f.} = 10$$
$$p \cong 0.32$$

$$\chi_d^2 = 7.85$$
$$\text{d.f.} = 3$$
$$p \cong 0.05$$

The Reliability Model Hypothesizing Equal Units of Measurement

$$\beta = \begin{pmatrix} 1.000 & 0 & 0 & 0 \\ 1.000 & 0 & 0 & 0 \\ 0 & 1.000 & 0 & 0 \\ 0 & 1.000 & 0 & 0 \\ 0 & 0 & 1.000 & 0 \\ 0 & 0 & 1.000 & 0 \\ 0 & 0 & 0 & 1.000 \\ 0 & 0 & 0 & 1.000 \end{pmatrix}$$

$$\phi = \begin{pmatrix} 2.438 & & & \\ 1.881 & 5.900 & & \\ 3.877 & 4.185 & 12.141 & \\ 1.391 & 0.378 & 1.743 & 4.362 \end{pmatrix}$$

$$\psi = (1.409,\ 1.441,\ 2.321,\ 1.479,\ 0,\ 2.753,\ 1.946)$$

$$\chi^2 = 19.35$$
$$\text{d.f.} = 13$$
$$p \cong 0.11$$

$$\chi_d^2 = 12.05$$
$$\text{d.f.} = 3$$
$$p \cong 001$$

The Reliability Model Proposing Parallel Forms

$$\beta = \begin{pmatrix} 1.000 & 0 & 0 & 0 \\ 1.000 & 0 & 0 & 0 \\ 0 & 1.000 & 0 & 0 \\ 0 & 1.000 & 0 & 0 \\ 0 & 0 & 1.000 & 0 \\ 0 & 0 & 1.000 & 0 \\ 0 & 0 & 0 & 1.000 \\ 0 & 0 & 0 & 1.000 \end{pmatrix}$$

$$\phi = \begin{pmatrix} 2.432 & & & \\ 1.865 & 6.034 & & \\ 3.872 & 4.424 & 12.141 & \\ 1.192 & 0.116 & 1.210 & 4.185 \end{pmatrix}$$

$$\psi = (1.425,\ 1.425,\ 1.946,\ 1.946,\ 0,\ 2.384,\ 2.384)$$

$$\chi^2 = 31.40$$
$$\text{d.f.} = 16$$
$$p \cong 0.01$$

Table 6.7

Individual Reliabilities, Composite Reliabilities, and Error Variances for the Variables

Variable	Reliability for First Operationalization	Reliability for Second Operationalization	Composite Reliability	Total Error Variance
Task-specific self-esteem	0.634	0.470	0.712	1.196
Job satisfaction	0.622	0.631	0.768	2.203
Sales performance	—	—	1.000	0.000
New business	0.481	1.000	0.674	4.119

of the findings for the individual reliabilities for $x_1 - x_7$, the composite reliabilities, and the total error variances will be performed after discussion of the results for the other reliability models.

The results for the equal units of measurement model are shown in the second column of Table 6.6. Although the overall model fits the data fairly well (i.e., $\chi^2 = 19.35$ with 13 degrees of freedom and $p \cong 0.11$), one must reject the hypothesis of equal units of measurement because the difference in the goodness-of-fit tests between the first and second reliability models produces an $\chi^2 = 7.85$ with 3 degrees of freedom and $p \simeq 0.05$.

Finally, the findings for the reliability model hypothesizing parallel forms are presented in the third column of Table 6.6. Because the difference in χ^2 tests between the second and third models given an $\chi^2 = 12.05$ with 3 degrees of freedom and $p \cong 0.01$, the hypothesis of parallel forms must be rejected.

Table 6.7 summarizes the results for the individual reliabilities, composite reliabilities, and total error variance. In general, as indicated by the values for the composite reliabilities, the operationalizations do a reasonable job of measurement.

Further Issues in Causal Modeling

In this section, three common problems in causal modeling are addressed. First, the issue of correlated errors across the indicators of separate theoretical variables is discussed. Second, the issue of correlated errors within theoretical constructs is addressed. Third, the topic of the comparison of causal models is treated.

The first problem can perhaps best be analyzed with an example. Consider the model in Figure 6.6 consisting of two exogenous variables ξ_1 and ξ_2 influencing a theoretical variable η_1, which in turn is reciprocally related to a second theoretical variable η_2. The error term for the second indicator of η_1, ε_2, is shown correlated with the error term for the first indicator of η_2, ε_3. Correlated errors across factors (i.e., theoretical variables) might arise as a result of memory effects, demand characteristics, or the occurrence of some unmeasured cause(s) producing systematic variation in the indicators in addition to that arising from η_1 and η_2.

The model of Figure 6.6 can be easily estimated using the procedures developed in Chapter 4. To employ the program LISREL, however, one must make a number of alterations to the structural equation specification. In particular, the equations for the model of Figure 6.6 become

$$\begin{pmatrix} 1 & -\beta_1 & 0 & 0 \\ -\beta_2 & 1 & 0 & 0 \\ -\beta_3 & 0 & 1 & 0 \\ 0 & -\beta_4 & 0 & 1 \end{pmatrix} \begin{pmatrix} \eta_1 \\ \eta_2 \\ \eta_3 \\ \eta_4 \end{pmatrix} = \begin{pmatrix} \gamma_1 & \gamma_2 \\ 0 & 0 \\ 0 & 0 \\ 0 & 0 \end{pmatrix} \begin{pmatrix} \xi_1 \\ \xi_2 \end{pmatrix} + \begin{pmatrix} \zeta_1 \\ \zeta_2 \\ \zeta_3 \\ \zeta_4 \end{pmatrix}$$

$$\begin{pmatrix} y_1 \\ y_4 \\ y_2 \\ y_3 \end{pmatrix} = \begin{pmatrix} 1 & 0 & 0 & 0 \\ 0 & 1 & 0 & 0 \\ 0 & 0 & 1 & 0 \\ 0 & 0 & 0 & 1 \end{pmatrix} \begin{pmatrix} \eta_1 \\ \eta_2 \\ \eta_3 \\ \eta_4 \end{pmatrix} + \begin{pmatrix} 0 \\ 0 \\ 0 \\ 0 \end{pmatrix}$$

$$\begin{pmatrix} x_1 \\ x_2 \end{pmatrix} = \begin{pmatrix} 1 & 0 \\ 0 & 1 \end{pmatrix} \begin{pmatrix} \xi_1 \\ \xi_2 \end{pmatrix} + \begin{pmatrix} 0 \\ 0 \end{pmatrix}$$

The following matrix must also be constructed to allow $r_{\varepsilon_2\varepsilon_3}$ to occur:

$$\psi = \begin{pmatrix} \psi_{11} & & & \\ 0 & \psi_{22} & & \\ 0 & 0 & \psi_{33} & \\ 0 & 0 & \psi_{43} & \psi_{44} \end{pmatrix}$$

where $r_{\varepsilon_2\varepsilon_3} = \psi_{43}$.

The value in representing correlated errors across theoretical constructs is twofold. First, if the true model is actually described by such correlations, then this may be the only way to accurately represent the underlying causal processes.

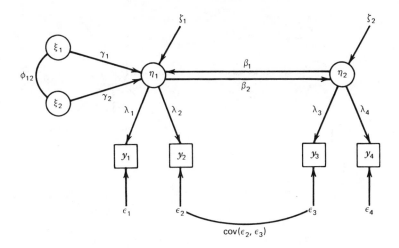

Figure 6.6. A simple causal model with errors allowed correlated across constructs.

Given that one has no further information as to the reasons for correlated errors and depending upon the nature and magnitude of such correlations, one will, in general, achieve inadequate fits for any model failing to allow for correlated errors that, in fact, are present.

A second benefit in the modeling of correlated errors across theoretical constructs lies in its use as a diagnostic tool. Costner and Schoenberg (1973), for example, investigate a number of variants of the model consisting of one theoretical variable influencing a second. For the case where both theoretical variables are operationalized with two measures, Costner and Schoenberg (1973) show that, if one investigates all possible sub-models with cross-construct correlated errors (using a procedure similar to that outlined above for Figure 6.6), it is possible to determine which pairs of cross-construct errors should be correlated. However, given only two indicators for each theoretical construct, one cannot determine the presence of (a) correlated errors between indicators of the same theoretical variable or (b) relationships between one theoretical variable and an indicator of a second theoretical variable. On the other hand, for the case where both theoretical variables are operationalized with at least three indicators, Costner and Schoenberg (1973) demonstrate that it is possible to discover cross-construct correlated errors, within-construct correlated errors, and relationships between one construct and the indicator(s) of another.

For correlated errors of indicators within constructs, consider the example illustrated in Figure 6.7. Again, to employ LISREL and the procedures

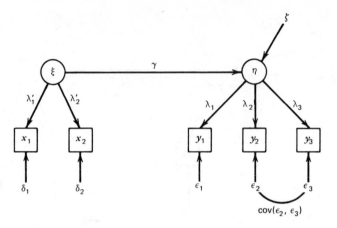

Figure 6.7. A simple causal model with errors for indicators allowed correlated within constructs.

developed in Chapter 4, the following alterations must be made to the structural equations:

$$\begin{pmatrix} 1 & 0 & 0 \\ -\beta_1 & 1 & 0 \\ -\beta_2 & 0 & 1 \end{pmatrix} \begin{pmatrix} \eta_1 \\ \eta_2 \\ \eta_3 \end{pmatrix} = \begin{pmatrix} \gamma \\ 0 \\ 0 \end{pmatrix} \xi + \begin{pmatrix} \zeta_1 \\ \zeta_2 \\ \zeta_3 \end{pmatrix}$$

$$\begin{pmatrix} y_1 \\ y_2 \\ y_3 \end{pmatrix} = \begin{pmatrix} 1 & 0 & 0 \\ 0 & 1 & 0 \\ 0 & 0 & 1 \end{pmatrix} \begin{pmatrix} \eta_1 \\ \eta_2 \\ \eta_3 \end{pmatrix} + \begin{pmatrix} 0 \\ 0 \\ 0 \end{pmatrix}$$

$$\begin{pmatrix} x_1 \\ x_2 \end{pmatrix} = \begin{pmatrix} \lambda_1' \\ \lambda_1' \end{pmatrix} \xi + \begin{pmatrix} \delta_1 \\ \delta_2 \end{pmatrix}$$

$$\phi = \text{var}(\xi)$$

$$\psi = \begin{pmatrix} \psi_{11} & & \\ 0 & \psi_{22} & \\ 0 & \psi_{32} & \psi_{33} \end{pmatrix}$$

where $\psi_{32} = \text{cov}(\varepsilon_2, \varepsilon_3)$, $\lambda_2 = \beta_1$, and $\lambda_3 = \beta_2$.

The final issue to be considered is the comparison of parameters and/or causal models within a particular population or across populations. Consider first the problem of the comparison of structural parameters within a causal model fitted to a specific population. As used throughout this monograph, the structural parameters representing linear relationships between variables are either standardized or unstandardized coefficients. The relationship between any standardized and unstandardized parameter can be represented as follows:

$$P_{ij} = b_{ij}\left(\frac{\sigma_j}{\sigma_i}\right)$$

where P_{ij} is a standardized parameter (also called a path coefficient) relating a dependent variable i to an independent variable j, b_{ij} is an unstandardized parameter relating dependent variable i to independent variable j, σ_j is the standard deviation of independent variable j, and σ_i is the standard deviation of dependent variable i. Notice that the standardized parameter is a function of both the unstandardized coefficient (which measures the contribution or effect of the independent variable upon the dependent variable in an absolute sense) and the ratio of standard deviations of independent to dependent variables.

The distinction between standardized versus unstandardized parameters has a number of implications. First, as Kim and Mueller (1976, p. 436) note: "standardized coefficients, but not unstandardized coefficients, are affected (even when there are no specification, measurement and sampling errors) by the following analytically distinct components of the variance-covariance structure:

1. The variance of the independent variable under consideration;
2. The variances of other variables that are explicitly identified in the causal system;
3. The covariances of the explicitly included variables; and
4. The variance of the variables not explicitly included in the causal system."

Standardized parameters are appropriate only when one desires to compare the relative contributions of a number of independent variables on the same dependent variable and for the same sample of observations. They are not appropriate and can lead to false inferences when one desires to make comparisons across populations or samples.

The unstandardized parameters, in contrast, are appropriate for comparisons across populations or samples because they are not affected by the above contaminating factors. However, as Schoenberg (1972) shows, unstandardized parameters may be inappropriate when:

1. There is random measurement error in the independent variable (and this is not taken into account).
2. There is nonrandom measurement error in variables (e.g., the error component of variables are intercorrelated or are correlated with other variables).
3. Important causes of the dependent variable are omitted.
4. The units of measurement for independent or dependent variable change from one population to another.

Using unstandardized parameters as a base, Specht and Warren (1975) develop a technique for comparing causal models and individual parameters across populations. The approach is essentially an extension of multiple regression, and it employs the F-test to examine hypotheses. The procedures assume no measurement error in variables, independent residuals within and between equations in the model, and homoskedastic error variances.

Summary

The multiple-indicator-multiple-cause (MIMIC) model is a common one in the behavioral sciences. The chapter began with an analysis of two special cases of the MIMIC model: the situation where the indicators of the unobservable are uncorrelated and the situation where they are correlated. Next, the MIMIC model was extended to include a fallible unobservable as a consequence of the original unobservable.

The presentation then turned to an illustration of the general linear model as a methodology for fitting and testing recursive models. Next, a general structural equation model for representing and testing reliability was derived and illustrated. Finally, the chapter closed with an introduction to problems in the comparison of causal models and structural parameters within and across populations and samples and the general problem of correlated errors both between and within constructs.

Note

[1]For a description of the full model and empirical results, see Bagozzi and Van Loo (1978).

SEVEN

STRUCTURAL EQUATION MODELS IN EXPERIMENTAL RESEARCH

Researchers have found the experimental design to be an effective method for testing theory. This chapter[1] derives and illustrates a structural equation approach for the development and analysis of theory using the experimental method. The causal modeling orientation provides the researcher with a means for discovering the existence of a causal relation (through a χ^2 goodness-of-fit test), the magnitude of this relation, the measurement error of constructs, and certain problems in the particular application of an experimental design (e.g., the existence of demand characteristics, evaluation apprehension, etc.).

The chapter begins with a brief introduction to the experimental method with particular emphasis given to problems with the usual methods of analysis and how a structural equation methodology might overcome some of these problems. Next, a basic structural equation model is derived for the situation consisting of a single experimental manipulation with a single treatment or multiple treatments (with multiple manipulation checks) and a single dependent variable with multiple operationalizations. The model is then illustrated with simulated data from a marketing experiment. Following this, the presentation turns to a derivation of a methodology for diagnosing experimental design problems. Finally, the chapter closes with a discussion of more complicated experimental designs and the role of structural equations.

The Experimental Method

Basic Considerations

Before development of the structural equation approach for analyzing experimental data, it is useful to illustrate features of the traditional experimental design. Consider the situation diagramed in Figure 7.1 consisting of one independent variable x, a single dependent variable y, and a causal relation from x to y (represented as β'). The figure represents one way for depicting the posttest-only control group design (cf., Campbell and Stanley, 1963, pp. 25–27). Suppose, for purposes of illustration, that the marketing researcher desires to test whether a change in x will produce a change in y. For example, one might wish to ascertain the effect of source credibility in an advertisement on subsequent attitude change. In general, x and y could each consist of qualitative variables (e.g., nominal or ordinal), quantitative variables (e.g., interval or ratio) or combinations of qualitative and quantitative variables.

In the typical two-group experimental design (cf., Keppel, 1973), test subjects are assigned randomly to either a control or treatment group, and the independent variable is manipulated in the latter. For perhaps the most common experimental situation, the independent variable is a dichotomous nominal variable, whereas the dependent variable is continuous. The analysis of variance technique is used most often in such cases, and the appropriate test is to examine the null hypothesis postulating equality in means between the two groups. By use of the F-test, a significant value indicates that the difference between means for the groups is statistically significant. An equivalent method of analysis for this two-group example can be performed using the multiple regression model. That is, by use of dummy variables to indicate which group a test subject is in, the regression model can determine whether there is a relation between x and y. The null hypothesis maintains that $R^2 = 0$, and a significant F-ratio indicates whether or not the value of R^2 is statistically significant. The equivalence of the analysis of variance and multiple regression models for analyzing such data is well known and will not be demonstrated here (cf., Kerlinger and Pedhazur, 1973; Scheffé, 1959; Woodward and Overall, 1975). However, it should be noted that, although the methods are interchangeable for the case in which the dependent variable is categorical (e.g., nominal), "multiple regression analysis

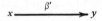

Figure 7.1. A simple two-variable model: one independent variable x and one dependent variable y.

is superior or the only appropriate method of analysis in the following cases: (1) when the independent variable is continuous, that is, experimental treatments with varying degrees of the same variable; (2) when the independent variables are both continuous and categorical, as in analysis of covariance, or treatments by levels designs; (3) when cell frequencies in a factorial design are unequal and disproportionate; (4) when studying trends in data: linear, quadratic, and so on" (Kerlinger and Pedhazur, 1973, pp. 113–114).

When looking for a possible causal relation between x and y, the researcher seldom will stop at the significance tests described above, however. Because the significance tests determine only the presence or absence of treatment effects, one would like additional information as to the nature of the causal relationship itself (particularly for the case of a quantitative independent variable and orthogonal comparisons for trend). As a result, methodologists have developed procedures and criteria for examining the character of β' in Figure 7.1. For example, when different levels of the treatment x are manipulated, useful information can be obtained from comparisons among treatment means. The marketing researcher may have five levels of source expertise (very low, low, medium, high, and very high). A significant F-test for the means of the five groups on the dependent variable y merely indicates that the five means are different. It tells nothing about the particular differences among the possible pairs of means or the shape of the function relating expertise to a dependent variable of interest. For this reason, it is often desirable to make comparisons among means and an analysis of trend in order to answer questions such as: (1) Do the *combined* experimental groups differ from the control group—that is, is there a general experimental effect? (2) Do the experimental groups differ among themselves? (3) What is the form of the function relating independent to dependent variables? The researcher has several options to follow in such cases including orthogonal analysis, trend analysis, and certain multiple comparisons. These topics are well known and are covered in standard texts on experimental design (cf., Keppel, 1973, Winer, 1971).

In addition to determining if a causal relation exists, one often would like to know the magnitude or strength of the relationship between x and y. The *omega squared* (ω^2) index is useful in this context. For the single-factor experiment, the index can be written as (e.g., Keppel, 1973)

$$\hat{\omega}_A^2 = \frac{\hat{\sigma}_A^2}{\hat{\sigma}_T^2} = \frac{\hat{\sigma}_A^2}{\hat{\sigma}_A^2 + \hat{\sigma}_{S/A}^2} \tag{7.1}$$

where $\hat{\sigma}_A^2$ is an estimate of the population treatment variance, $\hat{\sigma}_T^2$ is an estimate of the population total variance, and $\hat{\sigma}_{S/A}^2$ is an estimate of the within-levels variance. The index indicates the amount of variance explained or accounted for by the experimental treatment. In this case, it reflects the strength of association between x and y. Keppel (1973) presents the formulas for applying the ω^2 index to completely randomized designs and the fixed-effects model. Other researchers have treated cases in which random factors or repeated measures are used, among other issues (e.g., Fleiss, 1969; Keppel, 1973; Vaughan and Corballis, 1969).

The use of the experimental method for inferring causality goes considerably beyond the single-factor model illustrated above. The analysis of the effects of two or more independent variables in factorial experiments, repeated measures designs, and analysis of covariance models greatly increase the ability of the researcher to determine the existence and nature of causal relationships. Because the structural equation model below accommodates the single-factor and multiple-factor experiments as well as the analysis of covariance models, these topics are not discussed here in the interest of brevity. For discussions of these topics from the perspective of the traditional experimental design, the reader is referred elsewhere (e.g., Keppel, 1973; Winer, 1971).

Problems with the Traditional Experimental Method

The classical experimental method and traditional analysis of variance and regression models are fine as far as they go, but a number of shortcomings deserve mention. These shortcomings arise as a result of (1) the assumptions made in both the experimental method and data analytic procedures, (2) certain omissions with respect to the representation of cause-and-effect, and (3) limitations in the overall approach for diagnosing flaws in any particular application.

In order to discuss these shortcomings, consider first the issues of measurement error and the modeling of cause-and-effect in the context of an experiment. The traditional experimental design and experimental analysis assume that the independent and dependent variables are measured without error and that the causal relationship, if present, is between these measured variables. Thus, with these assumptions, the model of Figure 7.1 may be expressed in the following regression equation:

$$y = \alpha + \beta'x + u \tag{7.2}$$

where y and x are, respectively, the observed (i.e., measured) dependent and independent variables, α is an intercept, and u is an error term.

There are at least three reasons why the model in (7.2) or its analysis of variance equivalent may be incorrect, insufficient, or misleading. The first reason stems from the representation of the independent variable, that is, the experimental manipulation. Although a significant F-test indicates that a difference between means of a control and treatment groups exists, the difference may not be due entirely to the effect of the manipulation itself. For example, variation in the dependent variable may be due to factors independent of the manipulation such as demand characteristics, evaluation apprehension, or other artifacts.[2] Although the experimenter usually will try to control for these artifacts, application of the analysis of variance or regression model to experimental data consisting only of the measured independent and dependent variables can not determine whether (1) the significant F-test indicates that the manipulation alone produced the difference in means in the dependent variable, (2) artifacts alone produced the difference, or (3) both the manipulation and artifacts produced the difference. For this reason, many experimenters in recent years have attempted to obtain evidence (independent of the dependent variable) indicating whether the experimental manipulation was indeed effective. The evidence is typically in the form of self-report questions asking the respondent for his or her perceptions, comprehension, or some other psychological reactions to the manipulation(s). The questions are commonly referred to as manipulation checks. The logic of their use lies in the fact that a necessary condition for inferring causality from x to y is that subjects are exposed to x, and x, in turn, has some effect on a psychological state. The combination of controls designed to reduce artifacts with the use of manipulation checks provides the experimenter with stronger evidence for inferring causality. However, even in those few marketing studies using manipulation checks, the representation of the relation between the experimental treatment and the manipulation checks usually has not been modeled explicitly in the context of the entire experimental design. That is, the practice has been to see if the manipulation checks are significant and then to perform the usual experimental analysis using only the measured independent and dependent variables. A better practice would be to include the independent variables, dependent variables, and manipulation checks in a single model. As shown below, this procedure allows the researcher to represent better measurement error and causality.

The second problem with the traditional experimental design is the fact that the dependent variable is generally represented as measured without error. Ideally, one would like a model of the experimental design and analysis that explicitly represents the construct validity of the concepts being tested in one's theory (e.g., see Chapter 5 and Bagozzi, 1977d, 1978a; Campbell and Fiske, 1959). At a minimum, the analysis of the experiment should take into account the degree of correspondence between the dependent variables as a concept and the operationalization(s) used to measure that concept. Constructs that are not internally consistent in a theoretical sense, that are improperly operationalized, or that have low reliabilities in measurement will most certainly yield inaccurate and misleading findings. For a full interpretation of the nature of the causal relationship between variables, it is necessary to model the degree of measurement error in one's constructs (see the discussions in Chapters 4 and 5).

A third problem, though related to the first two, is more conceptual in nature. The experimental design is intended as a means of discovering, and testing for, cause-and-effect relationships. Although considerable debate exists as to the nature of the causal relation, most contemporary researchers using the experimental method assume a perspective that may be traced largely to the influence of Hume and Mill (see discussion in Chapter 1). Campbell (Campbell and

Stanley, 1963; Cook and Campbell, 1976) and Simon (1957) are two contemporary advocates of this tradition. As employed by these and other researchers, causation is conceived as a relation between variables or constructs in a theory and not between observed objects or events in the world of experience. Hence, unless one assumes or has reason to believe that one's variables in an experimental design are measured without error, there are a priori reasons for questioning the analysis of experiments that use only observed variables. As developed below, it is more sound from a theoretical standpoint to model cause-and-effect between theoretical variables that, in turn, are operationalized by measures of those variables.

In order to see why the above problems limit the traditional experimental design and make its application misleading in some instances, it will prove useful to compare the model of Figure 7.1 and Eq. (7.2) with a causal model explicitly representing manipulation checks, measurement error in the dependent variable, and the relationship between independent and dependent variables in a single overall structure. Consider the model of Figure 7.2 that depicts just such a structure. According to the conventions presented in Chapters 3–5, circles represent theoretical variables, squares illustrate operationalizations or other observed variables, and lines with arrowheads denote linear causal relationships. The model of Figure 7.2 may be interpreted as follows. The manipulation of the independent variable x ultimately causes variation in two observables. First, variation in x as a stimulus will cause a change in some psychological state in the test subjects (e.g., an emotion or thought). This will

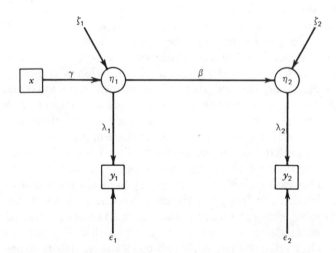

Figure 7.2. A causal model relating a single independent variable with one manipulation check to a single dependent variable with one operationalization.

be measured by the manipulation check y_1. The manipulation check, like all measurements of mental states, will be a fallible indicator of a theoretical construct η_1 (often referred to as an unobservable or true variable). The theoretical construct η_1 represents the true psychological state measured by y_1. The correspondence between this theoretical construct η_1 and the manipulation check y_1 is indicated by λ_1. The error in y_1 is represented by ε_1, while the error in equations (developed below) for η_1 is depicted as ζ_1. The impact of the manipulation x upon the true psychological state η_1 is represented as γ. The impact will be measured as a difference in means for categorical independent variables and as a parameter for continuous independent variables. Second, variation in x—given that the treatment has been effective—will produce a change in the observed value of the dependent variable y_2 (often referred to also as an indicator or operationalization). The true, unobserved dependent variable (for which y_2 is a measure) is indicated by η_2; ε_2 represents the error in y_2; λ_2 models the correspondence between η_2 and y_2; and ζ_2 is the error in equations term for η_2. Finally, the cause-and-effect relation between theoretical terms is represented by β. The dependent variable may itself be a psychological state or it may be an action or overt behavior. An example of a manipulation check in a persuasive communication study could be a measure of awareness or comprehension; while a dependent variable of interest might be attitude change, purchase intention, or actual purchase.

A number of advantages can be gained by using a model such as shown in Figure 7.2 rather than the regression model of Figure 7.1 (or its analysis of variance equivalent). First, rather than assuming that the experimental treatment has been perceived correctly and has produced its intended effect, the causal model of Figure 7.2 explicitly models the impact of the independent variable as reflected in the manipulation check. The representation of the manipulation check allows for measurement error and gives a direct index of the quality of the administration of the treatment (through the parameters γ, λ_1 and the variance of ε_1). Second, by portraying the dependent variable as both a construct and its operationalization, one is provided with a means of determining elements of construct validity (at least to the extent of convergent validity) and the degree of fallibility in one's measurement of the true dependent variable. To see why it is a good practice to model measurement error explicitly, consider the example of a continuous independent variable x and a continuous dependent variable y_2. If there is no measurement error in the dependent variable and if one can rule out artifacts such as demand characteristics, then a measure of the cause-and-effect relationship can be obtained as β' as shown in Figure 7.1 and Eq. (7.2). This model further assumes an errorless impact in the treatment. But suppose, as is often more realistic, that the operationalization for the dependent variable contains some error in measurement (due, for example, to the nature of the instrument used) and that the implementation of the treatment is not perceived perfectly as is assumed by the usual experimental design. Under these conditions, the cause-and-effect relation will be estimated as β as shown in Figure 7.2. In general, β will not equal β' except when $\gamma = \lambda_2 = 1$, that is, when the treatment is perceived exactly as intended and the dependent variable is measured without error (for a formal analysis of measurement error and the problems involved, see the discussion in Chapters 4 and 5). The procedures for estimating parameters in models similar to that in Figure 7.2 are derived in the next section. The model of Figure 7.2 offers the additional advantage of conforming to contemporary conceptions of causality in that cause-and-effect is represented as a relationship between theoretical variables, in contrast to the practice of the strictly empirical model of Figure 7.1. Finally, as will be developed in greater depth below, a model such as shown in Figure 7.2 (given certain additions needed to make it identified) can be used in a diagnostic sense to detect flaws in a particular experimental design application and to suggest ways for improving one's experiments. For the model of Figure 7.2 to be meaningful, at least two measures are required for η_1 and/or η_2.

The Basic Structural Equation Model

In this section of the chapter, a basic model is derived for the general experimental situation consisting of a single independent variable (for a single treatment or multiple treatments) with multiple manipulation checks and a single dependent variable with multiple operationalizations. A maximum likelihood procedure is used to determine parameter estimates, and the likelihood ratio technique is used to derive an overall χ^2 test-of-significance for the entire model.

Consider the model[3] illustrated in Figure 7.3 consisting of a single manipulated independent variable x, m manipulation checks $y_1, \ldots, y_m$, and $t - m$ operationalizations of a single dependent variable, $y_{m+1}, \ldots, y_t$. Using η_1 and η_2 to represent the true (i.e., measured without error) independent and dependent variables, respectively, the system of Figure 7.3 may be written as the following *structural form* equation:

$$\mathbf{B}\boldsymbol{\eta} = \boldsymbol{\Gamma}x + \boldsymbol{\zeta} \tag{7.3}$$

$$\mathbf{B} = \begin{pmatrix} 1 & 0 \\ -\beta & 1 \end{pmatrix}$$

$$\boldsymbol{\eta}' = (\eta_1, \eta_2)$$

$$\boldsymbol{\Gamma}' = (\gamma, 0)$$

$$\boldsymbol{\zeta}' = (\zeta_1, \zeta_2)$$

The structural form represents the relations among the observed experimental manipulation, the true independent variable, and the true dependent variable.

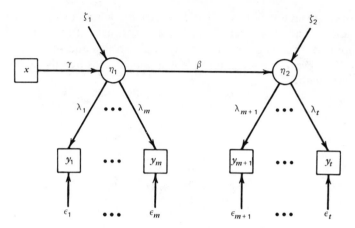

Figure 7.3. Basic model of an experiment with a single independent and dependent variable and multiple manipulation checks and operational indicators.

The parameter γ indicates the effect of the manipulated independent variable on the true independent variable, whereas β indicates the effect of the true independent variable on the true dependent variable. The error term ζ is a random vector of disturbances (i.e., errors in equations). Without loss of generality, it is assumed that $E(\eta) = E(x) = E(\zeta) = 0$. Similarly, **B** is assumed nonsingular, and ζ is assumed uncorrelated with x.

Next, consider the vector of observed variables

$$Z' = (y, \ldots, y_m, y_{m+1}, \ldots, y_t, x),$$

which can be written to represent the relationships between true independent and dependent variables and observed manipulation checks and operational indicators, respectively, as follows:

$$
\mathbf{Z} = \begin{pmatrix} y_1 \\ \vdots \\ y_m \\ y_{m+1} \\ \vdots \\ y_t \\ x \end{pmatrix} = \begin{pmatrix} \lambda & 0 & 0 \\ \vdots & \vdots & \vdots \\ 0 & & \vdots \\ \lambda_m & 0 & \vdots \\ 0 & \lambda_{m+1} & \vdots \\ \vdots & \vdots & \vdots \\ 0 & \lambda_t & 0 \\ 0 & 0 & 1 \end{pmatrix} \begin{pmatrix} \eta_1 \\ \eta_2 \\ \xi \end{pmatrix} + \begin{pmatrix} \varepsilon \\ \vdots \\ \varepsilon_m \\ \varepsilon_{m+1} \\ \vdots \\ \varepsilon_t \\ 0 \end{pmatrix} \tag{7.4}
$$

In this system of equations, the identity $x = \xi$ has been added to be consistent with the notation used in the general model presented in Chapter 4. In addition, the errors ε are assumed uncorrelated with each other and with the true variates η_1, η_2, and ξ. The parameters $\lambda_1, \ldots, \lambda_t$ are measures of the relationships (i.e., correspondence rules) between theoretical constructs and operationalizations. Finally, the observable indicators y are assumed measured as deviation scores from their means.

Letting $G' = (\eta_1, \eta_2, \xi)$, the vector of true variables, and

$$\Delta = \begin{pmatrix} \lambda_1 & 0 & 0 \\ \vdots & \vdots & \vdots \\ \lambda_m & 0 & \vdots \\ 0 & \lambda_{m+1} & \vdots \\ \vdots & \vdots & \vdots \\ 0 & \lambda_t & 0 \\ 0 & 0 & 1 \end{pmatrix} \tag{7.5}$$

the equations in (7.4) may be conveniently written at

$$Z = \Delta G + \varepsilon \tag{7.6}$$

The implied population covariance matrix of observed variables may then be expressed as

$$\begin{aligned} \Omega = E(ZZ') &= E[\Delta G + \varepsilon)(\Delta G + \varepsilon)'] \\ &= \Delta E(GG')\Delta' + E(\varepsilon\varepsilon') \\ &= \Delta \Phi \Delta' + \theta \end{aligned} \tag{7.7}$$

where $E(G\varepsilon') = 0$, $\Phi = E(GG')$, the covariance matrix of true variables, and θ is a diagonal matrix of error variances.

The system of equations in (7.4) is a special case of the general factor analysis model (Goldberger, 1974, p. 198). That is, it can be interpreted as a set of $t + 1$ observable variables $y_1, \ldots, y, x$, which are determined by $k = 2$ unobservable variables (η_1, η_2) and t independent disturbances (because x is assumed measured without error). Equation (7.7) represents a set of q' equations in p' unknowns, where $q' = (t + 1)(t + 1 + 1)/2 = (t + 1)(t + 2)/2$, and $p' = 3 + 2t.$[4] As an example of an overidentified model, consider the case for $m = 2$ manipulation checks and $t - m = 2$ operationalizations of the dependent variable. In this case, $q' = (5)(6)/2 = 15$ and $p' = 3 + 2(4) = 11$; hence, there are four overidentifying restrictions for the model (assuming the variances of the error terms for the true variables η_1 and η_2 have been standardized at one).

In order to estimate the parameters of the model (i.e., $\gamma, \beta, \lambda_1, \ldots, \lambda_t$, $\sigma_1^2, \ldots, \sigma_t^2$, and $\sigma_{\eta_1\eta_2}$), the values of Δ, Φ, and θ should be chosen to minimize

$$\ln|(\Omega)| + \text{tr}(\Omega^{-1}S) \tag{7.8}$$

where S is the sample covariance matrix, ln is the natural logarithm, and tr stands for the trace (Goldberger, 1974). In general, to minimize (7.8), an iterative procedure is required on a set of equations based on (7.8) (Goldberger, 1974). The estimates achieved by this procedure are maximum-likelihood estimates and are thus consistent and asymptotic efficient. Jöreskog's procedures are also applicable here.

Following the development due to Lawley and Maxwell (1971), one can derive a goodness-of-fit test for the model in Figure 7.3. This statistic, which is based on the likelihood ratio test, is equal to $N \ln[|(\hat{\Omega})|/|(S)|]$, where N is the sample size. The statistic is distributed χ^2 with degrees of freedom equal to $q' - p'$, the number of overidentifying restrictions. In particular, the test is a test of a specified model such as illustrated in Figure 7.3 versus the most general alternative hypothesis that Ω is any positive-definite matrix. Further indication of the degree of fit of a model can be determined from the standard errors of the parameter estimates and from the resulting residual matrix. The estimation procedures and goodness-of-fit test are illustrated below.

A Marketing Example

In order to illustrate the basic model, a set of data was generated to simulate the results of a typical experiment. For purposes of illustration, it is assumed that the data were obtained from a source credibility communication study consisting of a single manipulation for two levels of communicator credibility. Credibility might, for example, be manipulated by having two different speakers —one an expert and the other naive—present identical persuasive advertising appeals to separate experimental treatment groups. The two levels of the manipulation might then be termed high credibility and low credibility, respectively. For this hypothetical example, two separate manipulation checks each comprised of, say, three seven-point Likert scale questions are assumed to be obtained from each subject. The manipulation checks could be taken after an initial description of the speaker to the subjects but prior to the actual treatment, or could be taken at the end of the experiment, depending on the particular test design and circumstances. The actual manipulation check questions might tap perceived source expertise, knowledgeability, or other aspects of source credibility. It is assumed further that two measures of attitude (the dependent variable) toward a product advocated in the persuasive appeal were obtained from each subject (it is also conceivable that a pretest could have been taken in order to ascertain attitude change as a function of source credibility). The two attitude measures might be the belief and evaluative dimensions of attitude toward the act of using the product (cf., Lutz, 1975). The sample size

Table 7.1
Correlation Matrix of Variables for Hypothetical Credibility Experiment

Variable	Variable				
	y_1	y_2	y_3	y_4	x
y_1	1.00				
y_2	0.69	1.00			
y_3	0.39	0.43	1.00		
y_4	0.44	0.52	0.77	1.00	
x	0.71	0.82	0.41	0.48	1.00

for the experiment was 90. Table 7.1 presents the simulated zero-order correlations among the experimental manipulation (x), two manipulation checks (y_1, y_2), and two operationalizations of the dependent variable (y_3, y_4). The fact that the two manipulation check measures are correlated less between themselves than with the manipulation might be due to the fact that some error exists in the manipulation itself and/or that the zero-order correlation between the dichotomous manipulation and the continuous manipulation checks contains some error.

Using the structural equation approach derived for the basic model, maximum-likelihood estimates of parameters were determined.[5] The relevant structural equations for this model are

$$\mathbf{B\eta} = \mathbf{\Gamma}x + \zeta$$

or

$$\begin{pmatrix} 1 & 0 \\ -\beta & 1 \end{pmatrix} \begin{pmatrix} \eta_1 \\ \eta_2 \end{pmatrix} = \begin{pmatrix} \gamma \\ 0 \end{pmatrix} x + \begin{pmatrix} \zeta_1 \\ \zeta_2 \end{pmatrix}$$

and the reduced form is

$$\begin{pmatrix} y_1 \\ y_2 \\ y_3 \\ y_4 \\ x \end{pmatrix} = \begin{pmatrix} \lambda_1 & 0 & 0 \\ \lambda_2 & 0 & 0 \\ 0 & \lambda_3 & 0 \\ 0 & \lambda_4 & 0 \\ 0 & 0 & 1 \end{pmatrix} \begin{pmatrix} \eta_1 \\ \eta_2 \\ \xi \end{pmatrix} + \begin{pmatrix} \varepsilon_1 \\ \varepsilon_2 \\ \varepsilon_3 \\ \varepsilon_4 \\ 0 \end{pmatrix}$$

where, as before, the identity $x = \xi$ is specified in order to be consistent with the notation of the general model presented in Chapter 4. Table 7.2 lists the

Table 7.2
Parameter Estimates for Hypothetical
Credibility Experiment

Parameter	Standardized Value	Standard Errors
γ	0.92	0.20
β	0.55	0.16
λ_1	0.77	0.16
λ_2	0.89	0.19
λ_3	0.81	0.10
λ_4	0.96	0.13
$\sigma_{\eta_1\eta_2}$	0.06	0.13
θ_{ε_1}	0.64	0.06
θ_{ε_2}	0.45	0.06
θ_{ε_3}	0.59	0.08
θ_{ε_4}	0.30	0.20

maximum-likelihood standardized estimates, and the corresponding standard errors where it can be seen that the parameter estimates are highly significant. The χ^2 goodness-of-fit test for the model with 4 degrees of freedom is 0.30 with a probability level p of 0.99. As developed in Chapter 4, the p value gives the probability of getting a χ^2 value larger than the value actually obtained given that the hypothesized structure is true. The higher the value of p, the better the fit. In practice, values of $p \geq 0.10$ often give acceptable fits (cf., Lawley and Maxwell, 1971). Another indication of the goodness-of-fit can be obtained from the residual matrix (Table 7.3), which illustrates the difference between

Table 7.3
Residual Matrix for Hypothetical Credibility Experiment

Variable	Variable y_1	y_2	y_3	y_4	x
y_1	0.000				
y_2	0.000	0.000			
y_3	−0.012	0.007	0.000		
y_4	0.007	−0.003	0.000	0.000	
x	−0.001	0.000	−0.004	0.001	0.000

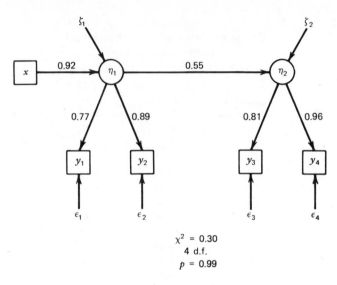

Figure 7.4. The basic model and maximum-likelihood parameter estimates for the hypothetical credibility experiment.

the actual and implied correlation matrices. Figure 7.4 summarizes the basic model for the hypothetical credibility experiment.

A number of conclusions may be derived from the foregoing results. From the χ^2 test and the parameter estimates and standard errors for γ and β, respectively, one can conclude that the experimental manipulation was effective and the independent variable (source credibility) had a significant positive effect on the dependent variable (attitudes). Thus, for example, the maximum-likelihood parameter estimate for β gives the direct effect the true independent variable has on the true dependent variable. A one unit change in the independent variable will produce a change of $\beta = 0.55$ units in the dependent variable. The unstandardized maximum-likelihood parameter estimates (not shown) give the effect variables have in an absolute sense and can be used to compare similar models in other populations. However, these estimates are tied to the measurement units of the variables they connect. Any change in the measurement scale for either independent of dependent variable changes the value, and, hence, comparability, of parameters across populations. A partial solution to this problem is provided by the standardized parameter estimates since all variables are in one sense measured on comparable scales when converted to variables with equal variances.[6] This procedure permits a comparison of parameters across experiments when the same population is under consideration. It also allows the researcher to compare the relative contributions of different independent variables on the same or different dependent variables within a particular experimental study. The standardized estimates are not suitable for comparisons across populations. The unstandardized estimates should be used in these cases (subject to the caution noted above). For detailed discussions of the pros and cons of standardized versus unstandardized parameter estimates, the reader is referred to Tukey (1954), Wright (1956), and Blalock (1967a), and Kim and Mueller (1976).

Finally, the results of the analysis of the experiment provide insights in regard to the degree of measurement error of operationalizations and the degree of construct validity achieved. In the model of Figure 7.2, y_1 and y_2 can be treated as indicators (i.e., measures) of η_1; and y_3 and y_4 may be viewed as indicators of η_2. An indication of the degree of correspondence between theoretical construct and operationalizations may be gained from the values and standard errors of the λ parameters, the amount of error in the model, and the goodness-of-fit test. Although the λ parameters for this hypothetical example are all significant, it can be seen that y_4 is relatively a better measure of its theoretical construct than, say, y_1 is of its construct (based on the magnitude and standard errors of parameters and estimated errors in variables). For a detailed discussion of construct validity, see the treatment in Chapter 5.

A rough indication of the specification validity of any model can be determined rather quickly by examining the observed correlations among manipulation checks and dependent variable operationalizations. For two-variable models such as shown in Figure 7.4, Costner (1969) derives an empirical rule of thumb—termed the "consistency criterion"—which, if satisfied, would indicate that unique estimates of parameters can be found for the model. For the model of Figure 7.4 (omitting x), the consistency criterion can be expressed as

$$(r_{y_1 y_3})(r_{y_2 y_4}) = (r_{y_1 y_4})(r_{y_2 y_3})$$

where the r's are the zero-order correlations between variables. As Costner (1969) shows, the consistency criteria is a necessary, but not sufficient, condition for the absence of a misspecified model. As an example, the consistency criterion for the data of Table 7.1 and Figure 7.4 can be expressed as follows:

$$(0.39)(0.52) = 0.20 \cong (0.44)(0.43) \cong 0.19$$

Since the equality approximately holds, one may conclude that the model is a reasonable fit; and most of the error in the model is random (i.e., the result of random error in equations and error variables) rather than due to a systematic misspecification of relationships. Because the consistency criterion tells nothing about how far the equality may deviate empirically, the maximum-likelihood procedures outlined above are preferable, even though they are more complicated and difficult to solve. Nevertheless, as a quick means for evaluating alternative causal structures, the consistency criterion is useful.

Diagnosing Problems in Experimental Research

If a researcher were to obtain results similar to the example of the preceding section, then he or she could, with a reasonably high degree of confidence, conclude that the experimental manipulation did indeed produce the predicted effect. But what is one to conclude if the expected hypothesis is not confirmed? It could be that there is no theoretical justification for such a causal prediction, and hence events fail to provide evidence. It could also be the case, however, that sufficient care was not taken in the choice, operationalization, and actual measurement of relevant variables in the study. Or the conduct of the experiment might have been such as to contain confounds or artifacts such as evaluation apprehension, demand characteristics, or other forms of reactivity (Cook and Campbell, 1976; Rosenthal and Rosnow, 1969). These alternative explanations need to be considered for a full interpretation of the results in any experimental research, yet they are not easily handled by the traditional means of experimental analysis. In the following paragraphs, a procedure is described that explicitly allows the researcher to determine certain confounds and rival hypotheses. Simulated data are used at points of the discussion to illustrate the technique.

Consider two experiments, A and B, on source credibility such as illustrated in the previous section. Tables 7.4 and 7.5, respectively, present the zero-order correlations among relevant variables. Using the procedures described above, estimation of parameters and analysis of the basic model yield the results shown in Table 7.6. Routine procedures of statistical inference lead to a rejection of both models since the χ^2, probability levels, and standard errors indicate a poor fit. An important question to answer is why do the data not support the proposed theory?

In order to answer this question, the steps outlined in Figure 7.5 may be followed. These procedures represent an expansion and modification of Costner's (1971) three-stage procedure and Alwin and Tessler's (1974) approach.

Table 7.4
Correlation Matrix of Variables for Experiment A

Variable	y_1	y_2	y_3	y_4	x
y_1	1.00				
y_2	0.79	1.00			
y_3	0.49	0.48	1.00		
y_4	0.38	0.39	0.71	1.00	
x	0.47	0.24	0.24	0.11	1.00

Table 7.5
Correlation Matrix of Variables for Experiment B

	Variable				
Variable	y_1	y_2	y_3	y_4	x
y_1	1.00				
y_2	0.36	1.00			
y_3	0.49	0.20	1.00		
y_4	0.18	0.39	0.25	1.00	
x	0.41	0.24	0.20	0.11	1.00

Table 7.6
Analysis of Parameter Estimates, χ^2, and Probability Levels for Experiments A and B

	Experiment A		Experiment B	
Parameter	Standardized Value	Standard Errors	Standardized Value	Standard Errors
γ	0.47	0.10	0.53	0.16
β	0.51	0.22	0.56	0.51
λ_1	1.00	0.10	0.78	0.16
λ_2	0.79	0.09	0.46	0.12
λ_3	0.96	0.13	0.68	0.46
λ_4	0.74	0.10	0.37	0.23
$\sigma_{\eta_1 \eta_2}$	0.00	0.38	0.32	0.64
θ_{ε_1}	0.00	—	0.63	0.13
θ_{ε_2}	0.61	0.07	0.89	0.07
θ_{ε_3}	0.29	0.27	0.73	0.14
θ_{ε_4}	0.67	0.08	0.93	0.08
	$\chi^2 = 9.83$		$\chi^2 = 11.06$	
	4 d.f.		4 d.f.	
	$p = 0.04$		$p = 0.02$	

Step 1. The first step begins with a test of the theoretical hypothesis of the experiment; that is, the determination of a causal relationship between independent and dependent variables. This step involves the application of the basic model derived above. A satisfactory fit of the model lends strong support to the proposed hypothesis. However, failure of the data to confirm the hypothesis should first lead to an analysis of (1) the effect of the experimental manipulation,

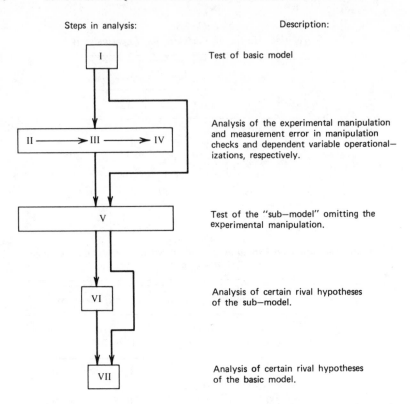

Steps in analysis:

Description:

I — Test of basic model

II ⟶ III ⟶ IV — Analysis of the experimental manipulation and measurement error in manipulation checks and dependent variable operational—izations, respectively.

V — Test of the "sub—model" omitting the experimental manipulation.

VI — Analysis of certain rival hypotheses of the sub—model.

VII — Analysis of certain rival hypotheses of the basic model.

Figure 7.5. An outline of steps in the analysis of problems in experimental research.

(2) measurement error in the manipulation checks, and (3) measurement error in the operationalizations of the dependent variables. This analysis is carried out below in Steps 2–4.

Before discussion of the analysis in these steps, however, it should be stressed that two necessary, but not sufficient, conditions must be met before the theoretical hypothesis of an experiment can be confirmed (or given the failure for confirmation of the hypothesis, before Steps 2–4 and the remaining procedures can be employed validly). The first condition is a strictly conceptual one. That is, in addition to the statistical criteria associated with the basic model, it is necessary that the relationship(s) between the theoretical constructs in one's theory and the corresponding operationalizations be sound from a logical or formal standpoint. Depending on one's preferences as to philosophy of science criteria, either of two positions may be maintained (see discussion on Observational Meaningfulness in Chapter 5). One school of thought associated primarily with the more positivistic scientists claims that the relationship between construct and operationalization is basically one of formal logic in the sense that operational definitions must be deducible from the theoretical constructs for which they are measures. A second school of thought rejects logical entailment in favor of a causal interpretation wherein an operationalization is related to a theoretical term by virture of its properties, characteristics, or nature. This perspective has been labelled "the realist view" in the philosophy of science literature. The important point to stress here is that a conceptual analysis must be made relating one's theoretical terms to operationalizations, and the criteria used to evaluate the relationships must be drawn from the standards in the philosophy of science (e.g., positivist or realistic rules of correspondence). For further discussion on this topic, the reader is referred to the treatment in Chapter 5 (cf., Brody, 1970; Hempel, 1965; Keat and Urry, 1975; Popper, 1959). The second necessary condition that must be satisfied before one can accept or reject an experimental hypothesis is a strictly empirical one. That is, the empirical operationalizations (e.g., manipulation checks, dependent variables) must be internally consistent and reliable. Measures of reliability such as the Cronbach α strive to determine the degree of internal consistency of one's operationalizations. Marketers have not always demonstrated the reliability of the measures used in their experiments, despite the necessity of such a criterion for inferring causality.

Steps 2–4. Given that the basic model does not fit the data (as in experiments A and B) and given that one has satisfied the necessary conceptual and empirical conditions outlined above, one next should check the empirical correspondence between observable variables and postulated theoretical constructs. Step 2 should consist of an investigation of measurement and specification error in the manipulation checks. This may be accomplished by determining the degree of single-factoredness in the manipulation checks as reflected in, say, a confirmatory factor analysis model (Jöreskog, 1969, 1970). By determining the χ^2 test and standard errors of parameter estimates for the model comprised of a true independent variable η_1 and its manipulation checks $y_1, \ldots, y_m$, one can judge whether it is reasonable or not to accept the single-factor model. Such a test requires at least three manipulation checks, however, for the model to be identified.[7] The parameter estimating procedures described in Chapter 4 are relevant here.

If Step 2 indicates a poor fit, one can conclude that the manipulation checks are indicators of more than a single common underlying dimension (i.e., more than the true independent variable). The nature of the other dimension(s) cannot be determined, however, without additional information. If Step 2 provides a good fit, indicating that the manipulation checks are each measuring the same construct, one should next check the causal model comprised of x, η_1, and $y_1, \ldots, y_m$. This test, labelled here as Step 3, may be accomplished by use of the mathematical development of the basic model (omitting β, η_2, and $y_{m+1}, \ldots, y_t$). At least two manipulation checks are required, and the χ^2 test and standard errors of parameters may be used to determine the fit of the model in Step 3.

If the fit in Step 3 is poor, one may test for certain rival hypotheses. Figure 7.6 illustrates one alternative explanation of a poor fit common to many experiments (e.g., Alwin and Tessler, 1974). The model of Figure 7.6 posits that the experimental manipulation x affects a manipulation check y_1 both through its intended path (e.g., a psychological state such as perceived source credibility η_1) and directly as γ_2 (e.g., due to demand characteristics or evaluation apprehension). In order to write the structural equations for the model of Figure 7.6 using the development found in Chapter 4, the following identities are necessary for certain parameters and variables in the figure: $\lambda_1 \equiv \beta$, $x \equiv \xi$, $y_1 \equiv \eta_2$. The structural equations then become

$$\begin{pmatrix} 1 & 0 \\ -\beta & 1 \end{pmatrix} \begin{pmatrix} \eta_1 \\ \eta_2 \end{pmatrix} = \begin{pmatrix} \gamma_1 \\ \gamma_2 \end{pmatrix} \xi + \begin{pmatrix} \zeta_1 \\ \zeta_2 \end{pmatrix}$$

$$\begin{pmatrix} y_1 \\ y_2 \\ y_3 \end{pmatrix} = \begin{pmatrix} 0 & 1 \\ \lambda_2 & 0 \\ \lambda_3 & 0 \end{pmatrix} \begin{pmatrix} \eta_1 \\ \eta_2 \end{pmatrix} + \begin{pmatrix} 0 \\ \varepsilon_2 \\ \varepsilon_3 \end{pmatrix}$$

$$x = (1)\xi$$

$$\Phi = 1.0$$

$$\psi = \begin{pmatrix} \psi_{11} & \\ 0 & \psi_{22} \end{pmatrix}$$

$$\theta_\varepsilon^2 = \begin{pmatrix} 0 & & \\ 0 & \theta_{\varepsilon_2}^2 & \\ 0 & 0 & \theta_{\varepsilon_3}^2 \end{pmatrix}$$

$$\theta_\delta^2 = 0$$

Given the above system of equations, there is one overidentifying restriction. The parameters may be estimated using the procedures developed in Chapter 4.

If the fit in Step 3 is adequate, one next should test the model comprised only of the true dependent variable and its operationalizations in order to determine the degree of measurement and specification error. This stage in the analysis is labelled Step 4 in Figure 7.5, and the computation procedures are identical to those noted for Step 2. One proceeds to Step 4 only if the models fit in Steps 2 and 3 in adequate (this is the case because certain rival hypotheses—discussed below—are possible whether the model of Step 4 is adequate or not, but not if the models of Steps 2 and 3 are rejected).

Step 5. Steps 2 and 4 require at least three operationalizations for each theoretical construct.[8] Steps 5–7 require only two. Step 5 investigates the adequacy of the "sub-model" of the basic model formed by the true variables η_1 and η_2 and

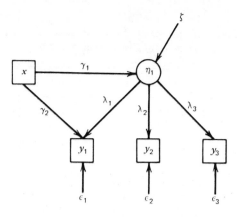

Figure 7.6. A model for testing an experimental manipulation with a rival hypothesis.

their respective indicators y_1 and y_2, and y_3 and y_4. The "sub-model" can be analyzed by the procedures derived in the beginning of the chapter by omitting x, the manipulation, and its parameter γ. This analysis was, in fact, performed for the example experiments A and B, and the results are summarized in Table 7.7. The sub-model of experiment A fits the data very well ($\chi^2 = 0.14$ with 1 d.f., $p = 0.71$), while the sub-model of experiment B does not ($\chi^2 = 11.05$ with 1 d.f., $p = 0.00$). Depending on the route the researcher used to get to Step 5. one of two conditions will result. First, if the researcher had a design with at least three operationalizations for each theoretical variable and thus progressed from Step 1 to Steps 2–4, confirmation of the sub-model for Step 5 (as in experiment A) leads to Step 7; rejection of the sub-model (as in experiment B) leads to Step 6. The former is the case because, given that the original basic model was rejected in Step 1 and given that Steps 2–5 confirmed segments of the model, it must be the case that either the rival hypotheses of Step 7 are present or else some unidentified and unmeasured confounding occurs. The latter is the case because, given that the original basic model was rejected and Steps 2–4 were confirmed, it must be the case that either the rival hypotheses of Steps 6 and 7 are present or else some unidentified and unmeasured confounding occurs. Second, if the researcher had a design with only two operationalizations for each theoretical variable and thus progressed directly from Step 1 to Step 5, confirmation of the sub-model for Step 5 (as in experiment A) leads to an algebraic verification check of the experimental manipulation; while rejection of the sub-model (as experiment B) leads to Step 6. For the former outcome, Costner (1971, p. 405) shows that two separate estimates may be derived for the parameter γ:

$$\gamma_1 = \frac{r_{xy_1}}{\lambda_1}, \qquad \gamma_2 = \frac{r_{xy_2}}{\lambda_2}$$

Table 7.7
Analysis of Parameter Estimates χ^2 and Probability Levels for the "Sub-models" of Experiments A and B

	Experiment A		Experiment B	
Parameter	Standardized Value	Standard Error	Standardized Value	Standard Error
β_1	0.58	0.14	0.89	1.00
λ_1	0.90	0.10	0.77	0.15
λ_2	0.88	0.10	0.47	0.12
λ_3	0.95	0.14	0.68	0.74
λ_4	0.75	0.10	0.37	0.38
θ_{ε_1}	0.44	0.11	0.64	0.16
θ_{ε_2}	0.47	0.11	0.88	0.08
θ_{ε_3}	0.32	0.22	0.74	0.14
θ_{ε_4}	0.66	0.08	0.93	0.08
	$\chi^2 = 0.14$		$\chi^2 = 11.05$	
	1 d.f.		1 d.f.	
	$p = 0.71$		$p = 0.00$	

Inconsistent estimates in the sense of differing values indicate the presence of confounding similar to that noted in the discussion of Step 3. As an example, consider experiment A:

$$\gamma_{A_1} = \frac{0.47}{1.00} = 0.47$$

$$\gamma_{A_2} = \frac{0.24}{0.79} = 0.30$$

where the λ values are those estimated in Step 1. Because these estimates of γ differ, one concludes that there is some direct effect from manipulation to manipulation check such as produced by demand characteristics. This effect cannot be identified or estimated because of insufficient information. It is interesting to note that the calculation of the manipulation check parameters for the hypothetical experiment of the previous section yields identical values of $\gamma = 0.92$. Finally, for the route of analysis going from Step 1 to Step 5, if Step 5 confirms the sub-model but inconsistent estimates of the manipulation γ arise, then no further analysis is warranted, and one must conclude that there is not enough information provided to make a sound judgment as to the failure of the basic model (other than ruling out what previously had been confirmed). If, however, consistent estimates of γ were found (in the sense noted above), one may proceed to Step 7.

Step 6. The only justification for performing an analysis of rival hypotheses of the sub-model (Step 6) is the rejection of the sub-model itself from the analysis of Step 5. Two cases are possible: (a) there are only two operationalizations each for the independent and dependent variables, and (b) there are three or more operationalizations each for the independent and dependent variables (the cases with two indicators for one variable and three or more for another require a hybrid analysis combining the principles already described in the previous steps with the two cases described below). For the situation of (a), there is only one rival hypothesis that may be tested unambiguously (Costner, 1969; Sullivan, 1974). This involves the alternative model that posits the addition of nonrandom measurement error across one indicator from the independent variable and one indicator from the dependent variables. Under this condition, the consistency criterion described above will not hold, indicating the presence of a confound. This model is essentially equivalent to hypothesizing the introduction of a common factor (i.e., unmeasured cause) across two indicators from the different constructs. For the basic model of (a), Costner (1971) describes one alternative hypothesis and Sullivan (1974) describes a second that, while meeting the consistency criterion, would cause one to reject the basic model. Unless one has additional information, the basic model does not allow the researcher to directly test for these alternative explanations (one can test for hypotheses similar to these for the model of case (b), however). Turning to situation (b), a number of analyses may be made. For the case of three indicators each for the independent and dependent variables, Costner (1971) presents criteria for the testing of three classes of rival hypotheses. These hypotheses encompass (1) differential bias across a pair of indicators, each indicator from a different theoretical construct (the single variable common factor case), (2) the addition of a direct effect from the true independent variable to an operationalization of the dependent variables, and (3) differential bias across three pairs of indicators across the two theoretical variables (the three variables common factor case). Tests for these hypotheses are derived algebraically from the observed correlations (e.g., Costner, 1971). Finally, given the situation in (b), analytic procedures exist for determining the rival hypotheses consisting of the addition of sources of common variance between pairs of indicators of the same theoretical variable combined with the differential bias and direct effect hypotheses above (Costner and Schoenberg, 1973). These procedures involve the analysis of the residual matrices for each hypothesis as a guide for selecting the subsequent alternative explanations, and the different χ^2 goodness-of-fit values are used to judge the acceptability of a model. The procedure resembles hierarchial hypothesis testing (discussed in Chapter 4) and is subject to certain limitations (e.g., Costner and Schoenberg, 1973). Rejection of the models of Step 6 leads to step 7.

Step 7. The final analysis to be made is the test for the presence of direct effects by the experimental manipulation x on either the true dependent variable or one

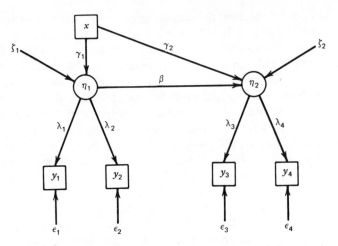

Figure 7.7. Rival hypothesis of a direct effect from the experimental manipulation to the true dependent variable.

or more of its operational indicators. As shown in Figures 7.7 and 7.8, two classes of rival hypotheses are possible. By setting different combinations of γ_1, γ_2, β, λ'_1, and λ'_2 equal to zero, Alwin and Tessler (1974, p. 92) derive six possible hypotheses. It is possible to test each of these hypotheses using the general model derived in Chapter 4. For Figure 7.7, one may write the structural equations as follows:

$$\begin{pmatrix} 1 & 0 \\ -\beta & 1 \end{pmatrix} \begin{pmatrix} \eta_1 \\ \eta_2 \end{pmatrix} = \begin{pmatrix} \gamma_1 \\ \gamma_2 \end{pmatrix} \xi + \begin{pmatrix} \zeta_1 \\ \zeta_2 \end{pmatrix}$$

$$\begin{pmatrix} y_1 \\ y_2 \\ y_3 \\ y_4 \end{pmatrix} = \begin{pmatrix} \lambda_1 & 0 \\ \lambda_2 & 0 \\ 0 & \lambda_3 \\ 0 & \lambda_4 \end{pmatrix} \begin{pmatrix} \eta_1 \\ \eta_2 \end{pmatrix} + \begin{pmatrix} \varepsilon_1 \\ \varepsilon_2 \\ \varepsilon_3 \\ \varepsilon_4 \end{pmatrix}$$

$$\boldsymbol{\Theta}^2_\varepsilon = \begin{pmatrix} \theta^2_{\varepsilon_1} \\ 0 & \theta^2_{\varepsilon_2} \\ 0 & 0 & \theta^2_{\varepsilon_3} \\ 0 & 0 & 0 & \theta^2_{\varepsilon_4} \end{pmatrix}$$

$$x = (1)\xi$$
$$\theta^2_\delta = 0$$
$$\phi = 1.0$$

$$\boldsymbol{\psi} = \begin{pmatrix} \psi_{11} \\ 0 & \psi_{22} \end{pmatrix}$$

The above system of equations has two overidentifying restrictions, and the

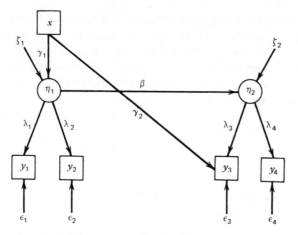

Figure 7.8. Rival hypothesis of a direct effect from the experimental manipulation to an indicator of the dependent variable.

parameters may be estimated with the procedures developed in Chapter 4. For Figure 7.8, the following identities allow one to write the structural equations using the development of Chapter 4: $\beta \equiv \beta_1$, $\lambda_3 \equiv \beta_2$, and $y_3 = \eta_3$. The equations then become:

$$\begin{pmatrix} 1 & 0 & 0 \\ -\beta_1 & 1 & 0 \\ 0 & -\beta_2 & 1 \end{pmatrix} \begin{pmatrix} \eta_1 \\ \eta_2 \\ \eta_3 \end{pmatrix} = \begin{pmatrix} \gamma_1 \\ 0 \\ \gamma_2 \end{pmatrix} \xi + \begin{pmatrix} \zeta_1 \\ \zeta_2 \\ \zeta_3 \end{pmatrix}$$

$$\begin{pmatrix} y_1 \\ y_2 \\ y_3 \\ y_4 \end{pmatrix} = \begin{pmatrix} \lambda_1 & 0 & 0 \\ \lambda_2 & 0 & 0 \\ 0 & 0 & 1 \\ 0 & 1 & 0 \end{pmatrix} \begin{pmatrix} \eta_1 \\ \eta_2 \\ \eta_3 \end{pmatrix} + \begin{pmatrix} \varepsilon_1 \\ \varepsilon_2 \\ 0 \\ 0 \end{pmatrix}$$

$$\boldsymbol{\theta}_\varepsilon^2 = \begin{pmatrix} \theta_{\varepsilon_1}^2 & & & \\ 0 & \theta_{\varepsilon_2}^2 & & \\ 0 & 0 & 0 & \\ 0 & 0 & 0 & 0 \end{pmatrix}$$

$$x = (1)\xi$$

$$\theta_\delta^2 = 0$$

$$\phi = 1.0$$

$$\psi = \begin{pmatrix} \psi_{11} & & \\ 0 & \psi_{22} & \\ 0 & 0 & \psi_{33} \end{pmatrix}$$

The above system of equations will have two overidentifying restrictions.

In summary, the structural equation approach to the analysis of experimental data allows the researcher to explicitly formulate and test a certain number of rival hypotheses. This property of the method can aid in the interpretation and analysis of experimental findings, the design of future experiments, and the comparison of findings across settings, populations, and time. For further treatments of the related topic of specification error, the reader is referred to Jacobson and Lalu (1974), Sullivan (1974), Werts, Linn, and Jöreskog (1974), and Althauser, Heberlin, and Scott (1971).

Structural Equation Models in More Complicated Experimental Designs

The general linear model developed in Chapter 4 is also applicable for a wide range of other experimental designs. In this section, two broad extension of the model are outlined.

Consider first the model developed earlier in the chapter where now the specification is extended to include $r > 1$ true independent variables and $s > 1$

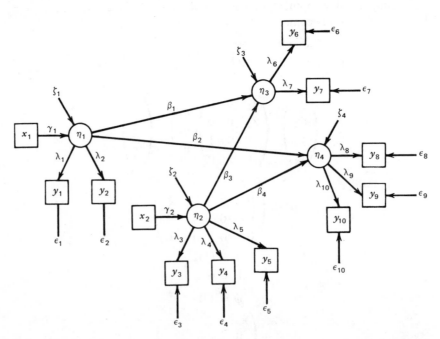

Figure 7.9. A causal model for the experimental situation consisting of two independent variables and two dependent variables.

true dependent variables with multiple manipulation checks for each independent variable and multiple operationalizations for each dependent variable. Figure 7.9 presents the case for two independent variables, x_1 and x_2, each affecting two true dependent variables, η_3 and η_4, through the respective true independent variables, η_1 and η_2. The effects of the two manipulated independent variables on the test subjects are represented, respectively, as γ_1 and γ_2, while the effects of the independent variables on the dependent variables are modelled as $\beta_1 - \beta_4$. The model of Figure 7.9 can be easily extended for $r > 2$ independent and $s > 2$ dependent variables.

The structural equations for the model of Figure 7.9 may be written as follows:

$$
\begin{pmatrix} 1 & 0 & 0 & 0 \\ 0 & 1 & 0 & 0 \\ -\beta_1 & -\beta_3 & 1 & 0 \\ -\beta_2 & -\beta_4 & 0 & 1 \end{pmatrix} \begin{pmatrix} \eta_1 \\ \eta_2 \\ \eta_3 \\ \eta_4 \end{pmatrix} = \begin{pmatrix} \gamma_1 & 0 \\ 0 & \gamma_2 \\ 0 & 0 \\ 0 & 0 \end{pmatrix} \begin{pmatrix} \xi_1 \\ \xi_3 \end{pmatrix} + \begin{pmatrix} \zeta_1 \\ \zeta_2 \\ \zeta_3 \\ \zeta_4 \end{pmatrix}
$$

$$
\begin{pmatrix} y_1 \\ y_2 \\ y_3 \\ y_4 \\ y_5 \\ y_6 \\ y_7 \\ y_8 \\ y_9 \\ y_{10} \end{pmatrix} = \begin{pmatrix} \lambda_1 & 0 & 0 & 0 \\ \lambda_2 & 0 & 0 & 0 \\ 0 & \lambda_3 & 0 & 0 \\ 0 & \lambda_4 & 0 & 0 \\ 0 & \lambda_5 & 0 & 0 \\ 0 & 0 & \lambda_6 & 0 \\ 0 & 0 & \lambda_7 & 0 \\ 0 & 0 & 0 & \lambda_8 \\ 0 & 0 & 0 & \lambda_9 \\ 0 & 0 & 0 & \lambda_{10} \end{pmatrix} \begin{pmatrix} \eta_1 \\ \eta_2 \\ \eta_3 \\ \eta_4 \end{pmatrix} + \begin{pmatrix} \varepsilon_1 \\ \varepsilon_2 \\ \varepsilon_3 \\ \varepsilon_4 \\ \varepsilon_5 \\ \varepsilon_6 \\ \varepsilon_7 \\ \varepsilon_8 \\ \varepsilon_9 \\ \varepsilon_{10} \end{pmatrix}
$$

$$
\theta_\varepsilon^2 = \begin{pmatrix} \theta_{\varepsilon_1}^2 \\ 0 & \theta_{\varepsilon_2}^2 \\ 0 & 0 & \theta_{\varepsilon_3}^2 \\ 0 & 0 & 0 & \theta_{\varepsilon_4}^2 \\ 0 & 0 & 0 & 0 & \theta_{\varepsilon_5}^2 \\ 0 & 0 & 0 & 0 & 0 & \theta_{\varepsilon_6}^2 \\ 0 & 0 & 0 & 0 & 0 & 0 & \theta_{\varepsilon_7}^2 \\ 0 & 0 & 0 & 0 & 0 & 0 & 0 & \theta_{\varepsilon_8}^2 \\ 0 & 0 & 0 & 0 & 0 & 0 & 0 & 0 & \theta_{\varepsilon_9}^2 \\ 0 & 0 & 0 & 0 & 0 & 0 & 0 & 0 & 0 & \theta_{\varepsilon_{10}}^2 \end{pmatrix}
$$

$$
\begin{pmatrix} x_1 \\ x_2 \end{pmatrix} = \begin{pmatrix} 1 & 0 \\ 0 & 1 \end{pmatrix} \begin{pmatrix} \xi_1 \\ \xi_2 \end{pmatrix} + \begin{pmatrix} 0 \\ 0 \end{pmatrix}
$$

$$\theta_\delta^2 = 0$$

$$\phi = \begin{pmatrix} 1.0 & \\ \phi_{21} & 1.0 \end{pmatrix}$$

$$\psi = \begin{pmatrix} \psi_{11} & & & \\ \psi_{21} & \psi_{22} & & \\ 0 & 0 & \psi_{33} & \\ 0 & 0 & \psi_{43} & \psi_{44} \end{pmatrix}$$

This system of equations may be conveniently solved using Jöreskog's procedures (see Chapter 4). Since there are 32 parameters to be estimated and 78 independent pieces of information, there will be 46 overidentifying restrictions.[9]

As a second extension of structural equation models in experimental research, consider the pretest-posttest control group design (cf., Campbell and Stanley, 1963, pp. 13–24). Figure 7.10 illustrates this situation where ξ_1 represents the true pretest scores measured by x_1 and x_2, η depicts the true posttest scores measured by y_1 and y_2, and x_3 models the experimental treatment. The parameter γ_2 represents the effect of the pretest on the posttest scores, while γ_1 shows the impact of the manipulation on the posttest.

Two general cases are possible for the model of Figure 7.10. The first occurs when the experimental treatment is a qualitative manipulation (e.g., a nominal or ordinal variable). When this is the case, the different treatment groups defined by x_3 may be used to construct sub-groups. For example, if x_3 were a 0–1 dichotomy (control group/treatment group), two sub-groups would be formed. The l sub-groups defined by x_3 can be used to specify l models each

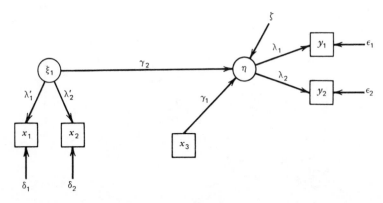

Figure 7.10. A causal model representing pretest and posttest scores with one single independent variable.

consisting of a pretest ξ_1 affecting a posttest η. By solving each of the l models, one may obtain an indication of the change in scores for the different subgroups. This may be found by comparing the slopes and intercepts for the regressions of η on ξ_1 and using the estimated mean vectors for η and ξ_1 and the estimated covariances for η and ξ_1 to derive contour ellipses for each subgroup. Sörbom (1974) develops a general model for determining differences in factor means and factor structure between groups that can be used in such cases.

The second case of interest for the model of Figure 7.10 occurs when the treatment x_3 is a continuous variable. Under these conditions, one may then estimate the parameters using the general linear model and procedures outlined in Chapter 4. The structural equations for the model of Figure 7.10 are

$$(1)\eta = (\gamma_2 \quad \gamma_1)\begin{pmatrix}\xi_1 \\ \xi_2\end{pmatrix} + \zeta$$

$$\begin{pmatrix}y_1 \\ y_2\end{pmatrix} = \begin{pmatrix}\lambda_1 \\ \lambda_2\end{pmatrix}\eta + \begin{pmatrix}\varepsilon_1 \\ \varepsilon_2\end{pmatrix}$$

$$\boldsymbol{\theta}_\varepsilon^2 = \begin{pmatrix}\theta_{\varepsilon_1}^2 & \\ 0 & \theta_{\varepsilon_2}^2\end{pmatrix}$$

$$\begin{pmatrix}x_1 \\ x_2 \\ x_3\end{pmatrix} = \begin{pmatrix}\lambda_1' & 0 \\ \lambda_2' & 0 \\ 0 & 1\end{pmatrix}\begin{pmatrix}\xi_1 \\ \xi_2\end{pmatrix}\begin{pmatrix}\delta_1 \\ \delta_2 \\ 0\end{pmatrix}$$

$$\boldsymbol{\theta}_\delta^2 = \begin{pmatrix}\theta_{\delta_1}^2 & & \\ 0 & \theta_{\delta_2}^2 & \\ 0 & 0 & 0\end{pmatrix}$$

$$\boldsymbol{\phi} = \begin{pmatrix}1.0 & \\ \phi_{21} & 1.0\end{pmatrix}$$

$$\psi = \text{var}(\zeta)$$

Since there are 11 parameters to be estimated in this system of equations and 15 independent pieces of information, there will be four overidentifying restrictions.[10]

Finally consider the model of Figure 7.11, which consists of a pretest ξ_1 a posttest η_2, a treatment x_3, and a true independent variable η_1, operationalized by two manipulation checks y_1 and y_2. The structural equations for this model

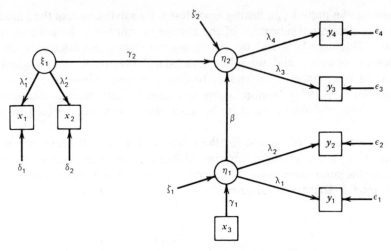

Figure 7.11. A causal model representing pretest and posttest scores with one single independent variable and multiple manipulation checks.

can be written as follows:

$$\begin{pmatrix} 1 & 0 \\ -\beta & 1 \end{pmatrix} \begin{pmatrix} \eta_1 \\ \eta_2 \end{pmatrix} = \begin{pmatrix} \gamma_1 & 0 \\ 0 & \gamma_2 \end{pmatrix} \begin{pmatrix} \xi_2 \\ \xi_1 \end{pmatrix} + \begin{pmatrix} \zeta_1 \\ \zeta_2 \end{pmatrix}$$

$$\begin{pmatrix} y_1 \\ y_2 \\ y_3 \\ y_4 \end{pmatrix} = \begin{pmatrix} \lambda_1 & 0 \\ \lambda_2 & 0 \\ 0 & \lambda_3 \\ 0 & \lambda_4 \end{pmatrix} \begin{pmatrix} \eta_1 \\ \eta_2 \end{pmatrix} + \begin{pmatrix} \varepsilon_1 \\ \varepsilon_2 \\ \varepsilon_3 \\ \varepsilon_4 \end{pmatrix}$$

$$\theta_\varepsilon^2 = \begin{pmatrix} \theta_{\varepsilon_1}^2 & & & \\ 0 & \theta_{\varepsilon_2}^2 & & \\ 0 & 0 & \theta_{\varepsilon_3}^2 & \\ 0 & 0 & 0 & \theta_{\varepsilon_4}^2 \end{pmatrix}$$

$$\begin{pmatrix} x_1 \\ x_2 \\ x_3 \end{pmatrix} = \begin{pmatrix} 0 & \lambda_1' \\ 0 & \lambda_2' \\ 1 & 0 \end{pmatrix} \begin{pmatrix} \xi_2 \\ \xi_1 \end{pmatrix} + \begin{pmatrix} \delta_1 \\ \delta_2 \\ 0 \end{pmatrix}$$

$$\theta_\delta^2 = \begin{pmatrix} \theta_{\delta_1}^2 & & \\ 0 & \theta_{\delta_2}^2 & \\ 0 & 0 & 0 \end{pmatrix}$$

$$\Phi = \begin{pmatrix} 1.0 & \\ \phi_{21} & 1.0 \end{pmatrix}$$

$$\Psi = \begin{pmatrix} \psi_{11} & \\ 0 & \psi_{22} \end{pmatrix}$$

Again, the above system of equations may be analyzed using Jöreskog's procedures. Since there are 18 parameters to be estimated and 28 independent pieces of information, there will be ten overidentifying restrictions.[11]

Other experimental designs may also be handled with the general linear model. The Solomon four-group design, for example, may be formed by combining the models of Figures 7.3 and 7.10. In addition, Jöreskog (1971) discusses a special case of the 2×2 factorial design with replications and a 2^3 factorial design.

Summary

This chapter investigated the use of structural equation models in experimental research. A basic model was derived for estimating parameters and testing hypotheses for the experimental situation consisting of a single experimental manipulation of a single or multiple treatments (with multiple manipulation checks) and a single dependent variable with multiple operationalizations. The model was then illustrated with data from a simulated marketing experiment.

Next, the use of structural equations as a tool for diagnosing problems in experimental designs was examined. Building on Costner's three-stage procedure, a seven-step methodology was derived and illustrated. Finally, two broad extensions to the basic model were developed. The first explored the problem of multiple independent and dependent variables. The second investigated the pretest-posttest control group design.

A structural equation approach to experimental design complements the usual orientations such as the analysis of variance. Specifically, the structural equation method allows the researcher to model measurement error separate from errors in equations, and it permits determination of the internal inconsistency of operationalizations. It also provides a means for explicitly representing flaws in experimental designs such as demand characteristics, evaluation apprehension, or other confounds. Since it accommodates experiments with continuous and/or categorical independent variables, it is in this sense more general than other procedures. Among other topics, the following chapter will examine the analysis of covariance and its relation to experimental and other research methodologies.

Notes

[1] This chapter is a revised and expanded version of the author's article appearing in the *Journal of Marketing Research* (Bagozzi, 1977b).

[2] Demand characteristics are cues in the experimental situation as to the role of the subject, the intent of the experiment, the expectations of the experimenter, and so on, all of

which act to stimulate a response in the subject independent of, or in addition to, the experimental manipulation (cf., Orne, 1969; Rosenthal and Rosnow, 1969). Evaluation apprehension is "an active anxiety-toned concern" that a test subject has as a result of the desire to "win a positive evaluation from the experimenter" or at least to avoid a negative evaluation (Rosenberg, 1969; Rosenthal and Rosnow, 1969). As with the broader concept of demand characteristics, evaluation apprehension can mask or augment the effect of the experimental manipulation. Other factors that have consequences similar to demand characteristics and evaluation apprehension include confounding variables (e.g., Aronson and Carlsmith, 1969) and forms of reactivity (Campbell and Stanley, 1963).

[3] In the following development, the derivation of the basic model is made for the case where the independent variable x is continuous. For the case where x is categorical, the appropriate model to test is the modification of Figure 7.3 and Eq. (7.3) consisting of the deletion of x and a comparison for each group of test subjects of the regression line relating η_1 to η_2. The comparison of intercepts for each test group allows one to determine relative differences in means for the dependent variable due to the experimental manipulation. In general, one might expect the slope of the regression line β to differ for each test group, and this also provides information as to the effectiveness of the independent variable (see discussion near end of chapter).

[4] This result differs slightly from that derived by Goldberger (1974, p. 198) for a number of reasons. First, the model in Figure 7.3 is restricted to two theoretical variables with multiple indicators. Second, the model has a manipulation x, which for purposes of determining the number of overidentifying restrictions can be treated as an errorless indicator of η_1. Thus the model of Figure 7.1 has $3 + 2t$ parameters to be estimated; that is, γ, β, λ_1, ..., λ_t, σ_1^2, ..., σ_t^2, and $\sigma_{\eta_1\eta_2}$, where the latter parameter is the covariance between the error terms of the true variables (the variances of the error terms of the true variables $\sigma_{\eta_1}^2$ and $\sigma_{\eta_2}^2$ are assumed standardized and thus are not estimated). The covariance between error terms of the true variables can also be fixed at zero and the resulting χ^2 compared to that found for the model not making this restriction in order to see the validity of the assumption that $\sigma_{\eta_1\eta_2} = 0$.

[5] The analysis was performed using Jöreskog's program, LISREL II.

[6] Although the independent variable in a laboratory experiment is manipulated and in this sense not free, the discussion on standardized parameter estimates is presented here since the topic is especially relevant to the natural or field experiments.

[7] The model with only two operationalizations will be identified also if one assumes that both the error variances and parameters relating the unobservable to operationalizations are equal; that is, $\lambda_1 = \lambda_2$ and $\theta_{\varepsilon_1}^2 = \theta_{\varepsilon_2}^2$.

[8] Except as noted in footnote 7.

[9] The illustration is performed for the quasi-experimental case where naturally occurring independent variables are allowed correlated (i.e., $\phi_{12} \neq 0$) and the error terms of the true independent variables are also allowed correlated (i.e., $\psi_{21} \neq 0$) as hypotheses. In a true experiment with complete randomization, $\phi_{12} = 0$, and hence, there will be one more overidentifying restriction.

[10] For the case of a true experiment, $\phi_{21} = 0$, and there will be one more identifying restriction.

[11] See footnote 10.

EIGHT

LONGITUDINAL AND PANEL ANALYSIS

This chapter is concerned with the analysis of causal relationships over time. The discussion begins with a simple model consisting of one theoretical variable measured at one point in time affecting a second theoretical variable measured at another point in time. The model is developed as an extension of the pretest-posttest experimental design discussed near the end of the previous chapter. That is, covariates are introduced in order to better explain the relationship between pretest and posttest measures, and the possibility of correlated errors in variables is discussed. Next, the cross-lagged panel correlation technique is presented as a means of determining the direction and magnitude of causality between the same two variables measured at two or more points in time. Finally, more complicated panel designs are considered including multiwave and one and two variable models and a general model for longitudinal data developed by Jöreskog and Sörbom (1977).

A Simple Longitudinal Model

Consider the situation where a researcher desires to ascertain the relationship between pretest and posttest attitudes. Figure 4.5 represents one causal model that can be used to determine the impact of pretest on posttest attitudes where this relationship is represented as γ. The model of Figure 4.5 suggests that posttest attitudes will be a function only of pretest attitudes and random error. It is often the case, however, that some other variable(s) systematically affects the

221

posttest scores such that the estimated relationship γ is contaminated by these factors when a model such as Figure 4.5 is employed. Common examples of variables that might systematically influence the posttest scores and produce a distortion in the estimation of the relationship modeled between pretest and posttest include differences in knowledge, intelligence, education, personality variables, or other individual differences in test subjects as well as systematic effects differentially impinging on people from the environment. Although the researcher will typically attempt to control for such systematic bias through randomization, it is not always practical or possible to do so. Under these conditions, one would like a methodology—analogous to the analysis of covariance—for controlling for and estimating the impact of systematic influences. The structural equation approach offers an efficient method for modeling these effects. The idea is that the explanation of variation in the dependent variable is adjusted for based on the impact of a control variable.

As an illustration, consider first the model in Figure 8.1, which consists of one theoretical variable η_1, the pretest, related causally to a second theoretical variable η_2, the posttest. A covariate x is shown affecting both pretest and posttest. This model explicitly allows the researcher to estimate and eliminate the effect(s) of x in order to discover the direct, uncontaminated effect of η_1 on η_2. Following the general model developed in Chapter 4, it is possible to write the structural equations for this model as follows:

$$\begin{pmatrix} 1 & 0 \\ -\beta & 1 \end{pmatrix} \begin{pmatrix} \eta_1 \\ \eta_2 \end{pmatrix} = \begin{pmatrix} \gamma_1 \\ \gamma_2 \end{pmatrix} \xi + \begin{pmatrix} \zeta_1 \\ \zeta_2 \end{pmatrix}$$

$$\begin{pmatrix} y_1 \\ y_2 \\ y_3 \\ y_4 \end{pmatrix} = \begin{pmatrix} \lambda_1 & 0 \\ \lambda_2 & 0 \\ 0 & \lambda_3 \\ 0 & \lambda_4 \end{pmatrix} \begin{pmatrix} \eta_1 \\ \eta_2 \end{pmatrix} + \begin{pmatrix} \varepsilon_1 \\ \varepsilon_2 \\ \varepsilon_3 \\ \varepsilon_4 \end{pmatrix}$$

$$\theta_\varepsilon^3 = \begin{pmatrix} \theta_{\varepsilon_1}^2 & & & \\ 0 & \theta_{\varepsilon_2}^2 & & \\ 0 & 0 & \theta_{\varepsilon_3}^2 & \\ 0 & 0 & 0 & \theta_{\varepsilon_4}^2 \end{pmatrix}$$

$$x = (1)\xi$$

$$\theta_\delta^2 = 0$$

$$\phi = \text{var}(x)$$

$$\psi = \begin{pmatrix} \psi_{11} & \\ 0 & \psi_{22} \end{pmatrix}$$

Since there are 15 independent pieces of information provided by the observed variances and covariances, and since there are 13 parameters to be estimated, it

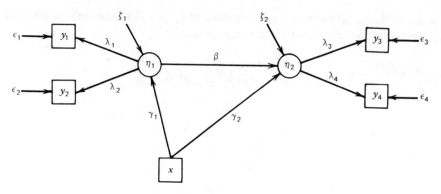

Figure 8.1. A simple causal model for a pretest and posttest design with one errorless covariate x.

can be shown that the entire model is identified with two overidentifying restrictions on Σ (see discussion on identification in Chapter 4 and Jöreskog and Sörbom, 1977).[1] The solution of the above equations and parameter estimates are easily obtained using LISREL.

Consider next the situation diagrammed in Figure 8.2 consisting of true pretest and posttest variables η_1 and η_2, and a true covariate ξ, measured with two indicators x_1 and x_2 (cf., Jöreskog and Sörbom, 1977). Again, one objective

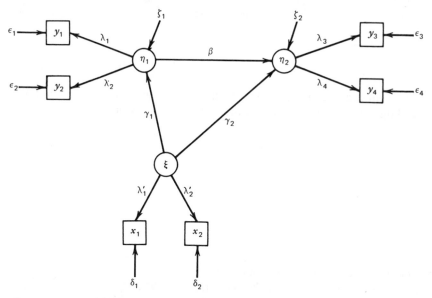

Figure 8.2. A causal model for a pretest and posttest design with one covariate ξ measured with two indicators.

of such a model is to obtain the direct effect of η_1 on η_2 by removing the effect of ξ. The structural equations for this model are

$$\begin{pmatrix} 1 & 0 \\ -\beta & 1 \end{pmatrix} \begin{pmatrix} \eta_1 \\ \eta_2 \end{pmatrix} = \begin{pmatrix} \gamma_1 \\ \gamma_2 \end{pmatrix} \xi + \begin{pmatrix} \zeta_1 \\ \zeta_2 \end{pmatrix}$$

$$\begin{pmatrix} y_1 \\ y_2 \\ y_3 \\ y_4 \end{pmatrix} = \begin{pmatrix} \lambda_1 & 0 \\ \lambda_2 & 0 \\ 0 & \lambda_3 \\ 0 & \lambda_4 \end{pmatrix} \begin{pmatrix} \eta_1 \\ \eta_2 \end{pmatrix} + \begin{pmatrix} \varepsilon_1 \\ \varepsilon_2 \\ \varepsilon_3 \\ \varepsilon_4 \end{pmatrix}$$

$$\boldsymbol{\theta}_\varepsilon^2 = \begin{pmatrix} \theta_{\varepsilon_1}^2 & & & \\ 0 & \theta_{\varepsilon_2}^2 & & \\ 0 & 0 & \theta_{\varepsilon_3}^2 & \\ 0 & 0 & 0 & \theta_{\varepsilon_4}^2 \end{pmatrix}$$

$$\begin{pmatrix} x_1 \\ x_2 \end{pmatrix} = \begin{pmatrix} \lambda_1' \\ \lambda_2' \end{pmatrix} \xi + \begin{pmatrix} \delta_1 \\ \delta_2 \end{pmatrix}$$

$$\boldsymbol{\theta}_\delta^2 = \begin{pmatrix} \theta_{\delta_1}^2 & \\ 0 & \theta_{\delta_2}^2 \end{pmatrix}$$

$$\phi = \text{var}(\xi)$$

$$\boldsymbol{\psi} = \begin{pmatrix} \psi_{11} & \\ 0 & \psi_{22} \end{pmatrix}$$

The identification of the model of Figure 8.2 may be determined as follows (Jöreskog and Sörbom, 1977). One first expresses the reduced form equations as

$$\eta_1 = \gamma_1 \xi + \zeta_1$$

$$\eta_2 = \gamma_2 \xi + \beta \eta_1 + \zeta_2$$

$$= \gamma_2 \xi + \beta \gamma_1 \xi + \beta \zeta_1 + \zeta_2$$

$$= \alpha \xi + u$$

where $\alpha = (\gamma_2 + \beta \gamma_1)$ and $u = \beta \zeta_1 + \zeta_2$. Assuming ζ_1 and ζ_2 are uncorrelated, the model contains 18 parameters to be estimated: β, γ_1, γ_2, λ_1, λ_2, λ_3, λ_4, λ_1', λ_2', $\phi = \text{var}(\xi)$, $\psi_{11} = \text{var}(\zeta_1)$, $\psi_{22} = \text{var}(\zeta_2)$, $\theta_{\varepsilon_1}^2$, $\theta_{\varepsilon_2}^2$, $\theta_{\varepsilon_3}^2$, $\theta_{\varepsilon_4}^2$, $\theta_{\delta_1}^2$, and $\theta_{\delta_2}^2$. The six variances and 15 covariances among the six observables (y_1, y_2, y_3, y_4, x_1, x_2) provide the information to solve for the parameters.

Beginning with the covariances among the observed covariates and the indicators of the pretest and posttest measurements, one finds the following:

$$\text{cov}(x_1, y_1) = \lambda_1 \gamma_1 \lambda_1' \phi$$

$$\text{cov}(x_1, y_2) = \lambda_2 \gamma_1 \lambda_1' \phi$$

$$\text{cov}(x_1, y_3) = \lambda_3 \alpha \lambda_1' \phi = \lambda_3(\gamma_2 + \beta\gamma_1)\lambda_1' \phi$$

$$\text{cov}(x_1, y_4) = \lambda_4 \alpha \lambda_1' \phi = \lambda_4(\gamma_2 + \beta\gamma_1)\lambda_1' \phi$$

$$\text{cov}(x_2, y_1) = \lambda_1 \gamma_1 \lambda_2' \phi$$

$$\text{cov}(x_2, y_2) = \lambda_2 \gamma_1 \lambda_2' \phi$$

$$\text{cov}(x_2, y_3) = \lambda_3 \alpha \lambda_2' \phi = \lambda_3(\gamma_2 + \beta\gamma_1)\lambda_2' \phi$$

$$\text{cov}(x_2, y_4) = \lambda_4 \alpha \lambda_2' \phi = \lambda_4(\gamma_2 + \beta\gamma_1)\lambda_2' \phi$$

Similarly,

$$\text{cov}(y_1, y_2) = \lambda_1 \lambda_2 \, \text{var}(\eta_1) = \lambda_1 \lambda_2 (\gamma_1^2 \phi + \psi_{11})$$

$$\text{cov}(y_3, y_4) = \lambda_3 \lambda_4 \, \text{var}(\eta_2) = \lambda_3 \lambda_4 (\alpha^2 \phi + \text{var}(u))$$

where

$$\text{var}(u) = \beta^2 \psi_{22} + \psi_{11}$$

Finally,

$$\text{cov}(y_1, y_3) = \lambda_1 \beta \lambda_3$$

$$\text{cov}(y_1, y_4) = \lambda_1 \beta \lambda_4$$

$$\text{cov}(y_2, y_3) = \lambda_2 \beta \lambda_3$$

$$\text{cov}(y_2, y_4) = \lambda_2 \beta \lambda_4$$

The above 14 equations determine $\beta, \gamma_1, \gamma_2, \lambda_1, \lambda_2, \lambda_3, \lambda_4, \lambda_1', \lambda_2', \phi, \psi_{11}$, and ψ_{22} with two overidentifying restrictions.[2] Finally, given the above parameter solutions, it is possible to solve for the error variances $\theta_{\varepsilon_1}^2 - \theta_{\varepsilon_4}^2$ and $\theta_{\delta_1}^2$ and $\theta_{\delta_2}^2$ using the following formulas: $\text{var}(y_i) = \lambda_i^2 + \theta_{\varepsilon_i}^2$ and $\text{var}(x_i) = \lambda_j^2 + \theta_{\delta_j}^2$ for $i = 1, 2, 3, 4$ and $j = 1, 2$. The models of Figures 8.1 and 8.2 are easily generalizable to two or more pretest and posttest variables with two or more covariates.

As a third extension of the pretest-posttest model, consider the diagram of Figure 8.3. In this situation, the errors for the measurements of the same indicators made at two points in time are allowed correlated. When the researcher has no or only partial control of the research setting (due to the absence of complete randomization, the failure to fully control for demand characteristics, etc.), it is often reasonable to expect the error terms for the measurements made at different times to be correlated. The covariation will be the result of some extraneous, unmeasured variable producing variation in the parallel

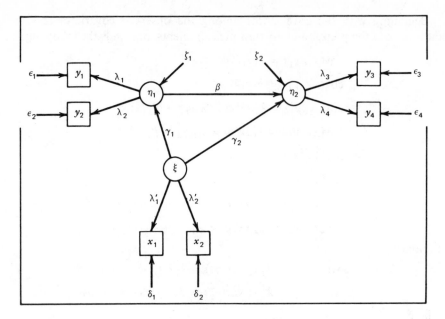

Figure 8.3. A causal model for a pretest and posttest design with one covariate, ξ, measured with two indicators and allowing for correlated errors between points in time.

measurements. For example, the calculated relationship between pretest and posttest attitudes might be a function of response sets aggravated by an improper questionnaire construction rather than a function of a true connection between attitudes.

To solve for the system of equations modeling Figure 8.3, the researcher must make a few changes in Jöreskog's procedure (e.g., Jöreskog and van Thillo, 1972; Jöreskog and Sörbom, 1977). The structural equations for the model may be written as follows:

$$\mathbf{B}\boldsymbol{\eta} = \boldsymbol{\Gamma}\boldsymbol{\xi} + \boldsymbol{\zeta}$$

In order to allow for correlated errors, the error terms $\boldsymbol{\varepsilon}$ are constructed as common factors. This yields the following equations:

$$
\begin{pmatrix}
1 & 0 & 0 & 0 & 0 & 0 \\
-\beta & 1 & 0 & 0 & 0 & 0 \\
0 & 0 & 1 & 0 & 0 & 0 \\
0 & 0 & 0 & 1 & 0 & 0 \\
0 & 0 & 0 & 0 & 1 & 0 \\
0 & 0 & 0 & 0 & 0 & 1
\end{pmatrix}
\begin{pmatrix}
\eta_1 \\ \eta_2 \\ \varepsilon_1 \\ \varepsilon_2 \\ \varepsilon_3 \\ \varepsilon_4
\end{pmatrix}
=
\begin{pmatrix}
\gamma_1 & 0 & 0 & 0 & 0 \\
\gamma_2 & 0 & 0 & 0 & 0 \\
0 & 1 & 0 & 0 & 0 \\
0 & 0 & 1 & 0 & 0 \\
0 & 0 & 0 & 1 & 0 \\
0 & 0 & 0 & 0 & 1
\end{pmatrix}
\begin{pmatrix}
\xi \\ \varepsilon_1 \\ \varepsilon_2 \\ \varepsilon_3 \\ \varepsilon_4
\end{pmatrix}
+
\begin{pmatrix}
\zeta_1 \\ \zeta_2 \\ 0 \\ 0 \\ 0 \\ 0
\end{pmatrix}
$$

$$
\begin{pmatrix} y_1 \\ y_2 \\ y_3 \\ y_4 \end{pmatrix} = \begin{pmatrix} \lambda_1 & 0 & 1 & 0 & 0 & 0 \\ \lambda_2 & 0 & 0 & 1 & 0 & 0 \\ 0 & \lambda_3 & 0 & 0 & 1 & 0 \\ 0 & \lambda_4 & 0 & 0 & 0 & 1 \end{pmatrix} \begin{pmatrix} \eta_1 \\ \eta_2 \\ \varepsilon_1 \\ \varepsilon_2 \\ \varepsilon_3 \\ \varepsilon_4 \end{pmatrix}
$$

$$
\boldsymbol{\theta}_\varepsilon^2 = \begin{pmatrix} \theta_{\varepsilon_1}^2 & & & \\ 0 & \theta_{\varepsilon_2}^2 & & \\ 0 & 0 & \theta_{\varepsilon_3}^2 & \\ 0 & 0 & 0 & \theta_{\varepsilon_4}^2 \end{pmatrix}
$$

$$
\begin{pmatrix} x_1 \\ x_2 \end{pmatrix} = \begin{pmatrix} \lambda_1' & 0 & 0 & 0 & 0 & 0 \\ \lambda_2' & 0 & 0 & 0 & 0 & 0 \end{pmatrix} \begin{pmatrix} \xi \\ \varepsilon_1 \\ \varepsilon_2 \\ \varepsilon_3 \\ \varepsilon_4 \end{pmatrix} + \begin{pmatrix} \delta_1 \\ \delta_2 \end{pmatrix}
$$

$$
\boldsymbol{\theta}_\delta^2 = \begin{pmatrix} \theta_{\delta_1}^2 & \\ 0 & \theta_{\delta_2}^2 \end{pmatrix}
$$

The appropriate variance-covariance matrix for ξ is then

$$
\boldsymbol{\phi} = \begin{pmatrix} \phi & & & & \\ 0 & \phi_{11} & & & \\ 0 & 0 & \phi_{22} & & \\ 0 & \phi_{31} & 0 & \phi_{33} & \\ 0 & 0 & \phi_{42} & 0 & \phi_{44} \end{pmatrix}
$$

where $\phi = \mathrm{var}(\xi)$, $\phi_{11} = \mathrm{var}(\varepsilon_1)$, $\phi_{22} = \mathrm{var}(\varepsilon_2)$, $\phi_{33} = \mathrm{var}(\varepsilon_3)$, $\phi_{44} = \mathrm{var}(\varepsilon_4)$, $\phi_{31} = \mathrm{cov}(\varepsilon_3, \varepsilon_1)$, and $\phi_{42} = \mathrm{cov}(\varepsilon_4, \varepsilon_2)$. The model is completely specified with $\boldsymbol{\psi}$ defined as follows:

$$
\boldsymbol{\psi} = \begin{pmatrix} \psi_{11} & & & & & \\ 0 & \psi_{22} & & & & \\ 0 & 0 & 0 & & & \\ 0 & 0 & 0 & 0 & & \\ 0 & 0 & 0 & 0 & 0 & \\ 0 & 0 & 0 & 0 & 0 & 0 \end{pmatrix}
$$

In sum, the model of Figure 8.3 allows the researcher to determine the relationship between pretest and posttest variables η_1 and η_2, while controlling for the influence of the covariate ξ, and at the same time allowing errors between successive measurements of the indicators of η_1 and η_2 to be correlated.

The final extension of the pretest-posttest design is shown in Figure 8.4. This model explicitly represents the addition of a treatment x_3 and a true independent variable η_3 measured with two manipulation checks y_5 and y_6. The structural equations for this model become

$$
\begin{pmatrix} 1 & 0 & 0 \\ -\beta_1 & 1 & -\beta_2 \\ 0 & 0 & 1 \end{pmatrix}
\begin{pmatrix} \eta_1 \\ \eta_2 \\ \eta_3 \end{pmatrix}
=
\begin{pmatrix} \gamma_1 & 0 \\ \gamma_2 & 0 \\ 0 & \gamma_3 \end{pmatrix}
\begin{pmatrix} \xi_1 \\ \xi_2 \end{pmatrix}
+
\begin{pmatrix} \zeta_1 \\ \zeta_2 \\ \zeta_3 \end{pmatrix}
$$

$$
\begin{pmatrix} y_1 \\ y_2 \\ y_3 \\ y_4 \\ y_5 \\ y_6 \end{pmatrix}
=
\begin{pmatrix} \lambda_1 & 0 & 0 \\ \lambda_2 & 0 & 0 \\ 0 & \lambda_3 & 0 \\ 0 & \lambda_4 & 0 \\ 0 & 0 & \lambda_5 \\ 0 & 0 & \lambda_6 \end{pmatrix}
\begin{pmatrix} \eta_1 \\ \eta_2 \\ \eta_3 \end{pmatrix}
+
\begin{pmatrix} \varepsilon_1 \\ \varepsilon_2 \\ \varepsilon_3 \\ \varepsilon_4 \\ \varepsilon_5 \\ \varepsilon_6 \end{pmatrix}
$$

$$
\boldsymbol{\theta}_\varepsilon^2 =
\begin{pmatrix}
\theta_{\varepsilon_1}^2 & & & & & \\
0 & \theta_{\varepsilon_2}^2 & & & & \\
0 & 0 & \theta_{\varepsilon_3}^2 & & & \\
0 & 0 & 0 & \theta_{\varepsilon_4}^2 & & \\
0 & 0 & 0 & 0 & \theta_{\varepsilon_5}^2 & \\
0 & 0 & 0 & 0 & 0 & \theta_{\varepsilon_6}^2
\end{pmatrix}
$$

$$
\begin{pmatrix} x_1 \\ x_2 \\ x_3 \end{pmatrix}
=
\begin{pmatrix} \lambda_1' & 0 \\ \lambda_2' & 0 \\ 0 & 1 \end{pmatrix}
\begin{pmatrix} \xi_1 \\ \xi_2 \end{pmatrix}
+
\begin{pmatrix} \delta_1 \\ \delta_2 \\ 0 \end{pmatrix}
$$

$$
\boldsymbol{\theta}_\delta^2 =
\begin{pmatrix}
\theta_{\delta_1}^2 & & \\
0 & \theta_{\delta_2}^2 & \\
0 & 0 & 0
\end{pmatrix}
$$

$$
\boldsymbol{\Phi} =
\begin{pmatrix}
1.0 & \\
\phi_{21} & 1.0
\end{pmatrix}
$$

$$
\boldsymbol{\psi} =
\begin{pmatrix}
\psi_{11} & & \\
0 & \psi_{22} & \\
0 & 0 & \psi_{33}
\end{pmatrix}
$$

Since there are 25 parameters to be estimated and 45 independent pieces of information, there are 20 overidentifying restrictions. LISREL can be conveniently used to estimate the parameters and test the model.

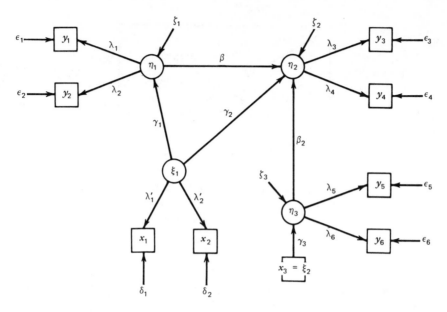

Figure 8.4. A causal model for a pretest and posttest design with one covariate ξ measured with two indicators, x_1 and x_2, one treatment, x_3, and two manipulation checks, y_5 and y_6.

The Cross-Lagged Panel Correlation Technique

The cross-lagged panel correlation technique is a quasi-experimental procedure for ascertaining the direction of causality between two variables measured at two or more points in time. Although first suggested in its primitive form by Lazarsfeld (e.g., 1948), the cross-lagged panel correlation technique owes its most recent development to the work of Donald T. Campbell and his colleagues (e.g., Campbell, 1963; Campbell and Stanley, 1966; Rozelle and Campbell, 1969; Cook and Campbell, 1976). Others in the causal modeling tradition have made important contributions also (c.f., Duncan, 1969, 1972, 1975; Hannan et al., 1974).

Figure 8.5 presents a typical cross-legged panel correlation design for two variables (x and y) measured at two points in time (1 and 2). For this model, there are six correlations of interest. The correlations $r_{x_1 y_1}$ and $r_{x_2 y_2}$ are known variously as concurrent, static, or synchronous correlations. They measure the contemporaneous correlations between the variables of interest at both points in time. The correlations $r_{x_1 x_2}$ and $r_{y_1 y_2}$ are called test-retest or autocorrelations. They indicate the stability over time of the two variables under scrutiny.

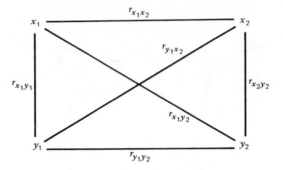

Figure 8.5. A cross-lagged panel correlation design for two variables (x and y) measured at two successive points in time (1 and 2) on the same sample of subjects.

Finally, the cross-lagged correlations $r_{x_1y_2}$ and $r_{x_2y_1}$ reflect the temporal association between different variables.

The inference of causality between x and y is based on the sign of the cross-lagged differential, that is, the sign of $(r_{x_1y_2} - r_{x_2y_1})$. Specifically, if the cross-lagged differential turns out to be positive, then one has some evidence for inferring that x causes y. A negative cross-lagged differential, in contrast, provides some evidence for inferring that y causes x.[3] The null hypothesis of the cross-lagged panel correlation technique may be tested using the model of Figure 8.6. This hypothesis maintains that the relationship between x and y is due to an unmeasured third variable (cf., Kenny, 1975). The null hypothesis model may be conveniently analyzed using the structural equation methodology developed in Chapter 4. More will be said about this and related models later in the chapter.

Duncan (1969) has analyzed the two-wave, two-variable model of Figure 8.5 from the perspective of path analysis. Figure 8.7 presents the general model for such situations where a, b, c, d, e, and f represent the path or regression coefficients of interest. Notice that there are seven parameters to be estimated but only six independent pieces of information. Therefore, since the model is under-identified, one must make some a priori assumption as to the value of one of the seven parameters in order to estimate the remaining parameters. The restriction(s) can be made based on theoretical considerations, past empirical findings, or methodological factors. For example, one may know, based on logical considerations, that a simultaneous effect from y to x is impossible. Thus, one might then eliminate parameter e from consideration in Figure 8.7.

One of the problems with the traditional cross-lagged panel design analysis is that it assumes that variables are measured without error. When measurement

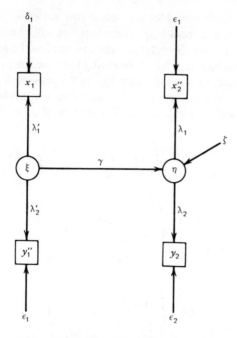

Figure 8.6. Null hypothesis model for cross-lagged panel correlation model of Figure 8.5.

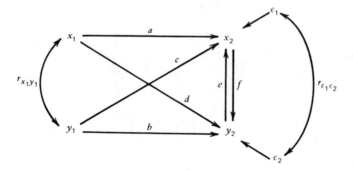

Figure 8.7. The general two-wave, two-variable model with no measurement error in variables.

error is present in one's variables and when this varies across time, the synchronous, test-retest, and cross-lagged relationships will be contaminated if one uses the standard analysis. Structural equation models, however, provide the researcher with a methodology for representing both measurement error and the relationships among variables over time. Figure 8.8 presents a general model for the two-wave, two-variable case with measurement error where each variable is operationalized with two indicators.[4] The structural equations for this model may be written as

$$\begin{pmatrix} 1 & -\beta_1 \\ -\beta_2 & 1 \end{pmatrix} \begin{pmatrix} \eta_1 \\ \eta_2 \end{pmatrix} = \begin{pmatrix} \gamma_1 & \gamma_2 \\ \gamma_3 & \gamma_4 \end{pmatrix} \begin{pmatrix} \xi_1 \\ \xi_2 \end{pmatrix} + \begin{pmatrix} \zeta_1 \\ \zeta_2 \end{pmatrix}$$

$$\begin{pmatrix} y_1 \\ y_2 \\ y_3 \\ y_4 \end{pmatrix} = \begin{pmatrix} \lambda_1 & 0 \\ \lambda_2 & 0 \\ 0 & \lambda_3 \\ 0 & \lambda_4 \end{pmatrix} \begin{pmatrix} \eta_1 \\ \eta_2 \end{pmatrix} + \begin{pmatrix} \varepsilon_1 \\ \varepsilon_2 \\ \varepsilon_3 \\ \varepsilon_4 \end{pmatrix}$$

$$\boldsymbol{\theta}_\varepsilon^2 = \begin{pmatrix} \theta_{\varepsilon_1}^2 & & & \\ 0 & \theta_{\varepsilon_2}^2 & & \\ 0 & 0 & \theta_{\varepsilon_3}^2 & \\ 0 & 0 & 0 & \theta_{\varepsilon_4}^2 \end{pmatrix}$$

$$\begin{pmatrix} x_1 \\ x_2 \\ x_3 \\ x_4 \end{pmatrix} = \begin{pmatrix} \lambda_1' & 0 \\ \lambda_2' & 0 \\ 0 & \lambda_3' \\ 0 & \lambda_4' \end{pmatrix} \begin{pmatrix} \xi_1 \\ \xi_2 \end{pmatrix} + \begin{pmatrix} \delta_1 \\ \delta_2 \\ \delta_3 \\ \delta_4 \end{pmatrix}$$

$$\boldsymbol{\theta}_\delta^2 = \begin{pmatrix} \theta_{\delta_1}^2 & & & \\ 0 & \theta_{\delta_2}^2 & & \\ 0 & 0 & \theta_{\delta_3}^2 & \\ 0 & 0 & 0 & \theta_{\delta_4}^2 \end{pmatrix}$$

$$\boldsymbol{\phi} = \begin{pmatrix} \phi_{11} & \\ \phi_{21} & \phi_{22} \end{pmatrix}$$

$$\boldsymbol{\psi} = \begin{pmatrix} \psi_{11} & \\ \psi_{21} & \psi_{22} \end{pmatrix}$$

Since there are 36 independent pieces of information provided by the observations and since there are 28 parameters to be estimated, there will be eight overidentifying restrictions.[5] The above system of equations may be conveniently solved using LISREL.

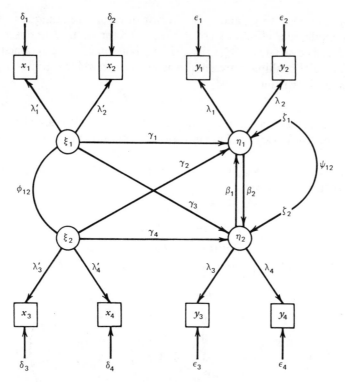

Figure 8.8. A causal model for a two-wave, two-variable model with measurement error—all variables operationalized with two indicators.

Jöreskog's General Model for Longitudinal Data

In this section, a general model for longitudinal data will be outlined. The model was first suggested by Jöreskog and Sörbom (1977), and it explicitly represents the relationships among two or more variables measured at two or more points in time. Further, it allows the researcher to model the influence of covariates such as individual differences, background variables, environmental stimuli, or other exogenous factors.

Consider the model consisting of p_t variables $\mathbf{y}'_t = (y_{1t}, y_{2t}, \ldots, y_{p_t t})$ measured at $t = 1, 2, \ldots, m$ occasions. The relationships between the true, unobserved variables $\boldsymbol{\eta}_t$ and their respective observed variables $\mathbf{y}_t$ may be expressed as follows:

$$\mathbf{y}_t = \mathbf{v}_{yt} + \boldsymbol{\Lambda}_{yt}\boldsymbol{\eta}_t + \boldsymbol{\varepsilon}_t$$

where $\mathbf{v}_{yt}$ is a vector of means for $\mathbf{y}_t$, $\boldsymbol{\Lambda}_{yt}$ is a matrix of parameters (i.e., factor loadings) relating $\boldsymbol{\eta}_t$ to $\mathbf{y}_t$, and $\boldsymbol{\varepsilon}_t$ is a vector of errors (i.e., unique factors). In order to model the effects of covariates, a vector of true unobservables $\boldsymbol{\xi}$ measured by q covariates $\mathbf{x}' = (x_1, x_2, \dots, x_q)$ is assumed to be obtained prior to $t = 1$. The relationships between the true unobserved covariates and their measures can be written as

$$\mathbf{x} = \mathbf{v}_x + \boldsymbol{\Lambda}_x \boldsymbol{\xi} + \boldsymbol{\delta}$$

where $\mathbf{v}_x$ is a vector of means for $\mathbf{x}$, $\boldsymbol{\Lambda}_x$ is a matrix of parameters, and $\boldsymbol{\delta}$ is a vector of errors. The true covariates $\boldsymbol{\xi}$ are modeled as determinants of the true variables $\boldsymbol{\eta}_t$.

The structural equations for the system of relationships among the $\boldsymbol{\eta}_t$'s and $\boldsymbol{\xi}$ may be written as follows:

$$\boldsymbol{\eta}_1 = \boldsymbol{\Lambda}_1 \boldsymbol{\xi} + \boldsymbol{\zeta}_1$$
$$\boldsymbol{\eta}_t = \boldsymbol{\Lambda}_t \boldsymbol{\xi} + \mathbf{B}_t \boldsymbol{\eta}_{t-1} + \boldsymbol{\zeta}_t$$

where $t = 2, \dots, m$. As an illustration, the system of equations for the general model with $m = 4$ time periods can be written as (e.g., Jöreskog and Sörbom, 1977):

$$\mathbf{B}\boldsymbol{\eta}_t = \boldsymbol{\Gamma}\boldsymbol{\xi} + \boldsymbol{\zeta}_t$$

$$\begin{pmatrix} \mathbf{I} & \mathbf{0} & \mathbf{0} & \mathbf{0} \\ -\mathbf{B}_2 & \mathbf{I} & \mathbf{0} & \mathbf{0} \\ \mathbf{0} & -\mathbf{B}_3 & \mathbf{I} & \mathbf{0} \\ \mathbf{0} & \mathbf{0} & -\mathbf{B}_4 & \mathbf{I} \end{pmatrix} \begin{pmatrix} \boldsymbol{\eta}_1 \\ \boldsymbol{\eta}_2 \\ \boldsymbol{\eta}_3 \\ \boldsymbol{\eta}_4 \end{pmatrix} = \begin{pmatrix} \boldsymbol{\Lambda}_1 \\ \boldsymbol{\Lambda}_2 \\ \boldsymbol{\Lambda}_3 \\ \boldsymbol{\Lambda}_4 \end{pmatrix} \boldsymbol{\xi} + \begin{pmatrix} \boldsymbol{\zeta}_1 \\ \boldsymbol{\zeta}_2 \\ \boldsymbol{\zeta}_3 \\ \boldsymbol{\zeta}_4 \end{pmatrix}$$

$$\mathbf{y}_t = \boldsymbol{\Lambda}_{yt} \boldsymbol{\eta}_t + \boldsymbol{\varepsilon}_t$$

$$\begin{pmatrix} \mathbf{y}_1 \\ \mathbf{y}_2 \\ \mathbf{y}_3 \\ \mathbf{y}_4 \end{pmatrix} = \begin{pmatrix} \boldsymbol{\Lambda}_{y_1} & \mathbf{0} & \mathbf{0} & \mathbf{0} \\ \mathbf{0} & \boldsymbol{\Lambda}_{y_2} & \mathbf{0} & \mathbf{0} \\ \mathbf{0} & \mathbf{0} & \boldsymbol{\Lambda}_{y_3} & \mathbf{0} \\ \mathbf{0} & \mathbf{0} & \mathbf{0} & \boldsymbol{\Lambda}_{y_4} \end{pmatrix} \begin{pmatrix} \boldsymbol{\eta}_1 \\ \boldsymbol{\eta}_2 \\ \boldsymbol{\eta}_3 \\ \boldsymbol{\eta}_4 \end{pmatrix} + \begin{pmatrix} \boldsymbol{\varepsilon}_1 \\ \boldsymbol{\varepsilon}_2 \\ \boldsymbol{\varepsilon}_3 \\ \boldsymbol{\varepsilon}_4 \end{pmatrix}$$

$$\boldsymbol{\xi}' = (\xi_1, \xi_2, \dots, \xi_n)$$

$$\mathbf{x} = \boldsymbol{\Lambda}_x \boldsymbol{\xi} + \boldsymbol{\delta}$$

As an example, consider the model in Figure 8.9 consisting of a four-wave, two-variable (y, y^*) design with uncorrelated errors and one true covariate (ξ) directly affecting only the first wave. The structural equations for this system are

$$\mathbf{B}\boldsymbol{\eta}_t = \boldsymbol{\Gamma}\boldsymbol{\xi} + \boldsymbol{\zeta}$$

$$\begin{pmatrix} 1 & 0 & 0 & 0 \\ -\beta_2 & 1 & 0 & 0 \\ 0 & -\beta_3 & 1 & 0 \\ 0 & 0 & -\beta_4 & 1 \end{pmatrix} \begin{pmatrix} \eta_1 \\ \eta_2 \\ \eta_3 \\ \eta_4 \end{pmatrix} = \begin{pmatrix} \gamma \\ 0 \\ 0 \\ 0 \end{pmatrix} \xi + \begin{pmatrix} \zeta_1 \\ \zeta_2 \\ \zeta_3 \\ \zeta_4 \end{pmatrix}$$

$$\mathbf{y}_t = \boldsymbol{\Lambda}_{yt} \boldsymbol{\eta}_t + \boldsymbol{\varepsilon}_t$$

$$
\begin{pmatrix} y_1 \\ y_2 \\ y_3 \\ y_4 \\ y_1^* \\ y_2^* \\ y_3^* \\ y_4^* \end{pmatrix} = \begin{pmatrix} \lambda_1 & 0 & 0 & 0 \\ 0 & \lambda_2 & 0 & 0 \\ 0 & 0 & \lambda_3 & 0 \\ 0 & 0 & 0 & \lambda_4 \\ 1 & 0 & 0 & 0 \\ 0 & 1 & 0 & 0 \\ 0 & 0 & 1 & 0 \\ 0 & 0 & 0 & 1 \end{pmatrix} \begin{pmatrix} \eta_1 \\ \eta_2 \\ \eta_3 \\ \eta_4 \end{pmatrix} + \begin{pmatrix} \varepsilon_1 \\ \varepsilon_2 \\ \varepsilon_3 \\ \varepsilon_4 \\ \varepsilon_1^* \\ \varepsilon_2^* \\ \varepsilon_3^* \\ \varepsilon_4^* \end{pmatrix}
$$

$$
\boldsymbol{\theta}_{\varepsilon_t}^2 = \begin{pmatrix} \theta_{\varepsilon_2}^2 & & & & & & & \\ 0 & \theta_{\varepsilon_2}^2 & & & & & & \\ 0 & 0 & \theta_{\varepsilon_3}^2 & & & & & \\ 0 & 0 & 0 & \theta_{\varepsilon_4}^2 & & & & \\ 0 & 0 & 0 & 0 & \theta_{\varepsilon_1^*}^2 & & & \\ 0 & 0 & 0 & 0 & 0 & \theta_{\varepsilon_2^*}^2 & & \\ 0 & 0 & 0 & 0 & 0 & 0 & \theta_{\varepsilon_3^*}^2 & \\ 0 & 0 & 0 & 0 & 0 & 0 & 0 & \theta_{\varepsilon_4^*}^2 \end{pmatrix}
$$

$$
\begin{pmatrix} x_1 \\ x_2 \end{pmatrix} = \begin{pmatrix} \lambda_1' \\ 1 \end{pmatrix} \xi + \begin{pmatrix} \delta_1 \\ \delta_2 \end{pmatrix}
$$

$$
\boldsymbol{\theta}_\delta^2 = \begin{pmatrix} \theta_{\delta_1}^2 & \\ 0 & \theta_{\delta_2}^2 \end{pmatrix}
$$

$$
\phi = \mathrm{var}(\xi)
$$

Since there are 55 distinct elements in Σ and 24 parameters to be estimated, there will be 31 degrees of freedom for the model.[6]

The model of Figure 8.9 assumes that the error terms for repeated measures of the same variables are not correlated. In many applications, this will not be a valid assumption since systematic (unmeasured) factors such as memory effects, demand characteristics, and other forms of bias may be present. Thus, it would be desirable to allow $\varepsilon_1^*-\varepsilon_4^*$ to be intercorrelated and also $\varepsilon_1-\varepsilon_4$ to be intercorrelated. For the four-wave, two-variable design (omitting the true covariate ξ), Jöreskog and Sörbom (1977) solve the system of equations allowing for correlations among repeated measures of the same variables. Unfortunately, the model is underidentified and can not be estimated. The authors then derive two models that may be used to represent possible causes of covariation in the error terms for repeated measures of the same variable: the test-specific factor model and the simplex error model. Both of these are briefly described below.

Figure 8.10 illustrates a test-specific factor model for the four-wave, two-variable design. The test-specific factors η_1^* and η_2^* might represent variables present at each measurement occasion causing common variation in the

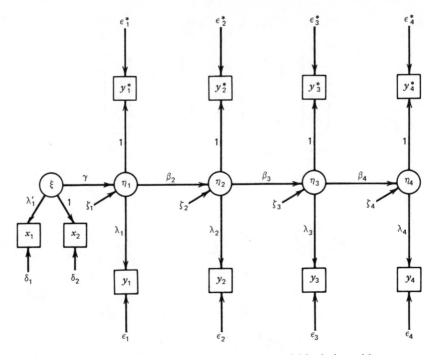

Figure 8.9. A causal model for a four-wave, two-variable design with uncorrelated errors and one true covariate affecting the first wave.

measures. The structural equations for this system are

$$\mathbf{B}\boldsymbol{\eta}_t = \boldsymbol{\Gamma}\boldsymbol{\xi} + \boldsymbol{\zeta}_t$$

Since there are no covariates specified, we find that

$$\begin{pmatrix} 1 & 0 & 0 & 0 \\ -\beta_2 & 1 & 0 & 0 \\ 0 & -\beta_3 & 1 & 0 \\ 0 & 0 & -\beta_4 & 1 \end{pmatrix} \begin{pmatrix} \eta_1 \\ \eta_2 \\ \eta_3 \\ \eta_4 \end{pmatrix} = \begin{pmatrix} \zeta_1 \\ \zeta_2 \\ \zeta_3 \\ \zeta_4 \end{pmatrix}$$

and

$$\begin{pmatrix} y_1 \\ y_2 \\ y_3 \\ y_4 \\ y_1^* \\ y_2^* \\ y_3^* \\ y_4^* \end{pmatrix} = \begin{pmatrix} \lambda_1 & 0 & 0 & 0 & \gamma_1 & 0 \\ 0 & \lambda_2 & 0 & 0 & \gamma_2 & 0 \\ 0 & 0 & \lambda_3 & 0 & \gamma_3 & 0 \\ 0 & 0 & 0 & \lambda_4 & \gamma_4 & 0 \\ 1 & 0 & 0 & 0 & 0 & \gamma_5 \\ 0 & 1 & 0 & 0 & 0 & \gamma_6 \\ 0 & 0 & 1 & 0 & 0 & \gamma_7 \\ 0 & 0 & 0 & 1 & 0 & \gamma_8 \end{pmatrix} \begin{pmatrix} \eta_1 \\ \eta_2 \\ \eta_3 \\ \eta_4 \\ \eta_1^* \\ \eta_2^* \end{pmatrix} + \begin{pmatrix} \varepsilon_1 \\ \varepsilon_2 \\ \varepsilon_3 \\ \varepsilon_4 \\ \varepsilon_1^* \\ \varepsilon_2^* \\ \varepsilon_3^* \\ \varepsilon_4^* \end{pmatrix}$$

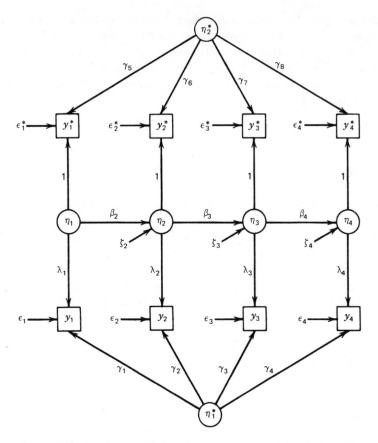

Figure 8.10. A causal model for a four-wave, two-variable design with two test specific factors η_1^* and η_2^*.

Finally,

$$\psi = \begin{pmatrix} \psi_{11} & & & \\ 0 & \psi_{22} & & \\ 0 & 0 & \psi_{33} & \\ 0 & 0 & 0 & \psi_{44} \end{pmatrix}$$

Jöreskog and Söbom (1977) show that the model of Figure 8.10 is overidentified with 9 degrees of freedom. In general, for $m \geq 3$ periods in time, the degrees of freedom for the model of Figure 8.10 may be computed as (Jöreskog and Sörbom, 1977): d.f. $= 2m^2 - 6m + 1$.

Finally, Jöreskog and Sörbom (1977) investigate the longitudinal model where error terms of repeated measures of variables are represented through a simplex structure. This involves introducing two factors for each set of variables such that the factors are causally related within each set of variables and each factor directly causes two of the repeated measures. For the derivation of the approach and an illustration, the reader is referred to Jöreskog and Sörbom (1977). Additional versions of the model and examples can be found in Wheaton et al. (1977).

Summary

Causal relationships among variables over time may be modeled in a variety of ways. The relationship between pretest and posttest variables, for example, can be easily represented using Jöreskog's general model. The approach is particularly effective for discovering the true effect between pretest and posttest after controlling for contaminating covariates. Four variants of the pretest/posttest model were examined: (1) the pretest and posttest design with one errorless covariate, (2) the pretest and posttest design with one fallible covariate measured by two indicators, (3) the pretest and posttest design with one fallible covariate measured by two indicators allowing for correlated errors across repeated measures, and (4) the pretest and posttest design with one fallible covariate and a single treatment with two manipulation checks.

Next, the cross-lagged panel correlation technique was presented as a means for discerning the direction of causality between two variables measured at two or more points in time. Both the errorless and measurement error versions of the cross-lagged panel correlation approach were investigated.

Finally, Jöreskog's general model for longitudinal data was developed. The special case of the four-wave, two-variable design with uncorrelated errors and one true covariate affecting the first wave was derived. In addition, the four-wave two-variable design with test-specific factors was outlined as one means for representing causality over time. For an extension of the general linear model to time-series studies, the reader is referred to Geweke (1977).

Notes

[1] Jöreskog and Sörbom (1977) suggest that, in longitudinal studies, it is often useful to fix the scales of η_1 and η_2 so that these are measured in the same units as one of the tests in both y_1 and y_2 on the one hand, and y_3 and y_4 on the other. This may be done by fixing $\lambda_1 = 1$ and $\lambda_3 = 1$ in Figure 8.1, for example. When these constraints are made, there will be four overidentifying restrictions for the model.

[2] Again, following the logic outlined in footnote 1, if one desires to fix scales of measurement, the following parameters could be restricted a priori: $\lambda_1 = \lambda_3 = \lambda'_1 = 1$. This will increase the number of overidentifying restrictions to five. Some analysts may also desire to standardize the variance of ξ at one, and this will increase the number of overidentifying restrictions to six.

[3] In addition to the sign of the cross-lagged differential, it is often maintained that, for x to cause y, $r_{x_1 y_2}$ should be statistically significant and greater than both $r_{x_1 y_1}$ and $r_{x_2 y_1}$ (cf., Pelz and Andrews, 1964). Others add the additional requirement that $r_{x_2 y_2} > r_{x_2 y_1}$ (cf., Wanous, 1974). All of these rules of thumb are insufficient, however, since one must make certain assumptions about models such as shown in Figure 8.5 (e.g., no measurement error) in order to make the model identified (cf., Duncan, 1969). Finally, Vroom (1966) suggests that one may rule out the counter hypothesis that the reason a cross-lagged differential exists is due to a third variable causing covariation in x and y. This may be done by examining the Pearson product-moment correlations between the change scores of variables x and y. A significant "dynamic" correlation lends additional support to the conclusion that a cross-lagged differential indicates a causal relationship between x and y.

[4] Duncan (1975) presents a simpler model for the two-wave, two-variable design where each variable is measured by a single indicator. He then discusses various restrictions that may be made in order to make the model identified. His model does not allow for measurement error, however.

[5] As discussed in footnotes 1 and 2, one may desire to fix the scales of ξ_1, ξ_2, η_1, and η_2 so that these are measured in the same units. This may be accomplished with the following constraints: $\lambda'_1 = \lambda_1 = \lambda'_3 = \lambda_3 = 1$. Under these conditions, there will be four additional overidentifying restrictions. Also, for most applications, either $\psi_{21} = 0$ or β_1 and β_2 both equal zero.

[6] For the simpler model consisting only of the four-wave, two-variable situation *without* the covariate ξ, Jöreskog and Sörbom (1977) show that the system is overidentified with 17 degrees of freedom. For $m > 2$ time periods, the number of degrees of freedom for this simpler model may be calculated as $2m^2 - 4m + 1$. In general, the model is a simplex or first-order autogressive one and may be expressed as

$$\eta_{i+1} = \beta_{i+1}\eta_i + \zeta_{i+1}$$

The variance-covariance matrix Φ for the first-order autoregressive model with four waves is

$$\phi = \begin{pmatrix} \phi_1 & & & \\ \beta_1\phi_1 & \phi_2 & & \\ \beta_1\beta_2\phi_1 & \beta_2\phi_2 & \phi_3 & \\ \beta_1\beta_2\beta_3\phi_1 & \beta_2\beta_3\phi_2 & \beta_3\phi_3 & \phi_4 \end{pmatrix}$$

where

$$\phi_1 = \psi_{11}$$
$$\phi_{i+1} = \psi_{(i+1)(i+1)} + \beta_{i+1}^2 \phi_i$$

and

$$\psi_{ii} = \text{var}(\zeta_i)$$

NINE

BUYER BEHAVIOR

Most contemporary models of buyer behavior fall into one of two classes. On the one hand, there are a number of models that attempt to capture the full range of buyer decision-making processes. Thus, the models of Nicosia (1966), Howard and Sheth (1969), and Engel, Kollat, and Blackwell (1973) are all similar in the sense that each conceptualizes buyer behavior to be a complex response to situational stimuli as a function of certain perceptual, learning, motivational, and information processing variables. At the other extreme, many theories of buyer behavior attempt to explain sharply delimited phenomena. For example, the Fisbein attitude model (e.g., Lutz, 1977) and advertising effect models (e.g., Wright, 1973) focus on narrow, well-defined cognitive responses of buyers.

The vast majority of buyer behavior models in marketing (including the above) are variants of the stimulus–organism–response paradigm (see discussion in Chapter 2). This chapter examines this paradigm in the context of causal modeling. Specifically, causal modeling permits the researcher to formally represent l stimuli as they impinge upon m perceptual, cognitive, or motivational processes in the buyer, and then models the impact of these m processes on n buyer responses (e.g., preference or choice). The entire pattern of relationships among the $k = l + m + n$ variables is represented with a structural equation model. After discussion of the general causal model, the overall procedure is illustrated on simulated data, and specific problems and uses of the approach are examined in a theory building and diagnostic sense.

The Model

Consider the general S–O–R model of buyer behavior outlined in Figure 9.1. In this model, a single stimulus (S) is shown as it affects three psychological constructs[1]—affect (A), cognitions (C), and behavioral intentions (BI)— and these, in turn, are modeled as determinants of a single behavior response (R). The model of Figure 9.1 can be easily extended to the general case for l stimuli, m psychological processes, and n responses, but will not be done here for simplicity.

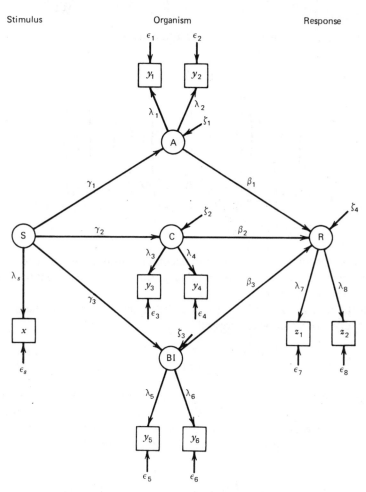

Figure 9.1. A causal diagram for the S–O–R model. *Note:* The covariances among certain error terms (i.e., ζ_1, ζ_2, and ζ_3) have been omitted from the diagram for simplicity.

To represent the system of relationships shown in Figure 9.1, two sets of equations are needed: (1) equations modeling cause-and-effect and/or functional relationships and (2) equations modeling the measurement relationships. Looking first at the cause-and-effect relations implied by Figure 9.1, it can be seen that these can be written as

$$
\begin{pmatrix}
1 & 0 & 0 & 0 \\
0 & 1 & 0 & 0 \\
0 & 0 & 1 & 0 \\
-\beta_1 & -\beta_2 & -\beta_3 & 1
\end{pmatrix}
\begin{pmatrix}
\mathbf{A} \\
\mathbf{C} \\
\mathbf{BI} \\
\mathbf{R}
\end{pmatrix}
=
\begin{pmatrix}
\gamma_1 \\
\gamma_2 \\
\gamma_3 \\
0
\end{pmatrix}
(\mathbf{S}) +
\begin{pmatrix}
\zeta_1 \\
\zeta_2 \\
\zeta_3 \\
\zeta_4
\end{pmatrix}
\tag{9.1}
$$

Similarly, the equations modeling measurement relations may be summarized as

$$
\begin{pmatrix}
y_1 \\
y_2 \\
y_3 \\
y_4 \\
y_5 \\
y_5 \\
z_1 \\
z_2
\end{pmatrix}
=
\begin{pmatrix}
\lambda_1 & 0 & 0 & 0 \\
\lambda_2 & 0 & 0 & 0 \\
0 & \lambda_3 & 0 & 0 \\
0 & \lambda_4 & 0 & 0 \\
0 & 0 & \lambda_5 & 0 \\
0 & 0 & \lambda_6 & 0 \\
0 & 0 & 0 & \lambda_7 \\
0 & 0 & 0 & \lambda_8
\end{pmatrix}
\begin{pmatrix}
\mathbf{A} \\
\mathbf{C} \\
\mathbf{BI} \\
\mathbf{R}
\end{pmatrix}
+
\begin{pmatrix}
\varepsilon_1 \\
\varepsilon_3 \\
\varepsilon_3 \\
\varepsilon_4 \\
\varepsilon_5 \\
\varepsilon_6 \\
\varepsilon_7 \\
\varepsilon_8
\end{pmatrix}
\tag{9.2}
$$

$$
x = S \tag{9.3}
$$

where the latter equation expresses the fact that the stimulus is assumed measured without error. The assumptions and conventions derived in Chapter 4 for the general linear model apply here also.

With the $\mathbf{w} = (\mathbf{y}', \mathbf{z}')$ and $\mathbf{t} = (\mathbf{w}', \mathbf{x}')$, the variance-covariance matrix of the eight observations can be experessed as

$$
\mathbf{\Sigma} =
\begin{pmatrix}
\mathbf{\Lambda}_w(\mathbf{B}^{-1}\mathbf{\Gamma}\phi\mathbf{\Gamma}\mathbf{B}'^{-1} + \mathbf{B}^{-1}\mathbf{\psi}\mathbf{B}'^{-1})\mathbf{\Lambda}_w' + \mathbf{\theta}_\varepsilon^2 & \mathbf{\Lambda}_w\mathbf{B}^{-1}\mathbf{\Gamma}\phi \\
\phi\mathbf{\Gamma}'\mathbf{B}'^{-1}\mathbf{\Lambda}_w & \phi
\end{pmatrix}
$$

where $\mathbf{B}$ is the matrix of β parameters designated in (9.1), $\mathbf{\Lambda}_w$ is the matrix of λ parameters expressed in (9.2), $\mathbf{\Gamma}$ is the vector of γ parameters shown in (9.1), ϕ is the variance of x, $\mathbf{\theta}_\varepsilon^2$ is the vector of error variances for the endogenous measurements, and the variance-covariance matrix for ζ can be written as

$$
\mathbf{\psi} =
\begin{pmatrix}
\psi_{11} & & & \\
\psi_{21} & \psi_{22} & & \\
\psi_{31} & \psi_{32} & \psi_{33} & \\
0 & 0 & 0 & \psi_{44}
\end{pmatrix}
$$

An Illustration

Methodology

As an empirical test of the model, a field experiment was simulated to model the effects of source credibility in a persuasive appeal on consumer attitudes and subsequent behavior. As background, the experiment was conceived as follows. Consider the problem faced by four churches of the same denomination in a small rural city. In an effort to increase both funds for special operations and the amount of food donated in the weekly food-for-the-needy program, the church elders decided to sponsor a one-time personal appeal at a future Sunday service. By varying the credibility of the communicator in each of the four churches, the elders hoped to evaluate the effectiveness of source credibility on attitudes and behavior. This was deemed necessary because the cost of hiring a speaker varied directly with credibility, and the elders desired to learn from the experience so as to optimize future appeals. Also, they were concerned with the feelings and cognitive evaluations of the church rank-and-file so as not to engender negative psychological reactions.

As a stimulus (S), the same message was presented at each service, but different levels of source credibility (high, medium, and low) and a no-message control were randomly assigned to the four churches. The affective component of attitudes was measured with a six-item Likert index (y_1) and an eight-item semantic differential scale (y_2); cognitions were indicated by five bi-polar items (y_3) and six Likert items (y_4); behavioral intentions were operationalized with two self-report pledges (y_5 and y_6) taken immediately after the manipulation and three days later in a mail questionnaire, respectively. Finally, two behavioral response measures were recorded on subjects over the period of one month. One measure was the actual increase in dollars donated (z_1), while the second was the actual increase in the value of food donated (z_2). The increase for each person was relative to the average given per month in the past six months.

Findings

The application of LISREL to the model of Figure 9.1 and the data of Table 9.1 yields the results summarized in Table 9.2. Notice first that the data fit the model very well, since $\chi^2 = 18.44$, d.f. $= 16$, and $p \simeq 0.30$. Second, the stimulus has the greatest impact on behavioral intentions, being about 30 percent and 8 percent more forceful on this variable than it is on cognitions and affect, respectively (assuming that the psychological states are measured on the same metric). Similarly, behavioral intentions are about 25 percent and 12 percent more powerful than are affect and cognitions, respectively, in their influence on behavioral responses. However, it should be noted that all of the γ and β effects are significant and of a relatively high magnitude. Given the results

Table 9.1

Pearson Product-Moment Correlation Matrix of Observations— Simulated Data Set #1

	y_1	y_2	y_3	y_4	y_5	y_6	z_1	z_2	x
y_1	1.000								
y_2	0.912	1.000							
y_3	0.362	0.386	1.000						
y_4	0.381	0.370	0.871	1.000					
y_5	0.424	0.411	0.333	0.341	1.000				
y_6	0.418	0.431	0.329	0.344	0.947	1.000			
z_1	0.638	0.627	0.601	0.649	0.692	0.680	1.000		
z_2	0.642	0.656	0.583	0.593	0.656	0.662	0.889	1.000	
x	0.513	0.572	0.452	0.446	0.612	0.595	0.616	0.594	1.000

N = 100.

Table 9.2

Standardized Maximum-Liklihood Parameter Estimates for the Model of Figure 9.1 and the Data of Table 9.1

Parameter	Standardized Estimate	Parameter	Standardized Estimate
γ_1	0.575	θ_{ε_2}	0.231
γ_2	0.473	θ_{ε_3}	0.422
γ_3	0.620		
β_1	0.347	θ_{ε_4}	0.278
β_2	0.389	θ_{ε_5}	0.179
β_3	0.435		
λ_s	1.000^a	θ_{ε_6}	0.271
λ_1	0.938	θ_{ε_7}	0.288
λ_2	0.973		
λ_3	0.907	θ_{ε_8}	0.372
λ_4	0.961	Ψ_{11}	0.669
λ_5	0.984	Ψ_{21}	0.140
λ_6	0.963	Ψ_{22}	0.777
λ_7	0.958	Ψ_{31}	0.088
λ_8	0.928	Ψ_{32}	0.074
θ_{ε_s}	0.000^a	Ψ_{33}	0.615
θ_{ε_1}	0.348	Ψ_{44}	0.171

$\chi^2 = 18.44$; d.f. = 16; $p \cong 0.30$.
[a] Constrained parameter.

summarized in Table 9.2, one may compare the gain in both revenue and value of food per unit change in stimulus to the costs of implementing the various levels of credibility. In addition, the causal model allows the researcher to ascertain which psychological states are most efficacious in influencing behavior and which are most susceptible to influence from the stimulus. This information can be used in product design and message and media planning decisions.

The above results indicate that the S–O–R model of Figure 9.1 fits the data of Table 9.1 very well. To illustrate the role of causal modeling as a diagnostic tool, consider the data of Table 9.3. The correlations in Table 9.3 are the same as those in Table 9.1 except for $r_{z_1y_1}$, $r_{z_1y_2}$, $r_{z_2y_1}$, and $r_{z_2y_z}$, which represent the correlations between the measures of affect and the measures of behavior. Notice that these changes represent inconsistent and relatively low correlations between measures of affect and subsequent responses—a finding perhaps not too unexpected in field research. The application of LISREL to the model of Figure 9.1 and the data of Table 9.3 produces $\chi^2 = 190.63$, d.f. $= 16$, and $p \simeq 0.00$, indicating a highly unsatisfactory fit.

One way to locate the source of the poor fit is to examine the three submodels shown in Figure 9.2. Table 9.4 summarizes parameter estimates and goodness-of-fit measures for these sub-models applied to both the data of Table 9.1 and the data of Table 9.3 and compares these findings to that found for the model of Figure 9.2. Notice first that the sub-models of Figures 9.2a and 9.2b fit both data sets very well. These findings are to be expected because neither sub-model contains any of the four changed correlations shown in Table 9.3. However, for the model of Figure 9.2c, the data fit very poorly, since $\chi^2 = 149.04$, d.f. $= 13$, and $p \simeq 0.00$. In sum, Figure 9.2b demonstrates that the psychological states have been measured accurately; Figure 9.2a indicates that source

Table 9.3
**Pearson Product-Moment Correlation Matrix of Observations— Simu-
lated Data Set #2**

	y_1	y_2	y_3	y_4	y_5	y_6	z_1	z_2	x
y_1	1.000								
y_2	0.912	1.000							
y_3	0.362	0.386	1.000						
y_4	0.381	0.370	0.871	1.000					
y_5	0.424	0.411	0.333	0.341	1.000				
y_6	0.418	0.431	0.329	0.344	0.947	1.000			
z_1	**0.110**	**0.212**	0.601	0.649	0.692	0.680	1.000		
z_2	**0.121**	**0.077**	0.583	0.593	0.656	0.662	0.889	1.000	
x	0.513	0.572	0.452	0.446	0.612	0.595	0.616	0.594	1.000

$N = 100$.

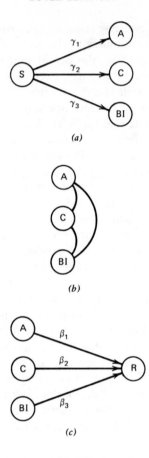

Figure 9.2. S–O–R submodels. (*a*) Stimulus and psychological processes. (*b*) Psychological processes. (*c*) Psychological processes and behavioral responses.

credibility systematically affects these states; and Figure 9.2*c* identifies the relationship between affect and behavior as the source of the inadequate fit. Next, notice that, while the parameter estimates using the data of Table 9.1 are relatively stable across models, this is not true for the data of Table 9.3. As shown in the final two columns of Table 9.4, for example, the low correlations between the measures of affect and the measures of behavior produce biased estimates in β_2 and β_3 as well as β_1. Similarly, as illustrated in the first two columns of Table 9.4, the estimates of γ_1, γ_2, and γ_3 are biased. Thus, the meaning

Table 9.4

Comparison of Selected Parameter Estimates and Goodness-of-Fit Measures for the Model of Figure 9.1 and the Sub-models of Figure 9.2

Parameters and Goodness-of-Fit Measures	Model							
	Figure 9.1		Figure 9.2a		Figure 9.2b		Figure 9.2c	
	Data Set #1	Data Set #2	Data Set #1	Data Set #2	Data Set #1	Data Set #2	Data Set #1	Data Set #2
γ_1	0.575	0.513	0.575	0.575	—	—	—	—
γ_2	0.473	0.503	0.481	0.481	—	—	—	—
γ_3	0.620	0.634	0.621	0.621	—	—	—	—
β_1	0.347	−0.424	—	—	—	—	0.350	−0.418
β_2	0.389	0.610	—	—	—	—	0.386	0.600
β_3	0.435	0.690	—	—	—	—	0.433	0.688
χ^2	18.44	190.63	10.75	10.75	7.04	7.04	13.51	149.04
d.f.	16	16	7	7	6	6	13	13
p	0.30	0.00	0.15	0.15	0.32	0.32	0.41	0.00

of the theoretical variables and hypothesized relations between them depend on the *entire* structure of theory and measurements in the research design. To look only at the observed relationships between some of the variables in the theory would yield inaccurate and misleading results. The problem is analogous to the omitted variables issue in regression analysis. The structural equation methodology presented herein provides the researcher with a procedure for modeling the complete system of hypotheses.

The results in Table 9.4 imply that the source of the poor fit with the S–O–R model lies in the hypothesized relationship between affect and behavior. Because of the evidence found for the model of Figure 9.1 and the first data set and the model of Figure 9.2b and the second data set, one may rule out measurement error in the behavioral responses and affect, respectively, as the source of the poor fit. Given this information, one must conclude that the model is misspecified and/or no evidence exists for relating affect to behavior in the study. Thus, the causal path β_1 must be removed from Figure 9.1 (given the data of Table 9.3).

As an example of measurement error in constructs, consider the data in Table 9.5 where the pattern of correlations suggests that the measures of affect (y_1 and y_2) may be poor ones. Table 9.6 summarizes the parameter estimates and goodness-of-fit measures for the models of Figures 9.2a and 9.2b applied to the data of Table 9.5 and the previous two data sets. Notice first that one must reject the model of Figure 9.2b for the data set of Table 9.5, since $\chi^2 = 45.31$, d.f. = 6, and $p \simeq 0.00$. This indicates a problem with the measurements and validity of the psychological states. When the stimulus is added as shown in Figure 9.2a, the data of Table 9.5 still fail to fit the model,

Table 9.5
Pearson Product-Moment Correlation Matrix of Observations—Simulated Data Set #3

	y_1	y_2	y_3	y_4	y_5	y_6	z_1	z_2	x
y_1	1.000								
y_2	**0.240**	1.000							
y_3	0.362	0.386	1.000						
y_4	**0.081**	0.370	0.871	1.000					
y_5	0.424	0.411	0.333	0.341	1.000				
y_6	0.418	0.431	0.329	0.344	0.947	1.000			
z_1	**0.110**	**0.212**	0.601	0.649	0.692	0.680	1.000		
z_2	**0.121**	**0.077**	0.583	0.593	0.656	0.662	0.889	1.000	
x	**0.152**	**0.349**	0.452	0.446	0.612	0.595	0.616	0.594	1.000

N = 100.

Table 9.6
Comparison of Selected Parameter Estimates and Goodness-of-Fit Measures for Figures 9.2a and 9.2b

Parameters and Goodness-of-Fit Measures	Model					
	Figure 9.2a			Figure 9.2b		
	Data Set #1	Data Set #2	Data Set #3	Data Set #1	Data Set #2	Data Set #3
γ_1	0.575	0.575	0.494	—	—	—
γ_2	0.481	0.481	0.452	—	—	—
γ_3	0.621	0.621	0.621	—	—	—
χ^2	10.75	10.75	51.37	7.04	7.04	45.31
d.f.	7	7	7	6	6	6
p	0.15	0.15	0.00	0.32	0.32	0.00

and parameter estimates for γ_1 and γ_2 are biased. Again, even though the correlations relating the stimulus to measures of cognition are valid, the errors in measurement for affect alter the estimate for the relationship between the stimulus and cognitions. Hence, this example shows that it is important to explicitly model measurement error in order to insure that the relationships to be tested in one's entire theory are not contaminated by errors in variables. The causal modeling methodology accomplishes this task in a straightforward way.

Summary

Causal models represent a unique way to estimate and test relationships in S–O–R theories. By formally modeling theoretical relationships among all variables, the methodology allows for the estimation and evaluation of the relative impact of the stimulus on psychological states and the relative influence of these states on behavioral responses. In this way, the stimulus (e.g., product, persuasive communication) can be better designed to have the optimal effect on behavior. Further, the procedures provide a means for separating errors in equations from errors in variables and thus permit a better diagnosis and theory building in research when compared to traditional methodologies such as the correlation, regression, and analysis of variance techniques. A drawback with causal modeling is that at least some of the variables in a theory must have multiple operationalizations.

Note

[1] For purposes of illustration, the three constructs are shown as parallel psychological responses. If one wanted to also represent BI as a function of A and C as suggested in the Fishbein model, then the model of Figure 9.1 could be modified by adding paths from A and C to BI. This was not done in the present discussion to keep the development simple. The inclusion of functional or causal relationships among psychological states can be easily accomplished with the proposed procedures, however.

TEN

CAUSAL MODELS IN SURVEY RESEARCH: THE CASE OF AN INDUSTRIAL SALES FORCE

This chapter illustrates the use of structural equation models in survey research. The particular example of an industrial sales force is chosen for investigation. In the first study, the effect of performance on job satisfaction is examined as the principal hypothesis. Included in the analysis are the effects of three antecedents: achievement motivation, task specific self-esteem, and verbal intelligence. In the second study, the influence of role ambiguity and achievement motivation on job outcomes is studied. Three broad job outcomes are modeled: task-specific self-esteem, performance, and job satisfaction.

Study #1: Performance and Satisfaction

Research into the relationship between performance and job satisfaction[1] has been largely inconclusive. Indeed, reviews of the literature suggest that the relationship has more often than not failed to appear, or that when it has, it has typically been quite low in magnitude (Herzberg, Mausner, Peterson, and Capwell, 1957; Locke, 1976; Vroom, 1964).

Locke (1976) maintains that the disappointing findings are due to an inadequate conceptualization of the relationship itself and a preoccupation with measurement. Specifically, two broad reasons are given for this state of affairs, depending on the causal ordering of the variables. For the performance → job satisfaction sequence, the lack of evidence is attributed to "(1) the failure to

251

identify individual differences in (task-related and nontask) values; and (2) the failure to measure differences in the rewards actually obtained for performance" (Locke, 1976, p. 498). Similarly, the lack of support for the job satisfaction → performance sequence is thought to be the results of "(1) the failure to measure attitudes toward the appropriate object, namely, production itself; (2) the failure to measure cognitive and value anticipations (with respect to future performance); and (3) the failure to take account of contextual factors such as the individual's total value system, his beliefs, and his interpretation of the total situation" (Locke, 1976, p. 498). Thus, the existence of a relationship between performance and job satisfaction is hypothesized to depend on the circumstances associated with individual differences and/or the situation itself.

A study by Wanous (1974a) provides some support for the idea that different types of values or rewards and individual differences in these values can account, in part, for the performance/job satisfaction relationship. Using a combination of cross-lagged and dynamic correlations in a longitudinal study, Wanous found that the causal ordering depends on whether one looks at extrinsic satisfaction (i.e., satisfaction resulting from the work itself—Herzberg's so-called "motivators" (Herzberg et al., 1957)) or intrinsic satisfaction (i.e., satisfaction resulting from the context of the work situation—"Hygienes"). Based upon a significant correlation between initial, intrinsic satisfaction and delayed performance ($r = 0.30$, $p < 0.05$), the author concluded that some support exists for the hypothesis that intrinsic satisfaction might effect performance. This support was regarded as minimal and inconclusive, however, because the dynamic correlation was not significant. On the other hand, based upon a significant correlation between initial performance and delayed, extrinsic satisfaction ($r = 0.37, p < 0.05$) and a significant dynamic correlation ($r = 0.30$, $p < 0.05$), the author concluded that performance affects extrinsic satisfaction.

A number of points deserve mention with respect to Wanous' study. First, assuming that extrinsic satisfaction results largely from attainment of nontask values, the finding that performance influences extrinsic satisfaction is consistent with Locke's (1976) analysis. Second, the failure to find a conclusive relationship between intrinsic satisfaction and performance might be the consequence of two factors. On the one hand, it might have been the case that either the people constituting the sample did not have a high need for task-related values and/or the job did not provide for these. Either possibility is to be expected for newly hired phone operators, the focal sample. Alternatively, it may be argued that the performance measures were not indicative of the intrinsic rewards actually obtained by the phone operators. Because performance was measured by a composite of supervisory ratings and company indexes (relatively extrinsic operationalizations), there is reason to question both the functional and cognitive connections between performance and the attainment of task-related values. Thus, failure for the intrinsic satisfaction → performance relationship to materialize may be the result of an absence of the necessary value anticipations on the job. Unfortunately, these cognitions were never measured, hence one cannot determine whether the failure to find the hypothesized empirical association was due to an inadequate theory or a poor methodology.

The importance of a cognitive connection between what one perceives in a job and what one values (as a necessary condition for the satisfaction/performance relation) can be seen in a recent study by Sheridan and Slocum (1975). Sheridan and Slocum used the cross-lagged correlational design to test for the direction of causality between work performance and job satisfaction for managers and machine operators. For the managers, some evidence was found for the performance → job satisfaction sequence. In particular, "job satisfaction developed from the managers' perception that previous performance had resulted in the presence of desirable facets on the job and provided the 'pull' for continued high performance" (Sheridan and Slocum, 1975). For the machine operators, in contrast, "need deficiency (measured as the difference between 'what should be' and 'what is' in regard to need satisfaction) provided the 'push' to improve performance and need dissatisfaction, not satisfaction, was directly related to later performance in a lead dissatisfaction → performance relationship" (Sheridan and Slocum, 1975).

Although a vast body of research exists on the performance/job satisfaction relationship in the general work setting, very little effort has been directed at the connection in the salesforce context. Except for the work of Churchill, Ford, and Walker (1976) investigating the impact of organizational climate on job satisfaction, very little is known about the causes and consequences of job satisfaction in sales people.

The research reported in the present study examines the impact of actual performance on job satisfaction for a sample of industrial salespeople. Of particular interest is the role of three individual difference variables as they affect the performance/satisfaction relationship. Specifically, self-esteem, motivation, and verbal intelligence are investigated in order to better model the nature of this relationship.

Theory

Job satisfaction is defined herein as "the pleasurable emotional state resulting from the appraisal of one's job as achieving or facilitating the achievement of one's job-values" (Locke, 1969, p. 316). Performance is thought to function as an antecedent because of its ability to provide things of desirable value. It does this either by supplying things valued in and of themselves or for their instrumental utility in obtaining other things of value. Typically, job satisfaction will be a function of the discrepancy between what one desires from one's job and what one perceives that the job offers. Because people tend to adapt to their success

and failures and form expectations therefrom, performance will often be correlated with the percept-value discrepancy (and hence with satisfaction),
although it need not as a matter of necessity. An important research question
to answer is, under what conditions will performance and job satisfaction be
related?

It is hypothesized in this study that both performance and job satisfaction
will be a function of individual differences and that a failure to take these into
account will bias the observed relation between performance and satisfaction.
In particular, three individual difference variables are posited as important
determinants: achievement motivation, self-esteem, and verbal intelligence.

Reflecting the notion that the intensity of one's values is as crucial as the
content, the degree of achievement motivation is used to indicate individual
differences in values toward specific outcomes on the job. The hypothesis is
that individuals will evaluate job outcomes differently and strive for different
quantitative performance goals and that these factors, in turn, will influence
performance and job satisfaction (Locke, 1969, 1970, 1976). The greater the
value placed on specific outcomes associated with the job, the higher the
performance of activities leading to these outcomes and the greater the satisfaction with subsequent attainment of these outcomes. Some support for this
hypothesis can be found in Wanous (1974b).

The foregoing hypothesis suggests an achievement motivation $\rightarrow$ performance $\rightarrow$ job satisfaction sequence. It is also conceivable that achievement
motivation can affect job satisfaction directly and not only through changes in
performance. The way that it might do this is through a self-attribution and
cognitive balance process. A person who believes that he is highly motivated
(versus one who is relatively low in self-awareness of his own motivation) may
come to interpret his level of felt satisfaction in a somewhat inflated sense
because such an evaluation may be both functional and cognitively consistent
with expectations that high motivation is "good" and leads to success. Although
one would expect this to occur only when one has performed well, the tendency
to strive for consistency between attributions of self-motivation and satisfaction
may be in addition to the hypothesized link between actual performance and
satisfaction. Both hypotheses are examined in this study.

A second important individual difference variable, self-esteem, is also posited
to affect performance and job satisfaction and the relationship between them.
To understand the rationale for this hypothesis, it is helpful to consider the
origin of this personal construct (Kelly, 1963). Korman (1968, 1970, 1974)
maintains that self-esteem arises from three sources. Chronic self-esteem is
viewed as "a relatively persistent personality trait that occurs relatively consistently across various situations" (Korman, 1970, p. 35). Task specific self-
esteem originates from past experience with a particular task or similar tasks
and is a reflection of one's felt degree of competence in performing that task.
Finally, socially influenced self-esteem is a function of another's expectations

for one's behavior. Korman (1970, p. 35) posits that all three dimensions of self-esteem function to determine an individual's level of "self-perceived competence and ability for the task at hand." Further, Korman hypothesizes that self-esteem directly influences the level of task performance. The manner in which this occurs is through a balance or consistency theory of cognition:

Individuals will be motivated to perform on a task or job in a manner which is consistent with the self-image with which they approach the task or job situation. That is, to the extent that their self-concept concerning the job or task situation requires effective performance in order to result in "consistent" cognitions, then, to that extent, they will be motivated to engage in effective performance [Korman, 1970, p. 32].

Greenhaus and Badin (1974) tested aspects of Korman's hypothesis on performance of anagram tasks in a laboratory setting. Of the three dimensions of self-esteem, only task specific self-esteem was found to be related significantly to actual task performance ($r = 0.31$, $p < 0.01$). No other studies in the work setting could be found examining the relationship between self-esteem and performance or job satisfaction.

In the present research, it is suggested that individuals will differ in their self-esteem as a function of aspects of the task at hand and that this self-esteem, in turn, will influence performance and job satisfaction. The greater the task specific self-esteem, the higher the performance of activities leading to valued outcomes and the greater the felt job satisfaction with subsequent achievement of these outcomes. The hypothesized sequence is task specific self-esteem ↠ performance ↠ job satisfaction.

The final individual difference variable, verbal intelligence, has received little, if any, attention in the literature, though some argument can be made for its inclusion as a determinant of performance and satisfaction in the industrial selling context (Pace, 1962). Verbal intelligence is defined herein as the cognitive ability to accurately and efficiently perceive, attend to, and process information related to conversations, written instructions, and other forms of communication associated with the job. It is not regarded as a measure of IQ or a psychological trait but rather reflects the cognitive capacities and competencies associated with an individual in his or her commerce with others and the environment. As Hunt et al. (1975, p. 176) note, "A person with 'high verbal ability' should be glib of tongue, quick to pick up nuances in the language, and generally alert to information conveyed by either written or oral speech. We also expect the 'higher verbal' to show superior performance in the basic perceptual and motor skills involved in speech." It is also thought that verbal intelligence is positively related to certain cognitive styles (e.g., information processing complexity, differentiation, etc.) and accommodative or coping styles (e.g., analytic vs. global functioning, leveling-sharpening, etc.).

A considerable body of research exists supporting the impact of verbal intelligence on various aspects of behavior (Hunt et al., 1975). In general, it has been found that high verbal individuals manipulate information in short-term memory (STM) more rapidly, reach STM faster, retain information in certain senses in STM more effectively, and access highly overlearned material in long-term memory more rapidly than do low verbals. Moreover, in their experiments, Hunt et al. (1975) found that high verbals showed superior recall, were more accurate in the perception of speech sound order, processed negation almost twice as fast, and were more accurate and more rapid on certain data manipulation tasks than were low verbals. Of particular interest was the finding that "superior abilities displayed by the high verbal is the ability to make a rapid conversion from a physical representation to a conceptual meaning" (Hunt et al., 1975, p. 223).

Because the cognitive skills associated with being high in verbal intelligence tend to be those necessary for interpreting and reacting to customer needs, planning and scheduling of work activities, and, in general, performing the managerial tasks connected with the selling job, it is hypothesized that verbal intelligence will be positively associated with both performance and job satisfaction. However, the hypothesis should be regarded as tentative and exploratory, given the lack of research in the work setting. The hypothesized sequence of relationships is verbal intelligence $\overset{+}{\rightarrow}$ performance $\overset{+}{\rightarrow}$ job satisfaction.

Research Setting and Sample

Data were obtained from a sample of industrial salespeople and information found in company accounting records. The focal sales force consisted of 135 men of whom 122 completed all items employed for a 90 percent response rate. These salespeople sell steel and plastic strapping and seals used in shipping and also small handtools used to apply strapping. For the most part, the customers include purchasing agents and material managers from a wide assortment of industries. The salespeople are each assigned to an exclusive geographical territory.

The particular selling job requires a considerable amount of skill and initiative. The salesperson must be versed in the technical and functional aspects of an extensive product line. Some product-form competition exists in the form of many substitute products (e.g., twine, wire, alternative packaging, etc.), and four or five competitors who manufacture similar products as the focal organization also exist in every market.

As a test of the hypotheses outlined above, the sample is ideal for a number of reasons. First, compared to many other organizational settings, the present context exhibits stronger contingencies between the efforts, abilities, and individual differences of the employees on the one hand and their job outcomes on the other. Second, the relative role of situational and environmental determinants of performance is less in the present setting than in many other occupations. The two above conditions are a result of the nature of the job and its position in the market and industry. That is, the products and customer needs are technical and well-defined; very little product differentiation exists within the industry; there is no price competition among firms for selling steel strapping, which constitutes the largest part of each person's sales; and advertising is minimal and does not appear to have a discernible effect on sales. Thus, there are a priori reasons for expecting that situational factors are not the major causes of performance but that the characteristics and behavior of the salespeople are significant determinants of job outcomes.

A third reason that the sample provides an ideal test of hypotheses lies in the structure of the task and employee-supervisor relationships. The performance of each salesperson is quantitative; highly visible; regularly monitored by management and the salesperson; and tied to salary, bonuses, promotions, and formal recognition in a company-wide publication. Further, as part of formal procedures on the job, each salesperson regularly appraises his or her own past and present performance against both personal and company standards. These factors tend to provide strong cognitive and functional connections between the behavior of salespeople and their outcomes experienced on the job.

Finally, the focal sample is ideal because a high level of self-esteem, motivation, and personal initiative is required for success. This is so, in part, because a high sales performance is required to achieve both intrinsic and extrinsic rewards, and this must occur under conditions of relatively high role tension and role ambiguity characteristic of the boundary spanning job. Moreover, because competition is keen and the work is demanding, one expects that individual differences will be operative as determinants of job outcomes.

Data Collection Instruments[2] and Procedures

Performance was measured as the dollar volume of sales each person attained for the year. The data were hand copied from company records, and steps were taken to adjust for or remove those salespeople who quit or were transferred. Also, care was taken to adjust for changes in territory size, shifts in accounts between territories, windfall accounts, and other confounds that occurred during the investigation period.

Job satisfaction was measured with an eight-item Likert scale. Job satisfaction measure #1 consists of four six-point items asking each salesperson for his feelings of satisfaction about promotion opportunities, the level of pay, the general work situation, and other dimensions of the job. Job satisfaction measure #2 contains four six-point items asking each salesperson for his feelings of satisfaction with the opportunity to demonstrate ability and initiative, job security, the degree of challenge on the job, and the amount of control over the work situation. Four of the items were those used by Pruden and Reese (1972), while four were explicitly designed for the specific sales situation in this study. The domain of the items encompass what Locke (1976) terms task-related and nontask values. The Cronbach Alpha reliability for the composite job satisfaction measures was 0.78 in the present study.

Task specific self-esteem was operationalized through six Likert items especially constructed for this study. Self-esteem measure #1 consists of two nine-point items and one five-point item asking each salesperson to rate himself in relation to the other salespeople in the company as to his quantity of sales achieved, potential for reaching the top 10 percent in sales, and quality of performance in regard to management of time, planning ability, and management of expenses. Self-esteem measure #2 is comprised of three nine-point items asking each salesperson to rate himself in relation to the other salespeople in the company as to his ability to reach quota, quality of performance in regard to customer relations, and quality of performance in regard to knowledge of own company and products, competitor's products, and customers' needs. The Cronbach Alpha reliability for the composite self-esteem measure was 0.77.

To measure achievement motivation, the eight-item Work Orientation Index was used (Duncan, 1969). This scale measures how committed one is to the general work situation. Four items indicate the degree to which the salesperson values work in an absolute sense, and four items measure the value of work relative to leisure and outside activities. The original yes-no format was changed to a five-point Likert scale for the present study. The Cronbach Alpha reliability for the composite measure was 0.60.

Verbal intelligence was measured with Borgatta's (1971) Word Association Form, a 30-item matched response scale. The scale measures verbal ability through the cognitive associations of words. Although the format of the scale does not permit the application of internal consistency measures of reliability such as the Cronbach Alpha formula, Borgatta reports correlations with the Verbal Power Test for three independent samples of 0.72, 0.70, and 0.61, respectively.

Table 10.1 presents the means, standard deviations, and intercorrelations for all variables used in Study #1.

Prior to the collection of performance measures and administration of the questionnaire and even before the final set of scales were selected, extensive interviewing and participant observation were conducted. Interviews were performed with the head of sales (a vice-president of the corporation), sales managers, salespeople, and a number of marketing research personnel close to the selling situation. The author also accompanied a number of salespeople as they made calls. Observation and discussion with the above people led to the design and selection of the instruments used in the study.

The questionnaire was sent to the salespeople by mail with a cover letter from the head of sales. The letter stated the overall purpose of the study in

Table 10.1
Pearson Product-Moment Correlations for Observed Variables

Variable	y_1	y_2	y_3	x_1	x_2	x_3	x_4	x_5	Mean	SD	No. of Items
Performance (y_1)	1.000								720.86	209.06	—
Job-satisfaction #1 (y_2)	0.418	1.000							15.54	3.43	4
Job-satisfaction #2 (y_3)	0.394	0.627	1.000						18.46	2.81	4
Achievement Motivation #1 (x_1)	0.129	0.202	0.266	1.000					14.90	1.95	4
Achievement Motivation #2 (x_2)	0.189	0.284	0.208	0.365	1.000				14.35	2.08	4
Self-esteem #1 (x_3)	0.544	0.281	0.324	0.201	0.161	1.000			19.57	2.16	3
Self-esteem #2 (x_4)	0.507	0.225	0.314	0.172	0.174	0.546	1.000		24.16	2.06	3
Verbal Intelligence (x_5)	−0.357	−0.156	−0.038	−0.199	−0.277	−0.294	−0.174	1.000	21.37	3.65	30

$N = 122$; $r_{0.05} = 0.175$.

rather vague terms, who was conducting the research, and directions for completing the questionnaire. The letter also stressed that the individual responses of salespeople would be kept strictly anonymous. To reduce the impact of evaluation apprehension and other forms of reactivity, a statement was included in the letter instructing the salespeople not to sign the questionnaire. Since no numbers or other identifying marks appeared on the questionnaire, the salespeople had no reason to believe that their individual responses would be known to anyone.

The Causal Model

To test the hypotheses, a causal modeling methodology was employed. Figure 10.1 illustrates one model that exhaustively depicts all of the proposed relationships. The causal model hypothesizes that achievement motivation (AM),

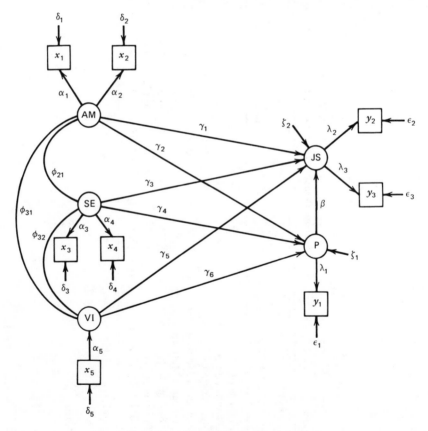

Figure 10.1. Causal model for testing hypotheses.

task specific self-esteem (SE), and verbal intelligence (VI) each affect job satisfaction (JS) and performance (P) and that performance also influences job satisfaction. Given the theory developed earlier, the hypothesized signs of key parameters can be seen to be:

$$\gamma_1 = + \qquad \gamma_4 = + \qquad \beta = +$$
$$\gamma_2 = + \qquad \gamma_5 = 0$$
$$\gamma_3 = 0 \qquad \gamma_6 = +$$

The structural equations for the theoretical relationships depicted in Figure 10.1 can be written as

$$\begin{pmatrix} 1 & 0 \\ -\beta & 1 \end{pmatrix} \begin{pmatrix} P \\ JS \end{pmatrix} = \begin{pmatrix} \gamma_2 & \gamma_4 & \gamma_6 \\ \gamma_1 & \gamma_3 & \gamma_5 \end{pmatrix} \begin{pmatrix} AM \\ SE \\ VI \end{pmatrix} + \begin{pmatrix} \zeta_1 \\ \zeta_2 \end{pmatrix}$$

The measurement equations are

$$\begin{pmatrix} x_1 \\ x_2 \\ x_3 \\ x_4 \\ x_5 \end{pmatrix} = \begin{pmatrix} \alpha_1 & 0 & 0 \\ \alpha_2 & 0 & 0 \\ 0 & \alpha_3 & 0 \\ 0 & \alpha_4 & 0 \\ 0 & 0 & 1 \end{pmatrix} \begin{pmatrix} AM \\ SE \\ VI \end{pmatrix} + \begin{pmatrix} \delta_1 \\ \delta_2 \\ \delta_3 \\ \delta_4 \\ 0 \end{pmatrix}$$

$$\begin{pmatrix} y_1 \\ y_2 \\ y_3 \end{pmatrix} = \begin{pmatrix} 1 & 0 \\ 0 & \lambda_2 \\ 0 & \lambda_3 \end{pmatrix} \begin{pmatrix} P \\ JS \end{pmatrix} + \begin{pmatrix} 0 \\ \varepsilon_2 \\ \varepsilon_3 \end{pmatrix}$$

Given the above specification, one can use the estimation and hypothesis testing procedures developed in Chapter 4 to examine the theory.

Results

Figure 10.2 summarizes the findings for application of LISREL to the data of Table 10.1 and the model of Figure 10.1. As shown by the goodness-of-fit test (i.e., $\chi^2 = 15.01$, d.f. = 14, $p \simeq 0.38$), the model fits the data very well. Notice first that the following hypothesized relationships were confirmed:

1. The impact of achievement motivation on job satisfaction (i.e., $\gamma_1 = +0.316$).
2. The effect of task specific self-esteem on performance (i.e., $\gamma_4 = +0.659$).
3. The absence of a direct effect from verbal intelligence to job satisfaction ($\gamma_5 = $ n.s.).

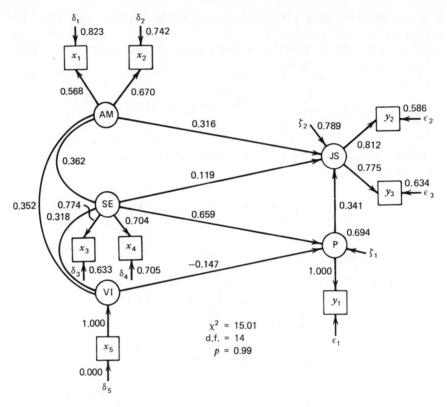

Figure 10.2. Findings for the model of Figure 10.1 and the data of Table 10.1.

4. The influence of performance on job satisfaction ($\beta = +0.341$), which is the key relationship under study.

Notice second that, contrary to expectations, (a) no relationship emerged between achievement motivation and performance (i.e., $\gamma_2 =$ n.s.), (b) a small, but significant, relationship[3] exists between task specific self-esteem and job satisfaction ($\gamma_3 = +0.119$), and (c) a negative relationship between verbal intelligence and performance resulted ($\gamma_6 = -0.147$), although this parameter is also small in magnitude.

Finally, a few comments on the relative impact of antecedents need to be menioned. First, the indirect effect of self-esteem on job satisfaction is about 1.9 times the direct effect (i.e., $\gamma_4 \times \beta = 0.225$ versus $\gamma_3 = 0.119$). Second, the impact of performance on job satisfaction is about 1.1 and 2.9 times the effects of achievement motivation and self-esteem, respectively, on this same variable. Third, self-esteem has approximately 4.5 times more influence on performance than does verbal intelligence.

Examination of Some Rival Hypotheses

Because the present research is a naturalistic field survey, it is not possible to infer causality with the certainty that experimental manipulation affords. However, the use of partial correlations with the variables in the study and certain control variables can be used to examine for spurious correlations and other confounds and thus, through a process of elimination of confounds, increase the internal validity of the findings. The logic and procedures for the nonexperimental control and basis for inference of causal relations can be found in Blalock (1964). It should be stressed, however, that future research will ultimately have to use naturalistic field experiments and/or longitudinal studies to verify the hypotheses derived in this research. Suggestions for this type of study are made in the Discussion and Conclusions where the limitations of the present research are discussed.

Consider first the relationship between performance and job satisfaction. As theory suggests, there is a positive relationship between the two variables as shown in Figure 10.2. It is important, however, to verify whether the relationship is a genuine connection between the two variables or whether it is a spurious one due to the influence of other factors. To see if the observed relationship is spurious due to generalized self-esteem, task specific self-esteem, role ambiguity, or job related tension, the following partial correlations were examined.[4] If the observed relationship is spurious, it should yield a zero partial correlation when the other variables are controlled for. First, the relationship between performance (1) and job satisfaction (2) was investigated controlling for generalized self-esteem (3) and task specific self-esteem (4). The data show $r_{12.3} = 0.45 (p < 0.001), r_{12.4} = 0.32 (p < 0.001)$, and $r_{12.34} = 0.33 (p < 0.001)$. Thus, it may be concluded that the relationship between performance and job satisfaction is not a spurious one due to generalized and task specific self-esteem. Second, the focal relationship was also examined controlling for job-related tension (3) and role ambiguity (4). The results show that $r_{12.3} = 0.25$ $(p < 0.003)$, $r_{12.4} = 0.42$ $(p < 0.001)$, and $r_{12.34} = 0.25$ $(p < 0.003)$. Hence, it may be concluded that the relationship between performance and job satisfaction is not a spurious one due to job related tension and role ambiguity.

Another key relationship to scrutinize is that between task specific self-esteem and job satisfaction. Recall that it was hypothesized that task specific self-esteem would influence job satisfaction only through its effect on performance. Yet, as shown in Figure 10.2, a weak, but statistically significant, direct relationship exists between task specific self-esteem and job satisfaction. When the partial correlation between these two variables is examined controlling for performance, the result is $r_{12.3} = 0.10$ (n.s.). Moreover, since the zero-order correlation between generalized self-esteem and job satisfaction is $r_{12} = 0.10$ (n.s.), and the partial correlation between these same two variables, controlling for performance, is $r_{12.3} = -0.06$ (n.s.), it may be concluded that the relationship between self-esteem and job satisfaction is spurious and under the influence of performance. Thus, the direct path from task specific self-esteem to job satisfaction in Figure 10.2 cannot be supported. This finding is consistent with the theory and hypothesis developed earlier.

Finally, another important relationship to analyze is that between task specific self-esteem and performance. As predicted by theory, the relationship shown in Figure 10.2 is positive. To examine the counterhypothesis that the relationship is spurious and under control of job satisfaction, job-related tension, and role ambiguity, the following partial correlations were examined. Looking first at the effect of job satisfaction (3), the partial correlation is $r_{12.3} = 0.55$ ($p < 0.001$). Second, the effects of job-related tension (4) and role ambiguity (5) yield: $r_{12.4} = 0.54$ ($p < 0.001$), $r_{12.5} = 0.57$ ($p < 0.001$), and $r_{12.45} = 0.54$ ($p < 0.001$). Thus, it may be concluded that the observed relationship between task specific self-esteem and performance is not a spurious one due to job satisfaction, job-related tension, or role ambiguity.[5]

Discussion and Conclusions

To explain job satisfaction, it is not sufficient to relate feelings of satisfaction to outcomes such as performance (or even to the percept-value discrepancy associated with a given individual and his or her performance). Rather, explanation requires that the meanings of a given performance outcome be ascertained and that characteristics of individuals be taken into account as explanatory concepts (e.g., Locke, 1970). Although job satisfaction was found to vary depending on the level of performance attained, individual differences also functioned as important antecedents influencing job satisfaction both directly and indirectly through performance outcomes.

The performance/satisfaction relation was shown to depend, in part, upon the degree to which individuals evaluate outcomes associated with the job. The greater the value placed on job outcomes (as indicated by one's achievement motivation), the higher the level of satisfaction with the attainment of subsequent rewards. Because people differ in their evaluation of task-related and nontask values, any observed relation between performance and satisfaction that fails to take these differences into account may yield biased and misleading estimates of parameters.

Task specific self-esteem is also an important individual difference variable affecting the relationship between performance and satisfaction. The findings show that self-esteem has a significant positive effect on performance. Further, the relationship between performance and satisfaction is attenuated approximately 35 percent when self-esteem is held constant, although it still has a significant impact (Bagozzi, 1979a). Apparently, even though salespeople perform and evaluate their satisfaction with the job in a manner consistent with their self-image (though processes of cognitive balance), their level of self-esteem affects the manner in which performance influences satisfaction. It may be, for example, that performance leads to satisfaction only for those relatively high in self-esteem (Korman, 1970; Greenhaus and Badin, 1974). Locke, (1976, p. 1325) hypothesizes that high self-esteem persons versus those low in self-esteem should "(1) be more likely to value challenging tasks; (2) find the pleasures resulting from achievement to be more intense and enduring; (3) be more likely to want promotions for reasons of justice and the more likely to want them for status reasons; (4) be less likely to value prestige, approval, and verbal recognition as sources of self-assurance ...; (5) be less emotionally affected by criticism; (6) experience fewer conflicts and feelings of anxiety on the job; (7) be less defensive and employ fewer defense mechanisms." Very little research, however, has been conducted into the relationship of self-esteem and job satisfaction.

The results for the hypothesis relating verbal intelligence to performance and satisfaction are inconclusive. Although no relationship was found between verbal intelligence and job satisfaction, a negative relationship was found between verbal intelligence and performance, opposite to that predicted by theory. However, the magnitude of the relationship was relatively small ($\gamma_6 = -0.146$). It may have been the case that, for those very high in verbal intelligence, the job was boring or in some other way nonchallenging, thus leading these individuals to devote less time and energy to the job at hand. In the participant observation phase of the research, the author noted that two subjects who were identified as among the very best salespeople in the company spent an unusual amount of time in extra-company pursuits. One individual, for example, used normal working time to complete course work toward an M.B.A. and to evaluate sites for an investment venture. The second person expressed feelings that the job was "somewhat" boring and has subsequently accepted a position with another firm. It is also possible that the verbal intelligence scale contains excessive amounts of measurement error. Future research should focus on task specific verbal skills rather than relying on a generalized measure.

Although this is one of the first studies to investigate the performance/job satisfaction relationship in the personal selling context, a number of caveats should be mentioned. First, as noted earlier, any conclusions as to cause and effect must be regarded as tentative. Although the findings constitute necessary conditions for inferring causality and eliminate some rival hypotheses, they are not sufficient. Replications, longitudinal studies, and quasi-experiments will be required to validate the present findings. Second, other causal sequences should also be investigated. It is possible that over time or for some individuals that current performance can influence future achievement motivation and task specific self-esteem. Similarly, current job satisfaction may influence future performance, although Locke (1976, pp. 1332–33) presents compelling arguments for not expecting this reverse sequence and the studies cited earlier by Wanous (1974a) and Sheridan and Slocum (1975) also cast doubt on this alternative. In any case, longitudinal studies will be required to ascertain the cause and effect sequence.

The performance/job satisfaction relationship has a number of implications for managers. The research suggests that—in addition to the organizational climate variables found by Churchill et al. (1976) to effect job satisfaction—performance and individual differences in achievement motivation, self-esteem, and verbal intelligence may also play a role. Salespeople tend to be more satisfied as they perform better, but the relationship is particularly sensitive to the level of motivation and positive self-image of the person. Although management may have no direct control over the performance achieved by salespeople, they can influence the level of motivation and self-esteem through effective incentive and sensitive supervisor-employee programs and thereby indirectly affect both performance and job satisfaction. If the goal is to enhance job satisfaction, the most direct way is to improve the level of motivation, while a change in self-esteem appears to work only indirectly through its impact on performance.

The central role of performance as a determinant of job satisfaction might indicate the importance of matching the salesperson to his or her territory. The discrepancy between the particular level of achievement motivation and task specific self-esteem in a salesperson and the level of difficulty of a territory would appear to be a key factor moderating satisfaction in the sales force. A small discrepancy between the abilities and self-awareness of salespeople on the one hand and the anticipated and actual experiences with customers in a territory, on the other, will tend to produce both higher performance and higher levels of satisfaction. It is thus important that salespeople be trained to recognize and evaluate performance goals in a realistic way in consonance with their own characteristics and those of their territory. For such a program to work, it is also necessary that salespeople be encouraged to cultivate a self-awareness of their own levels of motivation and self-esteem and that management provide the information necessary for the salesperson to realistically evaluate their own performance and goals. The latter might entail better distribution of workloads, better sales potential monitoring programs, and contrasts across territory and time to facilitate social comparison processes. Finally, a selection program should attempt to choose those higher in motivation, self-esteem, and the ability to assess their own strengths and weaknesses as well as the social situation in which they must operate.

Study # 2: Job Outcomes and Some Antecedents[6]

Modern managers realize increasingly that salespeople experience tangible and intangible outcomes as a consequence of their job and that the productivity of the sales force is directly related to the well-being of the individuals comprising it. In general, it is possible to identify at least three broad classes of job outcomes:

self-esteem, performance, and job satisfaction (Bagozzi, 1979b). The research reported in this section of the chapter examines these outcomes as they are influenced by role ambiguity and achievement motivation.

The Dependent Variables

Self-esteem is a particular kind of personal construct that refers to the manner in which individuals attribute and infer dispositions in themselves (Coopersmith, 1967; Kelly, 1963; Wells and Marwell, 1976). These dispositions typically deal with attributions of personal competence and self-regard. They entail both cognitive and affective psychological processes in that the person must peform an act of conceptual self-identification and form an emotional evaluation thereof. The emotional content may be positive or negative and will vary in intensity, depending on the situation and the person's attributions in relation to it. This study will limit inquiry to one type of self-esteem, namely, task specific self-esteem (see discussion earlier in the chapter and Korman, 1970). The antecedents to task specific self-esteem will be discussed shortly.

Performance outcomes refer to the actual events resulting from a salesperson's efforts. They thus connote objective happenings under the influence of the salesperson. Common indicators of performance include the total volume of sales achieved (in dollars or units), new business generated, percent of quota reached, improvement over the past year, sales relative to others with like experience, expenses incurred, and so on.

What constitutes performance is somewhat a normative and arbitrary issue. Management sets company and individual salesperson goals based, in part, on the history of sales, the costs of production and administration, profit expectations, estimates of territory potential, the ability and experience of the salesperson, competition, and other factors. The salesperson, in turn, perceives and interprets company goals in terms of his or her needs and the unique selling situation. For the salespeople under investigation in this study, the most relevant performance measure is the dollar volume in sales achieved by each salesperson. This measure of performance is the one most visible to management and the salespeople. Salaries, bonuses, rewards from contests, and recognition in a montly publication within the firm depend directly on these values. Hence, given the controls discussed earlier for the methodology of Study #1, there is reason to expect that this job outcome measure of performance will be connected to the efforts and activities of the salesperson.

The final class of job outcomes is job satisfaction (e.g., Locke, 1976). Whereas self-esteem refers to attributions toward the self as an object of focus, job satisfaction denotes specific cognitive and affective reactions toward the job as the object of scrutiny.

Employees react to a variety of dimensions of their jobs (e.g., Hackman and Lawler, 1971; Hellriegel and Slocum, 1974; and James and Jones, 1974). In the personal selling context, research indicates that the closeness of supervision, the perceived influence a salesperson has in determining the standards by which his or her performance is supervised and evaluated, the frequency of communication between salesperson and manager, the perceived opportunities for promotion, feelings of job security, and happiness with pay are all related to the experienced satisfaction with one's job (e.g., Bagozzi, 1978; Churchill et al., 1976).

In general, job satisfaction is expressed in two forms. The first is a strictly cognitive one in that specific aspects of the job are seen by the salesperson as a means for satisfying needs. The second is largely affective in content. That is, the salesperson is thought to form either positive or negative feelings toward dimensions of the job, with these feelings varying in magnitude depending on the person and situation.

Factors Affecting Job Outcomes

The self-esteem, performance, and job satisfaction experienced by salespeople are hypothesized to be affected by two broad determinants. First, they are posited to be a function of the nature of the social interactions the salesperson has with customers, sales managers, and significant others in his or her role-set. The social interaction variable studied in this investigation is role ambiguity. Second, job outcomes are hypothesized to be under the influence of the person. In particular, the motivation of the salesperson is regarded as a strong determinant of job outcomes in that it reflects the psychological and physical effort and commitment devoted to the job. Each of the above influences of job outcomes is discussed below.

Role Ambiguity

Although all members of organizations engage in many relationships with individuals and groups within the organization, salespeople seem to face a set of interactions that differ in both kind and degree. In addition to the normal encounters with supervisors, co-workers, and other agents of the home organization, salespeople must regularly deal with a large and diverse set of customers, gatekeepers, and acquaintances who are outside the organization, yet who are central to the selling job. Moreover, exchanges with customers are more intense and risky than the typical intrafirm encounter experienced by employees. This is the case for a variety of reasons. First, the salesperson-customer relationship usually transpires away from the salesperson's organization. The physical separation lessens the direct scrutiny of supervisors, and it tends to weaken normative constraints felt by the salesperson. It also mitigates any social control resulting from informal group affiliation in the home organization. Second, even though the actions of the salesperson are relatively hidden from the supervisor, the performance outcomes of exchanges, of course, are not. This condition coupled with the fact that the salesperson's livelihood depends directly on these outcomes make the salesperson vulnerable and dependent on the customer. Third, because of the nature of the functions performed by the salesperson and the presence of scarcity of resources and competition in the economic environment, he or she will be confronted with a set of conflicting expectations and demands. Customers bring pressures to bear to lower prices, expedite shipments, straighten-our paper work, and generally meet their needs; while management urges that sales expand, expenses decline, profits rise, and the company's needs be met. Overall, the selling situation is one where uncertainty and interpersonal conflict are great, and demand for coping exceed the norm for most occupations.

Role theory represents one paradigm for modeling the behavior of salespeople in organizations. Following Biddle and Thomas (1966, p. 29) a "role" is regarded herein as "the set of prescriptions defining what the behavior of a position member (in the organization) should be." As such, roles attempt to capture the social connections between the salesperson on the one hand and the home organization and customer organizations on the other hand. These connections are manifest in the expectations that the salesperson has of the organizations and their agents and the expectations the organizations and their agents have of the salesperson.

The concept of role ambiguity is useful for representing the impact of the organization on the salesperson. Role ambiguity is defined here as the degree of uncertainty the salesperson experiences with respect to customers, sales managers, and family expectations; limits to authority; and other dimension of the job role.

It is hypothesized that role ambiguity will be negatively related to self-esteem, performance, and job satisfaction. The mechanism is thought to arise through information processing activities. That is, as uncertainty in expectations increases, the ability of the salesperson to make accurate judgments decreases, while risk increases. The result is that performance is adversely affected and evaluations of the self and job decline. Some support for this hypothesis may be found in both the organization behavior (Hamner and Tosi, 1974; House and Rizzo, 1972; Rizzo, House, and Lirtzman, 1970; and Schuler, 1977) and marketing (Bagozzi, 1978; Churchill, 1975; Pruden and Reese, 1972) literatures.

Motivation

The final determinant of job outcomes is motivation. In general, two broad conceptualizations of motivation have been identified by industrial and organizational psychologists: (1) mechanical or process theories and (2) substantive or content theories (e.g., Campbell and Pritchard, 1976). Mechanical theories of motivation are perhaps best exemplified by instrumentality (Mitchell and Biglan, 1971) or expectancy-value (Campbell and Pritchard, 1976) approaches. Briefly, these models define motivation to be a multiplicative function of one's cognitive evaluation of various job outcomes times one's expectancies that (a) working hard will lead to the accomplishment of task objectives and (b) these, in turn, will lead to particular job outcomes (e.g., Staw, 1977). Substantive theories typically posit the existence of certain needs within individuals and then relate these to behaviors on the job such as performance. Herzberg's (1959) two-factor theory, McClelland's (1961) theory of need achievement, and Alderfer's (1972) hierarchy of needs model are three leading examples.

Motivation in the present study is conceptualized as a general cognitive evaluation of the importance of work in the everyday life of the salesperson (see discussion under Methodology). By attempting to capture the generalized valences for work in both an absolute and relative sense (with respect to leisure activities) and at the same time relating these to the needs of the salespeople, this investigation combines elements of both the mechanical and substantive approaches to motivation.

The hypothesis is that motivation will be positively related to self-esteem, performance, and job satisfaction. That is, the greater that salespeople value the positive dimensions of their jobs and the less they feel anxious about or devalue the negative dimensions of their jobs, the higher will be their self-esteem, performance, and job satisfaction. The rationale for the connections is based on both a balance theory of cognition and social learning theory (e.g., Mischel, 1973). Salespeople are hypothesized (1) to form cognitions of various dimensions of the job, (2) to evaluate these dimensions in terms of their own needs and expectations, and (3) to expend an amount of effort consistent with these cognitions and evaluations. Hence, the more motivated the salesperson is and/or the greater the probability that the job meets the needs and expectations of the salesperson, the higher will be the self-esteem, performance, and job satisfaction.

Methodology

The overall theory relating the antecedents to job outcomes was tested on the same sample as described in Study #1. Thus, the discussion there on Research Setting and Sample and on Data Collection Instruments and Procedures will not be repeated here. However, the role ambiguity scales were not discussed earlier and will be introduced now.

Role ambiguity was measured with a 12-item scale developed by Ford et al. (1975). Role ambiguity measure #1 is comprised of six five-point Likert items asking how certain/uncertain the salesperson is with respect to limits to authority, call norms, sales manager expectations for allocating time, sales manager evaluations of importance of activities, customer expectations for frequency of calls, and family expectations for time spent on the job. Role

Table 10.2
Pearson Product-Moment Correlations for Observed Variables

Variable	y_1	y_2	y_3	y_4	y_5	x_1	x_2	x_3	x_4	Mean	SD	No. of Items
Self-esteem measure #1 (y_1)	1.000									19.57	2.16	3
Self-esteem measure #2 (y_2)	0.546	1.000								24.16	2.06	3
Dollar volume of sales (y_3)	0.544	0.507	1.000							720.86	209.06	—
Job-satisfaction measure #1 (y_4)	0.281	0.225	0.418	1.000						15.53	3.43	4
Job-satisfaction measure #2 (y_5)	0.324	0.314	0.394	0.627	1.000					18.46	2.81	4
Role ambiguity measure #1 (x_1)	−0.335	−0.251	−0.188	−0.154	−0.175	1.000				12.77	2.71	6
Role ambiguity measure #2 (x_2)	−0.384	−0.426	−0.261	−0.163	−0.256	0.686	1.000			12.60	2.46	6
Motivation measure #1 (x_3)	0.201	0.172	0.129	0.202	0.266	−0.065	−0.041	1.000		14.90	1.95	4
Motivation measure #2 (x_4)	0.161	0.174	0.189	0.284	0.208	−0.078	−0.060	0.365	1.000	14.35	2.08	4

N = 122.

ambiguity measure #2 consists of six five-point Likert items asking how certain/uncertain the salesperson is with respect to the freedom to negotiate on price, power to modify delivery schedules, satisfaction of manager with own performance, general customer expectations, satisfaction of customers with own performance, and general family expectations. The Cronbach Alpha reliability for the composite role ambiguity measures was 0.80. Table 10.2 summarizes the intercorrelations among all of the variables used in the study.

The Causal Model

The causal model is shown in Figure 10.3 where the structural equations relating theoretical variables can be written as

$$\begin{pmatrix} 1 & 0 & 0 \\ 0 & 1 & 0 \\ 0 & 0 & 1 \end{pmatrix}\begin{pmatrix} SE \\ P \\ JS \end{pmatrix} = \begin{pmatrix} \gamma_1 & \gamma_4 \\ \gamma_2 & \gamma_5 \\ \gamma_3 & \gamma_6 \end{pmatrix}\begin{pmatrix} RA \\ M \end{pmatrix} + \begin{pmatrix} \zeta_1 \\ \zeta_2 \\ \zeta_3 \end{pmatrix}$$

The measurement equations are

$$\begin{pmatrix} x_1 \\ x_2 \\ x_3 \\ x_4 \end{pmatrix} = \begin{pmatrix} \alpha_1 & 0 \\ \alpha_2 & 0 \\ 0 & \alpha_3 \\ 0 & \alpha_4 \end{pmatrix}\begin{pmatrix} RA \\ M \end{pmatrix} + \begin{pmatrix} \delta_1 \\ \delta_2 \\ \delta_3 \\ \delta_4 \end{pmatrix}$$

Given the above specification, one can use the estimation and hypothesis testing procedures developed in Chapter 4 to examine the theory.

Results

Application of LISREL to the data of Table 10.2 and the model of Figure 10.3 yields the findings displayed in Table 10.3. Notice first that the overall model receives very strong support since $\chi^2 = 11.53$, d.f. = 16, and $p \simeq 0.78$. Also, each of the hypothesized relationships between the independent variables and job outcomes is as predicted by theory (see estimates for $\gamma_1-\gamma_6$ in Table 10.3). Of particular interest are the relative magnitudes of effects. For example, role ambiguity has about 1.5 times as much impact on self-esteem as does motivation, though both have strong effects. Similarly, role ambiguity and motivation affect performance with approximately equal magnitudes, and they are relatively less forcefull than the other causal paths in the model. Finally, motivation affects job satisfaction with about 1.4 times the force of role ambiguity, though both variables have strong effects.

Discussion and Conclusions

Based on the absolute and relative magnitudes of effects, a number of conclusions and implications can be made. Looking first at the absolute levels of

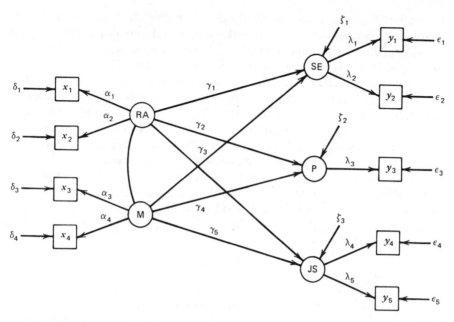

Figure 10.3. The effect of role ambiguity and motivation on job outcomes.

Table 10.3
Parameter Estimates and Goodness-of-Fit Test for the Model of Figure 10.3

Parameter	Standardized Parameter Estimate	Parameter	Standardized Parameter Estimate
γ_1	-0.528	λ_3	1.000^a
γ_2	-0.245	λ_4	0.785
γ_3	-0.229	λ_5	0.799
γ_4	0.347	θ_{δ_1}	0.710
γ_5	0.236	θ_{δ_2}	0.227
γ_6	0.478	θ_{δ_3}	0.783
α_1	0.704	θ_{δ_4}	0.809
α_2	0.974	θ_{ε_1}	0.665
α_3	0.622	θ_{ε_2}	0.683
α_4	0.587	θ_{ε_3}	0.000^a
λ_1	0.747	θ_{ε_4}	0.619
λ_2	0.731	θ_{ε_5}	0.602

$\chi^2 = 11.53$; d.f. $= 16$; $p \cong 0.78$.
^{a} Constrained parameter.

parameter estimates, it can be seen that role ambiguity and motivation are strong determinants of self-esteem, performance, and job satisfaction.

Evidence thus exists supporting the following propositions. Uncertainty in role expectations is inversely related to job outcomes. The greater the felt ambiguity, the lower the self-esteem, performance, and job satisfaction. The mechanism is hypothesized to be an information processing one wherein uncertainty functions as a cognitive disrupter of the ability to plan and cope with the job. Similarly, motivation is positively related to job outcomes. The greater the motivation, the higher the self-esteem, performance, and job satisfaction. The rationale here is a combination of balance theory and need theory in that salesmen are hypothesized to be more motivated and to experience higher levels of job outcomes the greater that they value the extrinsic and intrinsic rewards of the job (and/or devalue the costs) and the closer that they perceive the means-end relationships between working hard and attaining desired job outcomes.

Looking next at the relative impact of role ambiguity and motivation on job outcomes, a number of points deserve mention. First, role ambiguity appears to have the greatest adverse effect on self-esteem. That is, it has a strong negative impact on the self-regard and attributions of self-competence on the job. Motivation, in contrast, has the strongest effect on job satisfaction. The more motivated the salesperson, the more highly they evaluate and feel positive about specific dimensions of the job. Although somewhat lower in actual magnitude than other effects, the influences of role ambiguity and motivation appear to have about equal but opposite effects on performance.

In sum, role ambiguity and motivation have differential effects, depending on the particular job outcome examined. Although it might appear on the surface that the optimum action management could take is to reduce role ambiguity and increase motivation, such a policy may not always be possible. For example, the firm may have limited resources and be required to choose between one of two programs: one designed to reduce ambiguity, the second designed to enhance motivation. Under these conditions, then, the choice would depend (assuming both alternatives were expected to work) on the goals of the organization. If the goal was to increase the self-esteem of salesmen, then the reduction of role ambiguity should be the target; similarly, a program stimulating effort (say through incentives) would be the appropriate choice to increase job satisfaction. On the other hand, given the necessity of trade-offs, the firm would be indifferent between the two programs, if the increase in performance were the objective.

The choice between changing role ambiguity or motivation also depends on the nature of the selling job and the people involved. In many selling situations, for instance, motivation may be already relatively high because of a good selection and training program, an effective incentive system, a recent contest, or other factors. Under these conditions, the gain in motivation would be marginal, and management might focus on changing the uncertainty present in company policies, supervisor-salesman relationships, and other aspects of the organization. Further research should focus on the feedback and interaction, if any, among job outcomes. For example, performance may be enhanced indirectly through a program designed to increase job satisfaction. Although the present study was only concerned with the antecedents of job outcomes and made no assumptions as to the processes among them, the next logical step would be to study salesmen over time in order to identify sequences and interrelationships among self-esteem, performance, and job satisfaction.

Notes

[1] For a presentation of the full study, see Bagozzi (1979a).

[2] For a full description of the data collection instruments and their rationale, see Bagozzi (1976b).

[3] This relationship is a spurious one, however, as discovered through an analysis of partial correlations (see discussion under Examination of Some Rival Hypotheses).

[4] A description of the control variables and the rationale why they might be related to performance and job satisfaction are discussed more fully in Bagozzi (1976b).

[5] As further support for this finding, it should be noted that similar results arose for the same partial correlations substituting generalized self-esteem for task specific self-esteem (Bagozzi, 1976b).

[6] For a presentation of the full study, see Bagozzi (1979b).

REFERENCES

Aaker, D. A., and Bagozzi, R. P. 1979. Unobservable Variables in Structural Equation Models with an Application in Industrial Selling. *J. Market. Res.* 16.

Aaker, D. A., Bagozzi, R. P., Carman, J., and MacLaughlin, D. 1980. On Using Response Latencies to Measure Preferences. *J. Market. Res.* 17.

Addis, L. 1975. *The Logic of Society: A Philosophical Study.* Minneapolis: University of Minnesota Press.

Aiken, M., and Hage, J. 1968. Organizational Inter-dependence and Intra-organizational Structure. *Am. Soc. Rev.* 35 (Dec.): 912–930.

Ajzen, I., and Fishbein, M. 1973. Attitudinal and Normative Variables as Predictors of Specific Behaviors. *J. Person. Soc. Psych.* 27: 41–57.

———. 1977. Attitude-behavior Relations: A Theoretical Analysis and Review of Empirical Research. *Psych. Bull.* 84: 888–918.

Alderfer, C. P. 1972. *Existence, Relatedness, and Growth: Human Needs in Organizational Setting.* New York: Free Press.

Alderson, W. 1965. *Dynamic Marketing Behavior: A Functionalist Theory of Marketing.* Homewood, Illinois: Richard D. Irwin.

Allport, G. W. 1935. Attitudes. In *Handbook of Social Psychology,* edited by C. Murchinson, pp. 798–884. Worcester, Mass.: Clark Univ. Press.

Althauser, R. P., and Heberlein, T. A. 1970. A Causal Assessment of Validity and the Multitrait-Multimethod Matrix. In *Sociological Methodology 1970,* edited by E. Borgatta, pp. 151–169. San Francisco: Jossey–Bass.

Althauser, R. P., Heberlein, T. A., and Scott, R. A. 1971. A Causal Assessment of Validity: The Augmented Multitrait-Multimethod Matrix. In *Casual Models in the Social Sciences,* edited by H. M. Blalock, Jr., pp. 374–399. Chicago: Aldine.

Alwin, D. F., and Hauser, R. M. 1975. The Decomposition of Effects in Path Analysis. *Am. Soc. Rev.* 40 (Feb): 37–47.

Alwin, D. F., and Tessler, R. C. 1974. Causal Models, Unobserved Variables, and Experimental Data. *Am. J. Soc.* 80, No. 1 (July): 58–86.

Anderson, T. W. 1958. *An Introduction to Multivariate Statistical Analysis.* New York: Wiley.

Angelmar, R., and Pinson, C. R. A. 1974. Definitions of Marketing: The Fallacy of Misplaced Concreteness and Its Consequences. *Der Markt.* No. 50: 39–46.

Angelmar, Reinhard. 1976. Structure and Determinants of Bargaining Behavior in a Distribution Channel Simulation: A Content Analytic Approach. Ph.D. dissertation, Northwestern University, Evanston, Illinois.

Anscombe, G. E. M., and Geach, P. T. 1973. *Three Philosophers.* Oxford: Blackwell.

Aristotle. 1930. *The Works of Aristotle.* In *Physica,* translated by R. P. Hardie and R. K. Gaze, vol. 2. London: Oxford.

Aronson, E., and Carlsmith, J. M. 1968. Experimentation in Social Psychology. In *Handbook of Social Psychology* 2, edited by G. Lindzey and E. Aronson. Reading, Mass.: Addison–Wesley.

Ayer, A. J. 1973. *The Central Questions of Philosophy.* New York: William Morrow.

Ayers, M. R. 1968. *The Refutation of Determinism.* London: Methuen.

Bagozzi, R. P. 1974a. Marketing as an Organized Behavioral System of Exchange. *J. Market.* 38 (Oct.): 77–81.

———. 1974b. What is a Marketing Relationship? *Der Markt* (Vienna), 51: 64–69.

———. 1975a. Social Exchange in Marketing. *J. Acad. Market. Sci.* 3 (Fall): 312–325.

———. 1975b. Marketing as Exchange. *J. Market.* 39 (Oct): 32–39.

———. 1976a. Science, Politics, and the Social Construction of Marketing. In *Marketing: 1776-1976 and Beyond,* edited by K. L. Bernhardt. Chicago: American Marketing Association.

———. 1976b. Toward a General Theory for the Explanation of the Performance of Salespeople. Ph.D. dissertation, Northwestern University.

———. 1976c. Marketing at the Societal Level: Theoretical Issues and Problems. In *Proceedings of the Macromarketing Seminar 1976,* edited by C. Slater. Boulder, Colo.: University of Colorado.

———. 1977a. Comment: Populism and Lynching in Louisiana. *Am. Soc. Rev.* 42 (April).

———. 1977b. Structural Equation Models in Experimental Research. *J. Market. Res.* 14 (May): 209–226.

———. 1977c. Construct Validity in Consumer Research. Working paper. Schools of Business Administration, University of California, Berkeley.

———. 1977d. Convergent and Discriminant Validity by Analysis of Covariance Structures: The Case of the Affective, Behavioral, and Cognitive Components of Attitude. In *Advances in Consumer Research,* vol. 4, edited by W. D. Perreault, Jr. Association for Consumer Research.

———. 1978a. The Construct Validity of the Affective, Behavioral, and Cognitive Components of Attitude by Analysis of Covariance Structures. *Multivariate Behavioral Research* 13 (Jan.): 9–31.

———. 1978b. Marketing as Exchange: A Theory of Transactions in the Market Place. *Am. Behavioral Scientist* (March–April): 535–556.

———. 1978c. Exchange and Decision Processes in the Buying Center. In *Organization Buying Behavior,* edited by T. V. Bonoma and G. Zaltman. Chicago: American Marketing Association.

————. 1978d. Reliability Assessment by Analysis of Covariance Structures. In *Research Frontiers in Marketing: Dialogues and Directions*, edited by S. C. Jain. Chicago: American Marketing Association, 71–75.

————. 1978e. Salesforce Performance and Satisfaction as a Function of Individual Difference, Interpersonal, and Situational Factors. J. Market. Res. 15 (Nov): 517–531.

————. 1979a. Performance and Satisfaction in an Industrial Salesforce: A Causal Modeling Approach. Unpublished Working Paper. Massachusetts Institute of Technology.

————. 1979b. The Nature and Causes of Self-Esteem, Performance, and Satisfaction in the Salesforce. Unpublished Working Paper. Massachusetts Institute of Technology.

Bagozzi, R. P., and Burnkrant, R. E. 1978. Attitude Measurement and Behavior Change: A Reconsideration of Attitude Organization and Its Relationship to Behavior. In *Advances in Consumer Research*, vol. 6, edited by W. L. Wilkie. Ann Arbor, Michigan: Association for Consumer Research.

————. 1979. Attitude Organization and the Attitude-Behavior Relationship, *J. of Personality and Social Psychology*, forthcoming.

Bagozzi, R. P., Tybout, A. M., Craig, C. S., and Sternthal, B. 1979. The Construct Validity of the Tripartite Classification of Attitudes. *J. Market. Res.* 16 (Feb.): 88–95.

Bagozzi, R. P., and Van Loo, M. F. 1978. Toward a General Theory of Fertility: A Causal Modeling Approach, *Demography* (Aug): 301–319.

Bales, R. F. 1970. *Personality and Interpersonal Behavior*. New York: Holt, Rinehart and Winston.

Bandura, A. 1971. *Social Learning Theory*. New York: General Learning Press.

Barnes, J. A. 1972. *Social Networks*. Modular Publication in Anthropology No. 26. Reading , Mass.: Addison–Wesley.

Bartlett, M. S. 1951. The Effect of Standardization on an Approximation in Factor Analysis. *Biometrika* 38: 337–344.

Bass, F. M. 1974. The Theory of Stochastic Preference and Brand Switching. *J. Market. Res.* 11 (Feb.): 1–20.

Beauchamp, T. L., ed. 1974. *Philosophical Problems of Causation*. Encino, Cal.: Dickenson.

Becker, G. S. 1965. A Theory of the Allocation of Time. *The Economic Journal*, 75 (Sept.): 493–517.

Belk, R. W. 1975. Situational Variables and Consumer Behavior. *J. Consumer Res.* 2 (Dec.): 157–164.

Bem, D. J. 1970. *Beliefs, Attitudes, and Human Affairs*. Belmont, Cal.: Brooks/Cole.

————. 1972. Self-Perception Theory. In *Advances in Experimental Social Psychology*, edited by L. Berkowitz, vol. 6. New York: Academic.

Berger, P. L., and Luckmann, T. 1966. *The Social Construction of Reality*. Garden City, New York: Anchor.

Bettman, J. R. 1975. Issues in Designing Consumer Information Environments. *J. Consumer Research* 2 (Dec.): 169–177.

Bhaskar, R. 1975. *A Realist Theory of Science*. Leeds, Great Britain: Leeds.

Biddle, B. J., and Thomas, E. J. 1966. *Role Theory: Concepts and Research*. New York: Wiley.

Bishop, Y. M. M., Fienberg, S. E., and Holland, P. W. 1975. *Discrete Multivariate Analysis: Theory and Practice*. Cambridge, Mass.: *M. I. T.* Press.

Blalock, H. M., Jr., 1964. *Causal Inferences in Non-experimental Research.* Chapel Hill: University of North Carolina Press.

———. 1967a. Path Coefficients versus Regression Coefficients. *Am. J. Soc.* 72: 675–676.

———. 1967b. Causal Inferences, Closed Populations, and Measures of Association. *Am. Political Science Review* 61:130–136.

———. 1971. Causal Models Involving Unmeasured Variables in Stimulus-Response Situations. In *Causal Models in the Social Sciences,* edited by H. M. Blalock, Jr. Chicago: Aldine–Atherton.

———. (ed). 1971. *Causal Models in the Social Sciences.* Chicago: Aldine.

———. (ed.) 1974. *Measurement in the Social Sciences: Theories and Strategies.* Chicago: Aldine.

Blalock, H. M., Jr., Aganbegian, A., Borodkin, F. M., Boudon, R., and Capecchi, V. (eds.). 1975. *Quantitative Sociology: International Perspectives on Mathematical and Statistical Modeling.* New York: Academic.

Blau, P. M. 1964. *Exchange and Power in Social Life.* New York: Wiley.

———. 1974. Parameters of Social Structure. *Am. Soc. Rev.* 39 (October): 615–635.

Blumer, H. 1969. *Symbolic Interactionism: Perspective and Method.* Englewood Cliffs, N.J.: Prentice–Hall.

Bolles, R. C. 1974. Cognition and Motivation: Some Historical Trends. In *Cognitive Views of Human Motivation,* edited by B. Weiner, pp. 1–20. New York: Academic.

———. 1975. *Theory of Motivation,* 2nd ed. New York: Harper & Row.

Bonoma, T. V. 1975. *Conflict: Escalation and Deescalation.* Beverly Hills, Cal.: Sage.

Bonoma, T. V. and Bagozzi, R. P. 1977. Dyadic Marketing: The Second Plateau. Unpublished working paper. Graduate School of Business, University of Pittsburgh.

Bonoma, T. V., Bagozzi, R. P., and Zaltman, G. 1978. The Dyadic Paradigm in Marketing Thought. In *Organization Buying Behavior,* edited by T. V. Bonoma and G. Zaltman. Chicago: American Marketing Association.

Borgatta, E. F. 1971. Intelligent Word Associations. *Multivariate Behavioral Research* 6: 301–311.

Bowers, K. S. 1973. Situationism in Psychology: An Analysis and a Critique. *Psych. Rev.* 80 (Sept.): 307–336.

Box, G. E. P. 1949. A General Distribution Theory for a Class of Likelihood Criteria. *Biometrika* 36: 317–346.

Brand, M., and Walton, D. (eds.). 1976. *Action Theory: Proceedings of the Winnipeg Conference on Human Action.* Boston: D. Reidel.

Bridgman, P. W. 1927. *The Logic of Modern Physics.* New York: Macmillan.

Brody, B. A. 1970. *Readings in the Philosophy of Science.* Englewood Cliffs, N.J.: Prentice–Hall.

Bunge, M. 1959. *Causality.* Cambridge, Mass.: Harvard Univ. Press.

———. 1973. *The Methodological Unity of Science.* Boston: D. Reidel.

Burgess, R. L., and Bushell, D., Jr. (eds.). 1969. *Behavioral Sociology: The Experimental Analysis of Social Process.* New York: Columbia Univ. Press.

Burnkrant, R. D. 1976. A Motivational Model of Information Processing. *J. Consumer Research* 3: 21–30.

Burt, R. S. 1973. Confirmatory Factor-Analytic Structures and the Theory Construction Process. *Sociological Methods and Research* 2, No. 2 (Nov.): 131–190.

———. 1976. "Interpretational Confounding of Unobserved Variables in Structural Equation Models." *Sociological Methods and Research* 5: 3–52.

Campbell, D. T. 1960. Recommendations for APA Test Standards Regarding Construct, Trait, or Discriminant Validity. *Am. Psych.* 15: 546–553.

———. 1963a. Social Attitudes and Other Acquired Behavioral Dispositions. In *Psychology: A Study of Science* 6, edited by S. Koch. New York: McGraw–Hill.

———. 1963b. From Description to Experimentation: Interpreting Trends as Quasi-experiments. In *Problems in Measuring Change*, edited by C. W. Harris. Madison: University of Wisconsin Press.

———. 1969. Definitional Versus Multiple Operationism. *et al.* 2, no. 1 (summer): 14–17.

Campbell, D. T., and Fiske, D. W. 1959. Convergent and Discriminant Validation by the Multitrait-Multimethod Matrix. *Psych. Bull.* 56: 81–105.

Campbell, D. T., and Stanley, J. C. 1963. *Experimental and Quasi-experimental Designs for Research*. Chicago: Rand McNally.

Campbell, J. P., and Pritchard, R. D. 1976. Motivation Theory in Industrial and Organizational Psychology. In *Handbook of Industrial and Organizational Psychology*, edited by M. D. Dunnette. Chicago: Rand McNally, 63–130.

Campbell, K. 1970. *Body and Mind*. Garden City, N.Y.: Doubleday.

Caplow, T. A. 1968. *Two Against One: Coalitions in Traids*. Englewood Cliffs, N.J.: Prentice–Hall.

Carnap, R. 1936, 1937. Testability and Meaning. *Phil. Sci.* 3: 419–471; 4: 1–40.

———. 1950. *Logical Foundations of Probability*. Chicago: University of Chicago Press.

———. 1956. The Methodological Character of Theoretical Concepts. In *Minnesota Studies in the Philosophy of Science* 1, edited by H. Feigl and M. Scriven. Minneapolis: University of Minnesota. 38–76.

———. 1966. *An Introduction to the Philosophy of Science*. New York: Basic Books.

Cassady, R., Jr. 1974. *Exchange by Private Treaty*. Austin: Bureau of Business Research, University of Texas.

Caws, P. 1965. *The Philosophy of Science: A Systematic Account*. Princeton, N.J.: Van Nostrand.

Chadwick–Jones, J. K. 1976. *Social Exchange Theory: Its Structure and Influence in Social Psychology*. London: Academic.

Chestnut, R. W., and Jacoby, J. 1977. Consumer Information Processing: Emerging Theory and Findings. In *Foundations of Consumer and Industrial Buying Behavior*, edited by A. G. Woodside, P. D. Bennett, and J. N. Sheth.

Child, J. 1972. Organization Structure, Environment, and Performance: The Role of Strategic Choice. *Sociology* 6: 1–18.

Chisholm, R. 1955. Law Statements and Counterfactual Inference. *Analysis* 15: 97–105.

Churchill, G. A., Jr., Ford, N. M., and Walker, O. C., Jr. 1976. Organizational Climate and Job Satisfaction in the Salesforce. *J. Market. Res.* 13 (Nov.): 323–332.

Cohen, J. B., and Ahtola, O. T. 1971. An Expectancy Value Analysis of the Relationship between Consumer Attitudes and Behavior. In *Proceedings of the Second Annual Conference*. Association for Consumer Research.

Coleman, J. S. 1973. *The Mathematics of Collective Action*. Chicago: Aldine.

Cook, T. D., and Campbell, D. T. 1976. The Design and Conduct of Quasi-Experiments and True Experiments in Field Settings. In *Handbook of Industrial and Organizational Research*, edited by M. D. Dunnette, chap. 7. Chicago: Rand McNally.

Coombs, C. H. 1964. *A Theory of Data*. New York: Wiley.

Coombs, C. H., Dawes, R. M., and Tversky, A. 1970. *Mathematical Psychology: An Elementary Introduction*. Englewood Cliffs, N.J.: Prentice–Hall.

Coopersmith, S. 1967. *The Antecedents of Self-Esteem*. San Francisco: Freeman.

Costner, H. L. 1969. Theory, Deduction, and Rules of Correspondence. *Am. J. Soc.* 75 (Sept.): 245–263.

———. 1971. Utilizing Causal Models to Discover Flaws in Experiments. *Sociometry* 34 (Sept.): 398–410.

Costner, H. L., and Schoenberg, R. 1973. Diagnosing Indicator Ills in Multiple Indicator Models. In *Structural Equation Models in the Social Sciences*, edited by A. S. Goldberger and O. D. Duncan, 167–199. New York: Seminar Press.

Cox, D. R. 1970. *The Analysis of Binary Data*. London: Methuen.

Cronbach, L. J. 1951. Coefficient Alpha and the Internal Structure of Tests. *Psychometrika* 16: 297–334.

Danto, A. C. 1973. *Analytic Philosophy of Action*. Cambridge: Cambridge Univ. Press.

Davidson, D. 1967. Causal Relations. *J. Phil.* 64, no. 21 (Nov. 9): 691–703.

Davis, H. L. 1976. Decision Making Within the Household. *J. Consumer Research* 2 (March): 241–260.

Davis, H. L., and Rigaux, B. P. 1974. Perception of Marital Roles in Decision Processes. *J. Consumer Research* 1 (June): 51–62.

Davis, J. H., Laughlin, P. R., and Komorita, S. S. 1976. The Social Psychology of Small Groups: Cooperative and Mixed-Motive Interaction. In *Annual Review of Psychology* 27, edited by M. R. Rosenzweig and L. W. Porter. Palo Alto, Calif.: Annual Reviews.

Dawes, R. M. 1972. *Fundamentals of Attitude Measurement*. New York: Wiley.

Dawes, R. M., and Corrigan, B. 1974. Linear Models in Decision Making. *Psych. Bull.* 81 (Feb.): 95–106.

Day, G. S. 1970. *Buyer Attitudes and Brand Choice Behavior*. New York: The Free Press.

Descartes, R. 1931–1934. *The Philosophical Works of Descartes*, translated by E. S. Haldane and G. R. T. Ross, 2 vols. Cambridge: Cambridge Univ. Press.

———. 1966. *The Meditations and Selections from the Principles of Rene Descartes*, translated by J. Veitch. La Salle, Ill.: Open Court.

Doby, J. T. 1969. Logic and Levels of Scientific Explanation. In *Sociological Methodology 1969*, edited by E. F. Borgatta, 137–154. San Francisco: Jossey–Bass.

Donagan, A. 1966. The Popper–Hempel Model Reconsidered. In *Philosophical Analysis and History*, edited by W. H. Dray. New York: Harper and Row.

Doob, L. W. 1947. The Behavior of Attitudes. *Psych. Rev.* 54: 135–156.

Ducasse, C. J. 1951. *Nature, Mind and Death*. La Salle, Ill.: Open Court.

———. 1966. Critique of Hume's Conception of Causality. *J. Phil.* 63, no. 6: 141–148.

———. 1968. *Truth, Knowledge, and Causation*. London: Routledge, Kegan Paul.

———. 1969. *Causation and the Types of Necessity*. New York: Dover.

Dulany, D. E. 1968. Awareness, Rules, and Propositional Control : A Confrontation with S–R Behavior Theory. In *Verbal Behavior and General Behavior Theory*, edited by T. R. Dixon and D. L. Horton, 340–387. Englewood Cliffs, N.J.: Prentice–Hall.

Duncan, O. D. 1966. Path Analysis: Sociological Examples. *Am. J. Soc.* 72: 1–16.

———. 1969a. Contingencies in Constructing Causal Models. In *Sociological Methodology 1969*, edited by E. F. Borgatta, pp. 74–177. San Francisco: Jossey–Bass.

————. 1969b. Some Linear Models for Two-Wave, Two-Variable Panel Analysis. *Psych. Bull.* 72: 177–182.

————. 1970. Partials, Partitions, and Paths. In *Sociological Methodology, 1970*, edited by E. F. Borgatta and G. W. Bohrnstedt, 38–47. San Francisco: Jossey–Bass.

————. 1972. Unmeasured Variables in Linear Models for Panel Analysis. In *Sociological Methodology 1972*, edited by H. L. Costner, 36–82. San Francisco: Jossey–Bass.

————. 1975a. *Introduction to Structural Equation Models*. New York: Academic.

————. 1975b. Some Linear Models for Two-Wave, Two-Variable Panel Analysis, with One-Way Causation and Measurement Error. In *Quantitative Sociology*, edited by H. M. Blalock, A. Aganbegian, F. M. Borodkin, R. Boudon, and V. Capecchi, 285–306. New York: Academic.

Duncan, R. B. 1972. Characteristics of Organizational Environments and Perceived Environmental Uncertainty. *Admin. Sci. Quart.* 17 (Sept.): 313–327.

Ekeh, P. 1974. *Social Exchange Theory: The Two Traditions*. Cambridge: Harvard Univ. Press.

Emerson, R. M. 1976. Social Exchange Theory. In *Annual Review of Sociology*, edited by A. Inkeles, J. Coleman, and N. Smelser, 335–362. Palo Alto, Calif.: Annual Reviews.

Engel, J. F., Kollat, D. T., and Blackwell, R. D. 1973. *Consumer Behavior*, 2nd ed. New York: Holt, Rinehart and Winston.

Evans, F. B. 1963. Selling as a Dyadic Relation—A New Approach. *Am. Behavioral Scientist* 6 (May): 76–79.

Feigl, H. 1970. The "Orthodox" View of Theories: Remarks in Defense as well as Critique. In *Minnesota Studies in the Philosophy of Science* 4, edited by M. Radnor and S. Winokur, 3–16. Minneapolis: University of Minnesota Press.

Feyerbend, P. K. 1970. Against Method: Outline of an Anarchistic Theory of Knowledge. In *Minnesota Studies in the Philosophy of Science* 4, edited by M. Radnor and S. Winokur. Minneapolis: University of Minnesota Press.

Fleiss, J. L. 1969. Estimating the Magnitude of Experimental Effects. *Psych. Bull.* 72: 273–276.

Fletcher, R., and Powell, M. J. D. 1963. A Rapidly Convergent Descent Method for Minimization. *Computer J.* 6: 163–168.

Fishbein, M. 1963. An Investigation of the Relationship Between Beliefs About an Object and the Attitude Toward that Object. *Human Relations* 16 (Aug.): 233–240.

————. 1966. The Relationship Between Beliefs, Attitudes and Behavior. In *Cognitive Consistency: Motivational Antecedents and Behavioral Consequents*, edited by S. Feldman, 199–223. New York: Academic.

————. 1967a. A Consideration of Beliefs, and Their Role in Attitude Measurement. In *Readings in Attitude Theory and Measurement*, edited by M. Fishbein. New York: Wiley.

————. 1967b. Attitudes and the Prediction of Behavior. In *Readings in Attitude Theory and Measurement*, edited by M. Fishbein, 477–492. New York: Wiley.

Fishbein, M., and Ajzen, I. 1974. Attitude Towards Objects as Predictors of Single and Multiple Behavioral Criteria. *Psych. Rev.* 81: 59–74.

Fisher, F. M. 1966. *The Identification Problem in Econometrics*. New York: McGraw–Hill.

Foa, V. G. and Foa, E. B. 1971. *Societal Structures of the Mind*. Springfield, Illinois: Thomas.

Ford, N. M., Walker, O. C., Jr., and Churchill, G. A. Jr. 1974. Expectation-Specific Measures of the Inter-Sender Conflict and Role Ambiguity Experienced by Industrial Salesmen. *J. Business Research* 3: 95–112.

Galbraith, J. 1973. *Designing Complex Organizations*. Reading, Mass.: Addison–Wesley.

Galileo. 1974. *Two New Sciences*. Translated by S. Drake. Madison: University of Wisconsin Press.

Geraci, V. J. 1974. Simultaneous Equation Models with Measurement Error. Ph.D. Dissertation. Department of Economics, University of Wisconsin.

Goffman, E. 1959. *The Presentation of Self in Everyday Life*. Garden City, N.Y.: Doubleday.

———. 1974. *Frame Analysis: An Essay on the Organization of Experience*. Cambridge: Harvard Univ. Press.

Goldberg, D. 1975. Socioeconomic Theory and Differential Fertility: The Case of the LDCs. *Social Forces* 54: 84–106.

Goldberger, A. S. 1970. On Boudon's Method of Linear Causal Analysis. *Am. Soc. Rev.* 35: 97–101.

———. 1971. Econometrics and Psychometrics: A Survey of Communalities. *Psychometrika* 36, no. 2 (June): 83–107.

———. 1972. Maximum-Likelihood Estimation of Regressions Containing Unobservable Independent Variables. *International Economic Review* 13, no. 1 (Feb.): 1–15.

———. 1973a. Structural Equation Models: An Overview. In *Structural Equation Models in the Social Sciences*, edited by A. S. Goldberger and O. D. Duncan, 1–18. New York: Seminar Press.

———. 1973b. Efficient Estimation in Overidentified Models: An Interpretive Analysis. In *Structural Equation Models in the Social Sciences*, edited by A. S. Goldberger and O. D. Duncan, 131–152. New York: Seminar Press.

———. 1974. Unobservable Variables in Econometrics. In *Frontiers in Econometrics*, edited by P. Zarembka, 193–213. New York: Academic.

Goldberger, A. S., and Duncan, O. D. (eds.). 1973. *Structural Equation Models in the Social Sciences*. New York: Seminar Press.

Goldman, A. I. 1970. *A Theory of Human Action*. Englewood Cliffs, N.J.: Prentice–Hall.

Goodman, L. A. 1970. The Multivariate Analysis of Qualitative Data: Interactions Among Multiple Classifications. *J. Am. Stat. Assoc.* 65, no. 329 (March): 226–256.

Green, P. E., and Tull, D. S. 1975. *Research for Marketing Decisions*, 3rd ed. Englewood Cliffs, N.J.: Prentice–Hall.

Greenhaus, J. H., and Badin, I. J. 1974. Self-esteem, Performance, and Satisfaction: Some Tests of a Theory. *J. Appl. Psych.* 59: 722–726.

Griliches, A. 1974. Errors in Variables and Other Unobservables. *Econometrica* 42 (Nov.): 971–998.

Gruvaeus, G. T., and Jöreskog, K. G. 1970. A Computer Program for Minimizing a Function of Several Variables. Research Bulletin #70–14. Princeton, N.J.: Educational Testing Service.

Hackman, J. R., and Lawler, E. E. 1971. Employee Reactions to Job Characteristics. *J. Appl. Psych.* 55: 259–286.

Hamner, W. C., and Tosi, H. W. 1974. Relationship of Role Conflict and Role Ambiguity to Job Involvement Measures. *J. Appl. Psych.* 59: 497–499.

Hannan, M. T., Rubinson, R., and Warren, J. T. 1974. The Causal Approach to Measurement Error in Panel Analysis: Some Further Contingencies. In *Measurement in the Social Sciences: Theories and Strategies*, edited by H. M. Blalock, 293–323. Chicago: Aldine.

Hansen, F. 1969. Consumer Choice Behavior: An Experimental Approach. *J. Market. Res.* 6: 436–443.

Harary, F. 1969. *Graph Theory*. Reading, Mass.: Addison–Wesley.

Hare, A. P. 1976. *Handbook of Small Group Research*, 2nd ed. New York: Free Press.

Harmon, H. H. 1967. *Modern Factor Analysis*, 2nd ed. Chicago: University of Chicago Press.

Harré, R. 1972. *The Principles of Scientific Thinking*, 2nd impression. London: Macmillan.

Harré, R., and Madden, E. H. 1975. *Causal Powers: A Theory of Natural Necessity*. Totowa, N.J.: Rowman and Littlefield.

Harré, R., and Secord, P. F. 1973. *The Explanation of Social Behavior*. Totowa, N.J.: Littlefield, Adams.

———. 1975. In Defence of Ethogenic Methods in Social Psychology. *Phil. Soc. Sci.* 5 (Sept.): 299–303.

Hauser, R. M., and Goldberger, A. S. 1971. The Treatment of Unobservable Variables in Path Analysis. In *Sociological Methodology 1971*, edited by H. L. Costner, 81–117. San Francisco: Jossey–Bass.

Heath, A. 1976. *Rational Choice and Social Exchange*. Cambridge: Cambridge Univ. Press.

Heise, D. R. 1969a. Problems in Path Analysis and Causal Inference. In *Sociological Methodology 1969*, edited by E. F. Borgatta, 38–73. San Francisco: Jossey–Bass.

———. 1969b. Separating Reliability and Stability in Test-Retest Correlation. *Am. Soc. Rev.* 34 (Feb.): 93–101.

———. 1975. *Causal Analysis*. New York: Wiley.

Hellriegel, D., and Slocum, J. W., Jr. 1974. Organizational Climate: Measures, Research and Contingencies. *Academy of Management Journal* 17: 225–280.

Hempel, C. G. 1952. Fundamentals of Concept Formation in Empirical Science. In *International Encyclopedia of Unified Science* 11. Chicago: University of Chicago Press.

———. 1965. *Aspects of Scientific Explanation*. New York: Free Press.

———. 1970. On the "Standard Conception" of Scientific Theories. In *Minnesota Studies in the Philosophy of Science* 4, edited by M. Radnor and S. Winokur. Minneapolis: University of Minnesota Press.

———. 1973. The Meaning of Theoretical Terms: A Critique of the Standard Empiricist Construal. In *Logic, Methodology and Philosophy of Science IV*, edited by P. Suppes et al. Amsterdam: North Holland.

Henderson, J. M., and Quandt, R. E. 1971. *Microeconomic Theory*, 2nd ed. New York: McGraw–Hill.

Herzberg, F., Mausner, B., Peterson, R. O., and Capwell, D. F. 1957. *Job Attitudes: Review of Research and Opinion*. Pittsburgh: Psychological Service of Pittsburgh.

Herzberg, F., Mausner, B., and Synderman, B. 1959. *The Motivation to Work*, 2nd ed. New York: Wiley.

Hesse, M. 1970. "Is There an Independent Observation Language?" In *The Nature and Function of Scientific Theories*, edited by D. G. Colodny. Pittsburgh: University of Pittsburgh Press.

Hilderbrand, D. K., Laing, J. D., and Rosenthal, H. 1975. A Prediction–Logic Approach to Causal Models of Qualitative Variates. In *Sociological Methodology 1976*, edited by D. R. Heise, 146–175. San Francisco: Jossey–Bass.

———. 1976. *Prediction Analysis of Cross-Classifications*. New York: Wiley.

Hirsch, P. M. 1975. Organizational Analysis and Industrial Sociology: An Instance of Cultural Lag. *Am. Sociologist* 10 (Feb.): 3–12.

Homans, G. C. 1964. Commentary. *Sociological Inquiry* 34 (spring).

———. 1974. *Social Behavior: Its Elementary Forms*. Rev. ed. New York: Harcourt.

Hood, W. C., and Koopmans, T. C. (eds.). 1953. *Studies in Econometric Method*. New Haven, Conn.: Yale Univ. Press.

Hoult, T. F. 1972. *Dictionary of Modern Sociology*. Totowa, N.J.: Littlefield, Adams.

House, R. J., and Rizzo, J. R. 1972. Role Conflict and Ambiguity as Critical Variables in a Model of Organization Behavior. *Organization Behavior and Human Performance* 7: 467–505.

Howard, J. A., and Sheth, J. N. 1969. *The Theory of Buyer Behavior*. New York: Wiley.

Hsiao, C. 1975. Identification for a Linear Dynamic Simultaneous Error-Shock Model. Working paper. Berkeley: Department of Economics, University of California.

———. 1976. Identification and Estimation of Simultaneous Equation Models with Measurement Error. *Int. Econ. Rev.*

Hughes, G. D., and Guerrero, J. L. 1971. Testing Cognitive Models Through Computer-controlled Experiments. *J. Market. Res.* 8: 291–297.

Hull, C. L. 1943. *Principles of Behavior*. New York: Appleton–Century–Crofts.

Hume, D. 1739. *A Treatise of Human Nature*. Everyman's Library Edition. Introduction by A. D. Lindsay, 2 vols. New York: Dutton, 1911.

———. 1777. *An Enquiry Concerning Human Understanding*. La Salle, Ill.: Open Court Edition, 1963.

Hunt, E., Lunneborg, C., and Lewis, J. 1975. What Does It Mean to Be High Verbal? *Cognitive Psychology* 7: 194–227.

Hunt, S. D. 1976. *Marketing Theory: Conceptual Foundation of Research in Marketing*. Columbus, Ohio: Grid.

———. 1976b. The Nature and Scope of Marketing. *J. Market.* 40 (July); 17–28.

Jacobson, A. L., and Lalu, N. M. 1974. An Empirical and Algebraic Analysis of Alternative Techniques for Measuring Unobserved Variables. In *Measurement in the Social Sciences*, edited by H. M. Blalock, Jr., 215–242. Chicago: Aldine.

Jacoby, J., Speller, D. E., and Berning, C. K. 1974. Brand Choice Behavior as a Function of Information Load: Replication and Extension. *J. Consumer Research* 1 (June): 33–42.

James, L. R., and Jones, A. P. 1974. Organizational Climate: A Review of Theory and Research. *Psych. Bull.* 81: 1096–1112.

James, L. R., Singh, B. K. 1978. An Introduction to the Logic, Assumptions, and Basic Analytic Procedures of Two-Stage Least Squares. *Psych. Bull.* 85: 1104–1122.

Johnston, J. J. 1972. *Econometric Methods*, 2nd ed. New York: McGraw–Hill.

Jöreskog, K. G. 1966. Testing a Simple Structure Hypothesis in Factor Analysis. *Psychometrika* 31: 165–178.

———. 1967. Some Contributions to Maximum-Likelihood Factor Analysis. *Psychometrika* 32: 443–482.

————. 1969. A General Approach to Confirmatory Maximum Likelihood Factor Analysis. *Psychometrika* 34: 183–202.

————. 1970. A General Method for Analysis of Covariance Structures. *Biometrika* 57, no. 2: 239–251.

————. 1971. Statistical Analysis of Sets of Congeneric Tests. *Psychometrika* 36: 109–133.

————. 1973. A General Method for Estimating a Linear Structural Equation System. In *Structural Equation Models in the Social Sciences*, edited by A. S. Goldberger and O. D. Duncan, 85–112. New York: Seminar Press.

————. 1974. Analyzing Psychological Data by Structural Analysis of Covariance Matrices. In *Measurement, Psychophysics, and Neural Information Processing*, edited by D. H. Krantz et al., 1–56. San Francisco: Freeman.

Jöreskog, K. G., and Goldberger, A. S. 1975. Estimation of a Model with Multiple Indicators and Multiple Causes of a Single Latent Variable. *J. Am. Stat. Assoc.* 70 (Sept.): 631–639.

Jöreskog, K. G., and Sörbom. D. 1977. Statistical Models and Methods for Analysis of Longitudinal Data. In *Latent Variables in Socioeconomic Models*, edited by D. J. Aigner and A. S. Goldberger. Amsterdam: North-Holland.

Jöreskog, K. G., and Van Thillo, M. 1972. LISREL: A General Computer Program for Estimating a Linear Structural Equation System Involving Multiple Indicators of Unmeasured Variables. Educational Testing Service. Princeton, N.J.: Research Bulletin #72–56.

Kahane, H. 1973. *Logic and Philosophy*, 2nd ed. Belmont, Calif.: Wadsworth.

Kahn, R. L., Wolfe, D. M., Quinn, R. P., Snoek, J. D., and Rosenthal, R. A. 1963. *Organizational Stress: Studies in Role Conflict and Ambiguity*, New York: Norton.

Kant, I. 1961. *Critique of Pure Reason*, 2nd ed. Garden City, N. Y.: Doubleday.

Kaplan, A. 1964. *The Conduct of Inquiry*. Scranton, Penn.: Chandler.

Kaplan, M. F., and Schwartz, S. (eds.). 1975. *Human Judgement and Decision Processes*. New York: Wiley.

Keat, R., and Urry, J. 1975. *Social Theory as Science*. London: Routledge and Kegan Paul.

Kelly, G. A. 1955. *The Psychology of Personal Constructs*, 2 vols. New York: Norton.

————. 1963. *A Theory of Personality*. New York: Norton.

Kenny, D. A. 1973. Cross-Lagged and Synchronous Common Factors in Panel Data. In *Structural Equation Models in the Social Science*, edited by A. S. Goldberger and O. D. Duncan, 153–165. New York: Seminar Press.

————. 1975. Cross-lagged Panel Correlations: A Test for Spuriousness. *Psych. Bull.* 82, no. 6: 887–903.

Keppel, G. 1973. *Design and Analysis: A Researcher's Handbook*. Englewood Cliffs, N.J.: Prentice-Hall.

Kerlinger, F. N., and Pedhazur, E. J. 1973. *Multiple Regression in Behavioral Research*. New York: Holt, Rinehart and Winston.

Kim, J., and Mueller, C. W. 1976. Standardized and Unstandardized Coefficients in Causal Analysis. *Sociological Methods and Research* 4 (May): 423–438.

Kmenta, J. 1971. *Elements of Econometrics*. New York: Macmillan.

Kneale, W. 1950. Natural Laws and Contrary-to-Fact Conditionals. *Analysis* 10, no. 6 (June): 121–125.

————. 1961. Universality and Necessity. *British Journal for the Philosophy of Science* 12 (Aug.): 89–102.

Koestler, A., and Smythies, F. R. (eds.). 1969. *Beyond Reductionism: New Perspectives in the Life Sciences*. Boston: Beacon Press.

Korman, A. K. 1968. Task Success, Task Popularity, and Self-esteem as Influences on Task Liking. *J. Appl. Psych.* 52: 484–490.

———. 1970. Toward an Hypothesis of Work Behavior. *J. Appl. Psych.* 54: 31–41.

———. 1974. *The Psychology of Motivation*. Englewood Cliffs, N.J.: Prentice–Hall.

Kothandapandi, V. 1971. Validation of Feeling, Belief and Intention to Act as Three Components of Attitude and Their Contribution to Prediction of Contraceptive Behavior. *J. Personality and Social Psychology* 19: 321–333.

Kotler, P. 1971. *Marketing Decision Making: A Model Building Approach*. New York: Holt, Rinehart and Winston.

———. 1972. A Generic Concept of Marketing. *J. Market.* 36 (April): 46–54.

Kotler, P., and Levy, S. J. 1969. Broadening the Concept of Marketing. *J. Market.* 33 (Jan.): 10–15.

Kuhn, T. S. 1970. *The Structure of Scientific Revolutions*, 2nd ed. Chicago: University of Chicago Press.

Lachenmeyer, C. W. 1971. *The Language of Sociology*. New York: Columbia Univ. Press.

Lancaster, K. 1971. *Consumer Demand: A New Approach*. New York: Columbia Univ. Press.

Land, K. C. 1969. Principles of Path Analysis. In *Sociological Methodology 1969*, edited by E. F. Borgatta, 3–37. San Francisco: Jossey–Bass.

Lawley, D. N., and Maxwell, A. E. 1971. *Factor Analysis as a Statistical Method*, 2nd ed. London: Butterworth.

———. 1973. Regression and Factor Analysis. *Biometrika* 60, no. 2: 331–338.

Lawrence, P. R., and Lorsch, J. W. 1969. *Organization and Environment*. Homewood, Ill.: Irwin.

Lazer, W. 1971. *Marketing Management: A Systems Perspective*. New York: Wiley.

Lazarsfeld, P. F. 1948. The Use of Panels in Social Research. *Proc. Am. Phil. Soc.* 92: 405–410.

Lazarus, R. S. 1974. Cognitive and Coping Processes in Emotion. In *Cognitive Views of Human Motivation*, edited by B. Weiner. New York: Academic.

Lefcourt, H. M. 1976. *Locus of Control: Current Trends in Theory and Research*. New York: Wiley.

Leinhardt, S. 1977. *Social Networks: A Developing Paradigm*. New York: Academic.

Lerner, D. (ed.). 1965. *Cause and Effect*. The Hayden Colloquim on Scientific Method and Concept. New York: The Free Press.

Levy, S. J. and Zaltman, G. *Marketing, Society and Conflict*. Englewood Cliffs, New Jersey: Prentice–Hall.

Lewin, K. 1936. *Principles of Topological Psychology*. New York: McGraw–Hill.

———. 1938. *The Conceptual Representation and the Measurement of Psychological Forces*. Durham, N.C.: Duke University Press.

Locke, E. A. 1969a. Purpose Without Consciousness: A Contradiction. *Psychological Reports* 25: 991–1009.

———. 1969b. What Is Job Satisfaction? *Organizational Behavior and Human Performance* 4: 309–336.

———. 1970. Job Satisfaction and Job Performance: A Theoretical Analysis. *Organizational Behavior and Human Performance* 5: 484–500.

————. 1972. Critical Analysis of the Concept of Causality in Behavioristic Psychology. *Psychological Reports* 31: 175–197.

————. 1976. The Nature and Causes of Job Satisfaction. In *Handbook of Industrial and Organizational Psychology*, 1297–1349, edited by M. D. Dunnette. Chicago: Rand McNally.

Lord, F. C., and Novick, M. R. 1968. *Statistical Theories of Mental Test Scores*. Reading, Mass.: Addison-Wesley.

Lutz, R. J. 1975. Changing Brand Attitudes Through Modification of Cognitive Structure. *J. Consumer Research* 1 (March): 49–59.

————. 1977. An Experimental Investigation of Causal Relations Among Cognitions, Affect, and Behavioral Intention. *J. Consumer Research* 3 (March): 197–208.

Lyons, T. F. 1971. Role Clarity, Need for Clarity, Satisfaction, Tension, and Withdrawal. *Organizational Behavior and Human Performance* 6: 99–110.

McClelland, D. C. 1961. *The Achieving Society*. Princeton, N.J.: Van Nostrand.

McClelland, P. D. 1975. *Causal Explanation and Model Building in History, Economics, and the New Economic History*. Ithaca, N.Y.: Cornell Univ. Press.

McFadden, D. 1974. Conditional Logit Analysis of Qualitative Choice Behavior. In *Frontiers in Econometrics*, edited by P. Zarembka, pp. 105–142. New York: Academic.

McGuire, W. J. 1969. The Nature of Attitudes and Attitude Change. In *Handbook of Social Psychology*, vol. 3, G. Lindzey and E. Aronson (eds.). Reading, Mass: Addison–Wesley. 136–314.

————. 1976. Some Internal Psychological Factors Influencing Consumer Choice. *J. Consumer Research* 2 (March): 302–319.

McInnes, W. C. 1964. A Conceptual Approach to Marketing. In *Theory in Marketing*, 2nd series, edited by R. Cox, W. Alderson, and S. J. Shapiro. Homewood, Ill.: Richard D. Irwin.

Mackie, J. L. 1965. Causes and Conditions. *Am. Phil. Quart.* 2, no. 4 (Oct.): 245–264.

————. 1974. *The Cement of the Universe: A Study of Causation*. London: Oxford Press (Clarendon).

Madden, E. H., and Humber, J. 1971. Nonlogical Necessity and C. J. Ducasse. *Ratio* 13, no. 2 (Dec.): 119–138.

Malinvaud, E. 1970. *Statistical Methods of Econometrics*, 2nd ed. Amsterdam: North-Holland.

Maze, J. R. 1973. The Concept of Attitude. *Inquiry* 16 (summer): 168–205.

Mead, G. H. 1934. *Mind, Self and Society*, edited by C. W. Morris. Chicago: University of Chicago Press.

Meeker, B. V. 1971. Decisions and Exchange. *Am. Soc. Rev.* 36 (June): 485–495.

Merton, R. K. 1973. *The Sociology of Science*. Chicago: University of Chicago Press.

Metzer, B. N., Petras, J. W., and Reynold, L. T. 1975. *Symbolic Interactionism*. London: Routledge and Kegan Paul.

Mill, J. S. 1959. *A System of Logic*, 8th ed. London: Longmans.

Mischel, W. 1973. Toward a Cognitive Social Learning Reconceptualization of Personality. *Psych. Rev.* 80 (July): 252–283.

Mitchell, A. A., and Olson, J. C. 1975. The Use of Restricted and Unrestricted Maximum Likelihood Factor Analysis to Examine Alternative Measures of Brand Loyalty. Working paper no. 29. Pennsylvania State University.

Mitchell, J. C. 1974. Social Networks. In *Annual Review of Anthropology* 3, edited by B. J. Siegel, A. R. Beals, and S. A. Tyler. Palo Alto, Calif.: Annual Reviews.

Mitchell, T. R., and Biglan, A. 1971. Instrumentality Theories: Current Uses in Psychology. *Psych. Bull.* 76: 432–454.

Molnar, G. 1969. Kneale's Arguments Revisited. *Phil. Rev.* 78, no. 1 (Jan.): 79–89.

Morrison, D. F. 1976. *Multivariate Statistical Methods*, 2nd ed. New York: McGraw–Hill.

Mulaik, S. A. 1972. *Foundations of Factor Analysis*. New York: McGraw–Hill.

Murray, H. A. 1938. *Explorations in Personality*. New York: Oxford Univ. Press.

Nagel, J. H. 1975. *The Descriptive Analysis of Power*. New Haven: Yale Univ. Press.

Nerlove, M., and Press, S. J. 1973. *Univariate and Multivariate Loglinear and Logistic Models*. Santa Monica, Calif.: Rand.

Nicosia, F. M. 1966. *Consumer Decision Processes*. Englewood Cliffs, N.J.: Prentice–Hall.

Nowak, S. 1977. *Methodology of Sociological Research*. Boston: D. Reidel.

Orne, M. T. 1969. Demand Characteristics and the Concept of Quasi-Controls. In *Artifacts in Behavioral Research*, edited by R. Rosenthal and R. L. Rosnow, 143–179. New York: Academic.

Ostrom, T. M. 1969. The Relationship Between the Affective, Behavioral, and Cognitive Components of Attitude. *J. Experimental Social Psychology* 5: 12–30.

Pace, R. W. 1962. Oral Communication and Sales Effectiveness. *J. Appl. Psych.* 46: 321–324.

Parsons, T. 1960. The Analysis of Formal Organizations. In *Structure and Process in Modern Societies*, edited by T. Parsons. New York: Free Press.

Pelz, D. C., and Andrews, F. 1964. Detecting Causal Priorities in Panel Study Data. *Am. Soc. Rev.* 29: 826–848.

Petrie, H. G. 1971. A Dogma of Operationalism in the Social Sciences. *Philosophy of the Social Sciences* 1: 145–160.

Popper, K. R. 1968. *The Logic of Scientific Discover*. New York: Harper Torchbooks.

———. 1963. *Conjectures and Refutations*. New York: Harper Torchbooks.

———. 1972. *Objective Knowledge*. London: Oxford Univ. Press.

Posner, M. I. 1973. *Cognition: An Introduction*. Glenview, Ill.: Scott, Foresman.

Pruden, H. O., and Reese, R. M. 1972. Interorganizational Role-set Relations and the Performance and Satisfaction of Industrial Salesmen. *Admin. Sci. Quart.* 17: 601–609.

Rappaport, L., and Summers, D. A. (eds.). 1973. *Human Judgment and Social Interaction*. New York: Holt, Rinehart and Winston.

Reynolds, P. D. 1971. *A Primer in Theory Construction*. Indianapolis: Bobbs–Merrill.

Ritzer, G. 1975. *Sociology: A Multiple Paradigm Science*. Boston: Allyn and Bacon.

Rizzo, J. R., House, R. J., and Lirtzman, S. I. 1970. Role Conflict and Ambiguity in Complex Organizations. *Admin. Sci. Quart.* 15: 150–63.

Rokeach, M. 1968. *Beliefs, Attitudes and Values*. San Francisco: Jossey–Bass.

Rosenberg, M. J. 1969. The Conditions and Consequences of Evaluation Apprehension. In *Artifacts in Behavioral Research*, edited by R. Rosenthal and R. L. Rosnow, 280–349. New York: Academic.

Rosenthal, R., and Rosnow, R. L. (eds.). 1969. *Artifacts in Behavioral Research*. New York: Academic.

Rothenberg, T. J. 1973. *Efficient Estimation with A Priori Information*. New Haven, Conn.: Yale Univ. Press.

Rotter, J. B. 1954. *Social Learning and Clinical Psychology.* Englewood Cliffs, N.J.: Prentice–Hall.

Rozelle, R. M., and Campbell, D. T. 1969. More Plausible Rival Hypotheses in the Cross-lagged Panel Correlation Technique. *Psych. Bull.* 71: 74–80.

Rubin, J. Z., and Brown, B. R. 1975. *The Social Psychology of Bargaining and Negotiation.* New York: Academic.

Russell, B. 1912–1913. On the Notion of Cause. *Proc. Aristotelian Society* 13: 1–26.

Ryle, G. 1949. *The Concept of Mind.* New York: Barnes & Noble.

Sahlins, M. D. 1965. On the Sociology of Primitive Exchange. In *The Relevance of Models for Social Anthropology.* ASA Monographs 1, edited by M. Banton, 139–236. London: Tavistock.

Salmon, W. C. 1971. Statistical Explanation. In *Statistical Explanation and Statistical Relevance*, edited by W. C. Salmon et al. Pittsburg: University of Pittsburg Press.

Salmon, W. C., Jeffrey, R. C., and Greeno, J. G. 1971. *Statistical Explanation and Statistical Relevance.* Pittsburgh: University of Pittsburgh Press.

Scheffé, H. 1959. *The Analysis of Variance.* New York: Wiley.

Schoenberg, R. 1972. Strategies for Meaningful Comparison. In *Sociological Methodology 1972*, edited by H. L. Costner, 1–35. San Francisco: Jossey–Bass.

Schuler, R. S. 1977. Role Conflict and Ambiguity as a Function of the Task-Structure-Technology Interaction. *Organizational Behavior and Human Performance* 20: 66–74.

Sheridan, J. E., and Slocum, J., Jr. 1975. The Direction of the Causal Relationship between job Satisfaction and Work Performance. *Organizational Behavior and Human Performance* 14: 159–172.

Simon, H. A. 1954. Spurious Correlation: A Casual Interpretation. *J. Am. Stat. Assoc.* 49: 467–479. [Reprinted in Blalock (1971).]

———. 1957. *Models of Man.* New York: Wiley.

Skinner, B. F. 1953. *Science and Human Behavior.* New York: Free Press.

Smart, J. J. C. 1968. *Between Science and Philosophy.* New York: Random House.

Smelser, N. J. 1963. *Theory of Collective Behavior.* New York: Free Press.

———. 1976. *Comparative Methods in the Social Sciences.* Englewood Cliffs, N. J.: Prentice–Hall.

Sörbom, D. 1974. A General Method for Studying Differences in Factor Means and Factor Structure Between Groups. *British J. Math. Stat. Psych.* 27: 229–239.

———. 1975. Detection of Correlated Errors in Longitudinal Data. *British J. Math. Stat. Psych.* 28: 138–151.

Sosa, E. (ed.). 1975. *Causation and Conditions.* London: Oxford Univ. Press.

Specht, D. A., and Warren, R. D. 1975. Comparing Causal Models. In *Sociological Methodology 1976*, edited by D. R. Heise, 46–82. San Francisco: Jossey–Bass.

Spicker, S. F. (ed). 1970. *The Philosophy of the Body.* New York: Quadrangle.

Stapleton, D. C. 1977. Analyzing Political Participation Data with a MIMIC Model. In *Sociological Methodology 1978*, edited by K. F. Schuessler, 52–74, San Francisco: Jossey-Bass.

Staw, B. M. 1977. Motivation in Organizations: Toward Synthesis and Redirection. In *New Directions in Organizational Behavior*, 55–95, edited by B. M. Staw and G. R. Salancik. Chicago: St. Clair Press.

Sternthal, B., Tybout, A. M., Craig, C. S., and Bagozzi, R. P. 1976. The Construct Validity of the Tripartite Classification of Attitudes. Working paper. Evanston, Ill.: Graduate School of Management, Northwestern University.

Suchting, W. A. 1967. Popper on Law and Natural Necessity. *British Journal for the Philosophy of Science.* 18:233-235.

Sullivan, J. L. 1974. Multiple Indicators: Some Criteria of Selection. In *Measurement in the Social Sciences: Theories and Strategies*, edited by H. M. Blalock, 243-269. Chicago: Aldine.

Suppes, P. 1970. *A Probabilistic Theory of Causality.* Amsterdam: North-Holland.

Suppes, P., and Zinnes, J. L. 1963. Basic Measurement Theory. In *Handbook of Mathematical Psychology* 1, edited by R. D. Luce, R. R. Bush, and E. Galanter, 1-76. New York: Wiley.

Taylor, D. M. 1970. *Explanation and Meaning.* Cambridge: Cambridge Univ. Press.

Tedeschi, J. T., Schlenker, B. R., and Bonoma, T. V. 1973. *Conflict, Power, and Games: The Experimental Study of Interpersonal Relations.* Chicago: Aldine.

Theil, H. 1971. *Principles of Econometrics.* New York: Wiley.

Thompson, J. D. 1967. *Organizations in Action.* Chicago: McGraw-Hill.

Tolman, E. C. 1932. *Purposive Behavior in Animals and Men.* Berkeley: University of California Press.

———. 1951. A Psychological Model. In *Toward a General Theory of Action*, edited by T. Parsons and E. A. Shils. Cambridge, Mass.: Harvard Univ. Press.

Tucker, L. R., and Lewis, C. 1973. A Reliability Coefficient for Maximum-Likelihood Factor Analysis. *Psychometrika* 38: 1-10.

Tukey, J. W. 1954. Causation, Regression and Path Analysis. In *Statistics and Mathematics in Biology*, edited by O. Kempthorne, T. A. Bancroft, J. W. Cowed, and J. L. Lush, 35-66. Ames, Iowa: Iowa State College Press.

Turner, M. E., and Stevens, C. D. 1959. The Regression Analysis of Causal Paths. *Biometrics* 15: 236-258.

Vallier, I. (ed.). 1971. *Comparative Methods in Sociology.* Berkeley: University of California Press.

Vaughan, G. M., and Corballis, M. C. 1969. Beyond Tests of Significance: Estimating Strength of Effects in Selected ANOVA Designs. *Psych. Bull.* 72: 204-213.

Von Wright, G. H. 1971. *Explanation and Understanding.* Ithaca, N.Y.: Cornell Univ. Press.

———. 1974. *Causality and Determinism.* New York: Columbia Univ. Press.

Vroom, V. H. 1964. *Work and Motivation.* New York: Wiley.

———. 1966. A Comparison of Static and Dynamic Correlation Methods in the Study of Organizations. *Organizational Behavior and Human Performance* 1:55-70.

Walker, O. C., Jr., Churchill, G. A., Jr., and Ford, N. M. 1977. Motivation and Performance in Industrial Selling: Present Knowledge and Needed Research. *J. Market. Res.* 14: 156-168.

Wallace, W. A. 1972, 1974. *Causality and Scientific Explanation*, vols. 1 and 2. Ann Arbor: University of Michigan Press.

Wanous, J. P. 1974a. A Causal-Correlational Analysis of the Job Satisfaction and Performance Relationship. *J. Appl. Psych.* 59: 139-144.

———. 1974b. Individual Differences and Reactions to Job Characteristics. *J. Appl. Psych.* 59: 616-622.

Ward, S. 1974. Consumer Socialization. *J. Consumer Research* 1 (Sept.): 1–14.

Watson, J. B. 1930. *Behaviorism*. Chicago: University of Chicago Press.

Weber, M. 1964. *The Theory of Social and Economic Organization*. New York: Free Press.

Webster, M. 1973. Psychological Reductionism, Methodological Individualism and Large Scale Problems. *Am. Soc. Rev.* 38 (April): 258–273.

Weiner, B. (ed.). 1974. *Cognitive Views of Human Motivation*. New York: Academic.

Wells, L. E., and Marwell, G. 1976. *Self-Esteem: Its Conceptualization and Measurement*. Beverly Hills: Sage.

Werts, C. E. , and Linn, R. L. 1970. Path Analysis: Psychological Examples. *Psych. Bull.* 74: 193–212.

Werts, C. E., Jöreskog, K. G., and Linn, R. L. 1973. Identification and Estimation in Path Analysis with Unmeasured Variables. *Am. J. Soc.* 78, no. 6 (May): 1469–1484.

Werts, C. E., Linn, R. L., and Jöreskog, K. G. 1974a. Quantifying Unmeasured Variables. In *Measurement in the Social Sciences: Theories and Strategies*, edited by H. M. Blalock, 270–292. Chicago: Aldine.

――――. 1974b. Interclass Reliability Estimates: Testing Structural Assumptions. *Educational and Psychological Measurement*. 34: 25–33.

Wheaton, B., Muthen, B., Alwin, D. F., and Summers, G. F. 1977. Assessing Reliability and Stability in Panel Models. In *Sociological Methodology 1977*, edited by D. R. Heise, 84–136, San Francisco: Jossey-Bass.

White, L. A. 1949. *The Science of Culture: A Study of Man and Civilization*. New York: Farrar, Strauss, and Giroux.

Whitten, N. E., Jr., and Wolfe, A. W. 1973. Network Analysis. In *Handbook of Social and Cultural Anthropology*, edited by J. J. Honigmann. Chicago: Rand McNally.

Wiley, D. E. 1973. The Identification Problem for Structural Equation Models with Unmeasured Variables. In *Structural Equation Models in the Social Sciences*, edited by A. S. Goldberger and O. D. Duncan, 69–83. New York: Seminar Press.

Wiley, D. E., and Wiley, J. A. 1970. The Estimation of Measurement Error in Panel Data. *Am. Soc. Rev.* 35: 112–117. [Reprinted in Blalock (1971).]

Wilkie, W. L., and Pessemier, E. A. 1973. Issues in Marketing's Use of Multi-Attribute Attitude Models. *J. Market. Res.* 10 (Nov.): 428–441.

Willet, D. P., and Pennington, A. L. 1966. Customer and Salesman: The Anatomy of Choice and Influence in a Retail Setting. In *Science, Technology, and Marketing*, edited by R. M. Haas, 598–616. Chicago: American Marketing Association.

Wills, H. 1974. CDC XLOGIT 2.1 Users' Guide. Working paper No. 7412. Berkeley: Institute of Transportation and Traffic Engineering, University of California.

Winer, B. J. 1971. *Statistical Principles in Experimental Design*, 2nd ed. New York: McGraw-Hill.

Woodward, J. A., and Overall, J. E. 1975. Multivariate Analysis of Variance by Multiple Regression Methods. *Psych. Bull.* 82: 21–32.

Wright, S. 1960. Path Coefficients and Path Regressions: Alternatives or Complementary Concepts? *Biometrics* 16: 189–202. [Reprinted in Blalock (1971).]

Zald, M. 1970. *Organization Change: The Political Economy of the YMCA*. Chicago: University of Chicago Press.

Zaltman, G., and Burger, P. C. 1975. *Marketing Research: Fundamentals and Dynamics*. Hinsdale, Ill.: Dryden.

Zaltman, G., Pinson, C. R. A., and Angelmar, R. 1973. *Metatheory and Consumer Research*. New York: Holt, Rinehart and Winston.

Zetterberg, H. 1965. *On Theory and Verification in Sociology*, 3rd ed. Totowa, N.J.: Bedminster Press.

AUTHOR INDEX

Aaker, D. A., ix, 173, 276
Addis, L., 58, 276
Ahtola, O. T., 150, 280
Aiken, M., 60, 276
Ajzen, I., 120, 148, 150, 276, 282
Alderfer, C. P., 270, 276
Allport, G. W., 119, 276
Althauser, R. P., 133, 134, 214, 276
Alwin, D. F., 204, 208, 212, 277
Anderson, T. W., 103, 277
Andrews, F., 239, 289
Angelmar, R., 54, 59, 163, 277
Anscombe, G. E. M., 19, 277
Aristotle, 2, 277
Aronson, E., 220, 277
Ayer, A. J., 8, 40, 277

Badin, I. J., 255, 265, 283
Bagozzi, R. P., 32, 42, 52, 56, 57, 62, 70, 73, 76, 78, 80, 82, 84, 109, 111, 121, 127, 134, 136, 148, 152, 153, 173, 175, 176, 188, 193, 219, 264, 267, 268, 269, 275, 276, 277, 278
Bales, R. F., 52, 278
Bandura, A., 45, 278
Barnes, J. A., 54, 278
Bartlett, M. S., 104, 278
Bass, F. M., 25, 278
Beauchamp, T. L., 8, 14, 15, 30, 31, 278
Becker, G. S., 77, 278
Belk, R. W., 49, 278
Bem, D. J., 119, 278
Berger, P. L., 32, 59, 73, 278
Bettman, J. R., 49, 278
Bhasker, R., 19, 278
Biddle, B. J., 269, 278
Biglan, A., 269, 288

Blackwell, R. D., 46, 240, 282
Blalock, H. M., Jr., viii, 12, 97, 203, 263, 278, 279
Blau, P. M., 57, 62, 279
Blumer, H., 52, 279
Bolles, R. C., 44, 48, 50, 62, 279
Bonoma, T. V., 54, 58, 82, 279, 291
Borgatta, E. F., 258, 279
Bowers, K. S., 50, 279
Box, G. E. P., 104, 279
Brand, M., 61, 279
Bridgman, P. W., 16, 122, 279
Brody, B. A., 207, 279
Brown, B. R., 52, 82, 289
Bunge, M., 31, 37, 279
Burger, P. C., vii, 11, 292
Burgess, R. L., 45, 279
Burnkrant, R. E., 61, 109, 111, 121, 148, 152, 153, 278, 279
Burt, R. S., viii, 103, 106, 107, 112, 113, 153, 154, 155, 156, 157, 159, 161, 162, 164, 279, 280
Bushell, D., Jr., 45, 279

Campbell, D. T., 10, 11, 86, 112, 113, 119, 121, 123, 129, 130, 131, 133, 140, 143, 163, 190, 193, 194, 204, 216, 220, 229, 280, 289
Campbell, J. P., 269, 270, 280
Campbell, K., 38, 39, 61, 280
Caplow, T. A., 55, 280
Capwell, D. F., 251, 284
Carlsmith, J. M., 220, 277
Carman, J., 173, 276
Carnap, R., 7, 25, 30, 116, 117, 122, 125, 129, 163, 280
Cassady, R., Jr., 62, 280

Chadwick-Jones, J. K., 62, 280
Chestnut, R. W., 51, 280
Child, J., 60, 280
Chisholm, R., 14, 280
Churchill, G. A., 253, 266, 268, 269, 280, 282, 291
Cohen, J. B., 150, 280
Coleman, J. S., 54, 280
Cook, T. D., 112, 113, 194, 204, 229, 280
Coombs, C. H., 163, 280
Coopersmith, S., 179, 267, 281
Corballis, M. C., 192, 291
Corrigan, B., 70, 281
Costner, H. L., 106, 163, 185, 203, 204, 209, 211, 281
Craig, C. S., 153, 278

Danto, A. C., 61, 280
Davidson, D., 31, 281
Davis, H. L., 43, 52, 55, 281
Dawes, R. M., 70, 127, 163, 281
Day, G. S., 150, 281
Descartes, R., 38, 281
Doby, J. T., 85, 281
Donagan, A., 24, 281
Doob, L. W., 121, 281
Ducasse, C. J., 6, 12, 17, 30, 281
Dulany, D. E., 49, 281
Duncan, O. D., viii, 12, 60, 72, 73, 81, 91, 134, 229, 230, 239, 258, 281, 282

Ekeh, P., 62, 282
Emerson, R. M., 62, 282
Engel, J. F., 46, 240, 282
Evans, F. B., 52, 282

Feigl, H., 64, 123, 125, 129, 282
Feyerabend, P. K., 32, 282
Fishbein, 43, 119, 120, 148, 276, 282
Fisher, F. M., 98, 282
Fiske, D. W., 86, 123, 130, 131, 133, 140, 143, 163, 193, 280
Fleiss, J. L., 192, 282
Fletcher, R., 103, 179, 282
Ford, N. M., 253, 270, 280, 282, 291

Galbraith, J., 60, 282
Galileo, 3, 283
Geach, P. T., 19, 277
Geraci, V. J., 98, 283
Goffman, E., 52, 283
Goldberg, D., 170, 171, 172, 283

Goldberger, A. S., viii, 12, 83, 90, 100, 111, 165, 166, 168, 173, 198, 199, 220, 283, 284, 286
Goldman, A. I., 61, 283
Goodman, L. A., 108, 283
Green, P. E., vii, 11, 283
Greenhaus, J. H., 255, 265, 283
Gruvaeus, G. T., 83, 102, 103, 283
Guerrero, J. L., 150, 285

Hackman, J. R., 267, 283
Hage, J., 60, 276
Hammer, W. C., 269, 283
Hannan, M. T., 229, 283
Hansen, F., 150, 284
Harary, F., 54, 284
Hare, A. P., 55, 62, 284
Harré, R., 6, 9, 16, 19, 26, 27, 30, 31, 40, 52, 61, 62, 284
Hauser, R. M., 100, 168, 173, 284
Heath, A., 62, 284
Heberlein, T. A., 133, 214, 276
Heise, D. R., viii, 81, 284
Hellriegel, D., 267, 284
Hempel, C. G., 21, 22, 23, 24, 32, 64, 114, 116, 123, 125, 129, 163, 207, 284
Henderson, J. M., 82, 284
Herzberg, F., 251, 252, 270, 284
Hesse, M., 124, 284
Hildebrand, O. K., 108, 284
Hirsch, P. M., 59, 60, 285
Homans, G. C., 58, 62, 285
Hoult, T. F., 57, 285
House, R. J., 269, 285, 289
Howard, J. A., 46, 240, 285
Hsiao, C., 98, 285
Hughes, G. D., 150, 285
Hull, C. L., 47, 48, 285
Hume, D., 1, 4, 5, 6, 285
Hunt, S. D., vii, 255, 256, 285

Jacobson, A. L., 214, 285
Jacoby, J., 46, 51, 285
James, L. R., 91, 267, 285
Johnston, J. J., 70, 81, 111, 285
Jones, A. P., 267, 285
Jöreskog, K. G., viii, 54, 70, 83, 91, 92, 93, 95, 96, 98, 102, 103, 104, 105, 106, 108, 111, 135, 139, 164, 166, 168, 173, 178, 207, 214, 219, 221, 223, 224, 226, 233, 234, 235, 237, 238, 239, 283, 285, 286, 291

Kahane, H., 7, 23, 30, 31, 64, 81, 116, 286
Kant, I., 8, 30, 286
Kaplan, A., 37, 286
Kaplan, M. F., 56, 286
Keat, R., 19, 32, 57, 59, 61, 73, 123, 124,
    163, 207, 286
Kelly, G. A., 49, 179, 254, 267, 286
Kenny, D. A., 230, 286
Keppel, G., 190, 191, 192, 286
Kerlinger, F. N., 73, 190, 191, 286
Kim, J., 187, 203, 286
Kmenta, J., viii, 67, 69, 70, 81, 111, 286
Kneale, W., 14, 15, 30, 286
Koestler, A., 58, 286
Kollat, D. T., 46, 240, 282
Korman, A. K., 179, 254, 255, 265, 267, 286,
    287
Kothandapani, V., 113, 133, 136, 144, 145,
    146, 147, 148, 149, 163, 287
Kotler, P., 67, 287
Kuhn, T. S., 32, 287

Lachenmeyer, C. W., 118, 163, 286
Lalu, N. M., 214, 285
Lancaster, K., 77, 82, 287
Lawler, E. E., 267, 283
Lawley, D. N., viii, 90, 103, 104, 105, 111,
    178, 199, 201, 287
Lawrence, P. R., 60, 287
Lazarsfeld, P. F., 229, 287
Lazarus, R. S., 49, 50, 121, 287
Lefcourt, H. M., 66, 287
Leinhardt, S., 54, 287
Lerner, D., 12, 287
Lewin, K., 48, 287
Lewis, C., 106, 291
Linn, R. L., 133, 134, 214, 291
Lirtzman, S. I., 269, 289
Locke, J., 42, 44, 46, 50, 61, 62, 179, 251,
    252, 253, 254, 258, 264, 265, 267, 287
Lord, F. C., 127, 128, 176, 177, 181, 288
Lorsch, J. W., 60, 287
Luckman, T., 32, 59, 73, 278
Lutz, R. J., 43, 49, 120, 199, 240, 288

McClelland, D. C., 270, 288
McClelland, P. D., 12, 288
McFadden, D., 107, 288
McGuire, W. J., 43, 49, 50, 51, 82, 288
McInnes, W. C., 118, 288
Mackie, 12, 17, 30, 31, 288
McLaughlin, D., 173, 276

Madden, E. H., 16, 19, 26, 27, 30, 31, 284
Marwell, G., 179, 267, 291
Mausner, B., 251, 284
Maxwell, A. E., viii, 90, 103, 104, 105, 111,
    178, 199, 201, 287
Mead, G. H., 52, 288
Meltzer, B. N., 52, 288
Merton, R. K., 32, 288
Mill, J. S., 10, 11, 288
Mischel, W., 42, 49, 270, 288
Mitchell, J. C., 54, 288
Mitchell, T. R., 269, 288
Molnar, G., 13, 30, 288
Morrison, D. F., 111, 288
Mueller, C. W., 187, 203, 286
Mulaik, S. A., 177, 178, 289
Murray, H. A., 49, 289

Nerlove, M., 107, 289
Nicosia, F. M., 40, 46, 62, 289
Novick, M. R., 127, 128, 176, 177, 181, 288
Nowak, S., 82, 289

Orne, M. T., 220, 289
Ostrom, T. M., 113, 136, 139, 140, 141-148,
    163, 289
Overall, J. E., 190, 292

Pace, R. W., 255, 289
Parsons, T., 60, 289
Pedhazur, E. J., 73, 190, 191, 286
Pelz, D. C., 239, 289
Pennington, A. L., 52, 292
Pessemier, E. A., 61, 292
Peterson, R. O., 251, 284
Petrie, H. G., 122, 123, 124, 163, 289
Pinson, C. R. A., 59, 163, 277
Popper, K. R., 14, 28, 32, 125, 207, 289
Posner, M. I., 51, 289
Powell, M. J. D., 103, 179, 282
Press, S. J., 107, 289
Pritchard, R. D., 269, 270, 280
Pruden, H. O., 257, 269, 289

Quandt, R. E., 82, 284

Rappaport, L., 55, 56, 289
Reese, R. M., 257, 269, 289
Reynolds, P. D., 82, 289
Rigaux, B. P., 52, 281
Ritzer, G., 34, 289
Rizzo, J. R., 269, 285

Rokeach, M., 119, 120, 289
Rosenberg, M. J., 220, 289
Rosenthal, R., 11, 204, 220, 289
Rosnow, R. L., 11, 204, 220, 289
Rothenberg, T. J., viii, 96, 289
Rotter, J. B., 49, 64, 289
Rozelle, R. M., 229, 289
Rubin, J. Z., 52, 82, 289
Russell, B., 11, 12, 289
Ryle, G., 61, 290

Sahlins, M. D., 62, 290
Salmon, W. C., 23, 25, 290
Scheffé, H., 190, 290
Schlenker, B. R., 52, 82, 291
Schoenberg, R., 87, 106, 163, 185, 211, 281, 290
Schuler, R. S., 269, 290
Schwartz, S., 56, 286
Scott, R. A., 214, 276
Secord, P. F., 9, 36, 40, 52, 61, 62, 284
Sheridan, J. E., 253, 265, 290
Sheth, J. N., 46, 240, 285
Simon, H. A., 81, 194, 290
Singh, B. K., 91, 285
Skinner, B. F., 44, 290
Slocum, J. W., Jr., 253, 265, 267, 284, 290
Smart, J. J. C., 163, 290
Smelser, N. J., 11, 57, 62, 290
Sörbom, D., 217, 290
Sosa, E., 30, 290
Specht, D. A., 188, 290
Spicker, S. F., 38, 61, 290
Stanley, J. C., 10, 11, 190, 193, 216, 220, 229, 280
Stapleton, D. C., 173, 290
Staw, B. M., 270, 290
Sternthal, B., 153, 278
Suchting, W. A., 8, 30, 31, 290
Sullivan, J. L., 211, 214, 290
Summers, D. A., 55, 56, 289
Suppes, P., 12, 25, 163, 290
Symthies, F. R., 58, 286

Taylor, D. M., 16, 31, 290
Tedeschi, J. T., 20, 52, 53, 82, 291
Tessler, R. C., 204, 208, 212, 277

Thiel, H., viii, 68, 70, 81, 91, 97, 103, 104, 111, 291
Thomas, E. J., 269, 278
Thompson, J. D., 60, 291
Tolman, E. C., 47, 61, 62, 291
Tosi, H. W., 269, 283
Tucker, L. R., 106, 291
Tukey, J. W., 203, 291
Tull, D. S., vii, 11, 283
Tversky, A., 163, 280
Tybout, A. M., 153, 278

Urry, J., 19, 32, 57, 59, 61, 73, 123, 124, 163, 207, 286

Vallier, I., 62, 291
Vaughan, G. M., 192, 291
VonWright, G. H., 12, 18, 291
Vroom, V. H., 239, 251, 291

Walker, O. C., Jr., 253, 280, 282, 291
Wallace, W. A., 3, 19, 30, 31, 291
Walton, D., 61, 279
Wanous, J. P., 239, 252, 254, 265, 291
Ward, S., 45, 291
Warren, R. D., 188, 290
Watson, J. B., 44, 291
Weber, M., 35, 291
Webster, M., 58, 59, 291
Weiner, B., 42, 49, 121, 291
Wells, L. E., 179, 267, 291
Werts, C. E., 133, 134, 181, 214, 291
Wheaton, B., 238, 292
White, L. A., 58, 292
Whitten, N. E., Jr., 54, 292
Wilkie, W. L., 61, 292
Willet, D. P., 52, 292
Willis, H., 108, 292
Winer, B. J., 191, 192, 292
Wolfe, A. W., 54, 292
Woodward, J. A., 190, 292
Wright, S., 157, 203, 240, 292

Zald, M., 60, 292
Zaltman, G., vii, 11, 29, 73, 81, 85, 113, 114, 115, 124, 292
Zetterberg, H., 82, 292
Zinnes, J. L., 163, 290

SUBJECT INDEX

Abstraction, process of, 115-116
Action, 61
  social, *see* Social action
Activities, 34
Acts, 34
Affect, 40-41, 109-110, 241
Ambiguity, problem of, 118
Apprehension, 9
Attitude, 119-121, 124, 136-153, 199

Behavior, 61
  causal models of, 43-57
  definition of, 34-35
  explanation of, 35
  macrosocial, 56-57
  purposeful, 61
  purposive, 53
  small group, 54-56
  social, 51-57
Belief, 62
  moral, 41-42, 62
Buyer behavior, 240

Causal diagrams, 67-73
Causality, Aristotle's view of, 2-3
  as cognitive event, 5, 8-10, 13
  concept of in classical period, 4-11, 12
  concept of in early thought, 2-4
  conditions of, 16-19, 21, 22
  four types of, 2
  Galileo's view of, 3-4
  Harré & Madden's view of, 19-20
  Hempel's view of, 22-23
  Hume's rules of, 5-6
  Hume's view of, 4-6

  as illusion, 5. *See also* Causality, as cognitive event
  internal structure of, 19-20. *See also* Natural necessity
  Kant's view of, 6-10, 30-31, 50
  Mackie's model of, 17-18
  in macrosocial behavior, 56-57
  manipulability theory definition of, 18
  Mill's view of, 10-12
  as myth, 11-12
  as necessary connection, 4-6, 8. *See also* Natural necessity
  in organism-response model, 49-51
  problems with, 2, 4-5, 8-10, 11-12, 22-23, 57-60. *See also* Laws of nature, problems with
  realist and natural necessity definition of, 19-20
  as regularity of events, 4-5, 13-19
  regularity theory definition of, 18-19
  regularity theory view of, 13-19
  representation of, 63-73
  in response-response model, 49
  Russell's view of, 11-12
  in small group behavior, 56
  in social interaction models, 53
  in stimulus-response model, 43-46, 46-49
  Suppes' view of, 25
  triadic model of, 17
  von Wright's view of, 18
Causal knowledge, 3
Causal modeling, benefits of, 75. *See also* General linear model, strengths and limitations of
  definition of, 83-84
  illustration of, 109-110

philosophy and objectives of, 83-91. *See also*
    Causality, representation of; Explanation
Causal models, comparison of within and
    across populations, 186-188
Causal relation, functional form, 67, 69-70
    nonrecursive, 72, 92. *See also* Simultaneity
    recursive, 72, 92, 173-176
    spurious, 72
Causal relationships, types of, 72-73
Causal sequences, accidental, 6, 10. *See also*
    Generalization, accidental
Causation, four types of, 2-3. *See also* Causality
    history of, 2
Cause, efficient, 3
    final, 3
    as power, capacity, or liability, 19-20
Cause and effect, rules to judge, 5-6
COFAMM, 108
Cognition, 41, 120, 241
Concept, 64, 114-125
    classificatory, 116
    comparative, 116-117
    defined, 64
    derived, 64
    empirical, 64
    mental, 40-43
    observable, 122
    observational meaningfulness of, 121
    quantitative, 116-117
    social, 51-53, 58
    theoretical, 121-122, 153. *See also* Con-
        structs, theoretical
    theoretical meaningfulness of, 117-118
    types of, 116
Concept formation, 2
Condition, INUS, 17-18
Confirmation, 2, 20, 27-29, 119. *See also*
    Falsificationist model
Consistency checks, 127
Constant conjunction, 4, 9, 11, 45
Constructs, empirical, 59
    theoretical, 59, 64, 70, 80. *See also* Con-
        cepts, mental; Concepts, theoretical;
        Events, mental; Terms, theoretical; *and*
        Variables, theoretical
Contiguity, 9, 45
    in space and time, 11
    in time and place, 4
Contradiction, problem of, 119
Contrary-to-fact conditional, 14-15
Control, objective of in science, 73
Conventionalist models, 27, 32

Correction factor, small sample, 104
Correlated errors, 183-186, 226-227, 230-233
Correspondence rules, 64-66, 80, 92, 117, 122-
    125
    operational definition model of, 122
    partial interpretation model of, 122-124
    realist model of, 124-125
Counterfactual conditional, *see* Contrary-to-
    fact conditional
Counterfactual inference, *see* Contrary-to-fact
    conditional
Cronbach Alpha (α), 128, 180
Cross-lagged panel correlation technique, 229,
    233

Definable form, *see* Causality, four types of
Definition, extensional, 64
    intensional, 64
    operational, 64, 122
    ostensive, 64
Drive, 48. *See also* Affect
Dyad, 51. *See also* Exchange

EFAP, 108
Emotion, 120
Empiricism, blind, 29-30
Epistemology, 7
Errors in equations, 71, 92
Errors in variables, 71. *See also* Measurement
    error
Estimation, problem of in general linear model,
    102-103
Evaluation, 41-42
Events, cause and effect as instances of, 4-5,
    16-19, 21. *See also* Natural necessity
    mental, 48-49. *See also* Concepts, mental
Exchange, 20, 51-54, 76-81
Exchange relationship, characteristics of, 52-53
    52-53
Expectancy, 47. *See also* Cognition
Expectancy-value theory, 64
Experiences, subjective, 35-57
Experimental design, pretest/posttest with
    experimental manipulation, 216-219
    and covariate, 228-229
    structural equation model of, 196-199, 214-
        219
    traditional approach, 190-196
    two independent and two dependent vari-
        ables, 214-216
Experimental research, use of causal models in,
    189-220

Explanandum, 21, 23
Explanans, 21, 23
Explanation, 3, 14, 20, 31, 73, 84-85
  across levels of analysis, 57, 59-60
  causal, 14
  in causal modeling, 84-85
  Hempel's deductive-nomological model of, 20-25
  inductive statistic model of, 23-25
  levels of understanding in, 84-85
  positivist model, 20-25, 32
  realist model of, 25-27, 32
  statistical, 23-25
  in stimulus-response model, 44

Falsificationist model, 2, 28, 125. *See also* Confirmation

Generalization, accidental, 14-15
  nomological, 14. *See also* Laws of nature; Statements, lawlike
  universal, 13-14. *See also* Laws of nature
General linear model, 82-112
  strengths and limitations of, 107-109. *See also* Causal modeling, benefits of
Graph theory, 54

Hempel's deductive-nomological model, 20-25
How, question of, 25-27, 31. *See also* Why, question of
Hume's rules of causality, 5-6
Hypotheses, alternative, 104-105
  theoretical, 64-65
Hypothesis, null, 103-105
Hypothesis generation, 2
Hypothesis testing, in general linear model, 103
  sensitivity of to sample size, 106

Identification, example of, 88-90, 99-102
  problem of, 97-102
Induction, problem of, 14
Inductive statistical model, critique of, 24-25
Intelligence, verbal, 255
  measurement of, 258
  reliability of, 258
Interpretation, double process of, 37
  process of, 115-116
Interpretational confounding, 153-161

Job outcomes, *see* Performance; Satisfaction, job; *and* Self-esteem

Jöreskog's General Model for Longitudinal Data, 233-238

Law, 13, 21, 22, 23
  Humean, 15
  as part of explanans, 21
  statistical, 23-25
  universal, 5, 14
  see also Laws of nature
Lawlikeness, 14
Laws of coexistence, 22-23
Laws of nature, 13-16. *See also* Law
  problems with, 13-16
  in stimulus-response models, 45
Laws of succession, 22-23
Linear regression of model, 68-70
LISREL, 91, 107, 108, 111
Longitudinal models, 221-239

Manipulability theory, 18
Maximum likelihood technique, 102-103
  advantages of, 103
Meaning, observational, 114, 121-125
  theoretical, 114-121
Measurement, 125-126. *See also* Concept, empirical; Concept, observable; Correspondence rules; *and* Operationalization
Measurement, index, 126
  representational, 126
Measurement error, 68, 71, 86-90, 92, 127. *See also* Errors in variables
Method of agreement, 10
Method of concomitant variation, 11
Method of difference, 10
Methodological holism, 59
Methodological individualism, 58
Mill's methods, 11-12
Mind, behaviorist view of, 38-39
  causal theory of, 39
  as nonmaterial, 39-40
Mind-body problem, 37-43
Model, attitude, 40-43. *See also* Attitude
  organism-response, 49-51
  response-response, 48-49
  statistical relevance, 25
  stimulus-organism response, 46-49, 240-242
  stimulus-response, 43-46
Motivation, 48, 269-270
  achievement, 254
  measurement of, 258
  reliability of, 258

relation to job outcomes, 270
  see also Affect; Drive
Multiple-Indicator-Multiple Cause Model
    (MIMIC), 165-173
Multiple operationalization, doctrine of, 123,
    125. See also Operationalization
Multitrait-multimethod matrix (MM), 113-114,
    129-136
  causal modeling approach to, 133-136

Natural necessity, 6, 10-11, 19-20, 26
  in stimulus-organism-response models, 49
  see also Causality, as necessary connection
Norms, 53

Opacity, problem of, 118
Operationalization, 71
  internal consistency of, 125-128. See also
    Reliability
  see also Concepts, empirical; Measurement;
    Phenomena, observable; and Terms,
    observational

Parameters, constrained, 95
  fixed, 95
  free, 95
Performance, sales, antecedents of, 251-256,
    260-266, 268-270, 272-275
  measurement of, 257, 267
  relation to job satisfaction, 251-256, 260-
    266
Phenomena, observable, 13. See also Concept,
    empirical; Concept, observable; and
    Operationalization
Point variables, 157
Prediction, 73
Pretest/posttest models, 216-217, 221-229
Propositions, kinds of, 7
  nonobservational, 64, 80, 129

Questions, types of, 31. See also How, question
    of; Why, question of

Realist model, 19-20
  use in stimulus-organism-response models, 49
Reductionism, 57-59
Regularity theory, 13-19
  definition of, 18-19
  use in stimulus-organism-response models, 49
  use in stimulus-response-models, 43-46
Reification, 57, 59
Reinforcement, 43

Relation, deterministic, 67
  role, 54
  stochastic, 67
Relationship, causal, 12. See also Causality
  concept of in human behavior, 34-35
  concept of in social action, 35-36
  functional, 12
  means-end, 48. See also Cognition
  noncausal, 9
  spurious, 60
Reliability, 127-128, 176-183
  causal diagram of general model, 178
  example of using causal modeling, 179-183
  general causal model of, 177-179
  internal consistency method of, 127-128. See
    also Cronbach Alpha
  split-half method of, 127-128
  test-retest method of, 127-128
Reliability coefficient, 106, 109, 112
Role ambiguity, 268-269
  measurement of, 270, 272
  relation to job outcomes, 269
Rules of correspondence, 64-66. See also
    Correspondence rules

Satisfaction, antecedents of, 251-256, 260-266,
    268-270, 272-275
  job, definition of, 253
    measurement of, 257-258
    relation to performance, 251-256, 260-266
    reliability of, 258
Science, descriptive, 73
  distinction between natural and behavioral,
    36-37
  theoretical, 73. See also Explanation
"Scientia est cognito per causas," 3
Scientific research, 74-75
Self-esteem, 254, 267
  reliability of, 258
  task specific, measurement of, 258
Sentences, kinds of, 7
Simultaneity, 90-91, 93-96. See also Causal
    relation, nonrecursive
Single factor model, 88-90
Situation, role of in interaction models, 52
Social action, causal models of, 51-57
  definition of, 35-36
  explanation of, 35-36
Social facts, 34, 58. See also Reductionism;
    Reification
Social interaction models, 51-54
Social judgment theory, 55

Specification, problem of, 91-97. *See also* Causality; Explanation; *and* Theory
Standard construal, 64
  example of, 64-67
Statements, analytic, 7-8
  a posteriori, 7-8
  a priori, 7-8
  lawlike, 15-16. *See also* Law; Laws of nature
  synthetic, 7-8
Statistical relevance, 25
Structural equations, 67

Tautologies, sterile, 29-30
Temporal priority, 4, 9, 11, 45
Terms, logical, 117
  observational, 117. *See also* Concepts, empirical; Concepts, observable; *and* Phenomena, observable
  theoretical, 117, 129. *See also* Concepts, mental; Concepts, theoretical; Events, mental; *and* Variables, theoretical
Testability, 27
Theory, structure of, 63-67. *See also* Validity
Theory building, 2
Theory construction, example of, 75-81. *See also* Explanation; Theory, structure of
True causes (verae causae), 3-4
True-score, concept of, 176
Two-stage least squares, 91

Universal, accidental, 16. *See also* Causal sequences, accidental; Generalization, accidental
Universal laws, 14

Vagueness, problem of, 118
Validity, construct, 129
  definition of, 113-114
  convergent, 113-114, 129-136
    Campbell and Fiske definition of, 131
    causal modeling definition of, 133-136
    illustration of, 136-148
  discriminant, 113-114, 129-136
    Campbell and Fiske definition of, 131
    causal modeling definition of, 133-136
    illustration of, 136-148
  nomological, 113-114, 129
    example of, 148-158
Value, 47. *See also* Affect
Variables, intervening, 46-49
  nonobservable, 86-90, 92. *See also* Concept, theoretical
  theoretical, 77. *See also* Concept, theoretical
  unobservable, 86-90, 92. *See also* Constructs, theoretical
Variance-covariance matrix, model of in general linear model, 95

Why, question of, 3, 21, 25-27, 31, 84-85. *See also* Explanation; How, question of